SCHOOL'S
OUT

SCHOOL'S OUT

THE IMPACT OF GAY AND LESBIAN ISSUES ON AMERICA'S SCHOOLS
BY DAN WOOG

ALYSON PUBLICATIONS
LOS ANGELES

This is a trade paperback original from Alyson Publications Inc.,
P.O. Box 4371, Los Angeles, California 90078.
Distributed in the United Kingdom by Turnaround Distribution,
27 Horsell Road, London N5 1XL, England.

First edition: May 1995

5 4 3 2

ISBN 1-55583-249-0

Library of Congress Cataloging-in-Publication Data
Woog, Dan, 1953–
    School's out : the impact of gay and lesbian issues on America's
    schools / by Dan Woog.—2nd ed.
      p.   cm.
    Includes bibliographical references (p.)
    ISBN 1-55583-249-0
    1. Homosexuality and education—United States. 2. Gays—
Education—United States. 3. Gay teachers—United States. 4. Lesbian
teachers—United States. I. Title.
LC192.6.W66 1995
371.8'2664—dc20   95-5763
                                          CIP

To every gay or lesbian adult working in America's schools –
and every gay or lesbian human being who is now,
or ever has been, a student.

Contents

Part 3: Programs

Acknowledgments

Writing this book was one of the most uplifting – and exasperating – projects I have ever undertaken. It was uplifting because it allowed me to meet hundreds of wonderfully articulate, open, passionate people of all ages, gay and straight, in nearly every state. It was exasperating because nearly everyone I talked to eagerly referred me to two, three, or a dozen others. At times I felt that unless I spoke with every human being whose name I received, I would overlook some important aspect of gay and lesbian life in America's schools. Of course, speaking with so many thousands of people was impossible; to those I missed, I apologize.

Many people gave me good stories or good ideas, or pointed me toward good sources, but are not quoted directly in this book. Sincere thanks go, in absolutely no logical order, to Sandy Berman, head cataloger, Hennepin (Minnesota) Public Library, for his faithful and never-ending mailings; librarian Martha Carnog of Philadelphia; Wendy Thomas, public service librarian at the Schlesinger Library, Radcliffe College, and co-chair, American Library Association Gay and Lesbian Task Force; Merri Monks, coordinator of publications for the American Association of School Librarians and Young Adult Services Association, Chicago; librarian Chris Dodge of Minneapolis; social worker Debby King of Amherst, Massachusetts; Lea Dickson of Fairfield, Connecticut, and the Association for Supervision and Curriculum Development's Lesbian, Gay and Bisexual Issues in Education program; Wayne Pawlowski, director of training for Planned Parenthood in Washington, D.C.; George Neighbors of Parents, Families and Friends of Lesbians and Gays (PFLAG) headquarters in Washington, D.C.; Mitzi Henderson, national president of PFLAG; Mrs. G.A. Hawthorne of the Peninsula PFLAG chapter in San Jose, California; and Nancy McDonald of PFLAG Oklahoma.

Also: Christopher Rodriguez, coordinator of the Harvey Milk School in New York City; Akaya Windwood of the Pacific Center in Berkeley, California; Bob Riddle of the Crossroads School in Santa Monica, California; Paul Levy of the Georgetown Day School, Washington, D.C.; Ryan James of Linfield College in McMinnville, Oregon; Jeff Kornett and Eric Matthews of Ithaca College; Joseph Smith of

Charlotte, North Carolina; Jason Riggs of Granada Hills (California) High School; Charleen Cepek of Lyons Township High School in La Grange, Illinois; Maggie King, formerly of Mountlake Terrace High School in Washington State; Lee Neff of the Pacific Northwest Association of Independent Schools in Seattle; and Meade Thayer of the National Association of Independent Schools in Washington, D.C.

Also: Lily Eng of the *Philadelphia Inquirer;* Robert Jamieson of the *Seattle Post-Intelligencer;* Kay Longcope and Rich Brown of the *Texas Triangle* in Austin; Steve Biller, formerly of *TWN* in Miami; Dennis Delia, president of Gays United to Attack Repression and Discrimination (south Florida); Jim Klopfer of the Stonewall Speakers Association in Hartford, Connecticut; Jean Durgin-Clinchard of Lincoln, Nebraska; Joshua Cheney of Roxbury, Vermont; Tracy Phariss of Jefferson County, Colorado; Al Kielwasser, Project 21 co-coordinator, San Francisco; Joan Paul of Nova High School, Davie, Florida; Judy Elliott of St. Mark School in Cooper City, Florida; Robert Loupo of Dade County, Florida; and Jean Talpers.

Many faculty members at Staples High School in Westport, Connecticut — my alma mater, and the school at which I currently work in various capacities, including as lay reader for the English department, soccer coach, and co-adviser of the Gay/Straight Alliance — have been especially helpful and supportive during the year I spent writing this book. Special thanks go to Ann Friedman, Kate Dickstein, Sarah Herz, Fran White, and Candace McGovern.

Principal Gloria Rakovic has also been a dynamic force for multiculturalism at Staples; she embodies a rare blend of passion and power. On a personal level, she has been particularly supportive of me, and I truly appreciate that. Dr. Bob Selverstone — recently retired sexuality and values teacher, and former chair of the board of directors of the Sexuality Information and Education Council of the United States (SIECUS) — was for years one of Staples's most underappreciated assets; his support for me, on a personal level, has been both unstinting and incredibly important. To Dr. Gerald Kuroghlian, educator extraordinaire (and past president of the Connecticut Council of Teachers of English), I am overwhelmingly indebted. He read every word of this book, at every stage; his comments, criticisms, and insights were always honest, always on target, and always delivered with warmth and good humor.

Numerous friends also stood by me as I researched and wrote. Their support and enthusiasm — expressed and implied — meant a great deal to me. Sincere thanks go to Albie Loeffler, Peter Dickstein, Tim

Purcell, John Nathan, Jon Walker, Doug Nissing, Dan Kelly, Barb Schade, Scott Edwards, Lynn Berling-Manuel, John Morgan, Ari Edelson, and Olivier Goedert. My parents, James and Josephine Woog; my sisters Susan Woog Wagner and Laurie Woog; and their husbands, Stephen Wagner and Jay Goldring, also stood solidly behind me. Two supporters stand especially tall: Andy Stone, who has provided me with a special window into the life of a gay teenager in the 1990s (and is a wonderfully warm, wise, and witty young man to boot), and Jeff Garelick, former Staples High student, president of the Lambda organization at Vanderbilt University, and one of the most compassionate, courageous human beings I know. If all young people could be like Andy and Jeff, the world would be a far better place.

Naturally, I would like to thank Sasha Alyson, for providing me with the opportunity to write this book (we first met, fortuitously, at a National Education Association reception during the 1993 March on Washington), and Staples High School alumnus Adrien Saks, formerly of Alyson Publications, for his support too.

Yet my greatest appreciation is reserved for the many men and women who opened their hearts to me − and opened the eyes of readers − by the simple yet profound step of agreeing to be quoted by name. This book could not have been written without so many human faces. To the dozens of courageous teachers, students, principals, parents, and others − gay and straight − who were so willing to talk about such an important subject: Thanks. You made this book what it is.

Foreword

———>●<———

What's going on with gay and lesbian issues in America's schools?
It might be better to ask, what isn't going on? Scarcely a day goes
by without at least one incident like these:

- Maverick Shaw, a seventeen-year-old openly gay senior, is voted
  homecoming king at Austin, Texas's Westlake High School.

- A twelve-year-old Beaverton, Oregon, girl is shoved into lockers and beaten by older students. The reason: her mother is a
  lesbian.

- Matt Bell comes out as a sophomore at his suburban Philadelphia
  high school, proudly sharing important aspects of his life with
  classmates and teachers. But his physical education instructor
  refuses to believe it, and insists that Matt is not gay.

- Several teachers march fearfully in a gay pride parade, paper bags
  covering their heads. A television news crew films them later, sans
  bags, in a parking lot. When the tape airs, all expect to be fired.
  Instead, they receive overwhelming support, from principals and
  colleagues alike.

- A social service youth organization mails an ad, with payment,
  to school newspapers in northern California, reading: "Gay? Lesbian? Bisexual? Questioning? We know what that feels like. Join
  us for a weekly group where you can figure it out without any
  pressure to pretend you're someone else." They soon receive their
  first response: the journalism staff at Sarasota High rejects the ad.

- Northfield Mount Hermon Academy in Massachusetts convenes
  a conference of gay, lesbian, and bisexual private school groups.
  Nearly sixty students engage in wide-ranging discussions, with no
  untoward incidents.

- Across Washington State, more than two hundred gays and lesbians participate in a unique homecoming program: they return
  to their high school alma maters to tell their life stories.

- The mother of an eleven-year-old Ashland, Massachusetts, middle
  school student is incensed when her son portrays a homosexual in
  a class skit on prejudice, saying he felt humiliated. The teacher

responds, "If kids can see what it's like to be discriminated against for one day, can they imagine what it would be like to live that every day of their lives?"

All of which means – what? What conclusions can be drawn from the above examples (and hundreds more) detailing gay and lesbian life, and the lives of teachers, administrators, guidance counselors, coaches, librarians, nurses, custodians, and parents – gay, lesbian, bisexual, transgendered, straight, and uncertain – in the tens of thousands of public and private schools in America today?

Do we conclude that our buildings are breeding grounds for homophobia, or hotbeds of homosexual activism? That our teachers are terrified to raise gay and lesbian issues in their classrooms, or can't wait to do so? That our principals, superintendents, and school board members are terrified, prejudiced, and confused, or progressive, enlightened, and empathic? That millions of youngsters sit in school every day hearing words like "faggot" and "queer" – perhaps even using those taunts themselves – secretly wishing some adult will respond, and that sometimes someone does?

All of the above is true. The messages cascading around lesbian and gay issues – in newspapers and magazines; on television and movie screens; spoken by educators, implied by their silence and inferred from their gestures – are decidedly mixed. Some schools are awful places to be; others are, if not Edenic, at least safe and secure. Some faculty members are horrible people, with no business being around youngsters no matter what their sexual orientation; others are wondrous human beings who influence everyone they meet, and truly do their best to make the world a better place for future generations. Some gay and lesbian students are coming out earlier than ever before, forcing their classmates, teachers, and principals to confront the fact that life is filled with diverse people (some thrillingly different, others incredibly average, the sexual orientation of all irrelevant); other homosexual youngsters cower as deeply in the closet as their ancestors did twenty, fifty, one hundred years ago.

The messages, it is clear, are spectacularly unclear. They are mixed, mumbled, and mind-boggling. But that doesn't mean we should not attempt to decipher them.

This book attempts to do just that – from a human, anecdotal point of view. I have chosen to focus not on policy issues or curricular matters; instead, I have tried to zero in on the men and women, boys and girls whose stories personalize gay and lesbian life. After all, gay and lesbian issues are ultimately about human beings, not boards of education or faculty committees.

Although loosely organized into three broad categories – people, places, and programs – each chapter stands alone. Some are based on a common topic, such as athletics, guidance counselors, or private schools; some focus on a particular geographic area, like Washington State or Massachusetts, while others highlight individual gays and lesbians, and their heterosexual allies. But just as each individual gay man or lesbian woman draws strength from the larger homosexual community, so too does each chapter weave together to form the fabric of a greater book: the story of gay and lesbian issues in America's schools.

These stories are not intended to be all-inclusive; there is no way I could cover, let alone convey, every gay-related happening in our classrooms, auditoriums, playgrounds, playing fields, and principals' offices today. What I have tried to do is open readers' eyes and minds; to whet appetites, and induce a hunger to learn more.

In conducting nearly three hundred interviews for this book, I certainly learned plenty. I discovered there are gay and lesbian teachers in every school building in America – probably in numbers greater than our representation in the general population. Most are not out of the closet – though that is clearly becoming a less crowded place – but out or in, our schools are filled with gay men and women.

Many are excellent educators. They are devoted to their students. As marginalized members of society, gay and lesbian teachers relate to their youthful charges who are battling the stereotypes and preconceptions other adults impose on them. As human beings always vulnerable to attacks, they empathize with boys and girls who are constantly on guard (we all know how vicious classmates can be, and how quickly they can turn). And as former youths themselves, gay and lesbian teachers remember well the pain they felt as they struggled to identify who they were, and learn their place in the world. It is a struggle nearly every student fights, in some shape or form, nearly every day in school.

There are very few experiences that all Americans – gay and straight, male and female, black, red, brown, yellow, and white – share. School is one. But while differences of gender and race are readily apparent, those of sexual orientation are not. I wanted to find out what the school experiences of gays and lesbians – educators and students alike – are really like. I wanted to learn what we share with our heterosexual classmates and colleagues, and what is completely different.

To find out, I spoke to gays and lesbians around the country. I thought they would be hard to find. They were not. Virtually every man and woman I contacted referred me to others equally insightful and articulate, though often offering new twists. They were eager, almost painfully so, to share names, addresses, and numbers of colleagues who had felt the same feelings, fought the same wars, though on somewhat different battlefields. I often felt the book's subject was becoming a kaleidoscope: each time I looked at it from a slightly different angle I discovered new forms and was forced to reassess exactly what I was seeing. And, like a kaleidoscope, some images were more intriguing than others, yet all were worth peering at.

I found educators, students, and other school-related folks everywhere I turned. They're there in big cities, of course, but also in suburbs and small towns, and I soon realized it's impossible to draw conclusions from broad categories, such as where they grew up, live, work, or study. Each person's story is unique, and in the course of my research I came to understand that one can no more discuss a singular gay education experience than one can an all-encompassing straight, rural, or immigrant education experience (or anything else, for that matter).

Still, certain ideas recurred, interview after interview. I kept hearing about a sense of isolation when gay teachers and students are in the closet, and a powerful surge of freedom – accompanied by tremendous energy, creativity, and fulfillment – when that closet door opens. I came to recognize that gay and lesbian concerns touch not only homosexual and questioning students and staff, but also our straight colleagues and allies – everyone, in fact, in every school building in the country. I sensed sadness that so many gay and lesbian youngsters suffer so profoundly, because so many wounds are inflicted (both willfully and unwittingly) by so many supposedly enlightened adults. And in the end I came away exhilarated by the joy that so much is changing for the better. It is happening sometimes slowly, sometimes speedily, but school by school, in towns and cities across the nation, more and more people understand that gay and lesbian people and issues are here, are important, and are not about to go away.

I reached these conclusions by asking plenty of questions. Many of those questions, I was told, pushed people to think long and hard about their school experiences. But their initial reactions were just as intriguing: as soon as I introduced the topic, people reacted with wild enthusiasm. "That's great!" many said. "Fantastic!" "It's about time! How can I help?"

In fact, once they started thinking – and then talking – it was hard to get these folks to shut up. More than once people began telling incredible tales even before I asked permission to use their name. In fact, in two decades as a writer I have never met so many people so eager to talk for so long about so intimate a subject – and so willing to be quoted by name. And when I finished an interview by thanking the man or woman, boy or girl for his or her time, energy, enthusiasm, and insights, more often than not the response was some variation of "No, thank *you* for doing this. It's so important!"

Through this project I have met some of the most wonderful, intelligent, sharing, caring people in the education world. (I also got to experience Los Angeles's Northridge earthquake firsthand – but that's another book.) My only regret is that I could not include every single story here. I've had to leave out many intriguing people and omit many interesting tales, and for that I apologize. But I think I've included enough to give a flavor of where America's schools stand, homosexually speaking, today.

So what's the answer to the original question: What's going on with gay and lesbian issues in America's schools? You'll have to be the judge. After all, aren't reading, thinking, and learning what education is all about?

Dan Woog
Westport, Connecticut

PART 1

People

Schools Are People

"School" is one of the most powerful words in the English language. For nearly every American it conjures up images both pleasant and unpleasant, vivid and dim. School means buildings, big and imposing the first day we walk in, whose intricate rhythms and social structures some of us eventually master; others never do. School means the indefinable smells of the cafeteria, gym, and art room, and the indelible sounds of clanging lockers, jarring bells, and recess. School means walking up and down the same worn stairs day after day, sitting in the same hard seat month after month, feeling the same familiar emotions – of fear, security, exhilaration, stupidity, love, worthlessness, achievement, or boredom, depending on who you are, where you live, and a thousand other factors – year after year after year.

But ultimately school is not about places or things; school is much more than bricks, books, and backpacks. School is really about people – classmates, teachers, coaches, nurses, principals, everyone who makes up the communities in which we spend half our waking hours, three-quarters of the year, for over a decade of our lives.

Think about school reunions. After the initial squeals of recognition or puzzled looks, the talk turns backward in time. What do we talk about? Not buildings or courses, but boys and girls, men and women. We tell tales of who did what to whom; we remember remarks made years earlier; we trade stories of students and teachers, now seen through a long, strange lens.

The lens is different because, after our shared school experience, we live different lives. We leave our classmates and teachers, and head into the real world. Some of us follow the paths everyone thinks we'll travel, good or bad; others have greater or less success than a dozen years of school might indicate. Some of us lead happy lives, some sad. But our classmates remember us, we remember them, and hovering above us all, in spirit if not physically, are our teachers.

Our years away from school teach us many things, about ourselves and others. Some of us discover we're attracted to people of the same sex; others find out that friends or family members are lesbian, gay, or bisexual. Whatever the case, it's almost certain that we learn more about homosexuality after we leave school than while we're there.

But our schools are filled with homosexual people. Sexuality is not something we are handed, along with our diploma, on graduation day; it's there long before, even if we can't hang a name on it. Our high schools teem with young men and women who know they are gay, and more who think they may be but are not sure. Our middle schools pulse to the beat of hormone-filled adolescents; two of the most frequently heard pejoratives are "gay" and "fag." Even elementary school boys and girls are aware of sexuality, whether passing out valentines, playing on the monkey bars, or reading books about families.

Our schools are filled too with homosexual adults. Some are teachers or paraprofessionals; others coach teams, clean floors, run libraries. Some are in charge of the whole school, or even the district. Some are the targets of rumors; some no one would ever suspect. A few are open about who they are.

It is these people – these gay, lesbian, and bisexual educators, students, and parents (along with their heterosexual allies) – who determine how positive or negative a school experience will be for its gay students.

Often just one or two people can turn the tide. An outspoken girl who wears pink triangles and rainbow buttons and says to anyone who asks, "Yes, I am gay"; a teacher who stops class whenever the word "fag" is spoken, and explains why he is offended; a principal who puts a picture of her female lover on her desk; a parent who tells a teacher, "Heather has two mommies, so please make sure you put us both on the bulletin board" – these are the people who can send a message to the many other agonized students and teachers in their school that says, yes, there are gays and lesbians around; yes, we lead normal, productive, happy, healthy lives; and yes, we are proud of who we are.

In increasing numbers, these people are popping up in our schools. They have not yet reached critical mass, but across the country, at every grade level and in every state, one can find openly gay students, teachers, administrators, and other school community members.

The students are the ones driving the changes. In the past – just a few years ago, in fact – it was virtually impossible to find even one openly gay high school student. Admitting homosexuality was akin to committing social suicide, several gay men and women have said; who would invite a known "faggot" or "dyke" to homecoming, the prom, or even a weekend party? Who would work on a class project with one – what would everyone else in the room think? And who would ever want to play on the same football team, sing in the same chorus, or act on the same stage with a queer?

Apparently, in 1995, fewer students than ever seem to mind. Over and over again, high schoolers report that coming out has not had serious repercussions; rather, it is seen as a mark of individuality, a rare badge of courage or honor. Hard as it may be for older gays to believe, coming out actually improved at least one boy's social standing. "The girls all thought it was cool to have a gay friend," he said. "And the guys didn't want to alienate the girls, so they didn't say anything. I got invited to more parties than ever."

Gay and lesbian teachers are less concerned with social suicide than with professional work. Only eight states provide job protection for homosexuals; in all fifty states, teachers who come out in the workplace – whether to their supervisors, colleagues, selected students, or the school as a whole – may be regarded with suspicion, distrust, even downright fear.

But that too is changing. Teachers who have come out of the classroom closet describe the effects as exciting, liberating, almost intoxicating. By being more open about their own lives, past and present, they positively impact the lives of all those around them. They counsel gay, lesbian, bisexual, and questioning students, as well as raise the consciousnesses of straight ones; they act as sounding boards at faculty meetings, and confidants for colleagues in private sessions; they have a daily influence, great or small, on every corner of their school building, from the type of books stacked on their library's shelves to the type of language heard in their locker rooms.

And more and more teachers are feeling confident doing so. When I began my research in the summer of 1993, I kept hearing the name John Anderson; it was always followed by the appellation "the only openly gay teacher in Connecticut." A year later, he was being called "the first openly gay teacher"; several others had already followed his lead, and more were about to. And what was happening in Connecticut is being replicated, to varying degrees, in the forty-nine other states.

Nor is it happening only in academic classrooms or at the high school level. Coaches are coming out to their athletic directors and athletes (one woman in the Pacific Northwest estimated that half the teams in her league are coached by gay men or women); librarians are feeling secure enough to order gay-positive books and display them at the front desk; guidance counselors and nurses are forming support groups for students who need help; middle school and elementary educators are doing what they can too, limited, of course, by age-appropriate, commonsense restrictions.

Changes are also occurring above and below the teaching level. In the school hierarchy, teachers serve under administrators, and these men and women are coming out as well. Connecticut's John Anderson, the state's first openly gay teacher, is a life partner of Garrett Stack, the state's first openly gay elementary school principal. Across the country in San Francisco, Tom Ammiano was one of the first openly gay members of a local board of education — and served along with a lesbian colleague, Angie Fa.

Tomorrow's teachers are today's college students; in their education classes, they grapple with questions that both mirror those of tenured teachers ("If I come out in class, will I lose the respect of my students?") and present their own special dilemmas ("If I come out in a job interview, will I lose the chance of being hired?").

In ever-increasing numbers, gay men and lesbians are choosing to be open about their sexuality — open, out, and free. In ever-increasing numbers of schools, their openness is being accepted, if not welcomed. The choices they make do not come easily or painlessly, and their acceptance is far from complete. But for lesbian and gay youngsters and adults in schools today, the situation is healthier than it has been at any time in American history.

Our schools today are made up of all kinds of interesting, diverse people. Many are gay and lesbian; many more are gay- and lesbian-sensitive. A few of their stories follow.

Connie Burns Storms Out of the Closet

Most lesbian and gay schoolteachers never come out of the closet. Of the few who do, nearly all step tentatively: they test the waters for months, even years, seeking allies and developing strong support networks before finally revealing their sexual orientation to colleagues and administrators. Many out teachers draw a line between staff and students; it's one thing, they feel, to be open with adult faculty members, another entirely to have a schoolful of teenagers know (or imagine) intimate details of a teacher's sex life.

Connie Burns, on the other hand, came out one weekend on television and in the newspaper, and instantly the entire city of Buffalo knew.

The Riverside High School math teacher, heavyset and voluble, favors freedom rings, rainbow bracelets, triangle earrings, and message t-shirts. It's not hard to see she's a lesbian. But until the March on Washington in April 1993, Ms. Burns's gay life and school life existed on two entirely different planets.

In fact, it was not until relatively late – her midthirties – that she even realized there was a gay world to be part of. The second of five children of "incredibly Catholic" parents, Ms. Burns attended parochial grammar and high school, and would have gone on to a Catholic college had she not been convinced she wanted to teach in a public school. For the first time ever she opposed her mother and enrolled at Buffalo State College, where she earned bachelor's and master's degrees in secondary education.

Connie Burns taught in several different Buffalo buildings, including a school for girls with high pregnancy and dropout rates, an alternative school, an elementary school, and a magnet school, before transferring to Riverside half a dozen years ago. She describes it as "a neighborhood school in a really depressed part of town – a blue-collar, low-grade, almost redneck section of the city." Of Riverside's six hundred students, about half are in special education or are identified as at-risk. The magnet schools stole away much of the talent; many good students went elsewhere. It's the at-risk students that Ms. Burns loves to teach.

She has a good reason: as early as seven or eight, she figured out that she did not fit into her family or neighborhood. In college she participated in minor sexual experimentation with a female friend, but from age twenty until thirty-five Ms. Burns tried her hardest to be Heterosexual of the Year. That included two marriages, for a total of seven years; in between, she was promiscuous. She slept around, though not particularly enjoyably.

But as she and her second husband became friendly with another couple, things changed. One night the other wife confided that she probably was bisexual, and was deeply attracted to Connie. At that moment, Ms. Burns recalled, "My whole body became electric. It was like the pieces were falling instantaneously in place. I swear I was glowing in the dark."

She and her friend shared the news with their husbands. "They thought it was great," Connie said. "We came to find out most heterosexual men have fantasies of watching two women make love. They thought they'd stay married, reap the benefits, and everyone would be happy." Of course, it was not to be. The two women kissed for the first time on New Year's Eve; their feelings deepened, they spent more and more time together, and by the end of March they found an apartment and moved in.

But Ms. Burns's newly rapturous private life did not translate into joy at work. School was hell; now she cannot imagine how she got through the days. She knows she treated her students miserably. When she finally moved out of her house, she told classes that she and her husband had split up. Things got better then, although she was not yet out to them. She did tell her mother, however, describing the scene as "one of those blurt-it-out, I'm-leaving-my-husband-I'm-in-love-with-a-woman-I'm-a-lesbian-tell-Dad types of conversations."

Gradually, Connie and her lover became more active members of the gay community – but she was still not out at work. Part of the reason was that, working in an elementary school, she was aware of the problems that accompanied being a lesbian and teaching young children; part of the reason too was that her partner's son would soon enter kindergarten at her school.

Though she never lied, she also never said the l-word, and she suspected that people suspected. Her situation stayed that way – out in the gay and lesbian community, inhabiting a netherworld at school – until Christmas of 1992, when her relationship ended and she moved out of the home she and her lover had bought. In the agonizing months that followed, Ms. Burns recognized that to become herself again she needed to be truthful. She had always intended to come out to her students, but not until she began organizing Buffalo's contingent for the upcoming March on Washington trip was she spurred into doing so.

She did not decide on any one day to come out; rather, she recognized slowly an inner feeling that somehow Washington would be the vehicle for that to occur. She tried to talk to her principal the week before the march, to let him know where she was headed (emotionally as well as physically), but it was one of those hectic school weeks and they never connected.

The Thursday night before the march, Ms. Burns attended a rally and press conference in Buffalo. Knowing full well that cameras were panning her way, she made a conscious decision not to retreat behind the police barrier. It happened; she appeared on the late news for just a few seconds, but long enough to be easily recognizable. She spent the entire next morning in school waiting for someone to say something.

No one did. Finally, in the lunchroom, an aide told her that some students had mentioned seeing her on TV the night before. A male colleague whom Ms. Burns described as "one of the most right-wing, conservative teachers – the Rush Limbaugh of Riverside High School" overheard the comment and asked, "So, where were you? The Sabres game?"

"I thought to myself, of all the people in this school I'm going to say this to, it has to be this person, this guy who made me nuts all during Clinton's inauguration with comments about 'fags in the shower.' So I said, 'No, I was with the gays and lesbians, getting ready to go to Washington.'

"His mouth dropped to the floor. But then he recovered and said, 'No, really, where were you?' I said, 'I can't wait to march in Washington on Sunday.'

"He was absolutely stunned. I could almost see the stereotypes being smashed in his head, because even though we don't agree politically, we have respect for each other as teachers."

For the rest of the lunch period, her colleague was silent. However, he timed it so they walked upstairs together. All the way to class he sparred with her about gay issues. She enjoyed watching him react that way, letting her know in his own way that things were okay.

Ms. Burns did not hear another word about the subject all afternoon. On Saturday she flew to the capital (where she had "the typical, look-at-all-the-dykes-this-is-so-great reaction"), and at midmorning on Sunday she joined the New York State group preparing to march.

It was not long before she spotted the Washington bureau reporter for the *Buffalo Daily News*, gathering quotations for a local slant to his story. "I said to my friend, who was about at the same place I was, 'We're gonna talk to this guy and give him our names, aren't we?'" Connie recounted. "And he said, 'Yep, I think so.'" Not only did they talk to the reporter for an hour, but Ms. Burns made sure he wrote down her name, age, and school. She wanted him to get everything right; she had to make sure everyone reading the story understood that this was the same Connie Burns they knew.

The next day she flew back to Buffalo with a sinking feeling in her stomach. Her first act after returning home was to call the librarian, a good friend to whom she had come out several years earlier. The woman told her that people were indeed talking, but were treating the incident as no big deal.

The next morning, Ms. Burns felt she had to get her students to discuss it; otherwise they all would spend the rest of the school year avoiding the very large elephant in the room. She began homeroom, and all of her classes, by saying, "Before we do anything else, let's talk about something." The looks on her students' faces told her they knew what was coming. Some were uncomfortable. But she said simply, "Yes, some of you saw me on TV Thursday night. Yes, I went to Washington to march for gay and lesbian rights. Yes, I was in the paper yesterday. Yes, I am a lesbian. Now we have to talk about it."

She spoke about things she thought they could relate to. To the African-Americans she talked about the connections between the march and the civil rights movement. To the girls she addressed the fact that she and her partner had broken up at Christmas, how devastated she felt, and how if she had been straight (and straightforward) they would have understood. But she had not felt able to say that she and her girlfriend were splitting. Several of her students were in tears, and Ms. Burns was too — but they talked. In some classes that's all they did for the entire period.

The teenagers asked questions. They were stunned to learn that in New York State it is perfectly legal to discriminate against their teacher; she had no marriage benefits, no tax advantages, no legal rights at all. In every class a different African-American boy used the word "faggot." Each time she stopped the discussion, explained the concept of language, and emphasized that words can be either acceptable or offensive. She said, "I've never used this word in my classroom, and even in my life, but your using the word 'faggot' is the same as my using the word 'nigger.' I know you guys use it among yourselves, playing around, and that's fine. We use 'faggot' among ourselves too, but when someone else uses it, we find it offensive. So please, in the future, use 'gay' or 'lesbian.'" They understood, and began to police their language. When a student slipped and called someone a faggot, they would stop, look at their teacher, and say, "Oh! I'm so sorry! I didn't mean anything, Ms. Burns!"

After her eighth-period class, she was wiped out. But the students had been wonderful. It was one of those days when she knew exactly why she taught.

Two girls lingered after her final class. They hugged and cried together. It was a terrible day, one she never wants to repeat – but at the same time she felt wonderful. For the first time she wore double-woman earrings to school, and has every day since. As the days passed, students peppered her with questions about her freedom rings, rainbow bracelets, and slogan buttons. Sometimes it sparked discussions, sometimes it did not. But the most important thing to Ms. Burns was that so many students felt free to ask.

Among the things they wanted to know was how she was sure she was a lesbian, and whether she knew she was not attracted to men. They wondered about her life in general, and edged close to asking about sex. Whenever that happened, Ms. Burns would tell them it was inappropriate, noting they would never pose such questions of a straight teacher. However, she felt they were genuinely interested in learning, and that was important to her.

Some students sought her out to tell stories about gays in their own families; one boy confided that his mother was a lesbian. The outpouring of support, especially from students she didn't expect it from – or even know – was phenomenal. One girl had been in her homeroom for two years and math class for one; Ms. Burns thought of her as argumentative and bored with school. Several months later, another teacher told Ms. Burns that the girl had talked about how "neat" it was that she had come out, and had admired her teacher's courage. In fact, she told the other teacher, she even liked the way Ms. Burns taught. The math teacher marveled that this could be the same girl.

Some teacher-student relationships changed. "One girl, I swear she grew up because of this. Instead of talking about silly stuff like she had before, she'd come up to me in the hall and focus in on much more mature things. She asked questions about my gay buttons, or my jewelry. I could just see it was working in her head, and making a difference to her. By the end of the year I'd be making gay jokes to this kid, and she was getting them. That was really cool."

Teachers gave Connie plenty of positive feedback, including information on how students thought her classroom discussions had gone. Many reported that students felt genuine affection that she had the nerve to share such a private, important part of her life with them. The math instructor was also touched by expressions of support from staff members themselves, including colleagues she seldom saw. They went out of their way to stop by her room to exchange a few words, bring a copy of a newspaper article, or otherwise let her know they were on her side.

Though Ms. Burns did not feel she had been actively hiding her lesbianism, she realized as soon as she came out at Riverside that she had, in fact, been fairly closeted. Coming out unleashed an overwhelming sense of freedom, an almost physical sense of relief that she could wear whatever she wanted, say whatever she wished. Opening the closet door, and letting in fresh air, was the most powerful thing she had ever done.

In fact, Connie said, she knew of only one repercussion that could be called even faintly negative: central office administrators made a bit of noise about her dubious use of a sick day to attend the March on Washington. However, she never heard anything more, and assumes her principal took care of the issue.

The immediate, short-term personal rewards were obvious, but Ms. Burns also realized that by coming out she had assumed some long-term obligations at her school. "I feel I have to get information to kids that they're not now getting," she said. "For many of them, I'm the first person in their lives who has stood up and said, 'I'm a homosexual.' I know all the statistics about dropouts and suicides among gay kids, so I am aware that they need information that they're not alone; that they can grow up to be successful, happy, productive adults not condemned to horrible lives of doom and gloom. I can let them know that Eleanor Roosevelt was a lesbian, and that Michelangelo was probably gay.

"But more than that, straight kids have to understand all that stuff too. I can do that in the way I frame my own speech, challenge their comments, conduct my classes."

Ms. Burns hopes too to work with faculty groups to overcome their own internalized homophobia, and see how important it is for every student to see himself or herself reflected in the classroom. She plans to put together a homophobia course to be run out of the Buffalo teachers' center.

Ms. Burns would like to be appointed to the district multicultural committee, too. As the self-described only openly gay or lesbian instructor in the 4,000-teacher district, she calls herself a natural for the job.

Lesbian and gay education has been ignored in Buffalo, Ms. Burns noted. "Sex education is woefully lacking. For sixteen years we had a mayor who routinely used words like 'fags' and 'fruits' with no consequences whatsoever, and his school board is in that exact same mold. So the place to work is with faculty and curriculum – and I'm going to do it. I'm out now, and no one is going to shut me up."

As Buffalo's television viewers and newspaper readers – and then every staff member and student at Riverside High School – found out, getting lesbian teacher Connie Burns to keep quiet about her life is now impossible.

A Tale of Two Connecticuts

orey Canant does not look eighteen. Slim, freckled, dressed in clothes that straddle the thin line between Gap and grunge, he does, however, look like a typical suburban teenager.

His suburb is West Hartford, a haven for families of the insurance executives, bankers, and engineers who work for the many Connecticut companies that are heavily dependent on defense contracts. These men and women work in Hartford, but live in places like West Hartford. Connecticut is the second wealthiest state in the nation (Alaska's oil makes it number one); paradoxically, three of the poorest American cities lie there too: Hartford, New Haven, and Bridgeport. The Land of Steady Habits is one of the most segregated states in the U.S., with the line between city and suburb sharply drawn.

West Hartford's Hall High is a typically excellent upper-middle-class public school. There are enough computers, VCRs, AP classes, fine teachers, enrichment opportunities, special-needs programs, and other educational bells and whistles to stock a much larger school district; what there is not a lot of is diversity.

That makes it kind of tough to be a gay student. For two years at Hall, Corey Canant struggled with his sexuality; he tried to find friends, a niche in school, and inner peace. Yet he finished his Hall years as a happy, healthy high schooler, proud of himself and his place in his community, eager to assert himself and to educate any students, teachers, and administrators who cared to learn.

One summer afternoon Corey sat in the shade of West Hartford's Elizabeth Park, the site of Connecticut's annual gay pride festival, and talked openly and articulately about his Hall experience. Nearby was his other passion: an old blue VW, on which he did all the work himself. Like many Beetles, it was festooned with bumper stickers

Corey Canant came out in his junior year at Hall High School in upper-middle-class West Hartford, Connecticut. In retrospect, his only regret is that he didn't come out faster and stand up for himself sooner.

© JOHN GROO, 1993

advocating peace, love, and harmony; unlike most, it also bore a pink triangle.

An Austin, Texas, native who moved to Connecticut in sixth grade, Corey spoke in an accent that bore no trace of the Lone Star State. "I went to King Philip Elementary and Middle School. I had a horrible time growing up – but I don't know whether it's attributable to being gay or not. I think those years can be a horrible time for anybody."

Corey was not into sports, art, or anything else; he did not seem to fit in anywhere. He made no close friends until sophomore year. Long before that, he had recognized his attraction to males, but he had stereotypes: homosexuals wear leather and dresses, and sleep around with all their friends. He feared a miserable life if he turned out to be gay.

As a result, he dated females regularly, until he was thirteen. He never had sex with a girl, but he always had girlfriends. And they "fooled around"; he figured the more he did that, the greater the chance he'd enjoy it. In fact, it was enjoyable – but not fulfilling. Corey quickly recognized the difference.

For two years he had no sex at all. Then, when he was a fifteen-year-old sophomore, a very flamboyant freshman entered Hall. "He just couldn't hide the fact he was gay," Corey said. "He came out to everybody. He put up posters saying, 'Ten percent of the population is gay'; he came out in the local papers and the school paper, and on TV. I said, 'Wow! There's somebody who's gay in my high school!' I had no idea! I didn't know anything about ten percent, or anything like that.

"It triggered something in me. I said, 'I must be gay too.' But since I still had my stereotypes, I thought I had to start seeing this new boy, and sleep with him." The stereotypes came from Corey's friends, and his brother and his friends. They were, he recognized later, all myths.

Yet he didn't know that at the time, so he initiated a relationship with the younger boy. "It went on for a couple of weeks," Corey said, "but it didn't work out. He was very unstable, and I wasn't exactly stable at the time either. I really didn't like him at all." They soon went their separate ways.

Corey felt stuck. He realized he could not go back into the closet; he was already out to one or two friends. His parents had seen news articles about the freshman and were suspicious. His mother had always wondered if he was gay; his father always brushed the question aside. One night they called him into their bedroom and asked about his friend's homosexuality; Corey said he had no problem with it. They peppered him with questions: "Do you like men? Do you like women?" Eventually he slipped up. Corey did not want to break his parents' hearts, so he said he was bisexual. They said they wanted grandchildren.

Corey's mother took it well, though she seemed shocked. She told her son, "We'll always love you, and whatever you do we'll be happy with. I'm sure your father agrees." She looked at her husband, and he said nothing.

For half a year Corey didn't speak much to him.

***

Hall High School had a reputation as a rich, snotty school, Corey said. He found snobs and cliques, but also many wonderful people.

When the freshman began declaring his homosexuality, the school had just gotten a new principal. Though supportive of gay rights, she was also cautious. She chastised the freshman for putting up posters not approved by the administration.

Corey was not sympathetic to the newcomer's flamboyant method of fleeing the closet. "He was unstable. He threw it in people's faces. He alienated everyone around him. And because of that he was continually harassed." Eventually the boy dropped out of high school.

Not until a year later did Corey feel ready to tell the world at large that he too was gay. The sense of suppressing part of his life grew overwhelming; he was ready to get on with living, and begin a relationship. For a year he was very depressed.

As a junior Corey began writing a book about a boy who runs away from boarding school. It was so descriptive, a friend asked if the character was gay. Corey said he didn't know. Then the girl asked if the book was about himself. Again he said no. Finally she said, "Well, you're gay, aren't you?" Angrily, he repeated no.

A friend in the class stood up for Corey, and as he was leaving, he thanked her for it. Then he added, "I really am gay."

After that, his coming-out process took off. He told one other friend who told everybody. This time, however, Corey didn't mind; the issue had ceased to be as important as it once was.

In eleventh grade Corey also got involved in Hall's multicultural activities. He co-founded the Student Organization for Integration in Education, and joined a women's issues club. At the same time, he felt pressure from his parents to stay in the closet. They were not yet at the point of speaking publicly, or standing up for him to their friends. He had reached an impasse. His involvement with multicultural organizations was an indirect way of getting his point across, but he could not move beyond the discussions of race and ethnicity to other, gayer issues.

As part of his activities Corey tried to organize a speak-out program at Hall. He gave his principal information on the local Stonewall Speakers Association, but she opposed an assembly based solely on homophobia. She wanted it integrated with other issues. Her coldly professional manner gave Corey the message that she felt she already knew the extent of homophobia at Hall, and saw no need for further discussion.

What was the extent? Corey knew about ten gays and lesbians in the 1200-student school. Some were well out of the closet, while others came out only to him. One boy asked Corey about a pink triangle pin on his coat; when he explained its significance, the boy said, "Oh. Well, I'm gay too. I just didn't know how to tell you."

But Corey suspected there were many more closeted students at Hall. "I can almost pick them out," he said. "Sometimes it's how people react to me, or when they hear something about gays; sometimes it's eye contact. One person pretended to be gay, so everyone thought he wasn't, but he recently came out to me. It seems all my friends are coming out now," he laughed.

As junior year progressed, Corey came further and further out too. However, the results were not always positive. When people's assumptions were validated, some would not talk to him. Some refused even to look at him.

But the more out he became, Corey said, the more he realized it was no big deal. "It's how you present yourself. Even if you're not totally secure with yourself, if you present yourself as secure it makes a big impact on other people. I found myself standing up more and more for myself, for the gay community, for anything I didn't like."

He was out at work too – first at a restaurant, then at a video store. Several times he pulled aside employees, even managers, and explained to them that they were acting inappropriately. A fellow restaurant worker made fun of a flamboyant colleague; Corey got offended, and the worker said, "They're so easy to make fun of."

"Who?" Corey asked. "Flamboyant people or gay people?"

"Gay people," the co-worker replied.

"Well," Corey replied, "I hope you know I'm gay, and I don't want you to make fun of me."

From such incidents, Corey learned the importance of reining in his anger. Far better, he realized, to present a positive, upbeat image of gay people than a negative, combative one.

Though Corey did not have many opportunities to stand up for gay issues in school, he seldom let a good chance slip by. He mentioned statistics and facts in classes; he talked privately with a teacher who routinely called students "fags," and realized he made an impact when the teacher later mentioned seeing Corey on the cover of "some gay magazine."

Corey never had personal problems with homophobic teachers, though he knew they existed at Hall. More often the response to his openness was surprise or incredulity, followed by at least grudging respect. When his math teacher – a "big, dogmatic military man" – saw a note excusing Corey because he was attending a speak-out program at a nearby high school and asked him what the subject was, Corey told him matter-of-factly: gay rights. The teacher was stunned, but looked at his student through new eyes. And a French teacher signed his yearbook in French, "Thanks to you, diversity now has a face in the classroom."

———

What has Corey gotten out of being out? "It's really increased my self-confidence. Indirectly, it's blown the stereotypes I've had all over the place. It's made me real sensitive to other minority and disadvantaged people, and given me something to believe in. I'm more vocal on political and social issues. And in an odd way, it's allowed me to let other people have their own feelings. People have come up to me and said, 'I have a real problem with gays,' and I say, 'Fine.' I wasn't like that before I came out of the closet."

Did coming out change his status in school? "Yeah," Corey admitted. "I've had a lot of people I don't know well say, 'I really respect you,' or, 'You're really a strong person.' I know that's a pretty difficult thing to say to anyone."

Of course, he also noticed a few negative aspects to being so open about his sexuality, including avoidance, name-calling, and harassing phone calls. His junior prom created a problem too: he wanted to go with a male date but didn't feel that was an option, and his parents did not want him to do it either. So he did not go, a decision he later considered a mistake. He attended his senior prom with his best friend, a girl.

There were other awkward social situations as well. Much of the difficulty revolved around feeling out of place with his friends, as if he were the token gay. He felt unable to express himself as freely as they could. However, he acknowledged that as a self-imposed barrier, and as he grew older he felt less and less socially alienated.

Corey's friends came from many different groups. In retrospect, he recognized that there was a reason: he was making sure that if one friend turned against him, he would not then lose the support of his only group.

Because so much of high school conversation centers around relationships – who did what with whom, and how, when, and where – it is often difficult for gay and lesbian youngsters to participate in cafeteria and classroom banter. Corey found it easier to do that toward the end of his senior year.

Still, he had only one serious relationship with a Hall student, a petrified boy with homophobic parents. They pushed him so far into the closet that Corey fears the boy will never come out.

Most of Corey's gay friendships blossomed at Your Turf, a social and support group that draws gay teenagers from throughout northern and central Connecticut. A whole new world opened up for him. The Friday-night meetings, where he could finally be himself, were the highlights of his week. He became a student speaker – and one day, talking to health classes at a nearby high school, he saw a boy from Your Turf. Corey pretended not to recognize him.

Overall, Corey said, Hall students' awareness of lesbian and gay issues is mixed. A small majority know there are gay people there, but few have any idea of the numbers. Teacher awareness also varies. "Some are very aware, some are clueless – and some are in the closet. One woman brought a 'friend' to a school function. But I can't say anything. I'm not supposed to know."

Though no faculty members are out at Hall, Corey is adamant that the best thing a gay or lesbian teacher can do is come out of the closet, and be at the disposal of their students. It would say, "This is a safe place to be out." For students who feel in a void, who don't know anyone else who's gay, or about groups like Your Turf, out teachers could offer referrals, and talk to them about problems.

Corey reported that one student – the one who noticed his pink triangle – told the school psychologist he was gay, was having problems, and wanted to know where to go. The school psychologist said he had no idea.

"I was pissed!" Corey said. "So the next day I went to the psychologist with a handful of Your Turf flyers and said, 'My name is Corey Canant. I'm gay, and a friend said he came in with issues centering around homosexuality, and you didn't know where to send him. I don't want that to happen again.' I don't know if he's handing them out now, but at least he has them."

Corey's guidance counselor was one staff member to whom Corey did not come out. "I don't know whether he knew or not, and that was basically my parents' influence. They said, 'You still have to get a college recommendation from him, and we don't think you should tell him.' I was fed up with that. I was applying to some gay-positive schools, and one of the questions was, 'Has anything happened in your high school career that has changed your life?' What a wide-open question! But this was at the beginning of the year, and my parents said, 'You still have to get into college, and one asshole could read this and you wouldn't get in.'"

But Corey did let some college people know he is gay. While applying for scholarships, he mentioned the fact on any form that included a category for multiculturalism or minority students. He knew they didn't necessarily mean gays or lesbians, but he put it down anyway. He never heard anything about it, positive or negative.

———

After graduation, Corey offered some thoughts on how to make schools more gay- and lesbian-positive. Interestingly, his ideas focus outside the buildings themselves.

"Political groups need to put more pressure on school systems to bring in speakers, and make it as forbidden to call someone 'fag' as to call him 'nigger.' And they need to put pressure on schools to make sure someone is there to show people how to come out of the closet so they won't be harassed – or if they are harassed, to show them how to go to the principal, the school board, maybe even the courts. When you confront people, a lot of times the problems come to an end."

Yet Corey does not believe that every gay student should come out in school. "Not if it will risk your safety or health," he said. "But I think in general coming out is a good experience. It's worse to stay in the closet – it's a bad thing to do to yourself. I felt bad about letting people make fun of me, or the gay community, and not standing up for myself."

Overall, Corey considers his Hall experience to be fairly positive. His only regret is not coming out of the closet faster, and standing up for himself sooner. It took a year or two before he felt able to speak openly. He's made a promise to himself now that if anyone ever asks, he will not lie.

Corey Canant graduated from Hall High, and wore his pink triangle two months later to orientation at George Washington University. Many people asked him what it meant. "I'm gay," he told them, matter-of-factly yet proudly.

He saw plenty of other triangles, rainbow necklaces, and freedom rings at college. It was quite a different sight from his first day in high school. Then again, thanks to Corey and his friends, Hall is also a far different place now than it was when he entered.

————

Downtown Hartford lies just three miles from West Hartford's Elizabeth Park. Parts of the city are beautiful – the gold-domed statehouse is surrounded by broad lawns, and the Connecticut River winds slowly and broadly past gleaming office buildings. But other parts – the sections few tourists ever see – are just plain ugly.

The Hartford Public Library sits in between: a functional building that tries hard to inspire. It is the spot David Waterman chose to tell his story.

Though he too was eighteen at the time of the interview, David Waterman did not look like Corey Canant. David was much heavier, and wore an earring that said "Massive" in one ear; two studs adorned the other, and a small nose ring was clipped to one nostril. He carried a bass guitar, and had just come from an acting class. He was also a sculptor, working with wood and clay. Though his tone lacked Corey's passion, his quiet words were just as earnest and articulate.

There was one other way this teenager did not resemble Corey: David is black.

He grew up in Hartford, with four brothers and sisters; two other siblings died. He lives with his father in a housing project he proudly called "the nicest in Hartford." He feels closest to his thirty-year-old sister.

David realized he was gay in seventh or eighth grade. At first he ignored it; then he tried to suppress it. In ninth grade he entered the Regional Occupational Training Center in Manchester, Connecticut, a seventy-student vocational school for special students; his diagnosis was "schoolphobia." He specialized in woodworking, and his first couple of years went smoothly. During his third year, things changed.

In the winter he became depressed, anxious, and lonely. He was hospitalized for a week, and did not return to school until the following fall. Even then, problems remained until an outpatient therapist explored sexuality issues with him. That reached the heart of his depression.

He had two friends; one was straight, one bisexual. "Things happened" with his bi friend, David said. He became confused, and was hospitalized again. The relationship turned rocky, and the boy stopped attending school. His friend was summoned to a meeting with the principal; he brought his mother, and accused David of "making him do stuff." The school reported him to the state Department of Children and Youth Services; though the investigation was later dropped, the school felt they had to watch out for David. However, no one talked to him directly. Instead, the principal shared information not only with the social worker – the only one he should have told – but with the entire staff as well.

"He broke my confidentiality," David said. "Sexuality is very private. I wasn't even out to myself then."

After that, staff members treated him differently. They kept their eyes on him. He received none of the extra help he was entitled to; he was ignored. People who had looked up to him now glanced away. The social worker asked the wood shop teacher if he had made passes at anyone. Students in his auto class told him another teacher had called him a fag. David wondered how the man – not even one of his teachers – had heard such information.

One day David wore a pink triangle to school. A teacher asked if he realized what it meant. "Of course," he replied. The teacher told him that was not appropriate. "Your sexuality is private," he told David. "Don't flaunt it." David was so frustrated, he had an anxiety attack in school.

Seeking advice, he talked to a teacher he felt close to. She told him the best thing to do was to not seek out relationships – and if he had one, to keep it out of school. She told David that the staff had been told to keep an eye out for him, because of his problems.

David Waterman's struggle with his sexuality landed him in the hospital and in therapy. Encounters with unsupportive teachers and administrators left him angry. "The best thing I ever did was leave," he says of his high school years.

© JOHN GROO, 1994

The young man was appalled. "I could see if I had been convicted or arrested or something," he said. "But this was just the principal's word. They didn't even ask my side of the story."

A month before he was supposed to graduate, David was told by his principal and other school officials that he could not return to school. They told him he was a behavioral problem, and offered homebound tutoring. David was stunned, upset, and irate; he wanted to graduate with his class.

He filed reports with the state departments of Human Rights and Education. There were newspaper articles, in both the straight and the gay press. The entire school read about what was going on.

Yet when David returned to school, there was no harassment from students. "I even made more friends," he recalled. "People said, 'Wow! I didn't know!' Some of them asked, 'How do you know you're gay?' I just said, 'How do you know you're straight?' And they asked, 'How do you meet kids your age? What's it like being gay?'" Some students were more curious than others. "I think those ones have problems with their sexuality," David said.

David realized that any homophobic remarks he heard from his peers stemmed from ignorance. "They don't teach anything in school except the man's on top, the woman's on the bottom. Well, sexuality is a lot wider than that. Kids are not taught anything at all about homosexuality."

David said that at his school, he knows at least four gay or lesbian students. One girl is living a straight life because of her family. She told David she definitely would not come out after what happened to him.

In addition, David said, "there's one teacher who a lot of people say he's gay, but I don't know. People say he was married once, but that doesn't mean anything. And one woman teacher, they say she's a lesbian. She's a tomboy, the athletic type."

David discovered Your Turf; in fact, he and Corey became friends there. He also got involved with the Greater Hartford Gay, Lesbian, and Bisexual Inner City Youth Project and the House of Pleasure, which he described as "a second family for gay youth."

Back at school, he said, "a lot of people started looking at me as a demagogue – I think that's the word. It's a melting pot of races – I'm West Indian, and there's Asians, Dominicans, Italians. There are a lot of racial fights. I wanted to start a multicultural club, and we had three or four meetings. Then the gays in the military thing came up, and I spoke out about it. One kid said he was against it and I said, 'Don't flatter yourself. Every gay guy won't be attracted to you.' But at least we got people talking about it."

His advice to schools is to teach more about sexuality, and be more aware of everyone's feelings. He sees a need for neutral persons for students to talk to. The unprofessionalism of his school irks him; he cannot believe that they do not know how to deal with the changes happening in the world. He found his fellow students to be far more understanding than his teachers, social worker, and principal.

David cannot cite one positive element of his school experience. "The best thing I ever did was leave," he said. "I didn't feel I was accomplishing my potential. I wanted to go to college, and they told me I shouldn't. I don't know if that had to do with me being gay or not, but it just wasn't a supportive environment."

Lacking several credits to graduate, David transferred to a public high school, twenty minutes away. And then in the winter, his luck changed. He was accepted at the Hartford Academy of Performing Arts, a magnet school. His life turned around. He was among diverse people, in an atmosphere that, if not actually gay-friendly, was at least nonhomophobic. He became more focused than ever before. As the school year wound down he landed a role in the school production of *West Side Story* as a Shark. He got ready for a summer program at Wesleyan University's Center for Creative Youth.

And in June 1994, David Waterman graduated from high school.

JOHN ANDERSON & GARRETT STACK

One Teacher, One Principal, One Couple

S ome teachers come out because they feel impelled to be their school's counselor for anguished gay and lesbian students. Some come out for personal reasons: they're at a point in their lives where they must tell the world about themselves, or burst. Still others, involuntarily outed, suddenly find themselves sharing their secret in front of colleagues, supervisors, parents, and students.

John Anderson – Connecticut's first openly gay teacher – came out for none of those reasons. He simply saw a need as an educator to create a better, safer, more comfortable environment in his school, and he seized the chance.

He's one of those people who never doubted he would teach – and never stops learning. After earning his bachelor of arts from the University of Hawaii and his master of arts in teaching from the College of St. Thomas in St. Paul, Minnesota, he did graduate work in medieval studies at Catholic University. In 1972 he received his doctorate in Medieval Latin, with a minor in Middle English, then joined a private foundation that tests and advises students about college and career choices.

He met Garrett (Garry) Stack at a convention. Two years later John moved to Connecticut so they could be together, and the following fall he began teaching at a private Episcopal girls' boarding school. After three years he joined the Stratford public school system, where he has been for a decade. He describes Stratford as "a blue-collar town with a Valley cultural and social mentality." In Connecticut, "the Valley" is a pejorative term; as Dr. Anderson explained, "nobody would call it sophisticated. It's Republican, in no way progressive." As an example

John Anderson, Connecticut's first openly gay teacher, met his partner, elementary school principal Garrett Stack, at a convention.

he noted that Stratford's current schools superintendent was praised as unflashy, while his predecessor was considered too heady: he wanted to do too many exciting things.

Dr. Anderson, whose graying hair, glasses, and earnest demeanor mark him as a true academician, splits his Latin and English classes between two high schools, Stratford and Bunnell. He is one of the system's top educators, having been a Teacher of the Year finalist and the recipient of two Celebration of Excellence awards, at the state and regional levels. Dr. Anderson also writes books, poetry, and newspaper articles. In fact, he recalled while sitting on a spacious deck behind the red brick home he shares with Garry, it was his writing that moved him out of the closet.

Three years ago he got the opportunity to take over the male portion of the gay and lesbian column in the *New Haven Register,* with a piece every ten weeks (a voice for minority groups, the space rotates contributions by African-Americans, Hispanics, Asians, and Jews). He knew that by accepting the job, he would out himself.

The couple had many serious discussions about that – Garry Stack is an elementary school principal in Stratford, and it was obvious that the column's fallout would hit him too – before John decided to go ahead. "It's not that far from New Haven to Stratford," he said. "But I thought it was a lot farther than it is."

His first story appeared in October 1991. The same day a colleague handed him a copy of the paper, saying it had arrived from another teacher, via an administrator. The supervisor worked in the central office, clear across town.

"I think I blanched a little," Dr. Anderson recalled. "My stomach went tight. I thought, 'Oh God.' I had expected it would be several weeks before I had to deal with this. But it happened immediately, and word spread through the staff like wildfire."

Over the next several days he got strange, quizzical, sometimes angry looks from colleagues. However, no one said anything nasty; several made comments like, "I saw your piece in the paper. Great!" What impressed Dr. Anderson most was that many male teachers expressed approval, congratulated him, or patted him on the shoulder. He did not feel at all like a pariah.

As the months passed and the columns continued, other teachers made comments – always positive. One co-worker said, "I made a big effort to find you. I don't agree with everything you write, but I applaud your doing it." Dr. Anderson felt gratified by the tremendous support of his peers. It surprised him; he had expected at least some negative feedback.

He also was pleased by the initial reactions of his supervisors. Before he could hand a copy of the first column to the Bunnell principal, she beat him to it, noting with disgust the sleazy way it was delivered: someone had left it anonymously on her desk. Dr. Anderson was pleased she realized the inappropriateness of that.

Yet the source of his pleasure lay deeper than the moment: "A month earlier she had ripped me apart for an hour in her office, with my supervisor sitting next to me, because I wanted as my official evaluation goal for the year to examine the special needs of lesbian and gay students, and how the school system was meeting those needs. She absolutely refused; she said it was totally inappropriate for a high school teacher, and had nothing to do with the teaching of Latin. I just let her vent. At the end of the hour I told her I still wanted to do it."

After his first article appeared she called him back into her office and told him his goal would fly, after all, with a few changes. She'd gone to the superintendent and assistant superintendent; they were abuzz. In the meantime Dr. Anderson had contacted the union, and received their full support. Their only concern was that his high-profile activity might jeopardize Mr. Stack's reputation in town. When the teacher asked what their response would be in the event of a parental uprising, they assured him they would circle the wagons.

John Anderson pursued his educational goal all year. He talked with teachers, administrators, social workers, counselors, and nurses. He kept raising questions: What are we doing about gay and lesbian kids? What are we doing about homophobia? The answer was always the same: Nothing. He was stunned that while his fellow educators recognized these as legitimate issues, no one knew what to do about them – or who should take charge. Empowerment in an educational system, Dr. Anderson said, comes either from "a very strong sense of self, where you're willing to buck the system, or from the top. Well, we've never had any indication here in Stratford, from the principals, the assistant superintendents, or the superintendents, that this was a legitimate issue, or that we should deal with it in such-and-such a way. It's a taboo topic. It was never brought up. The wish is that it would go away; that by ignoring it, it's not real."

What exactly is "it"? "The plight of lesbian and gay kids trying to find themselves in an educational system that denies they exist," Dr. Anderson replied simply.

While he had never encountered any student he knew to be gay, Dr. Anderson assumed they existed at Bunnell and Stratford – and he knew the devastation that a hostile school environment could wreak on them. He listened to the "fag" jokes told by faculty members; he heard the word "faggot" in the halls, recognized it as the ultimate put-down in any school, and was angered by the ease with which the teaching profession ignored it.

He also knew that there were gay teachers and counselors (and, of course, at least one principal) in Stratford. A year earlier he had witnessed with horror what happened when a Bunnell teacher died of AIDS. "He never said he was gay or even that he had AIDS," Dr. Anderson recalled, "the latter because of insurance and keeping his job. But when he died it was treated extraordinarily different from any other faculty member's death. A group of students had to go to the principal in tears to ask that something be said over the intercom. I phoned the superintendent to tell him I was appalled by what was going on, and why weren't the flags at half-mast, as they would be for any other teacher who died? Well, he did act; the flags went down, and the next day a very brusque, peremptory announcement was made by the principal that a faculty member had died.

"We have in education what we call 'the teachable moment,'" Dr. Anderson continued. "That was 'the teachable moment' to deal with AIDS. Some teachers did things individually – but nothing as an institution was done." It was a defining moment in Dr. Anderson's decision to try to change the educational environment in Stratford.

⸻

He was the first openly gay educator in town; his partner was the second. Students at Dr. Anderson's two schools are aware that he and

Mr. Stack are a couple. A teacher at Bunnell put a *New York Times* interview of the Latin teacher on her bulletin board; students read it and said, "Oh, he's married to Mr. Stack." Dr. Anderson credited that colleague with creating an open, accepting environment.

In his other building, Stratford High, a girl told one of his closest female colleagues, "You and Dr. Anderson make a cute couple." Another student overheard the remark and asked if he was gay. Yes, the woman said; she added that if her marriage was half as good as Dr. Anderson's, she would be thrilled. "Well," the first girl said, "you and he still make a cute couple."

"To me, that's the goal," John Anderson said. "Being gay is just another item to her, like whether somebody's blue-eyed or brown-eyed, right-handed or left. Nothing more, nothing less."

But obviously it's not that simple or clear to everyone in Stratford, and so for a second year in a row Dr. Anderson selected as his educational goal an examination of the school system's environment for gay and lesbian students. The second time around was easier, he said. Teachers were getting used to it; they felt more empowered to deal with homosexuality. Colleagues told him about lesbian daughters, gay stepsons, bisexual sisters. They shared parts of their lives with him in ways they never had before.

Students, too, became more open with Dr. Anderson about homosexuality. One girl, sent by the school nurse, said she had a friend who had just come out to her. Dr. Anderson gave her pamphlets and penned a short note of encouragement; she tracked him down a few days later to thank him for his help. The boy remained too reticent to ever come to him, but that was all right; Dr. Anderson admired the girl's willingness to seek information and shepherd her friend through the process. His goal is not to be the only resource in school; he hopes students will talk to counselors too.

However, he added, "I'm still not convinced that all these counselors are trained, or comfortable, dealing with homosexual issues. Many of them in Stratford are excellent people – but the school system has never made an effort to train them on this issue. We have people teaching health classes, where homosexuality often comes up as an issue, who have never had a course or even a workshop on it. We wouldn't treat any other subject this way."

John has made it a habit to keep in touch with counselors and social workers, and they have become used to talking with him. They routinely share articles, information, and comments. If he hears they are making a presentation to parents, he suggests they include homosexuality, along with depression and suicide.

He has become quietly active in other ways, too. When students at his two schools were preparing articles for their newspapers about homosexuality, he worked closely with them. Both ended up positive pieces.

Dr. Anderson and Mr. Stack also bought half-page ads in the two Stratford high school yearbooks, plus the yearbook in the town in which they live, on behalf of PFLAG (Parents, Families and Friends of Lesbians and Gays). The organization's phone number is listed – but, said Dr. Anderson, "The ad sends a tremendous message even for kids who are not gay: 'Hey, maybe fags *are* human beings. It's here in my yearbook!'" In addition, Dr. Anderson made sure that the high school newsletter included information for parents of lesbian and gay children.

John Anderson has become active beyond Stratford, at the state level as well, again with satisfying results. He joined the teachers' group Educators and Friends of Lesbians and Gays. He has presented numerous workshops across Connecticut, to faculty, administrators, mental health professionals, counselors, and social workers. He has watched with satisfaction as the Connecticut Education Association hired a professional development coordinator to conduct free workshops for schools on issues of homophobia.

But he still grades Connecticut's handling of homosexuality at 15 on a scale of 100 – an F in any teacher's book – and that is why Dr. Anderson continues to count small incidents in his own classroom as important steps. For example, whenever he mentions Hadrian, he adds that the emperor was a homosexual. His students are less likely to giggle than others, because they know their teacher is gay too – and because he talks about Hadrian so unemotionally, so matter-of-factly. They hear it, and that's all he cares about.

Such opportunities arise randomly. When a boy brought in Benjamin Britten's *War Requiem* on CD, Dr. Anderson used that as a chance to talk about the use of Latin in church services; he then told his students that Britten was gay and had lived for over thirty years with the famous English tenor Peter Pears, and that when he died the Queen of England sent a letter of condolence to his lover.

Of course, there are occasional slips. "One kid will say the word 'faggot' in class, and the other kids look amused because they know what's coming," he recounted. "I'll say, 'Excuse me? What did you say?' and the kid will blush. Then I'll say, 'Call him something else – anything else – but not that.' One boy this year called President Clinton a faggot. I said, 'Whoa! Call him whatever you want, but I don't think he's a homosexual. And besides, I don't want to hear that word; it's a word just like "nigger."' I always include that, because they know 'nigger' is bad, but they don't know 'faggot' is bad. I mean, they know it's bad in the sense that they know 'faggot' really gets people when they say it, but no adult is telling them it's a no-no. I intervene that way, and some other teachers do too.

"But we're still not getting any word from the top to empower us, to tell us what to do, how to act – even whether we should do anything at all on this issue. We don't need directives, curriculum, policy; all we need is an *environment,* and that costs nothing at all. That's where there's a leadership vacuum."

What kind of leadership does John Anderson want? Going beyond a nondiscrimination statement in the student handbook would be good; he hopes teachers and administrators can actually *talk* about what those words mean. "We talk about gangs, sexual harassment, drugs, you name it – but we never say a word about creating a climate of approval or acceptance for people who are different, like gays or lesbians. That's what I want. I want the principals, when they meet with each class at the beginning of the year, to say, 'We don't want reductive language in our classes or halls. Nobody calls somebody a nigger; nobody calls somebody a faggot.' And they've got to say the f-word, or else they're just talking around the issue. The kids wonder: If it's not nice to be bad to gays, why isn't somebody saying so? Nobody is."

Dr. Anderson noted that his schools are rife with signs trumpeting every social issue. He looks forward to the day when one appears saying, "You may be gay, and it's okay." Or, "If you know someone who's gay, call..." Such posters never go up because administrators are scared of what he calls "the Christian Reich, and of parental reaction. And because they receive no signals from the board of education that this is something they should deal with, an informal conspiracy of silence ensues."

The "Christian Reich" is not, Dr. Anderson feels, a legitimate concern. "Nothing has happened in Stratford with parents, to my knowledge, over the fact that they have an openly gay high school teacher, and an openly gay elementary school principal. Nothing."

Which is not to say that there has been no reaction, period. Once, walking down the hall, he heard, "Hey, Dr. Anderson! Are you a faggot? I hear you're a faggot!" He turned, looked at a group of students fifty feet away, and headed straight to the principal's office. The girl who yelled was identified, spoken to, and reprimanded.

Several weeks later three or four boys passed Dr. Anderson. One hissed, "Faggot. Fuckin' faggots. I hate faggots." He turned, saw that one was a student of his, and hauled him down to the principal. Later that day, the boys appeared in his room to apologize. "I looked them in the eye and said, 'I'm gay. I'm not a fag, and I'm not a faggot,'" Dr. Anderson said. "I gave them a couple of other one-liners they needed to consider; then shook their hands and sent them out of there." Nothing similar has happened since.

The use of the word "faggot" continues, of course, at Stratford and Bunnell Highs. Dr. Anderson is not sure whether it is directed at him, and in vague situations he ignores it. He knows it is a word used nearly as often and casually as "like" or "whatever," but he does not want to have to put up with it. So he put his concerns in writing, sent them to the superintendent – and received no reply. He kept a log, created a paper trail, and considered filing a grievance, based on the fact that his school system was doing nothing to create a safe environment for him. Eventually he decided to wait for a different battle.

The issue, he believes, lies broader than talking to students on a case-by-case basis, and cuts deeper than one or two schools. "I know of a teacher at an intermediate school who is perceived as gay – and he is – who was harassed mercilessly," he said. "Kids said things at bus duty; they accessed messages from his answering machine, and made references to them in the middle of class. Eventually the superintendent and assistant superintendent had to intervene, because the principal is a macho pig who did nothing. There is absolutely no reason any teacher should have to go through that kind of agony. A black teacher wouldn't; we wouldn't allow that kind of crap with any other teacher either. Yet because it involved gay issues, it was allowed to continue for a long time."

Sometimes Dr. Anderson looks longingly north, where Massachusetts governor William Weld established a commission on gay and lesbian youth. "They produced a beautiful fifty-page document, filled with recommendations for schools," the teacher said. "We have the same document on a one-page sheet out of the state Board of Education, which has been pretty much ignored. And Governor Weld issued a directive to all schools, suggesting they come up with ways of dealing with homophobia. We have nothing like that here, and we're not that far from Massachusetts."

Dr. Anderson is adamant that all lesbian and gay teachers everywhere should leave the closet. "Absolutely," he said. "We're educators. We're in the business of educating children. To me, that means bringing them to knowledge. We're preparing them for careers, for life in a world filled with gay and lesbian people. They'll be working and living with homosexuals. If we don't teach them that there are gay people out there, and that that's okay, they won't be able to function in society. They'll lose jobs. They'll get their ass kicked, legally."

There is another reason John Anderson wants all gay and lesbian teachers to be out, and working to create a better educational environment: "If we're in the closet, we're cheating gay kids. We're denying them their whole psychosocial development, because they look around for a way to be who they are in school, and it ain't there. They look around to see at least one other gay person in the world, and it ain't there either.

"We need to be out," he continued. "That doesn't mean every gay teacher needs to be a counselor to gay kids. But it does mean kids need to know, 'He's gay' or 'She's gay' – just like we can see, 'He's black, she's Asian,' or whatever. It's part of the rich diversity of the culture we live in, and right now it's being denied to gay and lesbian students."

Finally, Dr. Anderson said, lesbian and gay teachers must be out for their own professional and personal peace of mind. "A gay person is not a full human being in the closet. I can't tell you the liberation that comes with being out. It's scary; it's hard; I've got bruises – but I'm free. I don't have to monitor what I say when I go back to work on Monday. When someone asks about my weekend, I don't have to think about the holy union I went to and say, 'I went to a wedding with, er, um, a couple of people I know.' I don't have to constantly watch my pronouns. My policy now is, 'If you ask, I'll tell.' So I'll say, 'I went to a holy union with Anita and Suzanne at Yale Divinity School, and it was great.' People ask, 'What'd you and Garry do this weekend?' just like I ask Pete about Sally. It's wonderful. It's living."

John Anderson paused. "I live for the day when we're included in everything. That's all I want: to be included. My favorite sign at the March on Washington was, 'No more. No less. Just equal.' That's it for me."

———————

Shortly after he was interviewed, Dr. Anderson addressed several important issues in his *New Haven Register* column. "It's been two years since Connecticut extended civil rights protection to include its gay and lesbian citizens," he began. "The lives of many people will never be the same because of this legislation. My life certainly has changed irrevocably. I'm out for life, in every meaning of this ambiguous statement.

My spouse, Garry, and I are drinking the cup of freedom, liberated from the duplicity of life in the closet."

The couple "put our faith and trust in the goodwill of our colleagues and have not been disappointed," he continued. "The people we work with are not extraordinary. We don't work in a particularly progressive town. We work in Stratford. It's a cross section of the country."

However, he noted, "the excitement of Garry's and my liberation is due to the ordinary decency of our co-workers and the parents of the kids we work with. They are learning to value us as a gay teacher and a gay principal because we gave them the chance to know us as we are."

Dr. Anderson called staying in the closet "selfish," then explained why. "We have an obligation to our families, our friends, our students to be who we are. There can be no healing without honesty. In the summer, Garry and I went to Hartford to register as domestic partners. We share that with our colleagues just as they share facts about their marriages. The Sunshine Fund at the high school gave us a present when I informed them we had something to celebrate. It's great to be 'part of' rather than 'excluded from.'"

"Garry and I are out for life," he concluded. "Come join us. The breathing is easy."

———————

The air at Franklin is fresh. It is, in many ways, a typical elementary school, nineties style. The halls are bright; carpeting covers the floors, and a cheerful mural accosts everyone who walks through the front door. "Happy Children Make Good Learners," it says, above an art teacher–type rendering of a gaggle of citizens who are, one supposes, learners. In typical elementary school fashion the mural's learners are black, brown, white, yellow, and red; they are tall and short, male and female and – this being Stratford, Connecticut, an hour from New York City – one even sports a Yankees cap. Are any of these learners gay or lesbian? Probably; after all, every school community includes homosexual students, staff, and parents.

And this particular school has a homosexual principal. An openly homosexual principal.

The principal, Garrett Stack – for fourteen years, John Anderson's partner – is clearly in charge here. Teachers, custodians, and parents pop by the office of the trim, tan, mustachioed administrator who carries himself with an almost military bearing; they report in, ask questions, seek counsel. But just as clearly he's in charge because he has earned their respect, not demanded it. There is a familiarity to his replies, an easy tone to his advice. A poster in his office says, "Please treat other kids the way y♥u want to be treated," and it is obvious that the words are not there merely for decoration.

It is not an easy school to be in charge of. A 1990 renovation brought the eighty-year-old building into the twentieth century, but a school is much more than bricks, blackboards, and bright lights. This one is filled with 450 boys and girls, kindergarten through sixth grade, and they represent a mix so diverse that their school and town are often studied by sociologists seeking an ethnic, economic, and social micro-cosm of the United States.

Stratford started out as an all-white, blue-collar suburb of Bridge-port, a city that in its prime was a driving force in America's industrial engine. But Bridgeport has fallen on hard times – it was one of the first major cities to teeter on bankruptcy – and Stratford too has changed. The school's population is now 31 percent African-American, His-panic, and Asian; many students live in single-parent homes, and nearly half the youngsters rely on free or reduced-fee lunch programs. But one thing has not changed: Franklin, just a few yards from the Bridgeport border, represents a step up for many residents. Moving from "the city" is a big deal for lots of residents – and many move for the schools.

Besides Franklin there are eight other elementary schools in Strat-ford, the town in which Garry Stack has spent his entire working life. In college he lived in New Haven and commuted to Western Connecti-cut State, nearly an hour away; his only request for a student teaching position was that it be as close to his house as possible. Stratford filled the bill; his training there was successful, and in 1968 he was offered a job in the district. At the time the salaries were the ninth highest in Connecticut; he started at $6,500 a year. Mr. Stack's classroom career covered fourth, fifth, and sixth grades, as well as the gifted program; after twelve years he moved into administration, and in 1991 he achieved his dream. He became an elementary school principal.

"I'm exactly where I want to be," he said with satisfaction. "I'm in a building, in the trenches. There's nothing else I'd rather do in education, nowhere else I'd rather be."

His move to Franklin coincided with his partner's opportunity to write a regular column on gay and lesbian issues for the *New Haven Register*. They made a conscious decision that if John would be out, Garry would as well. It was not a sudden change of heart: Garry Stack had been open about his homosexuality for a long time with many trusted colleagues. Some parents knew implicitly too. As far back as 1974 he'd come out to a principal he worked for when she asked about a rumor she'd heard. Garry remembers that incident as the first time he had to live up to a personal pledge never to deny who he was.

Mr. Stack's appointment at Franklin also coincided with the enactment, in October 1991, of a state law prohibiting discrimination on the basis of sexual orientation. No longer could homosexuality be used as a means of dismissal. After twenty-three years and an excellent record, he finally had the protection of the state of Connecticut behind him.

He decided that his Franklin staff should be the first people to share the bounty of that law. He came out to every adult in school – thirty teachers, classroom assistants, custodians, the secretary, the nurse – in a month-long series of one-on-one meetings. The sessions were natural for any new principal; he and the staff talked about the school, their roles in it, and their students. But at the end Mr. Stack would ask if they had a couple of more minutes to talk about something else. Then he told them that he was gay.

The reaction was unanimously positive. They knew him, or at least of him; he'd been in the system for twenty-three years, and that was the key. But beyond basic support, he heard more. Invariably, in the privacy of his office, people told stories: their brother was gay, their sister was a lesbian, their uncle was bisexual. He was not surprised. "If you believe that 10 percent of the population is gay – and I do – then it takes only ten people in a family for someone to be homosexual. And most families include at least ten people, when you count uncles and aunts and cousins and grandparents."

His next decision was to come out to the other community he works with: the parents. The first members of that community he told were the PTA co-presidents. Their reaction too was warm and accepting. And they too revealed personal information about their lives to him. He found that his honesty empowered people to share things they might have kept inside. That's good for everyone, he said. (It also earned him a number of fans and audience members for his most important extracurricular activity: president of the Connecticut Gay Men's Chorus.)

The goal in all this, Garry said, was for everything to be normal. He wanted to be able to say, "John and I," just as other people talked about their spouses. The staff at Franklin is very close; he found it silly to have to keep part of his life from such good friends.

That normalization process evolved well. "At first, when only a few people knew, they'd whisper, 'Did you see *Phil Donahue* last night?" he said. "Then, as more people knew, they'd ask it in a low voice. Now it's said in a normal tone, and in front of perfect strangers. One mother said, 'I could've killed that woman on *Sally Jessy* yesterday when they were talking about gay siblings and she didn't stand up for her lesbian sister!' Everyone looked around – she was really indignant."

While he doesn't feel it necessary to stand up at a PTA meeting and proclaim who he is, Garry Stack does believe it is important for people to know. People tend to assume that everyone else is heterosexual; they need to know that is not true, which is one reason he wears a wedding band. The father of a first grader was having trouble with his son, and went to Mr. Stack for advice. In the course of the conversation he noticed the ring, and asked the principal how long he'd been married and whether he had any children. "I'm on my second marriage, and this one has lasted fourteen years," Mr. Stack said. "But I'm married to a man; I'm a homosexual."

The man looked blank for a minute, then asked if he was kidding. Mr. Stack said no, adding that he has had kids – hundreds, in his twenty-six years in the schools. Then the conversation continued just as before. After five minutes the man told the principal that his father always said it takes a big man to be so open, and added that he respected Mr. Stack for that. Then they went back to talking about his son.

Incidents like that convince Garry that his course is the right one. A few days earlier a father had told the principal that he and a few other men were thinking of starting a Cub Scout troop at Franklin, and wanted his opinion. Garry replied that it was a great idea – he had been a Boy Scout himself – but added that he had a problem: not with scouting as a concept, but with the organization that ran it. He explained their policy on gays (the Boy Scouts of America do not allow homosexuals to serve in any capacity), asking what would happen if they set up a group and, after a few years, a thirteen-year-old boy came out to them and they had to kick him out. The father said that they knew about the policy, they thought it was wrong, and they were working on it. Mr. Stack gave his approval; the group is now attempting to effect change, together.

A couple of days before that – it had been quite a week – another father came to Mr. Stack because his son was being laughed at, tormented, and called "gay." The principal replied that no child should be subjected to any degradation, no matter what. "But then – and this is why it's so important for me to be out – I told him I was especially sensitive to this because I'm gay," he recounted. "The father nodded. I told him, 'I don't know your son's orientation; perhaps it's too soon to know. But if he *is* gay, what's most important is his parents' love and support. It's not a death sentence; he can have a happy, productive life with plenty of dreams and aspirations.' I told him about my family's love and support, and how that's allowed them to share in my successes. And then he nodded and assured me that this boy was his son, and he loved him no matter what.

"I want to be there so when people know me, and know I'm gay, they have to weigh me against any other stereotypes and beliefs they may have heard," Garry continued. "That's my whole purpose for being out."

He has learned that his partner John Anderson's credo – "The world is filled with good and decent people; give them credit" – is true. But adults are one thing; what about children? In elementary schools all over the country, after all, "faggot" and "gay" are the two harshest put-downs imaginable.

When he hears of such terms used by one of his students, Mr. Stack talks to the child. What he says depends upon the age. But his basic message is that it is a word meant to hurt somebody, and that at Franklin School hurting people is unacceptable. He does not stand up in an assembly and announce that the principal is gay. But he has told three students, in various ways ("so I guess I'm counting," he laughed).

The first time was when a fifth-grade girl told him high school students were saying he had left his wife to marry a man, and because of that they were going to beat her up. She had some facts wrong, but when Mr. Stack asked if she knew what "gay" meant she gave a good, rudimentary response. He asked if she liked him as a principal, and had he done nice things? She answered yes both times. So he told her those were the things to look at when you judge people. She accepted his answer.

The second incident came after he disciplined a worldly-wise sixth-grade boy who told Mr. Stack he'd heard a terrible rumor. Again the principal asked if the child knew what "gay" meant; this time the response was better than the girl's had been. Mr. Stack answered yes, then asked whether that made a difference. He said no – what else could he say to the principal?! – but the next day Mr. Stack made a point to talk to the boy again. "Now, I'm not sure what really went on in his head, but I had forced him to weigh me, and what he knew about me, against whatever he may have heard at home, in church, or on the street, and I think he came up with the right responses," Mr. Stack said.

The third situation arose with one boy who had been harassing another. The bully knew what "gay" meant, so Mr. Stack told him that the principal is gay, and he should think about who he might be hurting. Then they talked about the ways people are different – the boy happened to be very tall – and that was the end of that.

Coming out in school has had important implications, Garry Stack said, and those repercussions echo far beyond the Franklin community. A woman who worked in another Stratford school asked to speak to him in private. She wanted to know how to come out to the faculty, and Mr. Stack told her: One at a time. She said she had been afraid to come out for twenty years, but that after seeing Mr. Stack and his partner, and the way they lived their lives, she wanted people to know who she was.

A few months later, after an administrators' meeting, an administrator at another school asked to talk with him. She told Mr. Stack that her nineteen-year-old son had come out to her the previous weekend. She said she had started to cry, but then thought of the two educators she knew, and realized it was not such a terrible thing. Their happiness and success helped her accept her son's homosexuality. Since then, the woman and Mr. Stack have conducted "Invisible Minority" workshops throughout the district. One, held in a blizzard, drew even more attendees than had originally signed up.

But as important as that work is, it's inside Franklin School that Garry Stack feels most fulfilled. "I'm often told that when people walk into the building they find an immediate, recognizable, warm, welcome, friendly, human tone," he said. "People talk about the school with a lot of respect; teachers want to transfer in, and parents want their kids to go here. I think that's because people are more important than things here.

"One of the first things I did when I got here was to set up a Franklin School Set of Beliefs – twelve underpinnings of philosophy. They all relate to the belief that children count; that they deserve a place free from fear, threat, and all the other stuff lurking outside our bright doors. I'm not so naive to think that the outside doesn't have an effect on kids – we do have very damaged kids, who come in here missing very basic love and care – but I think children's needs are transparently simple. And anything that impinges on their happiness, I'm against it."

Which is why his message of care, respect, and love is the main focus of Franklin School, and why its principal's homosexuality is, in his words, a non-issue. "I love everything about this job and this place. I love the age group, the variety of activities, the enthusiasm little kids have for learning, the creativity they bring to the classroom that energizes their teachers. I have no aspirations for anything else. I want to stay an elementary school principal."

And, it is clear, Franklin's parents want their gay elementary school principal to stay there forever.

A Whole New Ball Game

Reggie Sellars was a football star at Yale. He spent two years as a dorm parent at a small boarding school; today he coaches football and wrestling, and teaches Spanish, at Noble and Greenough School in Dedham, Massachusetts. Naturally, everyone looks up to him, and he loves what he's doing. The openly gay, African-American role model is on top of the world.

Mr. Sellars, who says everyone calls him Reggie, speaks softly but articulately; the words flow slowly but steadily. He's like a football player churning out yardage: he'll carry the ball often and unspectacularly, but at the end of the day you suddenly realize he's gained over 200 yards and won the game. He's filled the role of solid, special person in many different settings and social situations, beginning as the youngest of six children in suburban North Carolina.

He has been athletic all his life: track, swimming, football. He knew he was gay almost as far back as he can remember, but never labeled his feelings that way. He did "the whole hetero thing, dating girls and whatnot," but after entering the elite Phillips Exeter Academy private school at sixteen, he found his first boyfriend. Yet he remained discreet, and did not come truly out until the summer before college, when he told his family and closest high school friends. As soon as he entered Yale, he confided in his new roommates; he wanted them to know who they were living with.

They accepted it easily – as, to his surprise, did his freshman football teammates. He expected to be kicked off the team, but it never happened. Instead, they accepted him and his homosexuality – so much so that by the end of the season they were trying to set him up with guys they thought he'd like.

As a sophomore he moved up to the varsity, and throughout his three-year Eli career, his homosexuality was never a football issue. He developed a good set of friends on the freshman team, and they stayed intense friends all through their varsity years. Yale has an Ivy League–wide reputation as a gay school, because so many students are so outspoken on the issue, and occasionally, other fans or bands made comments. The Dartmouth band once updated the "one in ten" slogan (purportedly the percentage of homosexuals in the general population), chanting, "One in four – maybe more!" at the Yale section. Reggie and his teammates took it as a joke, and laughed.

He was never politically active at Yale, preferring to channel his energy toward other less noticeable but equally important fronts, such as tutoring high school youngsters. He planned to head to Wall Street after graduation in 1990, but enjoyed tutoring so much that he changed his major to Spanish language and history, and searched for a teaching job. He had a special, personal motive as well: having spent four years in prep school himself, he sensed the need for more black role models there. He did not realize that he would soon serve as a gay role model too.

In his first weeks at Brewster Academy, a small boarding school in New Hampshire, he was one of several new young teachers. "Kids try to relate to you, find out who you are, right off the bat," he said. "I was working out a lot, playing basketball, and they kept asking if I was dating this or that woman teacher. I just said, 'No.' Then I starting hearing the words 'fag' and 'gay' used derogatorily in the halls. I spoke up, and told them to stop."

"Why? Are you a fag?" they asked.

"No," Mr. Sellars replied, "but it's offensive to me."

"I could rationalize that in my mind," he explained. "I could tell myself I wasn't a 'fag,' that I was 'gay,' but I realized that was just playing with words. So eventually I started speaking up even more."

As a co–dorm parent in charge of twenty junior boys, he was at first afraid of rejection. But he didn't want to live that way, so eventually he pulled some of the older boys aside and told them he was gay. They said they'd heard it already. At first they were nervous, but then they realized that if he could trust them with that information, they could trust him with important details about their lives.

Reggie became a conversational magnet for the boys. They confided everything in him: gay parents, gay siblings, molestation, drug and alcohol abuse. "That was pretty heavy for a 23-year-old," he admitted. "So many people were coming to me, it was like a flood. I guess they figured that gays were about the lowest people on the totem pole, so I knew what it was like to be different or have something on my own mind."

A boy wore a pink triangle on his jacket; Mr. Sellars told him he owned a lot of those symbols himself. The youngster brightened up, began paying more attention in class, and eventually came out to his teacher.

Eventually, Reggie Sellars came out to the entire school. He joined the Gay, Lesbian, and Straight Teachers Network (GLSTN), and learned why schools need teachers to be out. Before, he had not recognized how beneficial that could be for everyone. He had simply thought of being out in terms of his own life.

But though he experienced no overt problems or discrimination, Brewster was located in a small town, and the school was decidedly conservative. "When I came out to the headmaster he said, 'Fine, I respect you as a person, but don't tell anyone else,'" Reggie said. "But I already had. And he wouldn't let me mention GLSTN in my write-up in the profile of the school and faculty we send out to prospective students. He really tried to slow me and the school's progress down. He kept saying, 'Wait, wait, wait,' while the kids wanted and needed more, more, more."

After two years at Brewster, he still hoped he could effect change. But on the spur of the moment, while helping run a GLSTN workshop at Milton Academy in Massachusetts, he decided to interview at nearby Noble and Greenough. The interviewer jokingly asked how a teacher managed to get away in the middle of the week; Reggie replied that he'd been at a conference for gay and lesbian educators. For the next twenty minutes the administrator asked questions about Reggie's life and the workshop, and listened intently. He wanted to know what he could do about those issues at Noble. Thus began an excellent relationship with Noble; he knows now the decision to switch schools was the right one.

Because Reggie had worked there one summer, in a program for youngsters who were the first from their families to go to college, a few students and faculty members knew he was gay. Most, however, did not. He began work that fall excited about his new school, eager to get back to football as an assistant coach, but also feeling trepidation about athletics.

"Even though I'd had a great experience at Yale, football brought back a lot of homophobic fears I'd had about sports," he said. "I knew rumors would go around, and I didn't want anything to ruin my relationship with the players. So one day I told the two captains separately. They said, 'We already know. We've talked about it. We didn't know what to expect, but you're a good coach. You're a good guy. We're glad you told us yourself.'"

A few days later the largest boy on the team – a 235-pounder – confronted Reggie. "I had my preconceived notions," the coach said. "To me, this kid was the epitome of a football player. I stereotyped him, and unfortunately, because of his size, he'd been allowed to act like a typical football player all through school." The athlete asked Reggie what his pink triangle was for. "It means I support gay rights," he replied.

"Does that mean you're gay?" the boy continued.

"No, it doesn't," Reggie said. Retelling the story, he explains, "I could have copped out and stopped there, but I kept going. 'But I am,' I said. I was ready to fight, because I had this stereotype of him."

Instead, the boy said, "I thought so. I have one too!"

Now it was Reggie's turn to be surprised: "My mother's a lesbian," the boy explained.

"That incident taught me a lot about kids," the coach recounted. "I had had my own thoughts; I wasn't going to trust them to make the right decisions. Yet that taught me to just give kids the facts, and let them make their own decisions. We can't protect kids; it doesn't do anybody any good to shield them from anything. And it taught me not to stereotype anyone, just the way I don't want anyone stereotyping me."

Several days after that, Reggie was late for practice. The student manager, with whom he had a good, joking relationship, asked, "Where were you? Screwing a woman?" Reggie said, "First of all, that's none of your business; you're out of line. Second of all, why do you assume it's a woman I'd be screwing?"

The boy replied, "What are you, a fag?"

"No," Reggie answered, "I'm not a fag. I'm gay." And then he headed out to the field.

All through practice the manager looked at him. He later apologized, but asked if Reggie was kidding. When he said no, the boy refused to believe it. He asked Reggie why he was gay, since all the girls at school liked him. That led to a long discussion on sexuality. The boy, who wrote for the school newspaper, asked if he could do a story on Reggie. That was how the coach came out to the entire school. He was ready to answer any questions, but little happened immediately. His classes eventually had good, open discussions about Reggie and his sexuality, but it took a while. It had to sink in before people would talk about it.

When the football season was over, Reggie wanted to stay in shape. The wrestling coach invited him to help with preseason workouts; he then asked Reggie to stay with the wrestlers through the winter, because he would be a good role model.

While he'd had only a few qualms about the football team, wrestling was a different matter entirely. "It's not, obviously, a sexual sport – it's a physical sport – but people perceive it to be sexual," Reggie admitted. "I was nervous about being in close physical contact, especially with kids I didn't know."

But he decided that the best way to overcome his fears was to confront them, so he continued with the team. Though he weighs only 165 pounds, he wrestled with the heavyweight – the same boy who had told him during football season that his mother is a lesbian. People watched warily, to see how they interacted. Once they realized it was okay, everyone wanted to wrestle with Reggie, because they knew he'd be a good workout partner.

During football season Reggie had never showered in the gym; he lives near campus, and it was easier to change at home. In his first wrestling season he continued to shower there. But during his second year he realized that, because of the cold winter air after practice, it was healthier to do so in the gym. He had no idea what the athletes would think, and didn't want to cause any problems. But at the same time he realized he was cheating himself, because he had a right to shower in school. That marked one more important step on the long path to gay visibility. His wrestlers learned that, among other activities, gay people take showers – and that it's no big deal.

Reggie sees many parallels between his lives as a gay educator and as a black educator. Both grow from the same root: "Prep school is geared for the white, straight male. If you're black, gay, or female, there are ways to oppress you. There are very few forums in prep school to talk about or deal with being black, gay, or a woman. As the only black man on campus – which I was my first year at both schools – I've been very aware that whatever I do, I'm seen as speaking for all blacks, or all gays. In fact, I'm a southern black, and we're very different from northern blacks. And not all gays are the same either, of course. But I work as an adviser to both the Gay/Straight Alliance and the multicultural group, so I do what I can to break down myths in both areas. Believe me, there are a lot of them."

One way to shatter myths is by allowing students to ask questions. On the bus to a game, a boy asked if he could see the gay paper Reggie was reading. After some coaxing Reggie agreed, asking the boy not to laugh. The paper made the rounds of the bus and the players peppered him with questions, like why is a drag queen called he-she? They looked at the personals, and joked that he must have a huge phone bill. He felt good that he could share that part of his life with them, and that they in turn were mature and respectful enough to react as they did.

Such out-of-the-blue incidents help Reggie realize he made the right decision to come out of the coaching closet. Another occurred his first year at Brewster, while he was running the snowboarding team. "It's a sport that attracts kids who tend not to be part of the traditional crowd – different color hair, clothes, that sort of person," he explained. "We felt we could bond because we were all different from everyone else. We teased each other, affectionately, a lot. One day we were driving in the van, and I saw a guy I used to date. I just said so under my breath, but they yelled out, 'Oh my God, stop the van! Turn around! We want to meet him! Is he cute?' That thrilled me, that they wanted to meet him just because they knew he meant something to me."

Another casual encounter came while playing basketball in the gym with students; as often happens, there were side bets for pocket change. Reggie mentioned he had a date that weekend, and they began razzing him: "Well, too bad. We're gonna beat you in hoops and take all your money, and then you can't go out with him." Their casual use of the pronoun "him" meant a great deal to Reggie.

In all his coaching, however, he has never had a student actually come out. The closest incident occurred when a boy confessed he "might" be gay. "That was kind of hairy," Reggie said. "I worried he might just be emulating me, because he was so into football. I told him he was only sixteen, that it was okay to have questions, and that he didn't have to have all the answers about himself that very day." Most intimate talks about sexuality occur outside of the athletic environment, he said. He hypothesizes that because sports take up so much of a boy's time, there is little room left for heavy discussions.

With all that has happened, Reggie can recall only one untoward incident. A group of conservative Noble and Greenough mothers circulated a petition to end the Gay/Straight Alliance. Students heard, called the parents cowards for being anonymous, and challenged the mothers to a debate. As it turned out, a number of parents ended up supporting the group, and Reggie's right to lead it, so the end result was positive.

Though he loves what he is doing, Reggie is undecided about how long he'll continue to teach and coach. He is thinking of administration, because of the dire need there for gay and black faces. Perhaps, he jokes, he might do something fun for a while, like snowboarding or skiing. Right now, however, he continues to focus on teaching – what his headmaster calls "politicking."

And what others call affecting positively the lives of every athlete – and student – at Noble and Greenough School.

———

Equally out, equally comfortable, equally proud – and just a few miles away from Reggie Sellars – is Katherine Henderson, assistant director of athletics and, for ten years, volleyball and lacrosse coach at Phillips Andover Academy. That is the elite, 1200-student Massachusetts boarding school that boasts such famous graduates as George Bush and Jack Lemmon; it is now known too as the home of one of the most visible lesbian coaches in the country.

Ms. Henderson (who counts among her proudest accomplishments the co-founding of GLSTN) spent years quietly building support among colleagues. But the more she worked with gay students, the more the word got out. She began speaking up in faculty meetings, and wrote an article for the school paper on National Coming Out Day. That was more than five years ago.

In terms of athletics, the negative fallout has been minimal – even though, she laughed, "I'm a living stereotype: a dyke P.E. teacher!" She admitted that "perhaps people perceive me as a little bit tougher than I am. An English teacher told me that kids in class debated whether I could bench-press an entire stack of weights, and decided that I could. Sometimes I think people think of me as Amazon Woman, even though I change my haircut from butch to femme all the time."

But if there was little backlash when she came out, that does not mean she has not had an impact. Quite the contrary, she said: "One of the advantages of having an out lesbian coach is that young athletes learn not to fear the word. It's so important for all female athletes to disempower that name 'lesbian,' and see it as a positive word – or at least not a negative, so when someone uses it derogatorily it doesn't have that sting. Any female athlete in her late twenties or older remembers being called a dyke, whether it's true or not; that's why it's important to take away the negative connotations of that word."

When girls learn not to fear the word "lesbian," she continued, they grow as competitors. "If you have a group of homophobic female athletes, they may not bond closely or play as aggressively because they worry about being called lesbians, or manly. If they don't worry about the word, they bond and play aggressively." As proof, she pointed to Andover's 1993 fall season: four of the school's five teams, including her volleyball squad, won New England championships. The previous spring Ms. Henderson's lacrosse team was undefeated, and captured the New England title.

Although she is active in the school's Gay/Straight Alliance, she said that in more than five years she has seldom seen an athlete attend meetings. That is curious, she admitted, but athletes do come out to her and not go to meetings. Others come out later, after graduation, and let her know then. Reasons for this may include the homophobic nature of athletics, or the feelings of students who want to be part of a team that they cannot be different in any way. Or perhaps, she said, teenagers who are so wrapped up in sports just don't have time to examine who they really are.

When she first came out at Andover, Ms. Henderson worried about the reaction. She stood in front of the school and talked about being a lesbian, then approached practice warily. But the team beat her there – and decorated every volleyball and water bottle with a pink triangle. It was one of the prettiest sights of her life.

Earlier that day she thought about bringing pink triangles to her physical education class, but decided against it because someone might object. However, a girl asked whether she had any – her father wanted some. Ms. Henderson marveled that while the experiences of many gay people lead them to always expect the worst, being open to new situations can lead to wonderful insights.

Now every year – because National Coming Out Day occurs in the middle of volleyball season – she tells her team what she is going to write in the school paper before it appears. She invites questions, and reminds them that in only a handful of states can she be out and protected as their coach. In more than forty states she can be fired just for admitting she is a lesbian. The girls are stunned – and so she tells them that is exactly why she is doing what she's doing.

She believes that since she has come out to her teams, her relationships with her athletes have become closer. "Any coach in the closet keeps her distance. I'm a professional, but at times high school kids want to know about your life experiences, about what's going on with you. I can answer honestly now, and not skirt the issue. That makes for better feelings all around, which leads to better bonds and, ultimately better teams and better times."

Andover's administration and trustees have been very supportive, she said, although they tend to follow the cautious route that has served them well in the past. She is particularly proud of her personal relations with trustees. They tell her to keep doing what she is doing. They admit they don't always understand it, but they say they're trying – and that they appreciate it.

Parental feedback is equally positive. She receives notes that say how important she has been for the girls she has coached. She knows what's written between those lines. Parents admire her honesty, even if they are circumspect in their comments.

Ms. Henderson is honest about her life in ways both large and small. "In a boarding school, your living situation is so exposed," she said. "If an athlete stops by and I'm in the middle of dinner with my girlfriend, I don't have any worries now. I no longer get that sinking feeling in my stomach if I'm at the movies with a friend and half my team sits behind me.

"Kids today expect to grow up and have an intimate relationship with someone," she concluded. "To shut off that part of your life to an athlete does them a disservice. They need you as a role model, no matter who that relationship is with. It doesn't matter if you're gay or straight; if you can provide a good, loving role model to someone, you've done your job as a teacher or coach."

———————

Unfortunately, not every high school athlete has the chance to be coached by a Reggie Sellars or a Katherine Henderson. The vast majority of lesbian and gay coaches remain in the closet – and that's not just a wild guess. It's shown in voluminous research conducted by Dr. Pat Griffin, and the associate professor in social justice education at the University of Massachusetts knows what she's talking about: she herself was a closeted high school and college coach.

A self-described "pre-Title IX (women's equity) athlete," she played field hockey, volleyball, basketball, and softball while growing up, then participated in field hockey, basketball, swimming, and lacrosse as a University of Maryland undergraduate three decades ago. Dr. Griffin went on to coach high school field hockey, basketball, volleyball, and softball before moving to the University of Massachusetts, where she served as women's swim coach and a physical education teacher educator. Today she is a racquetball, tennis, and softball player; runner; biker; and rollerblader; and a Gay Games triathlete.

But although Dr. Griffin frequently raised race and gender equity issues while training young men and women to be phys. ed. teachers, it was not until the mideighties that she felt comfortable enough to add homophobia to the mix. Before that, it felt too close to home.

In 1987 she was part of the first American Association of Health, Physical Education, Recreation, and Dance (AAHPERD) workshop to include the word "lesbian" in the title – and the Las Vegas conference room was packed. There were four hundred people at the session, during which she and a graduate student came out. That freed Dr. Griffin to focus more frequently on issues of homophobia in physical education, to the point where it became her passion. She has since gained a national profile for putting lesbian and gay issues on the agenda of professional meetings and conferences.

Specializing in females in physical education, she has spotted three distinct generations of lesbians. The first consists of women her age and older who never identified themselves as lesbian, because they didn't like the word; they could not even conceive of being out. Next comes those who grew up in the 1970s. They may feel more comfortable identifying themselves as lesbians or feminists, and feel good about who they. are, but they don't necessarily feel safe being out. This group comprises the majority of coaches today.

The third group, according to Dr. Griffin, represents the new generation. They're coming out sooner, and are not willing to tolerate the culture of the closet. That closet culture has been dangerous, because it was passed down from coaches to athletes. Lesbian athletes learned by watching their coaches that they "had to" be closeted; they thought there was no alternative.

The risks of being openly lesbian were substantial, she said – and in many places, still are. She ticked off several: inability to land a job; job loss (either direct or, more likely, subtle, as when an athletic director or colleague makes coaching so difficult that a woman quits); lack of support; loss of credibility in a school or in an entire community.

Potential role models who remain in the closet bother Dr. Griffin. "Being lesbian or gay is for most kids still an isolating experience. No one talks about it, and they can't talk to anyone else. Even in 1995 it can be scary to be a lesbian or gay student – and that's particularly true for high school athletes." The close-knit nature of most teams inhibits same-sex relationships and contributes to youngsters' sense of isolation. It's rare, she noted, to see athletes of either gender at school support group or gay-lesbian-straight alliance meetings.

However, she detects flutters of hope in the wind. "I have no illusions things are going to be radically different anytime soon," she said, "but when I travel around the country for conferences I hear words like 'lesbian' and 'heterosexism' I never heard before. I get called to do workshops for school systems, and there are principals who are realizing it is an issue they have to address. I get a sense that things are starting to change."

Spoken like a true coach, preparing for her next big game.

———————

Gay by the Bay

Los Angeles is the home of Project 10, and New York points with pride to the Harvey Milk School. But it's doubtful any big city in America has more friends in higher places – places like the board of education and central school office, where curriculum and policy decisions are ultimately made – than San Francisco. It is those decisions, of course, that eventually ooze down through various levels of educational bedrock, affecting, first, building administrators; then, teachers; next, students; eventually, parents, guardians, and other family members; and, finally, entire communities. It is a slow process, driven by meetings, memos, and mandates, and it is easily ground to a halt despite constant vigilance from concerned citizen groups. But it is a process that works better in San Francisco than perhaps anywhere else in the country.

Big surprise. "Baghdad by the Bay" is home to a high percentage of homosexuals; according to one estimate, one-third of all San Franciscans are gay, and many of those citizens are proud, progressive, and proactive. They have learned how to use the system to make their voices heard – and more and more, those voices include their children. School politics in San Francisco revolves less around budget and building matters and more around student and family concerns than in most urban areas. In the 1990s, thanks to what Tom Ammiano has called "the gayby boom," many of the men and women who run San Francisco schools have realized that those family concerns also encompass gay and lesbian issues: students growing up with gay or lesbian parents or guardians. Yet even experienced teachers are unfamiliar with, or feel uncomfortable discussing, gay family issues. And because San Francisco is the homo-mecca of the universe, more gay, lesbian, and bisexual parents – and their school-age children – live there than in any other city of 750,000.

The Tom Ammiano who coined the term "gayby boom" is the same Tom Ammiano who makes his living as a stand-up comic in the Bay Area. He is the same Tom Ammiano who in 1990 was elected as the first openly gay member of the San Francisco Unified School District Board of Education, and the same one who two years later became its first openly gay chairperson. He held that position until late 1994, when he ran for – and won – a seat on the board of supervisors (the city council).

Sitting in his seat at the head of one of San Francisco's most influential tables, Mr. Ammiano symbolized an important trend in his city's education history (another member of the five-person board, Angie Fa, is openly lesbian). But his pedagogic roots lie deeper than the bureaucratic soil: he is a former special-education teacher who in 1975 helped found San Francisco's Gay Teachers Coalition. And in a third way too he represents the growing power and influence of the city's gay population: Mr. Ammiano is a gay father with a child in the same San Francisco school system that, despite its reputation for tolerance and progressivism, at times trivializes, undermines, and even shatters the self-esteem so vital to youngsters growing up gay or in gay families, and whose development is at least as important a part of the education process as the teaching of reading, writing, and computer skills.

His nearly lifelong concern about homophobia impelled Mr. Ammiano to make his run for the board of education, he recalled. Dressed informally on a weekday morning midway through his term, he delivered his comments rapid-fire in his book- and binder-strewn Van Ness Avenue office. The room had the look of a man who knew he belonged there – but a decade earlier there was no certainty his influence on board policy would ever extend beyond writing letters and speaking at meetings.

He was concerned with the usual things like class size and programs, but also got involved because although school board members solicited gay money and gay votes, they did not follow through with action benefitting the gay community. He saw the need for someone on the board with a gut feeling for lesbian and gay issues.

Plenty of voters agreed: Mr. Ammiano finished first in the election to the board of education post (which in practice is a full-time position, despite its paltry part-time pay of $500 a month). In his campaign he stressed that education issues cross many boundaries, affecting, among others, ethnic and racial communities, voters who have no children in school (including the elderly as well as gays and lesbians), and businesses that succeed or fail based on how well or poorly the schools educate each generation of workers.

Gay father (and stand-up comic) Tom Ammiano was the first openly gay member of the San Francisco Unified School District Board of Education and, later, its chairperson.

© STEVEN BARATZ, 1993

Tom Ammiano said that from the start he placed gay and lesbian concerns on a continuum; his aim was to integrate, not isolate them. One of the last frontiers in public education is gay and lesbian issues. That does not mean they should always be front and center, or stand apart from everything else that's going on; however, neither did it mean that Mr. Ammiano shied from shining the spotlight of publicity on issues of importance to the lesbian and gay community. "There's such a thing as positive fallout," he said. "Once these things are acknowledged and talked about, people can see how they relate to other issues in public education. We have to teach all kids, not just some: gay and lesbian kids, Afro-American kids, disabled kids. So while any particular issue might be gay- and lesbian-specific, at the same time there's a global need for inclusivity, whether it's curriculum, teaching staffs, or whatever."

What exactly are some "gay- and lesbian-specific" issues he was able to push, pull, or otherwise haul onto the board of education stage? Mr. Ammiano mentioned many, ranging from curriculum (providing supplementary resource materials to teachers in every school) to support services (hiring a director of support services for gay and lesbian students, designating a "gay- and lesbian-sympathetic staff person" in every middle and high school), and from policy (halting ROTC recruiting in the schools, kicking the Boy Scouts out of classrooms because they discriminate) to program (beefing up AIDS education, allowing condoms to be available in schools). Through everything, Mr. Ammiano said, one theme ran: he tried to institutionalize changes and attitudes, because that is how innovation thrives. While the school board had no problem with those issues, and the superintendent was supportive, there was no guarantee that would always be the case. The more he could help institutionalize lesbian and gay concerns, the better off the entire district would be.

Take the "anti-slur" policy. It's one thing to espouse some kind of vague "respect for all life" ideal; it's another to codify that in writing, stand behind it with rules specifically prohibiting name-calling, then back it all up with disciplinary guidelines. Mr. Ammiano prodded the San Francisco Unified School District to adopt a strong statement banning "the use of slurs by students, officials, and employees ... against any person on the basis of race, color, creed, national origin, ancestry, age, sex, sexual orientation, or disability." The statement explains, "Slurs are not always acknowledged as being painful and oppressive. Describing someone as a nigger, spic, faggot, or chink attacks a person's self-esteem. Further, use of these terms by students teaches that derogatory statements about others are acceptable." The statement also provides teachers with exercises for establishing classroom rules, beginning with student brainstorming about names they have heard, then following up with a discussion on how harmful prejudice can be. "You can control behavior in your classroom," the statement advises teachers. "By reacting immediately to slurs, students will feel safe in the classroom." The districtwide student handbook prescribes clear disciplinary guidelines if slurs occur.

Mr. Ammiano had his frustrations, of course. They ranged from administrators who failed to implement or follow well-intentioned policies, to the fiscal slash-and-burn educational philosophies of Presidents Reagan and Bush and Gov. Pete Wilson. He predicted that the effects of budgetary cutbacks in areas like guidance and counseling will be felt for years to come.

He was also displeased with much of the media coverage of his tenure on the board of education, though he adopted a philosophical tone when mentioning it. He believed few people thought he could win; when he did, they were jolted upright. A local paper went to his comedy show after he won, and tried to juxtapose what he said in his routine with his school board work. The thrust of the piece was, "Is this man appropriate to be on the school board?" At that point, he said, it was a bit late to wonder.

Mr. Ammiano found newspaper coverage of education to be poor in general. "They tried to sensationalize things," he said. "That's endemic to newspapers. And of course I'm gay, and a teacher, and progressive. For years the school board was the bastion of little white ladies. Now it's changing, yet the media is still conservative. So I was out there; I'm controversial, an easy target."

Tom Ammiano sidestepped the media, taking his ideas directly to his constituents. He tried to bring more parents into the schools – particularly gay and lesbian parents, because they are not always visible. He pointed out' that right-wing rhetoric always focuses on "parents" or "families," as if gays and lesbians were not parents and did not have families. He was proud to have given these people a voice, and delighted to watch their influence rise. As gay people – parents and nonparents – got involved in San Francisco's schools, they helped pass a bond measure for school maintenance and earthquake-proofing, along with a quarter-cent sales tax for schools to circumvent a $30 million cutback.

Mr. Ammiano pointed to two reasons that the lesbian and gay community has been supportive of San Francisco's schools: one is obvious, the other more subtle. "I think the gay and lesbian community is generally pretty progressive, and they realize the importance of public education," he said. "But they also remember their own school experiences. For many of them school was an awkward, painful time, and now that we're doing something to ensure the safety of self-identified gay students, to fully integrate nonjudgmental material and textbooks, to really blend cultural sensitivity with gay and lesbian sensitivity, they're responding."

Tom Ammiano did not accomplish all of that alone, of course, nor should all credit go to his allies on the board of education. The parents he helped empower have provided tremendous logistical, emotional, and financial support. And no one among the burgeoning lesbian and gay parent population of San Francisco has been more active or supportive than Valerie Schlafke.

A parent at Buena Vista Elementary School, where many other lesbians' children are enrolled, she became a catalyst for the citywide Lesbian and Gay Parents Association (LGPA). It is a lobbying and support organization begun – as so many groups are – for an entirely different reason. "The original parents got together because they didn't want to be the only lesbians at a school dance," she recalled. "Pretty soon, they weren't."

Pretty soon, they were doing more than dancing. In less than half a decade they made a significant impact on Tom Ammiano's board of education, and the school district he oversaw. The LGPA's most substantial accomplishments range from providing books on gay families to every elementary school, to mandating social studies curriculum emphasis on gay pride every June, to helping organize workshops on

Parents march in support of gay inclusion in San Francisco schools.

school issues for gay and lesbian parents. Other contributions seem less important, but in reality signal a sea change in the way schools view their students' families and lives: for example, the LGPA pushed the district to change the wording on all forms from "mother and father" to "parent or guardian."

Big or small, the LGPA's impact stems from one key fact, Ms. Schlafke said: people were scared to be out at their children's school because they thought their child would be hurt.

Even in San Francisco? "It was a major worry, and it still is," she insisted. "My kid is now a teenager so as a parent I'm invisible – that's an adolescent thing, not a lesbian thing – but in elementary school parents always volunteer for everything. There's a big focus on 'family' in elementary schools. Kids are starting to learn about who's different, who fits in where and who doesn't. Homophobia, racism – horrible stuff comes up on playgrounds."

Some stuff can't be classified as horrible; "stupid" is a better word. A child broke a wrist during school, and the mother could not be found. The substitute secretary refused to call the woman's partner. The principal was told but refused to make waves, claiming substitute secretaries are too hard to find. The LGPA learned two lessons from that, Ms. Schlafke said: the need to teach lesbian and gay parents how to deal with similar situations, and the necessity of making schools realize the importance of such incidents to everyone involved.

Prior to the arrival of the LGPA, awareness of gay and lesbian family issues was low. It's better now, though still not flying off the charts. During conferences, some teachers focus on the biological

Valerie Schlafke helped organize San Francisco's citywide Lesbian and Gay Parents Association.

parent and ignore the gay partner. A few won't even look the other person in the eye. In class some teachers constantly refer to "your mother and father," or put up posters of only two-parent, male-and-female families. Sometimes, of course, teachers are only too aware of gay and lesbian issues: when they hear the word "fag" used on the playground or in the classroom, they refuse to respond, fearful of addressing sexuality (or worried about guilt by association).

"Teachers are basically sensitive people, but they need to be sensitive to all diversity – disabled, Asian, gay and lesbian, whatever," Ms. Schlafke said. "They don't always get enough support to do that. One teacher, who's great at civil rights and feminism, said, 'God, they expect us to do everything.' That was his level of frustration. Well, we're ready to help him design curriculum. We have resources, we've got information readily available, and we can help him find it. We're not asking for huge curriculum redesign, even though it's badly needed; we're just trying to help teachers do the best job possible teaching sensitivity and diversity. We understand they have to do a lot themselves, with very limited resources."

Because so much of the elementary school curriculum is family-oriented, the LGPA has spent much of its time and energy helping teachers expand their definition of family beyond mother and father, into other shapes, sizes, and configurations. Material distributed by the group noted that families with lesbian or gay parents or guardians include two persons raising a child together; adoptive parents; one adult who is the equivalent of a stepparent; "divorced" parents or guardians (used figuratively, since lesbians and gay men are not allowed to marry); single parents; foster parents; and grandparents serving as parents or guardians. Among the LGPA's suggestions: "When meeting the lesbian or gay parents or guardians of a student, take cues from the adults as to what terms they use for themselves. If two men introduce themselves as 'Sarah's dads,' then in the future they should be referred to as 'Sarah's dads.' It is also important to validate the student, and let her or him know that she or he is accepted by you. In Sarah's case, after meeting them it would be very affirming to let her know that you enjoyed meeting her dads."

One way the LGPA has worked to frame issues, and thus find ways to sensitize educators, is its annual conference. The first, held for three hours on a Saturday morning in August 1992, bore a generic title: "Gay, Lesbian and Bi-sexual Families to Address Discrimination in S.F. Schools." Panelists included Mr. Ammiano; Bill Rojas, the newly appointed school superintendent; San Francisco supervisor Roberta Achtenberg; and Cynthia Chan, coordinator of the gay-lesbian parenting program for the Lyon-Martin Clinic. Over sixty adults discussed what gay parents needed from the school district. (The attendees brought thirty-five children, for whom childcare was provided.) A second meeting was held two months later, and the group continued to meet on a regular basis. Members spoke with school district personnel about such issues as inclusive curricula and sensitivity training for administrators and staff; they also initiated a quarterly newsletter called "The Report Card."

An important question that arose at each meeting was whether or not parents should be out at their children's schools; a majority indicated they were not. The discussions encompassed many factors, including the child's feelings, age, gender, and ethnic background; coming out to other parents; and the fact that each year involves a new set of school personnel. Related to those issues were problems that result from trying to raise children with a family secret, including feelings of confusion, isolation, low self-esteem, and fear.

Those meetings led to an all-day workshop in October 1993 called "Out of the Closet, into the Classroom?" Fliers said, "Attention Lesbian, Gay, Bisexual Parents." That scared some principals; LGPA members copied it for them, so they wouldn't have to do it themselves. The group felt it was important that the flyer go home with every child in every school, to serve as a policy statement that something necessary, and supported by the district, was going to happen.

Approximately seventy-five men and women attended the workshop. After an overview of "coming out as parents," including the different levels of outness involved and the issues that then spring up, attendees broke into groups of three to discuss a host of questions, ranging from the differences between coming out as a couple or an individual, to children's perceptions of gay parents. Each group reported back to the whole, and wrote their responses on large sheets of paper; everyone was invited to add comments during the lunch break.

A panel followed, featuring the fifteen-year-old son of a gay man and a twelve-year-old daughter of two lesbians. "You could really feel the boy's pain," Ms. Schlafke noted. "He didn't pretend it was easy. But he was grounded, not tragic. The girl has been on CNN; she was very articulate, and talked about the differences between her old working-class school and her current elite private school." Three parents also participated, each telling personal stories. Most of the questions were directed at the youngsters; as Ms. Schlafke pointed out, "Everyone always wants to know about the children's point of view. Even gay people want to hear about gender identification, role modeling, and security."

A second panel, after lunch, included Ms. Schlafke; Kevin Gogin, San Francisco's director of support services for gay and lesbian students; Laura Hurley, a straight woman who as head counselor at Balboa High School serves as a strong advocate for all youngsters; and Marcia Gallo, a lesbian affiliated with the American Civil Liberties Union. They told more stories: Ms. Schlafke spoke about subtle heterosexism in schools, Mr. Gogin about his daughter. Ms. Hurley noted that of the three gay students she counseled last year, two have dropped out of school because of conflicts with their parents, while Ms. Gallo discussed custody cases and civil rights. Postpanel questions centered around parents' legal rights, and the importance of strong familial relationships.

That led to a talk about the importance of lesbian and gay parents working hand in hand with the San Francisco Unified School District – and the risks of doing so. Ms. Schlafke noted that parents can alienate themselves from their child's school if they project anger, but offer no solutions. Pulling a youngster out of school, as she did, is not always the wisest course.

The workshop ended with networking. Ten agencies offered literature; Valerie Schlafke's group handed out phone numbers of key people at every level in the school district; there were books for sale; and two counselors who do free or low-cost counseling for children of gay parents passed out cards.

However, the LPGA's work can go only so far. For all their investment of time and money, for all they have done to make San

Francisco's schools more gay- and lesbian-sensitive, the group cannot help some people. Ironically, Ms. Schlafke related, one of her daughter's worst teachers was a lesbian. She was young, overworked, and unwilling to take chances. It had nothing to do with being gay – she simply was not a good teacher. But that frustrated the Lesbian and Gay Parents Association founder all year long.

———◦◦◦———

Besides a gay-sensitive board of education and an active lesbian and gay parents' organization, San Francisco's educational community wields one other potent weapon in the battle against homophobia, ignorance, and invisibility: Kevin Gogin.

Since 1990 he's served as the school district's first and only director of support services for gay and lesbian students. It's an amorphous title but – working largely on his own, in a position budgeted for only twenty hours a week – Mr. Gogin wasted little time proving that the position packs power.

There are three major elements of his work. One is working with gay, lesbian, bisexual, and questioning students, and their families. Signs at every middle and high school say, "A safe place for questions," and list his phone number; other posters have been donated by Levi Strauss. Mr. Gogin noted that the students he sees are those in conflict; the ones who are more comfortable never call.

His one-on-one work runs the gamut from crisis counseling to general support, such as suggesting where teenagers can meet other gay, lesbian, bisexual, and questioning youths. He has taken some youngsters to talk to priests, and driven others across the city to meet peers. He also visits hospitals to talk with teenagers who have attempted suicide.

Mr. Gogin's work is not limited to adolescents. He assists parents of gay teens by providing information, answering questions, and assuring them that having a gay child is hardly the worst thing in the world.

For youngsters and parents alike, he suggests reading materials and distributes brochures about community resources. In one eight-month period he recorded over a hundred personal contacts with high school and middle school students and their parents.

Mr. Gogin's second assignment is handling teacher and counselor training. Twice a year he runs voluntary in-service workshops dealing solely with lesbian and gay issues in high school and middle school. He leads sessions on development issues, including the genesis of homosexuality, for science and family life teachers; makes presentations to physical education teachers and coaches; and meets regularly with each school's "designated gay- and lesbian-sensitive adult." (These are men and women in every high school and middle school, appointed by the principal, who agree to be available to students in school; promote enforcement of the district's anti-slur policy; provide information about sexuality, sexually transmitted diseases, and substance abuse; link students and families with community resources; collaborate with other school personnel in assisting gay students; and refer students to Mr. Gogin's support services – in other words, to do whatever is necessary to provide a safe environment within each school for youngsters with gay-related questions or concerns.)

He also offers training and guidelines for teachers and counselors in such areas as establishing trusting, confidential relationships with students; becoming aware of one's own strengths and limitations in working with issues of sexual orientation and alternative lifestyles; assessing health risks (including suicide, substance abuse, sexually transmitted diseases, and HIV infection); gaining skills to confront anger and violence; utilizing the vocabulary of gay and lesbian youth for better adult-student communication; expanding classroom discussions to include issues of homosexuality when appropriate; collaborating on crisis response training; and increasing awareness of San Francisco's anti-slur policy. As part of his professional outreach he talks to groups as diverse as the American School Health Association, Western Regional College Board, California Peer Helper Convention, and Gay Asian Pacific Islanders.

Mr. Gogin's third charge is academic: he develops lesson plans and resources on name-calling, family diversity, and homophobia for teachers in grades six through twelve. He even teaches the lessons for teachers who feel uncomfortable.

How does Mr. Gogin, who is also a licensed psychotherapist with a private practice (not to mention the father of a young adopted daughter) manage to accomplish all this – on a part-time basis, yet? He has no idea, but it gets done. In 1993 he was given an even less part-time assistant, a female middle school counselor, and he collaborates closely with school nurses and such groups as the Lesbian and Gay Parents Association. Essentially, though, he was given the job and told, "Do it."

The position of director of support services for gay and lesbian students was created following the release of a federal report on gay and lesbian youth suicide. San Francisco already had in place its "designated gay- and lesbian-sensitive adult" program, but training was intermittent. Some principals resisted it altogether.

When the district decided a more concerted effort was needed, a battle ensued involving the school board and the public. After much debate the new position was approved, in late spring of 1990. Mr. Gogin, who had been an active member of the LGPA while home full-time raising his daughter, called Tom Ammiano; the board of education chair encouraged him to apply. Mr. Gogin never expected to be interviewed, because he was not a school employee. He was stunned to be selected from over twenty applications, although he believes his psychotherapy, AIDS work, and teaching background helped.

He was handed a nebulous blueprint, and told to create a program with substance and impact. Along the way he had to assuage parents' concerns about "recruitment" – everything had to be age-appropriate.

His impact was immediate. A high school senior came to his office, devastated. He could not say "gay," and could barely say "homosexual." He was Asian, and homosexuality just didn't happen in his culture – or so he thought. He wanted to be a doctor, and figured that dream was gone. By the end of the year he had won a BANGLE (Bay Area Network of Gay and Lesbian Educators) scholarship; today he is a premed college student.

Another early incident involved an eighth grader, whose father found him with another boy. The father beat him, and the boy was harassed at school. He would not tell Mr. Gogin his name, but they talked for hours. He was obviously in danger, but Mr. Gogin recognized the boy was ready to find the support he would require to survive.

He told one more success story. A sophomore girl who was very out at her school stood up in front of the San Francisco Board of Supervisors and said that the gay and lesbian program saved her life. "I can't ask for more than that," Mr. Gogin said proudly. "Now I can retire happy."

Of course, he has no intention of quitting soon. Too many unresolved issues remain, including devising better ways to reach students, expanding on-site counseling, and defending the program against budget-cutters, the radical right, and folks who simply have no idea what Mr. Gogin does.

"I think most teachers and administrators are glad there's a program in place," he said. "They see it as a way to hook up with resources they don't know about, and end everyone's isolation. They know we're not flakes.

"Parents, for the most part, are supportive once they hear what we're about and what we try to do. But there is still a small but vocal minority who think homosexuality shouldn't be talked about, and people who call me a pimp or say I'm training kids to go on the streets. As long as they're around I've got to keep working.

"I've seen so much in the few years I've been doing this. There are the parents who say, 'Do we have to talk about this?' They still have the assumption that a kid wakes up one day at nineteen and is suddenly a sexual being. They worry that I'm creating problems; they don't see that I'm solving them.

"And it's always hard to deal with the fundamentalist right, who believe you're wrong and that they have the one truth. I've realized there's little I can do about that. I haven't come to peace with it, but I've learned to stop beating my head against the wall. Now I've learned how to go around the wall. It's hard to believe some people think being gay means a life is not worth anything. I expect adolescents and preadolescents to be homophobic; I can deal with that. But I kind of expect more from adults."

Asked why he does this work, Mr. Gogin parried, "Why not? It's so important. Gays and lesbians are frightened by the same feelings their classmates find so exciting. Their feelings of attraction to members of the same sex can cause confusion, isolation, and fear. They can be victims of verbal or physical violence, or shunned by former friends. Some of them may also be ostracized from their families – told they're unwanted and unloved.

"But these gay, lesbian, and bisexual kids are an invisible minority. They look like any other student. Most people never recognize the isolation or loneliness they feel. We may never witness the verbal and physical harassment they face. Anyone who grew up gay knows what I'm talking about – but too many other teachers and administrators never think about it."

Mr. Gogin loves his job for another, even more personal reason: his daughter. One day, he said, "Someone is going to turn to her and say, 'Your dad's a fag.' That shouldn't happen, and I'm trying to make sure it doesn't. It used to be a luxury to teach diversity; now it's a necessity. We can't afford not to."

He paused. "Besides, it's a challenge – and lots of fun!"

Three Teachers, Three Stories

There is no such thing as a "typical" gay teacher, any more than there is a "typical" American state. Just as every man has his own story of when, where, how, and why he came out, and every woman tells her own tales of dealing with homophobic administrators, giggling students, and that one girl who needs to share her secret, so too is every place in the U.S. special. Massachusetts is not Michigan, Maryland, Montana, or even, despite its geographic proximity, Maine.

The Bay State is unique in many ways. It gained national prominence (and notoriety) when Gov. William Weld appointed a special commission to study issues of importance to gay and lesbian youths; the governor then forged ahead and actually followed through on his task force's recommendations – urging his department of education to conduct workshops, run training sessions, and implement programs, all aimed at minimizing the frustrations and fears felt by gay and lesbian students. But in many ways Massachusetts is not unlike any other state. Its teachers are still not emboldened enough to celebrate their gayness over the intercom their first day on the job; the word "faggot" still echoes as the ultimate put-down in school halls from the Berkshire mountains to the fishing villages near Cape Cod; and parents still retain enough power and prejudice to force all but a few lesbian and gay teachers into the classroom closet.

Yet for those who have come out to administrators and colleagues, even in some cases parents and students, the rewards have outweighed the risks. In interviews across the state teachers talked, as do out gays in all walks of life, of the feelings of honesty, serenity, and empowerment that have made their lives so much more complete. But they also spoke of becoming better teachers. Being open about their sexuality has made them more compassionate and less authoritative; they now take greater risks in their classrooms, speak more forcefully in faculty meetings, involve themselves to a deeper degree in their educational communities. The result, which they said makes all the travail worthwhile, is that their schools are now safer, more supportive places for all students, gay and straight.

Unfortunately, others who have spoken openly about their sexuality are no longer teaching.

There are no easy answers to how and why these teachers do it. Every success, every failure, every motivation and hesitation is uniquely their own. Each teacher's story is different – but taken together, the three men and women profiled here provide an intriguing look at what it's like to be gay, out, and a classroom teacher in Massachusetts.

Allan Arnaboldi is not a Bay Stater by birth; he grew up in Port Jefferson, New York, and attended college in the Midwest, earning a B.A. in speech and hearing therapy from Ohio University and a master's in audiology from Northwestern. Nor is he is someone who always knew he was born to teach. He spent many years as a speech pathologist and audiologist before realizing that short-term connections with children weren't for him; he needed sustained contact to see results and feel accomplishment.

Allan Arnaboldi certainly does not fit the male teacher mold. He obtained his second master's degree, in early childhood education, from Smith College; then, after working for several more years with preschoolers, he landed a job as a first-grade teacher at Fort River Elementary School in Amherst. Male primary school teachers, though recently increasing in number, remain rare; rarer still are those who are gay. The number who are open about their orientation is infinitesimal.

Mr. Arnaboldi came out first to his wife, whom he divorced while in his early thirties. Next, he told his brother and sister and their families, his parents and close friends, and then his twelve-year-old daughter.

At the time he worked at a day care center filled with homosexual colleagues; it was a supportive environment in which to come out, and he experienced no problems. He moved on to a private school in Greenfield for six- to eight-year-olds, and was out to the staff there as well. But when he entered public education, Mr. Arnaboldi felt he had to retreat back into the closet. "In a private school if parents didn't like the fact that a teacher was gay, they could remove their kids," he explained. "In the public sector there are more repercussions." Consequently, he watched his step.

Before he was hired, he spoke frankly with the first-grade teacher he would be working with. She said his homosexuality would be no problem. Another teacher was supportive too. After he was hired, he came out slowly. The first person he told was a lesbian paraprofessional, whom he noticed sitting with her partner when he gave a workshop on diversity.

One day another teacher asked if he had someone special in his life. He said yes, and that he was waiting for him for dinner. "Oh, I'm so glad," she said. "I knew you must have someone special, but you never talk about yourself in the faculty lounge. It must be hard not to talk." The next day Allan thanked her. She said she was worried she'd been intruding, but he told her he was glad he'd found another ally.

By his fourth year in Amherst – after receiving tenure – Mr. Arnaboldi was ready to come out to the entire staff. At a curriculum meeting, a black teacher on the crisis team began talking about the frustrations he felt because the rest of the faculty assumed he always wanted to deal with every racial matter that arose. A colleague noted how few minority groups were represented there.

When the principal asked how many teachers considered themselves part of a minority group, Allan raised his hand. People looked at him strangely. He told them he was a gay father. Then he spoke about the difficulty of not talking at lunch about his life with his partner. He added that as part of an invisible group, he empathized with the students at Fort River who could not be open about their families, and suffered as a result.

That sparked plenty of reaction – and action. After the meeting people shook Mr. Arnaboldi's hand, hugged him, congratulated him on his "brave, trusting" move, and mentioned that they had already gained new insights into him and his world.

Since he is part of one himself, diverse families have become Allan Arnaboldi's consuming interest. When he puts magazine photos on his wall, he makes sure some of them depict two men or two women. When he goes to workshops or gives presentations, he always mentions that there are gay families in every school – whether visible or not – and shows how to include them.

Every September, Mr. Arnaboldi introduces his "Person of the Week" bulletin board by starting with a picture of his partner and himself at their home. Though not labeled as his partner or lover, he is clearly part of Mr. Arnaboldi's family. Not only have there been no repercussions; on the contrary, several lesbian couples have requested him as a teacher. They feel his classroom is a safe place for their children-to-be, and want him as a role model for their children.

He is pleased too with the little, spur-of-the-moment things he can do to raise all students' awareness of gay issues, and to increase the self-esteem of children who may come from "different" families. For example, when Arthur Ashe died of AIDS, Mr. Arnaboldi read *Come Sit with Me,* a book about a child who died of the disease.

Still, from time to time he has felt the need to reach out to groups such as GALE (Gay and Lesbian Educators). "Support is important," he said, "because gay and lesbian teachers often feel they have to do 150 percent, so nobody can ever accuse them of not being a good teacher. The support I've gotten from Pat Griffin's collaborative research project with fifteen gay and lesbian teachers has been important too. It's helped me realize that being gay has made me a better teacher. I realize I'm sensitive, I don't buy into stereotypes, and that's good."

Of course, one stereotype of male elementary school teachers is that they're a bit – well, you know... Mr. Arnaboldi is well aware of that. "I've wondered whether people would think I was trying to indoctrinate little boys," he admitted. "But in some ways, the fact that I'm out to the staff counters that. They know who I am; there are no secrets among us."

He makes sure he is rarely alone with students, but has not altered what he described as his physical, affectionate style of teaching. "Kids respond to that," he said. "I don't hold back; I just treat all the kids the same. Boys in particular who don't have a father crave affection. Their parents request me as a teacher, and the kids seek me out. I'm not going to say no. That's just foreign to me."

Mr. Arnaboldi knows that having a daughter helps legitimize him in the eyes of some members of the school community. He has felt no resistance from parents, and his encounters with students have been equally positive.

One day two daughters of a colleague were discussing his newly pierced ear. The fifth grader told her younger sister that musicians do it, and so do gays. She didn't think Allan was a musician, so she figured he must be gay – and that was the end of the discussion.

Another time one student called a friend "gay." Mr. Arnaboldi asked the boy if he knew what that meant; "Happy," he said. "Well, that's not how you meant it," the teacher replied. "So the other boy said, 'It's when two men love each other.' I said, 'That's right, and I don't want to hear it used in a hurtful way in my classroom. You know how names can be used to make people feel bad? That name makes gay people feel bad. You need to think about the words you use." He wondered whether his talk would precipitate more usage of the word, but he did not hear it again.

Allan Arnaboldi realizes that his situation at Fort River Elementary School is good; colleagues at other Amherst schools report homophobic comments from staff members, and are not out. Yet, being out, he said, has been immensely helpful to him in both his professional and his personal lives. He urges other elementary school teachers to leave the closet – slowly and only partially, if necessary. Finding allies in the school is helpful. So is taking little risks at first to test the waters; bigger ones come later. The outcome is empowerment and a feeling of safety, because exposure is no longer a risk. "I don't make a big announcement to families, but I don't hide anything either. I don't say, 'I'm a gay teacher, and you're going to respect me' – but I'm much more myself now, and that's important."

He concluded by relating the story of a mother who met with him early one school year. She and the woman with whom she was co-parenting were concerned because their son's father was absent, and sometimes the boy felt out of place. The mother asked Mr. Arnaboldi if he would be willing to read a book about nontraditional families to the entire class. He quickly agreed, adding that as a gay father, he knew how important it was for children to hear that.

"Oh, I'm so happy!" the woman replied. "This is going to be so much easier than I thought!" Many things are easier for the boys and girls – from all types of families – lucky enough to have Allan Arnaboldi as their first-grade teacher.

Nancy "Satch" Hoff also knows a thing or two about breaking stereotypes. An out lesbian for many years, she is visible in both Goshen, Massachusetts, where she lives and served two terms on the select board (town council), and Mohawk Regional High School in Shelburne Falls, where she has taught industrial arts for nearly a decade.

With Ms. Hoff, what you see is what you get. Ten years ago she decided she had to be out or quit teaching. She was out in every other aspect of her life; she thought it was crazy to be out at night and at home, then close herself off during the day. She came out at school by taking strong stands: condemning faculty sexism, railing against student t-shirts that carried inappropriate messages, decrying classroom name-calling.

And if anyone missed her signals, several years ago she took her partner to the senior prom. "It was a very blatant and obvious move," she recalled. "Some kids didn't look at me all night, but that's their problem. I'm sure there was scuttlebutt and talk, but no one said I ruined their prom. There was absolutely no backlash that I knew of."

Being out at Mohawk Regional is easier than in some places, harder than in others. It's not far from the Five Colleges area (Amherst, Hampshire, Mt. Holyoke, Smith, and the University of Massachusetts), which Satch describes as a haven of political thought and ferment. At the same time, it is very rural, with strong political, economic, and social polarities. Parts are very poor, almost like Appalachia, yet Bill Cosby owns a home with hundreds of acres in the district.

Interestingly, Ms. Hoff is unable to categorize her students' views based on their backgrounds. It is hard to tell which kids come from where. One of the most overtly supportive girls came from the poor side, and was raised in a foster home. She has learned not to pigeonhole people at all.

Yet, she is aware that people pigeonhole female industrial arts teachers. She deals with stereotypes straightforwardly: because all seventh and eighth graders must take a minicourse in her wood shop, she talks about preconceptions on day one. Nowadays youngsters take her talk in stride; in the early days, when she was less sure of herself and not as open about her sexuality, she got into frequent power conflicts with students. Being out has made her a better teacher. She is less defensive with students, more relaxed, compassionate, and willing to let them challenge her.

She cited name-calling as an example of what's different. "When I used to hear 'faggot,' 'queer,' 'Polack,' 'Jew,' I'd challenge from an authoritative place," she said. "My attitude was, 'I'm greater than thou.' As an authority figure, they couldn't challenge me or question my voice. Now I'll take kids aside, talk about expectations, discuss what they're hearing at home, actually talk about my expectations of them, and why and how words like that can be hurtful and painful. This way, they're actually learning about oppression – not just about authority."

Though Ms. Hoff has let her school's guidance counselors know that she is available to talk to students unsure of their sexuality, she has never yet had a boy or girl ask direct questions. Yet she knows that she has had an effect on Mohawk Regional.

A young girl came to her as a seventh grader, ostensibly looking for glue. They ended up in a long discussion, during which the girl revealed that her mother was a lesbian. The day she graduated, Ms. Hoff asked if she remembered that day, and asked why she came to talk. The girl replied, "I knew you'd be safe."

Other youngsters have spoken about lesbian and gay issues to Ms. Hoff without ever saying the words; she does not mind at all. "They're not typical, hang-out-in-the-wood-shop kids, but they come here anyway," she noted. "They're probably here because they're questioning their sexuality, and I feel real good they're here. I never had that safe place to go when I was growing up." Fortunately for dozens of Mohawk students – whether adept at wood shop or king of the klutzes – Satch Hoff now provides it.

Michael Quercio never had a safe place either. The son of an Italian father who abandoned his family when Michael was a baby, he heard plenty of taunts after his Irish-Catholic mother married a black man. The teasing would surely have turned brutal if the youngsters in his Worcester neighborhood had known Michael was gay.

He related his story the same way he talks about everything else: in paragraphs. They are sometimes digressive, often angry, but always passionate paragraphs. Michael Quercio packs plenty of power into each one. He has to: he knows he doesn't have much time to say everything that wells up inside. He has AIDS – a disease that has brought him both the richest rewards and the bitterest disappointments of his life.

He received his HIV-positive diagnosis in February 1991, while working for an insurance company. He flew to the Virgin Islands to tell his mother, who screamed and fell to the ground when she saw him. After he returned to Massachusetts, he spent four months feeling sorry for himself. "I lay on that couch and I sobbed," he said, pointing to a corner of the well-decorated second-floor apartment he shares with his partner, not far from downtown Worcester. "I mean, I bawled. I wailed. I let everything out." And then Michael Quercio got on with his life.

He went back to running. He began speaking out about AIDS, giving up to three talks a day to anyone who would listen: local clubs, religious groups, state psychiatric hospitals. And schools.

Michael likens the state of HIV awareness by adolescents today to a medical cadaver. "The educational system doesn't even deserve an F, because that's 50 or above," he said. "It's lower than an F. A cadaver just lies there, not living or breathing or doing anything. That's where our schools are today when it comes to HIV."

When he talked to student groups, he pulled no punches. Always straightforward and honest, he was not about to change simply because the topic was AIDS. He brought the gay component into every talk he gave – a subject many AIDS educators pussyfoot around. "Sex is very exciting, very erotic," he told youngsters. He spoke about making love and abstinence, both of which he believes in very deeply. And he told his young listeners not to be ashamed of having heavy desires, whatever those desires are. However, he warned them about the dangers of acting impulsively or irresponsibly on those desires. "It wasn't a message that came out of nowhere, a bolt from the blue," he said. "Seventy percent of students are not abstaining from sex. It's not like I was suddenly introducing them to the notion of sex for the first time."

By April of 1992 Michael Quercio had given two hundred AIDS talks (and run in two postdiagnosis marathons). His extensive press coverage sparked the interest of a nurse at Worcester Academy, a private school a century and a half old that sits atop one of Worcester's seven hills, its red brick buildings ringing a large green. The school is handsome – but as the city changed it has become an oasis of sorts, for the surrounding neighborhood is one of abject poverty. That anomaly is repeated inside the school: at first glance the students are, in Michael's words, "all lily white and squeaky clean," yet closer inspection reveals a small international contingent. Abbie Hoffman is one of Worcester Academy's most famous graduates, but today's students are more conservative and career-oriented. Michael Quercio – a Worcester native who never had the chance to attend such an elite private school – saw an opportunity to knock the harsh reality of AIDS into these privileged students' lives. He quickly accepted the school nurse's offer.

That spring he spoke four times in the Worcester Academy theater. "I was the three-dimensional face of AIDS," he said. "I talked about everything: rage, the ravages of the disease, the way it was transmitted, and the way I felt. And I talked about the denial of AIDS, which is as much a pandemic as the disease itself. I don't use a podium; I walk into the audience, Oprah-style. I touch kids on the shoulder. I'm not an in-your-face, ACT UP person, but I do it to show that AIDS is here among us, among all of us. I guess I blew them away with my sensitivity and compassion and tears."

Receiving lines followed each talk; Michael described them as incredible. "One boy, a big football bruiser type kid, looked very hostile the entire time I was speaking. But he came up to me afterward, he looked me right in the eye, and he said, 'You've got balls. I could never have done that.'"

Those four talks led to an invitation to develop a special AIDS curriculum for Worcester Academy. He planned a twelve-session course that was, he said, the first AIDS class anywhere taught by someone who was AIDS-infected. He did not plan a one-shot appearance by an AIDS poster boy; this was to be the real thing.

The course – which came to be known as "Michael's class" – was mandatory for all Worcester Academy students, grades nine through postgraduate, on a pass-fail basis. It was conducted sixties seminar-style, like a rap group. And it was intense.

"It was a very visceral course," he admitted. "I told the students to leave their brains at the door, and to bring in their hearts. It's passion that gets you under the sheets, so it's passion that has to be changed." He brought in speakers, including a gay black policeman ("just to break down some of the stereotypes"), and he led discussions about everything associated with the disease: denial, epidemiology, diversity, spirituality, mortality. There were talks about "making love" versus "having sex," and debates on current events and social issues. One was about whether AIDS-infected students should be allowed in school classrooms. A new student, an African-American who had missed the first three sessions, said, "Yo, dude, we should just shoot 'em all." Michael asked the boy to repeat what he'd said; the boy, who did not know that his teacher had AIDS, did. The class watched, mortified yet transfixed. Michael appointed him head debater for the keep-them-out-of-school side. Three days later Michael addressed him privately. He told the boy he knew all about prejudice, because of his black stepfather, his homosexuality, and his AIDS diagnosis, then added that he was on the boy's side. The youngster cried. A strong friendship ensued; the two ate together, played basketball together – and sweated together. When the boy's grandmother died, the teacher he turned to was Michael.

Other students confided other things in Michael (who, he said proudly, was "the only teacher they called by their first name"). One athlete came to him panic-stricken: he had had unsafe sex with a prostitute. Michael helped him get tested. The result came back negative, but the boy was so moved by the experience he became a peer educator, appearing on radio shows. If he had not been tested he might have assumed he was positive, acted accordingly – and then might well have *become* positive, Michael noted.

The two courses he taught each morning between eight and ten – many days while on morphine – were not the only things Michael did in the spring of 1992. He also worked full-time at a youth outreach center, as a pre- and post-test counselor. And he got involved in Bill Clinton's presidential campaign. Michael met the Arkansas governor at a dinner. As he related his stories about Worcester Academy, he sensed that the candidate was listening — and reacting. Finally, the activist thought, we've got a chance to elect someone who will do something about AIDS.

That summer Michael met with his headmaster, to discuss the direction the AIDS course would take the following fall. The headmaster liked what Michael was doing, but said he had no money to fund it. Michael received a go-ahead to fund-raise on his own. He and a few supporters spoke to teachers, friends, even vendors to the school, and raised enough money to continue teaching the AIDS curriculum.

Meanwhile, the media noticed what was going on at the school on the hill. Charles Kuralt, the BBC, all the Boston television stations asked for interviews. "Worcester Academy got great press every time I spoke," he said. "I made sure everyone knew that we were doing something, something courageous and innovative and good, that was not being done anywhere else in the country." But already the situation was unraveling.

While Michael was hospitalized with an AIDS-related fever, the school doctor approached the headmaster with three concerns. "One was that I was 'teaching rebellion,'" Michael said. "Another was that I was 'promoting my lifestyle' — he wanted to know why I wasn't teaching that AIDS is punishment to gays for having gay sex. And the third was safety. We were lighting candles in class in memory of people who had died, and that was deemed a hazard." Michael solved the third issue by having students blow out the candles as soon as they were lit — just a gesture, but an important one — yet the others were more difficult to reconcile. Tensions rose during the fall and early winter.

They eased a bit with Bill Clinton's election. Michael Quercio had hitched his wagon to a star, and the star responded in kind. The president-elect named the AIDS educator Massachusetts's "Face of Hope" — there was one from each state, men and women accomplishing extraordinary things under difficult circumstances — and January of 1993 passed in a blur for him. He traveled to Washington for a week of inaugural festivities. He sat across from Mr. Clinton at a gala lunch, and was in the front row for both the concert and the inauguration. Perhaps best of all, he joined Mr. Clinton during his final jog as a private citizen.

In every interview, Michael Quercio credited Worcester Academy for its progressive outlook on AIDS education. Back home, however, he continued to chafe. There were symbolic, as well as substantive, issues. One centered around where the classes met: in Dexter Hall on the periphery of the campus, downstairs next to the boiler room. Michael felt embarrassed bringing a film crew there.

The National Association of Independent Schools (NAIS) asked him to give a talk at their annual convention in New York, on the development and implementation of his course. "I shoot from the hip — tactfully and with integrity, but honestly," Michael explained. "I don't sugar-coat, especially about something as dangerous as AIDS. My speech was ninety-five percent praising the school, and five percent about the obstacles I faced. I wanted to show it was not easy to introduce an AIDS course in a private school. They wanted to hear that; the people who were there wanted the truth." In his speech, Michael said he acknowledged the headmaster's courage — and his presence in the audience. But he also noted that there were problems. He heard plenty of praise. At the same time, he knew it might be political suicide.

Back in Worcester, the headmaster put Michael on strict probation, ordering him not to discuss the school with the press. Michael also found that, as the new semester began, his four classes — each with fifteen to twenty-five students — had shrunk to two. One had three students, the other just one. Two sections had no students at all. "They told me it was scheduling difficulties!" Michael said in disgust. "But there were plenty of kids who still hadn't taken the course, and plenty who wanted to. I knew they were putting the squeeze on me." Yet he continued to teach the course because he was committed to it, and because he believed that reaching students — no matter how few — was important.

When Michael met with the headmaster later that spring to ask about fall plans for an advanced AIDS course, and pre- and post-test counseling right on the Worcester Academy campus, he was told that funding posed a problem. The headmaster insinuated he would not be teaching anymore. He said he was not firing him; rather, he was not renewing his contract for the following year.

As word circulated that Michael would not be back — some rumors attributed it to health problems, others to his demands for more money — the teacher asked for an opportunity to address the school. He stood up at an assembly and told everyone why he was not returning. "I said I respected the head for allowing me to teach, and the faculty for supporting me, but I also said, 'I am not being allowed back by the headmaster.' On the walk back down the aisle I cried. And then I left, to thunderous applause."

One student was so incensed that he leaked the news to a Boston television station. "The phone calls started, and I just said, 'No comment,'" Michael recalled. "But finally, without a lot of forethought – and this was right, but also wrong – I acceded to their reporter. As soon as that happened, lots of other TV stations and newspapers started calling."

The headmaster was quoted too. "Michael decided he didn't have to comply with checks and balances," he told the Associated Press. He said that Michael refused to cooperate with the school doctor, declined to write up a curriculum for the course, and stated publicly that he would not follow a curriculum. He added, "Kids know that adults live by rules, but because Michael failed to do those things the advantages he brought us were being outweighed by the disadvantages he gave us as a role model."

When the headmaster called him in, Michael admitted violating his instructions about talking to the press. But he also claimed he told the truth. Several students planned a sit-in; the headmaster called an emergency meeting and quelled the uprising. He told the students that Michael had made the school look bad in his New York talk.

The faculty reaction, Michael noted, was mixed. He attributed that to the headmaster's power to hire and fire. Michael received a few calls of quiet support, but many older teachers – some of whom wondered why he had been there in the first place – were not about to rock the boat. He felt particularly hurt when a former ally, a woman with whom he had worked closely, turned on him. She feared for her job.

Among the calls he did not receive were any from the Massachusetts-based Gay, Lesbian, and Straight Teachers Network (GLSTN). "I wasn't a member," Michael said, "but I was openly gay, and a teacher, and no one even picked up the phone. That speaks to me of what's wrong with the gay community: there are so many divisions, too many turf wars."

Michael Quercio is no longer at Worcester Academy, yet he continues to be an effective AIDS educator. "I'm a full-time national speaker," he said. "I go all over the country; I'm very much in demand. I'm not falling apart simply because I have AIDS. If I think about the b.s. I went through long enough, it conjures up a lot of emotions, including anger. But I've moved on. When I was in the hospital with pneumocystis I was visited by some former colleagues, and I told them I wanted closure. They encouraged me to call the headmaster, so I did. I told him I could begin to understand his position, that I was wrong for thinking I was completely right just because I told the truth, and I said I hoped he would forgive me for that.

"I lost my home base. The students suffered because I was so strict adhering to my integrity. You've got to learn to dance if you want to be part of the system. I know I did important things. People told me I saved lives. And now there's no AIDS education at Worcester Academy at all.

"I think it would be a fairy-tale ending if the headmaster and I could sit down and say, 'Let's do this again,'" Michael concluded. "I would do this again. I loved what I did. It was important what I did. But like I said, that's just a fairy tale."

Help or Hindrance?

They're often portrayed as caricatures. On TV, in movies – even in many schools – guidance counselors are seen as comically incompetent, if well-meaning. Refugees from the football field or driver education, they creak under enormous student loads; the advice they give is limited to "stay in school, graduate, go to college/join the service/work." They are, stereotypes would have it, the last people to whom students would pose questions about real life – say, sexuality.

Welcome to the Gay Nineties. Guidance counselors have become integral staff members of many buildings – right up there with once similarly shunned professionals like school nurses and health teachers – and they are indeed some of the first people to whom adolescents turn when they face problems like who am I, where do I fit in, uh-oh-I've-got-a-crush-on-a-guy-on-my-baseball-team.

Among the new breed of guidance counselors is Frank Colasonti, Jr., an articulate, insightful man in his early forties. He grew up in a blue-collar Detroit neighborhood; his father toiled on the Chrysler assembly line for forty years, while his mother worked at J.L. Hudson department store. It was a loud, Italian family: very caring, very loving, very supportive. Their support followed him through to adulthood, a fact in which he takes great pride.

Mr. Colasonti went through the Detroit public schools during what he calls their glory days, when they were "fine institutions with excellent teachers." He describes himself as a top student. He took part in many activities, and his popularity cut across all groups. He dated occasionally, but sex was not in the forefront of his life.

He graduated from Wayne State University with a B.A. in political science, then earned a teaching certificate and master's degree in guidance and counseling. He settled into the Catholic school system for

Guidance counselor Frank Colasonti, Jr., unexpectedly came out to his school district when the *Detroit Free Press* featured an article about the local PrideFest celebration he had helped organize.

ten years, at one point even thinking of becoming a priest, and rose through the ranks to become a principal. He was, he said firmly, absolutely not out as a gay man at work. He spent many years in a state of self-loathing; he experienced the gay lifestyle, but internally was very homophobic. He seemed happy-go-lucky on the outside, but inside he was hateful and bitter.

After a decade in parochial schools, he realized he would one day retire without much of a pension, so he began interviewing in the public system. He snapped up an offer as a guidance counselor at Wylie E. Groves High School – in Michigan, it's hard to beat the Birmingham district.

The Birmingham Public Schools encompass ten large residential communities due north of Detroit, including elite Southfield and Bloomfield. What Mr. Colasonti calls its "bizarre configuration" keeps the district largely white, and middle to upper class. The parents are very involved in education. The district ranks near the top of the state in such measures as per-pupil expenditure and test scores.

Birmingham is the only suburb in Michigan that bans housing discrimination based on sexual orientation. There are two high schools in town; Groves, much more diverse, enrolls about a thousand boys and girls in grades nine through twelve. Ninety percent of the student body is white; 90 percent go on to college, the counselor estimates. It's very competitive, almost like a private high school with public funding. It is the kind of school parents dream about.

When Frank Colasonti was hired by Groves, he was an active participant in Detroit's lesbian and gay community, but he was not worried. He had hidden his homosexuality well, and planned to continue to do so.

But conflicts began when he took on major homosexual projects. "I realized the hypocrisy of recognizing gay and lesbian pride but not being out publicly. It became very hard to justify," he said matter-of-factly. In 1988 he helped found the annual PrideFest celebration; two years later he served as its chair. It was a great learning experience. The straight people he met were not as homophobic as he had expected. And as an educator he realized what a great opportunity it could be to teach people about homosexuality.

That year he invited the media to cover PrideFest, and agreed to an interview with Frank Bruni of the *Detroit Free Press*. When the reporter asked to use his name, Mr. Colasonti agreed. He thought the story would be buried somewhere next to the obituaries.

It wasn't. It ran on the front page of the second section on a June Monday – and he was "so freaked out" to see his name in print, he did not go in to school.

He had no idea what to do. He called the National Gay and Lesbian Task Force in Washington and the Michigan Organization for Human Rights to ascertain his legal options in case he was terminated; he did not have many options, they said. He had accrued tenure, and was an employee in good standing – but that did not prevent Mr. Colasonti from spending a harrowing day. He fielded calls from friends at school. "What are you doing?!" they asked. "Are you trying to get fired?" He found out that the person who had discovered his name in the article and passed it around school was a woman who had come on to him – to no avail – when he first arrived at Groves.

It was a Groves tradition to post news clippings with faculty members' names in the teachers' lounge. Realizing he could not stay away forever, Mr. Colasonti arrived at school at six a.m. Tuesday, an hour and a quarter earlier than usual, in order to prepare himself for the onslaught from parents, teachers, and administrators. His first stop was the faculty lounge; to his relief, the article was nowhere to be seen. Then he went to his office, and waited.

The reaction, when it came, was totally unexpected. "What I received was congratulations from many, many colleagues," he recounted. "People shook my hand and hugged me – men, I'm talking about, hugged me. Parents called to see if I was okay. It was the complete opposite of what I had expected. It was like a huge black cloud of depression that was over me had lifted."

He heard only one comment from an administrator, and that came in a humorous, offhand way. "So, are you starting a scrapbook?" a supervisor asked.

A few days later a student came out to him. "Thank God you're here," the boy said. It was, Mr. Colasonti noted, quite an emotional week.

Still, he thought, when school resumed following summer break he would be working entirely with girls. He figured the parents of every boy would uproot their sons to different counselors. Yet that did not happen either. Mr. Colasonti lost only two counselees – both girls, whose parents were ministers or fundamental Christians. The following year he lost only one student, a boy whose father was a preacher.

"On the reverse side," he said proudly, "I have gained more students than the other four counselors – all of whom are extremely responsive professionals. But kids have transferred to me, because some parents preferred it. It has nothing to do with the kids' sexual orientation; it's just the kind of person I am perceived to be. I guess it's because we have a lot of sophisticated, educated parents here, who know gays and lesbians in their personal and professional lives, and are not threatened by it."

When school began again in the fall, Mr. Colasonti expected to hear from his principal. That meeting did not occur for several months, and when it did the administrator asked first what the counselor was looking for. No changes, Mr. Colasonti replied; all he wanted was that gay people be included in anti-harassment policies, and that everyone be treated equally during the hiring process. The principal then wondered about the wisdom of counseling students behind closed doors. The counselor explained the difference between homosexuality and pedophilia, wielding the statistic that 90 percent of child molestation is cross-gender. He said if he were a parent, he would be more concerned about male staff and daughters. He left the meeting feeling that his principal and supervisor were determined to learn more and were willing to accept him for who he is: a competent employee, well liked by students, staff, and parents.

Frank Colasonti's self-description is not off the mark. In 1992 the Groves senior class selected him as one of the Top Ten Most Influential Educators in the school; the following year the *Detroit News* named him one of fourteen Michiganians of the Year – the first gay man so honored in the award's two decades. In being so named he joined such luminaries as Rosa Parks and Anthony Wendell, head of the Detroit NAACP. He felt proud and humbled.

Since he came out, several youngsters have approached Mr. Colasonti with their own questions. One was definite about his sexuality; others were questioning. That is appropriate for high school, he noted. About 1 percent know for sure; about 10 percent are confused or searching. In addition, he has counseled one student with a transvestite parent, and another whose father is gay. Had he not been out, he never would have learned that information. It added a great deal to his understanding and handling of the family dynamics.

Mr. Colasonti said that coming out has also enhanced his relationships with the faculty. Before, he felt a vast gulf separated him from others; now his rapport with the entire staff, including secretaries, aides, and custodians, is much closer. Of his nearly one hundred colleagues, only two or three have not been supportive.

But Groves High is in many ways an ideal school, and the Birmingham district is in many ways an ideal place. How does Mr. Colasonti assess the overall state of guidance counseling, with respect to lesbian and gay students?

"Generally speaking, it's poor," he admitted. "I've spoken to literally hundreds of classroom and health education teachers about homosexual youth, and the one group that has not invited me to appear is the counselors' association. I've approached them to speak, or offered to bring in other speakers, but so far there's been no response." At a recent statewide meeting, he noted, the counselors did have the opportunity to attend a short workshop featuring a gay speaker.

His district is fortunate, because most counselors are well versed on the subject, and the rest know where the proper resources are. But, he said, in many places counselors are just beginning to deal with sexuality – of any kind – as it relates to self-esteem. Younger counselors are aware of the issues, but older ones are not.

Older counselors, he noted, have not had any background or training in sexuality. "It just wasn't discussed when many of us were being educated. And many counselors have not kept up with the latest teachings on modern sexuality. It's not a conspiracy of any sort; it's just a lack of knowledge."

Unfortunately, he added, most of them do not care to know. "We're creatures of habit. This is out of the ordinary, so it disrupts their routine to learn about it. Massachusetts is doing a lot – but I don't know if anything like that will ever happen here in Michigan."

He hopes things will change. Youngsters need to find a counselor they can confide in. Birmingham offers a three-day unit on homosexuality for eleventh and twelfth graders, but as Mr. Colasonti notes, many students need it as early as eighth grade. The sophisticated ones get information from the media, but most do not. Many have nowhere to turn, which is reflected in dropout and suicide rates.

He does find rays of hope. The Michigan Education Association has a gay and lesbian caucus, of which Mr. Colasonti is an active member, and the Michigan Federation of Teachers has one too. Health teachers in the state have brought sexual orientation issues to the forefront, and some school districts now include it in anti-harassment policies.

The key, Frank Colasonti, Jr., said, is for lesbian and gay educators – not necessarily only guidance counselors, but school personnel everywhere – to come out. "They don't have to do it as publicly as I did," he laughed, "but they do have to be visible. As trite as it sounds, education will be the key to our acceptance by the entire fabric of American society."

––––––

Of course, most guidance counselors – like most students and staff members – are not homosexuals. That does not mean, however, that straight counselors cannot help gay, lesbian, bisexual, or questioning boys and girls.

Angela McLean is typical of those who can, though students seldom seek her out. Several years ago the Northfield (Vermont) High School counselor attended an adolescent sexual identity workshop at St. Michael's College. She learned that most public schools don't deal with those issues – and realized with surprise that that was true in her own small school of 420 seventh through twelfth graders. Indeed, it was even the case in her own counseling office.

"Where do kids who are going through a sexual identity crisis get the message that it's okay to go to a counselor or teacher to discuss these concerns?" she wondered. "They so internalize their feelings. The workshop addressed the need for Vermont schools to get the word out."

Ms. McLean can recall only two instances in over twenty-five years in education when youngsters came to her with concerns about their sexuality. One boy began having difficulties in seventh grade; he was already experiencing harassment from other students because he was effeminate. But it was not until several years later that he approached Ms. McLean with specific worries. She said this is typical. Students with questions about themselves find school to be an uncomfortable place, yet they do not know where to turn for support. In this case the problem was obvious, but it can be exacerbated when teenagers cover up, in order to be accepted by their peers.

Northfield tried every option available to keep that boy in school, Ms. McLean said, ranging from a vocational program, to a transfer to another school, to residential placement. He took the counselor's advice to seek counseling, and get support for himself and his family. Ultimately, however, Northfield was unsuccessful. The boy took some of the suggestions, and his parents tried to be supportive about school, but eventually he dropped out. Ms. McLean believes the school let him down. He felt he could not go through the system – and that is not unusual. She takes solace, however, that he looks back on her as at least one person who was helpful.

Angela knows of similar situations in neighboring towns. There are no workshops to speak of. Health programs deal with many different issues, but Vermont youngsters are not ready to have healthy conversations on homosexuality without feeling self-conscious and defensive.

She believes schools should do more to advertise that students can talk to their guidance counselors. Posters would help, yet she has none. "I tried to put up Outright Vermont's mini-posters," she explained, "but before I knew it they were covered with graffiti and ripped down, so I didn't try again. There's no anonymity here. When that boy was going through what he went through, everyone talked about him, everyone hassled him. This wasn't a safe place. You'll have that in rural areas, where everyone knows everyone else. I think it would take a very brave soul to feel he could trust a teacher or counselor." Ms. McLean does keep Outright Vermont information on hand, in case a student asks.

"We should do more, I know," she admitted. "Counselors are open to any discussion, in a confidential atmosphere. We're here to serve the public. But if the public doesn't come to us..." Her voice trailed off.

"We have no control if a student doesn't choose to talk about a sexual identity crisis," she began again. "On the other hand, I feel schools in general don't present the whole story to kids. We have a student support team of nurses, psychologists, and other people; we have a peer support team. Within these groups, information on sexual identity can become available; substance abuse problems often mask sexual identity problems. But I'm not sure if the word is getting out to enough kids. The local community paper now includes PFLAG (Parents, Families and Friends of Lesbians and Gays) meetings in the announcement section, and a former graduate just announced at work that he's HIV-positive, so people *are* becoming more aware. But these kinds of things are still not really discussed publicly around here."

Ms. McLean noted, for example, that gay and lesbian concerns have never been addressed at a Northfield faculty meeting – though the close friendship of two girls arose as an issue at several sessions of the student support team. They were not publicly affectionate; they were just together all the time, and everyone assumed they were a couple. When it first came to the attention of the administration, it was looked on as creating a problem in school. Ms. McLean and others pointed out the *girls* were not the problem; the harassment they were suffering was. Counselors, along with nurses and the school psychologist, did a good job of educating administrators on that issue, Angela felt. They saw that a counseling session could not "correct the problem." She is pleased that the incident opened some minds.

On the other hand, educators in Vermont still talk about AIDS without discussing sexuality. Teenagers still feel unable to discuss sexuality concerns with their guidance counselors. Angela McLean knows there is a dire need for many more workshops, much more education. While some minds are opening up, many more eyes remain closed.

———

Another guidance counselor with an insight into lesbian and gay issues is Norm Walker of Yakima's Davis High School. Yakima is a small city of some 50,000, nestled between two mountain ranges in south-central Washington; not far away lie fertile apple orchards and an enormous U.S. military firing range. Mr. Walker described the 1600-student school as "multicultural, multiethnic, and multisocioeconomic – truly a spectrum." Several openly gay youngsters walk the halls, with no ongoing harassment. The student body is fairly tolerant.

Yet, the counselor noted, the school faces obstacles similar to those in many other communities: "The far right comes flying out of the woodwork, and the administration gets real nervous." The three-person counseling staff, however, is able to work with lesbian, gay, bisexual, and questioning students on an individual basis – and they do so in a very up-front way.

He thinks that is the case with many counselors, attributable in part to the ethical standards that guidance counselors are supposed to obey. "Our primary loyalty is to each student," he said. "We treat them and their needs with respect and dignity, regardless of race, creed, and all that other stuff. Trouble comes when counselors don't agree that a student's homosexuality is natural or innate – they think it's a choice or a perversion, something that can be 'fixed' – but I also think most counselors are able to overlook that. The American Association of

School Counselors has taken the stand that we need to address these issues, for all kids, and their support has been important."

The religious right has generally remained away from the issue of counseling individual gay students, he said, "although they view group counseling as an evil, Satanic front to undermine family values." He and his Davis colleagues have each worked with youngsters who had questions about sexual orientation; however, when several of the students expressed interest in a support group and Mr. Walker began to organize one, red flags went up. Rather than wage a pitched battle, he started the group outside of school. Mr. Walker is a registered counselor in the state of Washington, so there was no problem with that. It was advertised in other schools, and ran for a couple of years. The original student members moved on, and other youngsters did not want to continue it. At the time he was interviewed, the counselor had not had any inquiries for several months.

However, Norm Walker firmly believes that any issue that teenagers want support for belongs in the school. There are support groups around drugs and alcohol; sexual orientation issues are even more basic than that. He is uncomfortable working sub rosa; he wants to be up-front. But he has learned that in the current Washington climate he cannot advertise such a support group, so he does what he can. And he hopes it helps.

Yet for every Frank Colasonti, Jr., Angela McLean, and Norm Walker, there are men and women like the random sample of 289 members of the American School Counselor Association (ASCA) who responded, anonymously and confidentially in the winter of 1991, to a questionnaire concerning their perceptions of adolescent homosexuality. They were 61 percent female and 39 percent male; only 3 percent claimed to be homosexual or bisexual. Seventy-one percent had earned master's degrees and 20 percent education specialist degrees, while 7 percent had their doctorates. This was not a stupid bunch.

While almost two-thirds of the respondents estimated that 1 to 5 percent of students in their high schools were gay or lesbian, about one in six believed there were no gay students at all. Seventy-one percent reported they had counseled a homosexual student during their guidance careers; they said they assisted those students primarily by helping them deal with their friends (81%) and family (79%).

James H. Price and Susan K. Telljohann analyzed that data, and plenty more, in a *Journal of School Health* article. Only one in five of the respondents found counseling gay or lesbian students "gratifying," while almost the same number said that counseling a homosexual student about gay issues would not be "professionally gratifying." Seven percent reported that homosexuality was offensive to them, while 16 percent believed a gay lifestyle is not a healthy lifestyle.

The counselors received their knowledge of homosexuality from a variety of sources, including professional journals (81%), mass media (44%), workshops or professional conferences (40%), textbooks (37%), on-the-job training (34%), and college classes (31%). However, what they knew did not always jibe with current knowledge about homosexuality: only 67 percent believed gay and lesbian students are more likely than most students to feel isolated and rejected; just 31 percent felt that gay students are more likely than their peers to attempt suicide, and a mere 8 percent perceived homosexual students as more likely than most students to abuse drugs. "The research supports, and it is important for all school personnel to understand, that adolescent homosexuals are at 'high risk' for some negative behaviors," including suicide and drug abuse, the authors wrote.

They were encouraged to find that "more of the younger and less experienced counselors reported receiving more training in the area of adolescent homosexuality from their college classes and textbooks." Perhaps, the authors continued, today's counselor preparation programs are dispelling some of the myths surrounding the topic.

However, in their conclusion, the authors recommended that professional preparation of school counselors should include more information about adolescent homosexuality. They advised school districts to provide in-service training so that educators could become more sensitive to the needs of homosexual students. And they wrote that school counselors need more professional literature directed toward them on gay and lesbian issues; that school districts "may want to provide support groups for adolescent homosexuals," with school counselors, health teachers, or school nurses facilitating such groups; that guidance counselors "may need to work with health teachers and school nurses to present this issue in a nonthreatening way in health classes so stereotypes and information about homosexuality can be openly discussed"; and that similar studies should be repeated with school administrators, teachers, and nurses. "Only with a comprehensive perspective of the perceptions of all school personnel regarding adolescent homosexuality," they concluded in perfect educationalese, "can the negative environment that exists in some schools regarding this population be minimized."

———>●<———

On the Front Lines

School nurses: they're not just aspirin dispensers and temperature takers anymore.

No longer do these women – and it is still an overwhelmingly female profession – spend their days in sterile-smelling offices, padding around in starched white uniforms waiting to patch skinned knees and examine sore throats. Today they're also asked to counsel pregnant girls, diagnose sexually transmitted diseases, and provide emotional support for youngsters grappling with a panoply of woes, ranging from physical abuse to drug and alcohol addiction.

Today more than ever before, the first person these students turn to is the school nurse. The guidance counselor is too busy with college transcripts and paperwork, the favorite teacher just won't understand, and no one even knows the social worker exists. But the school nurse – with her sanctuary of an office, complete with couch, closed door, and the promise of a late pass – provides an easily overlooked, often crucial role for youngsters in crisis.

An array of youngsters with a wide range of problems appear every day at Kay Williams's door. She is a school nurse at Central High School in Saint Paul, Minnesota. The two thousand ninth through twelfth graders are multiracial and multiethnic; they're enrolled in a variety of magnet school courses, including performing arts and a gifted and talented program; but they share the concerns of teenagers everywhere. It is those worries that often drive them to Ms. Williams's office. Many times they are concerned, sometimes even terrified, about same-sex attractions.

When she started a support group for gay and lesbian students, the first five students who showed up were familiar. They were frequent visitors, always claiming to be sick or wanting to go home. School was just too much for them, so they spent a lot of time in the nurse's office. That did not bother her. Ms. Williams said that she, like most school nurses, sees her role as being an advocate for youngsters, no matter what else is going on at school or in their lives. Though other professionals in a building also see themselves as advocates – teachers, guidance counselors, and coaches, for instance – Ms. Williams believes that nurses are uniquely positioned to play that role. While wary of generalizing, she noted that because many guidance counselors are men, and males generally have a tougher time with gay issues than females, it is taking awhile for counselors to make inroads with lesbian and gay students. Teachers and coaches seldom help, because they have few opportunities to study or learn about homosexuality. Nurses, on the other hand, have been trained to handle a variety of health-related subjects – including sexual orientation.

School nurses can deal with sensitive subjects in sensitive ways, Kay Williams added, and that contributes to the safe feeling her office provides. "When I talk to students about STDs, I always use gay-sensitive words. I say 'your partner,' not 'your boyfriend' or 'girlfriend.' I've learned you can't make assumptions that sexual partners are always opposite-sex. I don't pass judgments on how someone contracts an STD, because that's not the important thing. The important thing is to treat it, and gain the student's confidence while doing so. And I say 'your parents,' not 'your mother' or 'father,' because again you never know if someone's parents are straight."

Ms. Williams is able to communicate her sensitivity about gay and lesbian issues in other ways too. She stocks her office with brochures that answer questions about sexuality; frank posters line the walls. If she hears homophobic comments in her waiting room, she quietly lets the offender know why those words are inappropriate.

Nor does she confine her work to students. The nurse frequently consults and shares information with teachers – not breaching confidentiality, but raising awareness about issues they might ignore, or never consider. After listening gratefully to Ms. Williams, teachers ask questions. She recognizes that adults often have as little information about homosexuality as teenagers, and she welcomes the opportunity to provide answers for all.

But perhaps her most important work at Central revolves around the gay and lesbian group. It began four years ago, after a thirteen-year-old girl requested some kind of support. Weekly meetings attract anywhere from two to a dozen students who identify themselves as gay or lesbian; some are out of the closet, others not. All seek support. At first the group met in a room deep in back of Mrs. Williams's office suite. Then, as students felt safer, they moved to a conference room nearer the front. The nurse takes great pains to protect members' anonymity, and is always surprised when someone walks into the office and yells, "Are we having the group today?" Still, she is careful not to tell anyone on the staff – even her fellow nurses – what day of the week the group meets. To attend, students must ask her when and where they get together. In the beginning, members worried about harassment, but there has been none. No one comes to gawk. "It's a pretty big decision to talk to me about coming; it's not a fun thing to do," she said.

The first order of business at each meeting is to check what's gone on that week. A student who has been out for a while might be coping with an unexpected epidemic of harassment; those who are not open may be dealing with rumors or innuendoes. Minnesota has harassment laws, so the group may discuss how to use them the right way. Over forty different speakers have addressed the students, on topics ranging from religion to safe sex.

Sometimes the members simply sit, talk, and enjoy a good time. A few times each year the little family extends its reach, joining four or five similar groups in the Twin Cities area for joint activities. The membership constantly evolves. Whenever the numbers dwindle, it seems someone new walks through the door.

Youngsters learn about the group through posters, announcements, articles in the school newspaper, and area social service groups. In 1994 the yearbook ran a photo of two members, giving it heightened visibility.

Kay Williams believes it is important to have a co-facilitator, but was concerned at first that none of the leaders was gay. However, when she asked the teenagers about it, they said they were happy to take whatever they could get. She feels badly that gay teachers at Central do not feel comfortable participating, noting that even with Minnesota's human-rights legislation, homosexual adults are afraid of being identified with gay youth.

So the students bring their concerns to the school nurse – and not always during the group sessions. They ask questions at all hours of the school day; the word is out that her office is a safe place, and they flock to it.

The administration has been, she said, semisupportive. "I think they've pretended I'm not here – they haven't said I can't do it! The first few years they weren't really gung ho, but now I think they're kind of getting on the bandwagon. I think they realize it's important to have services for everyone, so that kids can get through school, feel good about themselves, and graduate."

Ms. Williams did not want to talk about her colleagues in other schools, but noted the positive feedback she received after presenting a workshop on gay and lesbian groups at a national school nurses' convention. "I realize not everyone is completely comfortable dealing with gay and lesbian issues, but I think most school nurses – at least the ones I know – are aware that they exist, and they have to be addressed. We've been doing that for a while, at least here in Minnesota, and I think it's something we should be doing."

Which is why lesbian and gay students at Central High School continue to head toward Kay Williams's office for a lot more than aspirin, Ace bandages, and an occasional late pass.

In or Out:
Two Teachers' Decisions

To be or not to be (out): that is the question. It is a question every gay, lesbian, bisexual, transgendered, and unsure-but-wondering teacher faces, at some point in his or her career – often at many points. Every teacher answers it his or her own way, or ways; obviously, it is not as simple a question as it seems, and the answer is never black or white. The shades of gray – the subtleties of being out of the closet, or in – appear limitless.

For example, Alan Miller responded this way when asked whether he is out or in: "Yes and no." The Berkeley (California) High School English instructor added, just as confusingly, "I've come out before, and I'm getting ready to come out again. It's something you have to do over and over and over."

Many people are surprised to find the act of coming out in a school situation to be so complex. Mr. Miller explained, "I'm out to my senior classes, but I've made it a point not to be out to my freshmen. The seniors are there 'cause they want to be; the freshmen are locked into their classes. I'm a difficult, confrontational teacher, and I don't want to give ninth graders any excuse to get out of my class."

He is out to the members of Berkeley's gay-lesbian-straight club, which he serves as a coordinator. He is out to anyone who walks into the school library and sees Mr. Miller's chapbook of poems. (He noted, however, that it took three years before anyone checked it out.) He is out to any students in other classes who hear him guest-read his poems (he described one as "haiku set in a black gay bar. There's nothing straight about it at all!"). And he is out to the Berkeley staff, some of whom attend his poetry readings around town.

Berkeley, California, high school teacher Alan Miller believes that coming out is a continual process.

It may seem that once a teacher is out, he or she is out for good – especially someone as vocal and visible as the six-foot-two, 200-pound Alan Miller. However, that is not the case. Each year brings swarms of new students and staff members to Berkeley High. They have no idea who's who, so each semester Mr. Miller has to get to know, and be known by, new youngsters and colleagues.

He does not announce on the first day of class that he is gay. "I don't generally want to come out early in the semester," he explained, "because I don't want to be stereotyped. I don't have a problem being known as a gay man, but I also don't want it to be my only identity. I'm plenty of other things too, and I want people to know me for my writing, my political activism, and the other things I do. I'm a big, black, gay man, and I enjoy fucking with their minds by breaking down lots of different stereotypes."

He's been breaking stereotypes for quite a while. Before coming to Berkeley he taught in the nearby Richmond district, where he showed his students *Tongues Untied,* the Marlon Riggs movie about black gay men. There was a special, added attraction: Mr. Miller appeared in it. He experienced "minor fallout" – a couple of parents objected – but, he noted, "I didn't strap the kids into their seats. They had the option of going to the library instead. In that school if you were talented, creative, and willing to work, your sexuality didn't matter that much. In an inner-city school like that, sexual orientation was less important than competence."

Berkeley High is more diverse than that Richmond school, he said. "We've got a mix of classes – a *clash* of classes – here now. Upper class to lower class. Hefty percentages of blacks and whites, with growing

Asian, Latino, and Native American populations. And of course there's the whole political history of the city hanging over the school, in good and bad ways." Mr. Miller invites a host of speakers to address topics of diversity, ranging from Pomo Afro Homos to Japanese performance artists and female coal miners. He has even taught Asian-American literature.

Yet, he remarked, when it comes to gay and lesbian issues, even enlightened Berkeley is not Eden. His gay-straight club's signs have been torn down, the group was denied funding for a simple poster project, and there have been incidents of verbal and physical harassment in the halls. None of that shocks him. "I've lived here twelve years, and the veneer of civility is only a veneer. When I heard homophobic and anti-Semitic comments made about a faculty member who died of AIDS – and the comments were made by another teacher – then it's not surprising what the kids pick up."

He said he is one of only a few teachers in the 2700-student school to introduce AIDS and gay issues as normal classwork topics. He has many closeted colleagues, but only one or two have followed his lead by coming out. His principal is supportive – though without, Mr. Miller noted wryly, "ever saying the words 'gay' or 'lesbian' to me. I think the term used is 'those people.'" Most administrators ignore the gay-straight group, but the adviser acknowledges they are burdened with many responsibilities.

Though he is out to most of the school, Mr. Miller played down the idea of being a role model. "That's a lot to put on anybody," he said. "I know that people do model their behavior on the way I behave, one way or another. But I just want to have my life, as a gay person, a black person, a poet, and a political figure. If I can have all that and *also* be a 'role model,' whatever that means, then okay."

However, he knows that he influences his students. A young Filipino lesbian from Richmond recently tracked him down and told him she was getting her teaching credentials, in part because she was so impressed with what he had accomplished in the classroom. That made him realize that he will indirectly affect students for decades to come.

That influence extends beyond his students. A girl once called him a "faggot" in class; he threw her out until she returned with a parent. When she showed up with her grandmother, the woman backed Mr. Miller one hundred percent, telling her daughter she had acted completely inappropriately. Such are the advantages of being out – even if the process of coming out must be repeated, over and over again, every single semester.

Down the coast in the Los Angeles Unified School District, Ignacio
Ruiz is far less open about his homosexuality now than before. "When
I was younger I was fully out," the middle school art teacher said. "It
was very important to me then. Now it's not so important. I don't think
I'm as out in school today as I used to be."

Yet that does not mean he ignores the subject. "I camp it up a lot in
class, and kids make comments. I just go along with them," he said. "If
they insinuate that I'm gay, I make jokes too. I just go along with the
program. But as far as coming out – it's none of their business. It really
isn't."

He is, however, able to connect with youngsters who are called
"gay" or "faggot." "I know how rough it can be – I was out before it
was in, when I was fifteen or sixteen," he said. "So I don't necessarily
come out to them, but I let the kids know that I got teased too when I
was young, because – this is what I say – I 'chose a different route.' I'll
praise the flamboyant kids, tell 'em to keep smiling. Whenever I see
someone who is possibly gay, I sort of help them out as much as I can."

Why is he no longer out? "I'm not afraid to be seen – there's a gay
bar not far from school, and I go there – but at a certain point it became
just not important to me anymore," he reiterated. "Teachers don't talk
about being heterosexual, and parents don't talk about how many times
they have sex, so why should I talk about being gay? Gay is so much
more than being sexual. When I was younger I felt oppressed, and at
that point it was a big deal, but now it's just sort of faded away."

Mr. Ruiz did come out to one student. After school one day, a boy
working in the main office started talking to him about movie stars
who were gay, so the teacher asked if *he* was. "Sort of," he replied.
When Mr. Ruiz said that he himself is gay, the boy admitted he was
too. They went into the art room to talk about AIDS and self-esteem.
Mr. Ruiz learned the boy had already come out to some odd people
– a Mormon teacher who talked incessantly about religion, and a
cousin who was a Jehovah's Witness – so he told the youngster that
God was on his side.

Ignacio took the youth under his wing. The boy felt comfortable in
the art room, even when Mr. Ruiz chastised him for having unsafe sex
with unknown partners. When he graduated from middle school, Mr.
Ruiz was a bit relieved: the boy's needs had become a bit burdensome.
But one day during summer school, he reappeared, and asked for a ride
home. Mr. Ruiz took him to lunch; the boy soon showed up at the
teacher's house, and told him he was in love.

"I asked with who, and he said, 'Someone in this room.' Well, we were the only two people there, so I said, 'I'm glad you're in love with yourself. It looks like this self-esteem stuff worked!' He said I was making fun of him. I told him to come back when he was twenty-one – he was only fifteen – and then he'd realize how old I was. Needless to say, he's twenty-one now – and he has a boyfriend. A good boyfriend."

Mr. Ruiz recognized that the youngster was looking for someone to talk to, and desperately needed attention and advice. "We went through a lot of scolding," he said. "I let him know he was making lots of wrong choices. He rebelled against me, and that hurt – but he kept coming to me. Now he's in college, and doing really, really well."

As the relationship progressed, Mr. Ruiz grew worried. "I got so scared of everything," he admitted. "Hell, yes. One time he talked to me on the phone about his boyfriend. His brother was listening in on the other line, and told their mother. I called Virginia Uribe [the founder of Los Angeles's Project 10 for gay and lesbian youth] and asked her what to do. She said, 'Nothing. You're a teacher; you can listen to whatever kids say. Just don't touch them, or advocate something like sex with an older person.' I was scared, and I didn't hear from him for four days. I went through trauma, but when he called, he explained that everything was fine. He said he'd talked to his mother, and blamed everything on himself." The mother was embarrassed that her son was sharing such personal things with a teacher.

Another time the boy's mother found information on coming out, and called Mr. Ruiz, to find out why he'd sent it. "Because your son asked for it," the teacher replied. She accused him of encouraging the boy's homosexuality, rather than helping him overcome it. "I'm not," he said. "He's gay, and he can't do anything about that. I'm helping him accept it, and accept himself."

Despite those calls, the teacher and the boy's mother had a good relationship – so good, in fact, that when she moved to Miami she signed full custody of her sixteen-year-old son over to Mr. Ruiz. "He was going to the High School for the Arts," the teacher explained. "He didn't want to lose that opportunity, so I offered to let him stay with me. But I told her I had to have full custody, for insurance purposes and everything." However, the mother surprised them both by leaving earlier than expected – and her son cried all night.

"He decided he didn't want to stay after all," Ignacio said. "So he spent two years in Miami, but we communicated. He came back for vacations here, and I went there. I was like a father to him. He realized he wanted to spread his wings, and she was holding him down." When he graduated from high school he returned to California to live with Mr. Ruiz. "It was not easy," he recalled. "We fought a lot about who he was hanging around with. He thought maybe I had the hots for him, but it was just that I was being overprotective, like his mother. Now he's found the right boyfriend. He realizes I saved him from a lot of crap that goes on in the gay community. There are a lot of weirdos out there, you know."

Another student to whom Mr. Ruiz came out was his brother-in-law's nephew, who attended his school – and whose grandmother thought he might be gay. "I spotted him before I knew his name," the teacher said. "He was a flamboyant queen. Two weeks later he asked me how I knew who his grandmother was, and I told him. He told the whole school I was his uncle, and started hanging around me."

At Halloween Mr. Ruiz gave him candy left over from his classes; another time he sent the boy a postcard from Tucson, as he did with many pupils in his classes, while a third time he took photos of the boy – also something he often did with students. The boy's mother called the school, and said she did not want her son to be around a homosexual. "She said I was giving him candy, sending him postcards, and taking his picture." Again, Mr. Ruiz called Dr. Uribe; again she said, "Don't worry. You're a teacher. You can't close the door on kids who need you." After Mr. Ruiz told the principal the circumstances surrounding the candy, postcards, and photos, the principal ended up telling the mother it was her job to control her child.

The principal knew the art teacher was gay. Years before, a girl had accused him of looking up her dress. Mr. Ruiz came out to the principal and assistant principal then, saying, "I'm gay. I have no reason to look up any girl's dress." He added, "That shut them up. Nobody ever spoke about that again!"

But most of Mr. Ruiz's interactions with lesbian and gay students are quieter and much less visible – like the time he intercepted a note in class, from one girl to another. "It was so suggestive," he said, "about what they wanted to do together. I just told them they were lucky I saw it, and not another teacher. I told them to keep that stuff out of school. If it fell into the wrong hands they would get sent off to counseling."

So Ignacio Ruiz, the formerly open art teacher, remains for the most part back in the closet. It is a place he feels happy – most of the time. "The L.A. School District has designated June as Gay and Lesbian Month," he concluded. "I'm in charge of the display cases here. Some of my colleagues at other schools put up displays each June, but I haven't had the guts to do anything like that here." He thinks about decisions like that every day of his life — just as tens of thousands of gay, lesbian, and bisexual teachers do in buildings across the country. Their actions may vary from semester to semester, class to class, even student to student. "Are you out of the closet?" is certainly not a true-false question; it's subjective, and the essay that answers it takes an entire career to write.

Alone in the Lone Star State

Just when you think things are looking up for lesbian and gay youngsters – right after you've finished reading chapters about openly gay students taking dates to the prom and being elected homecoming king, about openly lesbian teachers serving as assistant athletic director, about curricular changes and speakers' bureaus and all the other actions, large and small, that make you realize our schools are indeed capable of moving close to the twenty-first century – at that moment you read the story of Myk Simpson, and you remember that in some parts of America, the Dark Ages are not just ancient history. They're real life.

Myk (pronounced "Mike") was born in Austin, Texas, but moved to Corpus Christi when he was young. That's where he grew up, though not particularly happily: his childhood included sexual abuse, physical abuse, drug and alcohol use – and the knowledge, starting when he was four years old, that he was different.

"I didn't really know what it was that made me feel the way I did until I was in fourth grade," he said. "But I always knew it was something." That year he had a sex education course – "strictly heterosexual sex ed.," he noted – and was finally able to put a word to his feelings. Myk Simpson was gay.

He first attempted suicide in sixth grade; he tried to kill himself once or twice a year for the next six years. He was hospitalized several times, in Corpus Christi and Austin – always with bad results. No one wanted to deal with the source of his pain; no one knew how to help a teenager who was gay.

In his junior year at Tuloso-Midway High School in Corpus Christi, he found one good friend. His feelings finally overpowered him, and he came out to the friend – even though it took thirty minutes of silence, then crying, on the phone before he finally was able to say the words. In the end he just blurted out the news, then hung up. The friend called right back, to say it was okay – he was gay too! Myk had his first homosexual relationship.

Unfortunately the violence escalated, at home and at school. Tuloso-Midway was, he said, "a very conservative, very uppity suburban school. It was excellent as far as education goes, but there was no support for anyone, no matter what your problem was." Though Myk described himself as "not nell or anything – I was quite butch," he was harassed unmercifully. "Everyone needed someone to feel better than," he explained. Though he served on the student council, was vice president of Students Against Drunk Driving, and sang in the all-state choir, his classmates zeroed in on the student who'd always felt different.

He had achieved so much – all, he emphasized, without the support of his family – yet it was not enough. "I wanted to be someone," he said. "I wanted to be Myk the student council representative, Myk the all-state choir member, not Myk the homosexual, but it didn't happen. I was still Myk the homosexual." He had not, he noted, come out at school. "It was just that anyone in choir was considered a homo, and I was the person in choir everyone knew."

Unable to take school anymore, he downed a bag of pills. He flipped out in class and was sent to a psychiatric hospital. He did not divulge his secret there; every conversation revolved around straight sex. Myk became a superb liar, which depressed him even more. His mother and stepfather disowned him; he was adopted by his father – whom he had not seen in twelve years – and moved to Austin. But his father was abusive, Myk said, and that arrangement did not last even a month.

He moved again, this time to South Padre Island, where he lived with his grandmother. He enrolled in Port Isabel High School, and quickly learned that one of his teachers was alleged to be homosexual; he had been seen in that resort town's lone gay bar. Desperate to fit in in his new environment, Myk recalls that he joined his classmates in "doing everything possible to make this teacher's life miserable. We totally humiliated this man. We teased him, we glued his stuff to his desk, we did everything we could think of. It was pathetic. If I was in his shoes, I think I would've quit the profession." Myk also dated women, and had sex with as many as he could.

But hiding his sexual orientation took its toll, and he knew he could not live a lie forever. When a friend invited him to move in, Myk went back to Austin. He started his senior year at Anderson High, which he felt was a good school. He was fed up with hiding, burned out with lying, and decided to start being himself. On the first day of school he wore a pink triangle and freedom rings. He was not physically abused at Anderson, but he suffered verbal harassment, so he transferred to Round Rock High School a few miles north. The school came highly recommended; people called it "an awesome school," he said. But, they warned him: "Stay in the closet."

Again Myk played the heterosexual role; again he could not stand the charade. When he saw an actress come out on *Married ... With Children,* he knew he had to do it too. So one Friday morning he wore his pink triangle, his freedom rings, and his OutYouth Drop-In Center t-shirt to school. "I explained what everything was," he said. "All hell broke loose. By Monday, everybody in school knew that the new kid was a homosexual."

The week was filled with taunts and threats. As he walked down the hall he heard "Kick his ass!" and felt shoves from behind. A girl he had never seen before told him he was going to die. When he asked who was going to kill him, she replied, "My boyfriend is one of them." On his daily two-mile walk home from school, cars slowed when they saw him. "Faggot! Queer!" the passengers yelled.

Myk told his guidance counselor what was happening. "You chose that lifestyle," she said. "This is what happens. You just have to take it." Myk said he didn't choose it; he was born that way. She shook her head and said, "I'm sorry. There's nothing I can do."

His choir teacher assigned him to the worst seat. "I was a state qualifier; I ranked higher than any other kid in the school, and she put me second to last, with the freshmen." Not only did no one speak to him; no one even shared music.

One person did care: the school psychologist, his crisis counselor. She arranged for a therapist, but even that did not make Round Rock more bearable. The counselor told Myk her job would be on the line if people knew what she doing, so her intervention with teachers and administrators was minimal.

Myk sent a note to the principal, describing what was happening. "I saw him after that, and he was very threatening," the boy said. "He said something like, 'You and I have to talk!' But I didn't go in because I know I would've hit him, and you can really get in trouble for hitting a principal."

Around that time, a controversy erupted in Williamson County. Commissioners voted to deny a tax abatement to Apple Computers because its domestic partnership policies did not discriminate against homosexuals; the nation's media focused negative attention on the county, and many students responded defensively. They lashed out at the only visible target: gay student Myk Simpson. He checked himself into a hospital for depression – and when he got out, he found his teachers were piling on the work he'd missed. "I had like eighteen pages of algebra, twenty pages of geometry, three chapters of government, three chapters of economics," he recalled. "I went to after-school tutoring. I tried, I really tried. But I just couldn't do it."

Myk's first report card at Round Rock was filled with 50s and Incompletes. He had been an honor roll student. But they gave him those grades because they said he just could not keep up.

On December 6, 1993, Myk left Round Rock – and slit his wrists. It was a halfhearted attempt at suicide – "I told myself I couldn't die just because of this" – and he moved back to Austin. He dropped out of school, but filled his time by attending as many conferences, debates, and speak-outs about gay and lesbian teenagers as he could. Once out of school, his life became filled with a purpose: talking about homosexual youth. In March, he began taking evening courses to get his high school diploma.

Why was homophobia so rampant at the schools Myk attended? "This is major Bible Belt," he began. "The religious right is pathetic, but strong here. They don't educate people on 'love thy neighbor' – they choose to leave a certain segment of society out. And parents – they teach their kids prejudice."

Schools, he added, "won't teach the facts about homosexuality. They're afraid if they even mention facts about it, the religious right will accuse them of trying to turn kids gay. It's in some health books, and they're supposed to have to teach it, but a lot of teachers think if they even mention it, kids will think they're homosexual. There's so much ignorance – kids and teachers think homosexuality is just about AIDS and screwing in the street. They don't know it's really about love."

Schools, he said, "should teach the facts about *everything*. If they mention heterosexual sex, they should mention homosexual sex. And anytime someone threatens somebody else, they should be punished. There shouldn't be two standards of punishment, based on whether someone's gay or not."

He would like to see anyone employed in education – as a principal, counselor, teacher, or superintendent – asked if they can be open to *all* kinds of people. "It doesn't matter if someone has a problem with drugs, or they've been abused, or they're gay," Myk said. "If you can't face those problems, you shouldn't be hired. Because that's what education's all about – teaching people about life. Right now principals and superintendents just care that the grades are high and their reputation is number one. They don't care about the people in the school. But a school is the people in it, and there are gay people in schools, too."

Myk noted that his story is not unique. "Most gay, lesbian, and bisexual people I know have gone through things just like this," he said. "It's a shame. It's pathetic. I'm fortunate I haven't lost my life. I've had to walk alone for so long. Since 1991 I've had absolutely no support from my family. I've lived completely on my own; I haven't had any support from my schools. Nobody can take any credit for what I've done or who I am, because there's been absolutely no one there for me. Not my family, not my schools – nobody. Whatever I've accomplished, I've done on my own."

And that too – as much as the many "success" stories that fill this book – speaks volumes about lesbian and gay issues in America's schools in the 1990s. The millennium has not yet arrived.

Student Teachers Learn More Than Taking Roll

Psychologist Stan W. Ziegler said that for many gay and lesbian teachers, working in a school environment is like "returning to the scene of the crime where so much pain and suffering occurred." Why would any gay man or woman voluntarily go back to a place he or she knows teems with homophobic comments and rumors, or choose a career that – in addition to its everyday stresses – is filled with anxiety for homosexuals?

For some teachers, those obstacles are also attractions. These men and women are drawn to a profession they feel enables them to make a difference in people's lives; they're motivated by the opportunity to help youngsters in a way they themselves may (or may not) have been helped when they were growing up. Younger educators especially, who grew up in an era of relative enlightenment and openness about gay issues, may not feel as cowed by stereotypes. And, like any good teacher, they enjoy challenges.

Those challenges often begin early – perhaps the first day of education school. Suddenly, the new students are faced with questions that have no easy answers: What happens when lesbian and gay issues are not addressed in teacher training classes? How out should I be to my professors? To my classmates? To my classes when I'm student teaching? To my interviewers when I'm looking for a job? "Uh-oh," many teachers-to-be start thinking. "This isn't as simple as I thought." To use an analogy familiar to every student, education school isn't a gut with a couple of true-false tests you can cram for; it's a ball-buster, and you've got to study hard for some tough, subjective problems you never anticipated.

Theresa Urist faced many of those issues while studying at Harvard University's Graduate School of Education in a year-long teacher certification program. She grew up on eastern Long Island, and while her high school experience was not particularly painful, her best friend's was. He was gay, and the target of a torrent of abuse.

At Stanford University, she came to terms with her lesbianism. She majored in American studies, and because she loved history – particularly American women's history – she decided to teach it. "I think a lot of issues are ignored, or not addressed, in schools," she said. "Lots of teachers feel uncomfortable bringing things up – not just gay and lesbian issues, but also race and current events, like condoms in schools. It seems a lot of older teachers don't give time in their classes to the daily realities of students' lives."

Her search for a progressive program led her to Harvard. She liked Boston's similarity to the San Francisco Bay Area. But she also encountered a few surprises when her classes in the School of Education began. Though her 120 fellow students in the Teaching and Curriculum program were diverse – they came from all fifty states, and at an average age of around thirty, many had already worked in a variety of jobs – she was apparently the only lesbian.

She was surprised to find her professors addressing gay issues in the opening summer component of the program, and just as astonished to learn that many classmates had never dealt with such issues before. "We were back at square one," she said. "Here I was, twenty-two, one of the youngest people there, but it seemed my background at Stanford had tuned me in to a lot more sensitivity stuff than these older people had had. It was pretty alarming. We'd be in our discussion sections, and people would be amazed that gay and lesbian stuff was in the curriculum. They were saying they didn't think it was their job as teachers to deal with things like that!"

It was in a section meeting that Theresa first came out at Harvard. "People were real surprised," she said. "I found some allies, but a lot of people were clueless. Not intolerant, but naive."

She felt more comfortable after that, and gave high ratings to the program overall. "I think it's pretty progressive," she said. "Homosexuality is definitely dealt with, and I'm pretty happy with the way it was addressed. There were speakers and seminars, and Arthur Lipkin's class on gay and lesbian educational issues in the classroom was very informative. But I still don't get the feeling that a lot of teachers were comfortable addressing it. It's one thing to have knowledge of homosexuality; it's another to stand up in front of adolescents and actually talk about it. The high school environment is still rampantly homophobic, and I'm not sure how well teachers are prepared to deal with that."

She ran smack into homophobia as soon as she started student teaching. Originally assigned to suburban Newton South High School, which boasts an active gay-straight alliance, Theresa – whose aim was to teach in a San Francisco school – requested a more urban environment. She got it: Boston English High, whose student body is 40 percent Latino (mostly from the Dominican Republic), 40 percent black (primarily Jamaican, Haitian, and Somali), and 20 percent from all over the rest of the world.

She never came out at English, a decision she termed "very, very difficult. As a student teacher there for twelve weeks, I felt I should establish a certain level of trust and respect in the classroom before I came out. Then I felt, because of the attitudes I heard and observed, that being out would discredit me. I didn't know if I could reach the level, in just twelve weeks, to be able to talk so personally to kids, and break prejudice down."

Theresa called Boston English "a tough place to work. The kids were really, really rude, and it was hard to get them to focus on an activity. I had to deal with that first, before I could tackle other things like homosexuality."

But that didn't stop students from raising the subject. "I have very short hair, I seldom wear skirts, and I carry myself a certain way," Theresa noted. "I had kids bring up gay issues in a mocking way, and some have guessed I'm gay. One of them asked, 'Are you gonna march with the gays in the St. Patrick's Day parade?' The best thing I could say was, 'That's really inappropriate here in class.' In the ideal world, I guess I'd say, 'Why are you asking me that? What are the real issues here? Let's talk about that.'"

She went home that afternoon feeling defeated. "I was upset at not being able to have a forum to discuss things. I knew the issue would come up again. Kids aren't stupid; they're really perceptive. They pick up on a lot of things. When I said right off the bat we'd be doing a lot of women's stuff, because women are 52 percent of the population, I got this: 'Ms. Urist, why do you hate men?' I had to make a lot of instant decisions in the classroom, and I was not always happy with the decisions I made. But that's part of teacher training, I guess."

She thought about what she would say if a student asked, point-blank, if she is a lesbian. She decided that she would try to find out why the question was asked, before saying anything.

Contributing to her hesitancy about coming out was her mentor teacher, a conservative male who did not create a comfortable atmosphere for her. The school was filled, she said, with people like him: old-guard, traditional teachers, very set in their ways. The teaching force in Boston is still filled with Irish-Catholic men and women with traditional backgrounds and attitudes, and the discussions she heard in the faculty room, about gays marching in the St. Patrick's Day parade and serving in the military, left her uncomfortable. She even sat in on a teacher who was openly homophobic in class: pulling out a pink ruler, he called it "faggoty." Though she did come out to one woman – a biology teacher who seemed on her wavelength – her overall experience at Boston English was nightmarish. She had thought an urban environment would be more open.

But that has not quenched her desire to teach in an urban school. She planned to spend a year in Latin America, learning Spanish so she could communicate better with students, and then search for a job. Would she interview as a lesbian?

"That's a real tough question," she sighed. "To me, it's real important to be out eventually in my work environment. I came home seething, and that's not good. I've realized that I can't work in a place where I can't be myself. I think I will be out eventually, but in an interview ... I don't know."

She paused, then continued. "Obviously, it's not asked on job applications. And I don't want to walk in and say, 'Hi, I'm Theresa Urist, I'm a lesbian.' But, yet, it's an essential part of my identity. I think I'll probably feel the place out first – ask questions about the philosophy of the school, get a tone of the place – and then ask about how they deal with diversity issues, including students' sexuality."

She paused again, still mulling over the many questions that gnaw at men and women poised to begin teaching careers. "Had I stayed as a student teacher at Newton South, I think I'd be very, very out," she said. "Boston English was an extremely difficult climate, because the kids come from all different social and cultural backgrounds. But I am interested in urban education, and I don't think schools should be enclaves set apart from the real world. You know, this posed a lot of difficult issues for me, and I'm still really just trying to work them through."

Torey Wilson, one of Theresa Urist's classmates at Harvard Graduate School of Education, is different from her in many ways. He was born and raised in Galveston, Texas, and attended Trinity University, a small liberal arts college in San Antonio. He is an African-American male. And he did his student teaching at Cambridge Rindge and Latin School, a progressive place profiled often in the national media as the home of the Project 10 East gay, lesbian, and bisexual program.

But Torey, like Theresa, enrolled at Harvard for certification to teach history and social studies. He too struggled with questions of being out in education school. And he also observed two sides of gay issues as they apply to teacher training.

"Where I come from I didn't see anything about gays and lesbians discussed in the classroom, even in college," he said. "Then I came here, and I took a course in anti-homophobia education. It was touched on in other classes too – in our multiculturalism class we spent two days on homosexuality. I wrote about gay issues in that class, and in my adolescent sexuality class."

However, he noted, gay topics were often not dealt with until he brought them up. "The subject wasn't exactly avoided, but I definitely had to take the initiative a lot of times," he said. "Then when I did it raised the awareness of my straight peers, who hadn't realized these things were school issues."

Torey added that even when lesbian and gay issues were addressed, they were not always integrated into the curriculum; it sometimes felt as if they were discussed separately, or tacked on as an afterthought. When the class talked about multiculturalism, he felt he had to be the one to tell the professors to include it. Invariably, reading lists contained only one article, out of many, many books. That held true, he noted, even in the adolescent sexuality class – "which was bizarre, because the professor is a lesbian!"

Reactions, too, were mixed. "The first time I came out as a gay person at Harvard, and talked about my experiences as a gay adolescent, was very hard," he said. "I didn't know anyone yet. It was in the summer component, and it was a big risk. Some people were very interested and wanted to know more, but others were clearly uncomfortable dealing with any sexual issues whatsoever." He found it distressing that these classmates would be dealing with adolescents once they received their teaching certificates.

Though he was not the only gay person in his multiculturalism class, he was the only one whose project dealt with homosexuality and the curriculum. He created a history curriculum that included lesbian and gay issues, though it did not focus on them; they were merely included as part of the cultural revolution of the sixties. His work received positive feedback, he said; people reported it was good, but not overly threatening.

In an ideal curriculum, Torey said, lesbian and gay issues would be handled as well as African-American themes have been in recent years. "Great strides have been made to make people aware of black history," he said. "That's not neglected anymore. I feel more people need to understand gay and lesbian issues, and see them on a par with racial and other minority issues." The invisibility of young gays and lesbians contributes to this marginalization. "When I stand in front of a class-room, I can see the African-American kids. But I don't know the one or two students who are gay or lesbian or bisexual. A lot of teachers don't even know they're there. But we can't overlook them."

He was openly gay at Cambridge Rindge and Latin – in fact, he attended meetings of Project 10 East, calling them "an eye-opening experience" – but as he began applying for teaching positions, he said, that might change. "It's not a subject I bring up in interviews, because I don't want doors shut in my face. My main thrust is to get into the classroom. I don't want being gay to stop me from getting in; it's really only a small part of who and what I am. It wasn't until I came to Massachusetts that I realized I could be a gay person in a classroom. In Texas I couldn't be gay without fear of losing my job." He added that once he finds a position, "I'll prove to be a very competent teacher. Then I'll probably feel more comfortable coming out."

A third member of Harvard's graduate school does not plan to go directly into a classroom – she's in the individualized master's program, working on a degree combining education and law – but she has passionate feelings on teacher training. A native of a conservative midwestern town who delivers her opinions in fast, staccato bursts, she prefaced her discussion of Harvard with some background about her childhood. (She asked that her name not be used, to protect her parents' privacy.)

"When I was in high school there were two female teachers that everyone knew lived together, but no one ever discussed them as lesbians, so that information was never available to me. A couple of my friends in the theater crowd were known as lesbians, but that was never discussed either. I never had a clue about myself – but I also never dated. At the same time I was anorexic and in the academic fast track, so not dating was okay – because I was studying, because I was the newspaper editor, and because I was really feminine."

Then she entered all-female Wellesley College – "and guess who came out in big way?!" she asked with rhetorical glee. "At first people wondered why I was going there, was I gay, and I said, 'No! Of course not!' But then all of a sudden I saw this vibrant gay community, and my best friend there was a lesbian. My sophomore year I developed a really big crush on her. I came out then, and I came out to my parents my junior year. Then there was a huge homophobic incident at Wellesley, and I came *really* out! It was a painful time to be a lesbian there, and I ended up running the gay group." At that point she found Harvard's individualized program. After completion, she hopes to land a job involving civil rights, education, and law.

There are, she said, "a *lot* of gay teachers and educators" at Harvard's education school. However, she also found just as much homophobia about being gay, and working with kids. "Some of it is real – if I went to Louisiana to teach, I *could* get fired – but some of it is also self-imposed. Teachers worry a lot about themselves, without realizing how important it is for kids to have out role models."

In her multiculturalism class of about fifty students, at least six attended meetings of the gay, lesbian, and bisexual student group she co-chairs with Theresa Urist. Yet, she said, the professor never brought homosexuality up. "She said there were too many other issues to talk about. But you can't separate out, pick and choose, minority and multicultural issues; they're all interconnected. But she's the teacher; what can you do?"

The omission grew more and more aggravating. One day during a section meeting, she exploded. "I said we were doing exactly what we said we were trying to avoid: marginalize students. It just so happened that same day, two other students in two other sections also randomly reached the same blowup points!" That led to several people choosing homophobia as the theme of their final project. "I spent eighty dollars of my own money to Xerox the best readings I'd found about issues gay kids face," she said. "I told everyone in the class they needed to read these things, because we hadn't dealt with them in class. I'd been the Gay Voice at Wellesley, and I didn't want to be the Gay Voice of Harvard, but it was just something I felt I needed to do."

Equally ignored at Harvard were discussions of what it means to be a gay teacher. "That's as major an issue as dealing with gay youth," she noted. "I've heard horror stories about kids who were dying – they *knew* there were gay and lesbian teachers in their school, but the teachers said nothing, absolutely nothing, to them. As an educator, your primary responsibility is to your students, not to yourself, and I don't think we talked about that at all. I've seen what the closet can do to teachers. We've all been there; we've all seen what alcohol and lying does. If you reach that point, you can't be of any use to *anyone,* and what kind of teacher are you then?"

She has discussed with several classmates the agonizing personal decision of how honest to be about sexual orientation when interviewing for that important first position. "One of my good friends is not out at all," she said. "She doesn't feel safe. We've got so much to wrestle with in our twenties, and then this on top of that. Is it better to be in, to get there and *then* come out and support kids, or is it better to be truthful, and maybe not get the job? As a new person, the low person on the totem pole, is it worth it to be out?"

She includes her activist work on her resume, but not without qualms. "It's an issue for me," she admitted. "The fact that I work with gay, lesbian, bisexual, and transgendered students (as an assistant to Al Ferreira's Project 10 East at Cambridge Rindge and Latin High) is great for my commitment to diversity, but does it flag that I'm a lesbian? I don't know; I don't really know. Everyone handles it differently. You hate being in the closet, but..."

For the first time in the entire interview, she fell silent. A few seconds later, she became animated again, and completed her thought. "But you know, there are *so many* gay and lesbian people involved in education. I just walk around the ed. school, and my gaydar goes off all over the place. We really are everywhere – especially in education. So I guess eventually people *are* making the right decisions."

Helping them make those decisions is Arthur Lipkin, Ed.D. In addition to serving as head of the Project for the Study of Gay and Lesbian Issues in Schools (formerly the Gay and Lesbian High School Curriculum and Staff Development Project) at Harvard's Graduate School of Education, where he develops curriculum materials for schoolteachers around the country, Dr. Lipkin teaches a course on gay and lesbian issues. Its title – "T210A: Staff and Curriculum Development for Anti-Homophobia Education" – is dry, yet its content is anything but banal. Introduced in 1993 and believed to be the only graduate-level education course dealing specifically with gay and lesbian concerns, it represents one small step on the path toward teaching teachers about homosexuality. The aim of the eight-week, four-credit elective course is twofold: to raise new teachers' awareness about gay and lesbian issues, and to give them the tools to incorporate what they've learned into their lesson plans.

The syllabus ranges far and wide, in order to "explore the current scene politically and nationally as it relates to gay education," Dr.

Lipkin said. The reading list spans books, anthologies, and periodicals, including both *Commentary* and *The Advocate*. Selections cover categories from anthropology to sociology, from history to fiction; authors range from Anna Quindlen to Audre Lorde, from Martin Duberman to Midge Decter. Students delve into theories of causation; adolescent identity formation; the problems lesbian and gay youth face with parents, families, race, and ethnicity; gay teachers; curricula; and the movement for school change.

"It is so important to train teachers about these issues *before* they begin teaching," Dr. Lipkin said. "It is a huge responsibility to touch on such an important area before the students get away. But this has never been done before. We've always been playing catch-up, giving workshops to teachers who have been trained years before. Most college graduates are not exposed to this type of material. Yet if we expect teachers to deal with gay and lesbian issues, and gay and lesbian students, in the classroom, then we have to give them the expertise to do it. And expertise not just in methodology, but in the meat of the subject."

The initial year, Dr. Lipkin said, Staff and Curriculum Development for Anti-Homophobia Education was predominantly, though not exclusively, filled with students who identified themselves as gay or lesbian. That did not surprise him. "Any course given for the first time is a crapshoot," he noted. "It will always be taken by a 'special-interest constituency.'" Interestingly, teaching lesbian and gay material to lesbian and gay graduate students was not preaching to the choir. "Most of them were not – are not – very well informed on this subject," he said. "Some of them were not out in college, and didn't want to take gay and lesbian courses. Others never had the opportunity. And even those who might have taken a gay lit. course in college might not have read the theoretical stuff. A lot of it was new to many of them. They really appreciated it, according to their reviews." And, he added, the straight men and women in the course also gave it thumbs-up reviews.

In the years ahead, the seats in Dr. Lipkin's lecture hall will no doubt be filled with more and more heterosexuals. There will be less and less stigma attached to taking a course with the word "homosexuality" in the title. And Dr. Lipkin's students, together with their lesbian and gay classmates, will learn information they can then pass on to the thousands of youngsters, straight and gay, who will soon sit before them in classrooms of their own.

PART 2

Places

INTRODUCTION

Here, Queer, and Everywhere

You can find gay, lesbian, and bisexual staff and students at every school level from kindergarten through high school, and at every type of school, from public to private to parochial. And you can find them not only in all categories of school, but actually in every school. It is doubtful there is any school in the entire nation that does not have at least one homosexual member.

That's easy to say. Finding them is a bit harder.

It's one thing to be open about one's sexuality in San Francisco, Los Angeles, New York, or Boston; it's another to be openly gay in medium-sized cities, or the suburbs. And in the small towns and rural communities that still make up a significant part of America, it's a different story entirely.

It's one thing to be open about one's sexuality in high school, another in junior high. It's one thing to say, "I'm gay and I'm proud" in a large high school where no one really knows anyone anyway; it's another to proclaim it on a private school campus where a small, inbred group of classmates studies, eats, sleeps, and showers together twenty-four hours a day. It's even one thing for a teacher to say, "I'm straight, but I support the rights of my gay colleagues and students to exist in a safe school environment" on the East or West Coast, another to do so in America's heartland or in the wilds of Montana.

But as hard as it is to be out, or even gay-positive, in some parts of the country, people are. And every school day, their numbers grow.

Teachers are banding together in ways unimaginable even a few years ago. In northern California, a group called BANGLE – Bay Area Network of Gay and Lesbian Educators – grew so large it split into five chapters; across the country in Virginia, a teacher had the same idea for an educators' support group but found the going a good deal more difficult. Word of the first meeting was passed surreptitiously; participants worried about their safety, so two people patrolled the neighborhood to guard against trouble.

In Washington State, a group of lesbian and gay coaches gathers together informally to share stories. They are foes on the field, but friends off it; bound together by a force stronger than competition, they gain strength by talking about common concerns – their sexuality, their openness at work, their student athletes undergoing their own private torments over same-sex attractions.

In Omaha and Lincoln, Nebraska, guidance counselors and health teachers are raising gay and lesbian issues in their schools; their populations are not as diverse or sophisticated as Chicago, San Francisco, or New York, but they are cities nonetheless, and educators in Omaha and Lincoln know that homosexuality is a fact of life in their streets and their schools. Meanwhile, in smaller Nebraska towns like Grand Island, a few teachers are saying, "We're not Omaha or Lincoln, but we know homosexuality is an issue for at least some of our students, and we've got to address it as intelligently as we can." And at the same time there are tiny dots on the map like Holdrege, crossroads that make Grand Island look as big as Omaha, and even there men and women are speaking openly about homosexuality, so that teenagers won't have to struggle as desperately as they themselves once did.

Parts of Montana make Nebraska seem positively urban, of course, but even in Big Sky Country there are teachers willing to face up to the fact that not every cowboy, rancher, miner, and trucker is straight, nor may their children be. It's not easy finding people ready to speak openly about it – one gay teacher in Billings had to reach clear across the state to find a heterosexual ally willing to travel to Washington, D.C., for a workshop on homosexuality – but such people do exist. And that bodes well for every gay boy and girl growing up in Montana today.

One other "place" on the map of American education is more a state of mind than an actual state: private schools. Plenty of good things are happening there too, ranging from lesbian and gay support groups (and a New England conference bringing them together) to gay and lesbian alumni associations. The 1990s have seen openly gay chaplains and openly lesbian dorm parents. Heads (nee headmasters) have stood up to recalcitrant boards of directors in order to hire and promote gay faculty members; boards have prodded slow-moving heads to increase the number of gay students.

Not all of these advances and attitude readjustments have come easily, nor are all of them uniformly accepted. Examples of two steps forward and one step back abound: the case of the gay dorm parent is countered by the tale of the lesbian teacher denied on-campus housing; the inspiring story of the Nebraska phys. ed. teacher whose consciousness was raised by an AIDS speaker is negated by an incident in the same state in which a small-town superintendent and principal refused to shake the hand of a PFLAG speaker.

But the backward steps, petty and pitiful as they sound, are important, because it is through them that forward progress may be measured. The story of gay men and lesbians in America's schools is certainly the story of ordinary people doing extraordinary things. In states and schools across America, gay people are finding their voices. Sometimes it's teachers: their words may inspire students to follow, or administrators to take action. Other times it's the young taking the first bold steps: they become the teachers, leading their elders along the path to openness and honesty. In a few cases the catalyst for change arises outside the building, with lesbian and gay parents, or a church group of concerned heterosexuals.

Their words may be loud, strong, even deviant – or quiet, unsure, perhaps deferential. Their actions may be bold and broad, or tentative and tightly focused. Yet wherever they come from, and wherever they lead, one fact is inescapable: gay and lesbian issues are no longer addressed only in the most diverse city high schools or the most progressive private schools; they've burst out of the closet and spilled onto the table in virtually every school in the country. There's no turning back.

Courageous men and women, heroic boys and girls have helped place lesbian and gay issues in the forefront of school consciousness. Some have done so at great personal risk; others simply felt the time was right, or it was the right thing to do. Some of their stories are inspiring, some are heartbreaking. Each is unique. Taken together, they paint a vivid picture of an intriguing American landscape. An invisible minority has suddenly turned up in all fifty states – and if they haven't already, they'll be coming out soon, at a school near you.

BANGLE Blankets the Bay

Leave it to San Francisco to serve gay teachers like nowhere else.

The city that gave the world the Castro, homosexual supervisors, and a half-million-strong Pride Day parade led each year by dozens of wheelie-poppin' Dykes on Bikes is the same city that spawned a support and advocacy network for teachers and administrators so vast it split into five separate branches. BANGLE (Bay Area Network of Gay and Lesbian Educators) is the granddaddy of all teacher groups; similar acronyms and organizations abound, from SANGLE (Sacramento Area Network...) to WAGLE (Washington Area...), but in sheer numbers, programs, and impact, BANGLE rules. Scarcely a teacher, administrator, student, or parent in the sprawling San Francisco Bay Area has not heard of BANGLE; no school district has remained untouched by one of its five chapters. What the NAMES Project is to AIDS, BANGLE is to education.

The BANGLE story begins with Rob Birle, an Atlantan who moved west to attend the San Francisco Arts Institute. He graduated with a master's degree in performance video in 1983, and planned to teach art at the college level. But the job market was limited, so after receiving his teaching credential from San Francisco State University he took aim at secondary schools.

Being gay was never an issue with Rob Birle; out even as a student teacher, one of his first professional tasks was to plug into the Gay and Lesbian School Workers Coalition. That organization had a long, respected history in San Francisco, but by the mid-1980s had become relatively inactive; with so much focus on AIDS and political activism in the city, and plenty of social opportunities for gays and lesbians of all stripes, there seemed little need for a support group aimed specifically at teachers.

But Rob hoped to form bonds with others in his profession, and with a small group of like-minded men and women he founded what was first called the Bay Area Sexual Minority Educators. "Sexual Minority Educators" soon became "Network of Gay and Lesbian Educators," with both "gay and lesbian" and "educators" loosely defined. "We didn't limit it just to gays and lesbians – we also wanted bisexuals, transgendered people, heterosexuals who were interested in what we were doing," Mr. Birle recalled. "And educators was pretty broad too: administrators, community activists doing in-service training, youth workers – really anyone involved in any form of education. We consciously didn't limit it to just certified staff."

The organization mushroomed from a small number of student teachers into a larger group that included full-time teachers; meetings quickly outgrew Mr. Birle's house. The focus soon shifted from social support to advocacy for students as well as educators, and from the city of San Francisco out toward the rest of the Bay Area. Those two developments were linked, Mr. Birle said.

"I felt gay teachers in San Francisco already had lots of avenues for support and activities, but with the growth in the suburbs there were a lot of new teachers out there who did not. And I realized that in terms of helping kids, most gay and lesbian youth are not in the city but in suburban areas, because that's where kids generally live.

"You can effect change in suburban districts by giving information to kids and families, and get them to talk about issues where they live. Suburbs are real communities, with families that talk – but there's been too much silence about the issue of homosexuality. That leads to isolation, and fear among kids. Some of them run off to San Francisco and find support in youth groups, or get into the bar and hustler scene, which isn't healthy. It's better to deal with the issue of homosexuality in their home schools and communities. That's how BANGLE started moving out into the suburbs." Within a few years there were chapters in East Bay (Oakland), South Bay (San Jose), and Contra Costa and Sonoma Counties.

The mailing list exploded from a few dozen names to several thousand, including supportive straights, local professors of education, and social service contacts. Members received a monthly newsletter filled with information on educational programs, controversial issues, and teachers' potluck dinners throughout the Bay Area. And as BAN-

GLE grew, it groped along on its own. Each chapter networked with the others, but there were few kindred organizations in the country to turn to for advice.

"There was nothing really to model ourselves on," Mr. Birle said. "We had a little contact with a teachers' group in Los Angeles, and we knew a group existed in New York, but I can't recall any others. So at meetings we identified local concerns, then structured each group to address those needs. I think what evolved was right for the Bay Area."

Early debates swirled around the primary focus of BANGLE: should it be an advocacy group or a social organization? Rob advocated advocacy, but realized the importance of providing a social setting for educators. "About ninety percent of the people who attended our picnics, parties, and monthly get-togethers were closeted," he said. "Social events are fun and informal, but they were good places to network too. Administrators came, and that was a big help for the student teachers. We would get fifty or sixty people at some events. That's amazing."

But advocacy soon became BANGLE's main thrust. Group members met with superintendents of schools, board members, union officials, and the state superintendent of instruction; they embarked on a video project and, in conjunction with PFLAG (Parents, Families and Friends of Lesbians and Gays), coordinated training workshops called "Gay and Lesbian Teens: Facing the Facts, Meeting Their Needs" for administrators, teachers, and youth service workers.

Ironically, one major obstacle BANGLE faced was fear on the part of teachers themselves. Many – including tenured staff members – were reticent to get involved in a gay organization; they were frightened they'd be singled out by administrators. Thus, Mr. Birle said, the hundreds of names on BANGLE's mailing list represent only a fraction of the lesbian and gay teachers in the Bay Area.

Administrators represented another stumbling block. "That's part of the political landscape, even though it's shifted somewhat recently in urban areas," Mr. Birle said. "Homosexuality covers some hugely controversial issues, and it scared administrators to death. Gay and lesbian harassment was epidemic, even in San Francisco – I heard teachers use the word 'faggot' without even knowing it was a slur. For an administrator to take the initiative to address this homophobic environment was risky. They had to be pushed and prodded. But BANGLE, along with the NEA (National Education Association) and AFT (American Federation of Teachers), have taken stands and raised this issue, and it's finally beginning to impact even smaller districts."

The activity Rob points to as having perhaps the greatest impact is not BANGLE's work alone, although it had its roots in the organization. It's called Project 21 (for the twenty-first century); begun in 1991 as a joint effort between BANGLE, the San Francisco chapter of GLAAD (Gay and Lesbian Alliance Against Defamation), and the San Francisco Gay and Lesbian Youth Advocacy Council, it is an inclusion effort aimed at making textbooks and curriculum information available to all schools. After a decade in San Francisco, Rob Birle followed his partner to Kansas City, and finds the Midwest a convenient place to work full-time on Project 21. ("We also bought a house here for a realistic price," he laughed.)

But his legacy – in the form of five BANGLE chapters – lives on throughout northern California.

————

By all accounts, the most active BANGLE chapter is in Contra Costa, the booming county north and east of Oakland that includes such white-collar suburbs as Walnut Creek and Concord, along with older, more industrial towns like San Pablo. A pair of retirees – Joe Torp, who taught high school art, and Conrad Smith, a speech pathologist who worked with students from preschool through high school – co-chair the Contra Costa chapter. Though out only to friends while they taught, today everyone knows they're gay. ("It's easy," Mr. Torp said. "Now we don't feel that our jobs may be in jeopardy.") He and Mr. Smith form a good team, as well they should: they've lived together for forty-three years.

The Contra Costa chapter counts thirty paid members, though many nonmembers show up for group activities. Mr. Torp noted that perhaps three times as many more gay teachers are out to them but not to their districts. Not long ago a chapter member, a probationary teacher, was not rehired because of his homosexuality. His principal told him that he didn't want gays on his faculty. But there were no witnesses, and the teacher was not willing to fight. For reasons like that, the thirty active members of Contra Costa BANGLE have dedicated themselves to a stunning variety of activities.

The most wide-ranging is a book project. By spring of 1993 the chapter had donated seventeen books, plus the BANGLE-sponsored *Gay Youth* video, to all twenty-three county high schools and nine continuation or alternative highs. It was the culmination of an effort undertaken in 1990, when chapter members began reviewing sixty books dealing with such topics as self-esteem, coming out to parents, and the historical contributions of gays and lesbians. Book selections include *Gay Men and Women Who Enriched the World, Beyond Acceptance, Coming Out to Parents, How to Find Information about AIDS, Trying Hard to Hear You, Fried Green Tomatoes at the Whistle Stop Cafe, Profiles of Gay and Lesbian Courage, Positively Gay,* and *Lucky in Love.* In addition, the group contributed two sets of *Tales of the Closet,* informative stories published in comic book format by the Hetrick-Martin Institute of New York.

"It was touch and go, but all the books are now on the shelves," Mr. Torp reported. "Some schools did not accept *Tales of the Closet,* because they didn't like the comic book format and the street language, but the books are all there. When we started by donating two books to schools in 1989, some of the districts 'lost' them before they could be placed in the libraries. BANGLE yelled, 'Censorship!' in our local papers, and suddenly the books were found. The Traditional Values Coalition is strong here, and in our selection of books we had to make sure there were no overt sexual passages or obscenities. What's okay in San Francisco is not okay in Contra Costa County."

The project appears to be a success. After the initial donation to high schools was publicized, the principal of a 300-student continuation school called and asked where her shipment was. "That made us think," Mr. Torp said. "We realized a lot of gay kids ended up in her building after dropping out of traditional high schools, so we added alternative schools to our list."

Contra Costa BANGLE followed up each shipment with a survey sent to librarians. It included a request for information on checkout rate; observed frequency of material usage in addition to checkouts; when and how materials were made available to students and staff (for example, special showcases); student, staff, and parent comments; and suggestions for further projects. Survey returns indicated that the books were displayed, not hidden; were found by students, were used – and were used often.

The book project has an impact far beyond youngsters who may be questioning their sexuality, Mr. Torp noted. "Of course we're educating gay students and all staff this way, but we're also trying to reach nongay students. They may or may not pick up the books and look at them, but just having them on the shelves makes the issue less invisible. It makes them stop and think, 'Hey, maybe there are gay kids here.' It's a long, slow process, but it's an important one."

The Contra Costa chapter also helped sponsor the *Gay Youth* video mentioned above. Forty minutes long – designed to fit into a normal class period – it addresses in frank, sometimes terrifying fashion the homophobic attitudes and actions that are often encouraged in public schools. Videomaker Pam Walton contrasts the suicide of Bobby Griffith – a gay 21-year-old who threw himself from a freeway overpass into the path of an oncoming truck, after the taunts and abuse of family members and classmates had unraveled his self-esteem – with the courageous life of seventeen-year-old Gina Gutierrez, an out lesbian who lives in nearby Santa Clara.

In addition to those stories, the video presents lesbian and gay youngsters talking about family rejection, homelessness, drinking as a release from sexual orientation problems, attempted suicide, supportive parents, and the value of community youth groups. But it is Bobby Griffith's segment that is most compelling to Contra Costa viewers: he was a dropout from Walnut Creek's Las Lomas High School.

In an ironic demonstration of the ingrained attitudes BANGLE battles against, one of the most hesitant librarians worked at Las Lomas High. "He questioned and questioned why we were doing this project," Mr. Torp said. "Eventually, of course, he came around. And after working with us, he ended up being photographed in the local paper putting the books and video on his shelves!"

The success of *Gay Youth* spurred Contra Costa BANGLE to sponsor a second video. *Be True to Yourself,* filmed in a question-and-answer format, is currently in production.

Bobby Griffith's legacy lives on in another way too, thanks to BANGLE: in conjunction with the Diablo Valley chapter of PFLAG, the organization awards an annual $500 scholarship in his name to a graduating senior from a Contra Costa County high school; other BANGLE chapters have similar programs. Honorees need not be gay; in fact, the first recipient was not a lesbian, but demonstrated a strong desire to work for equal rights for all youths. The next two scholarship winners were both homosexual: an out boy who went on to New York University, and a lesbian who attended college in Washington State.

Applicants are solicited through letters and brochures sent each year to the scholarship coordinator at every Contra Costa high school. Though budget cutbacks have eliminated many guidance counselors, Mr. Torp is pleased at the number of applicants: over a dozen each year.

The local BANGLE chapter also participates in workshops, and speakers serve on panel discussions. One memorable four-hour session featured Mr. Torp and Mr. Smith; Mary Griffith, Bobby's mother; another mother and her gay college-age son; a sheriff; and a minister.

The group maintains close contact with Mrs. Griffith, who accepted her son's homosexuality and became an activist only after his suicide. She runs the Diablo Valley PFLAG chapter, which joins BANGLE as co-sponsor of many activities. "We never hear directly about BANGLE's impact, but through PFLAG we know we're reaching students and families," Mr. Torp said. "One boy came out at thirteen; he's now the facilitator for groups in Walnut Creek. He told PFLAG that our books are there in the high school, and they're being read. They're either checked out, or carried into the stacks and looked at there."

All of Contra Costa BANGLE's activities cost money, of course. Luckily, the chapter has some. The county United Way earmarked $40,000 for gay issues; BANGLE applied, and has been granted funds each year. Additional sources include direct-mail solicitations for the Bobby Griffith Memorial Scholarship, and dues of $15 to $25. BANGLE applied for and received 501(c)(3) status; as a nonprofit organization, contributions it receives are tax-deductible.

———————

Just west of Contra Costa lies Alameda County. The East Bay, as it's familiarly called, centers around Oakland, a city once famous for Gertrude Stein's line, "There is no there there"; later, it became known as the home of Black Panther activists. Today, downtown Oakland is racially diverse and, despite California's hard economic times, steadily growing; million-dollar homes line its high hills. Bordering Oakland is Berkeley, with its exotic mix of University of California students, radical politicians, and hippie refugees from the sixties. South of Oakland lie the middle-class suburbs of Hayward and Fremont. In this ethnic, racial, and economic jumble, East Bay BANGLE thrives.

The group's two main focuses, said spokesman Ben Backus (a former math teacher at the Oakland Street Academy public high school, now a graduate student at Cal-Berkeley), are social and advocacy. "East Bay BANGLE is a meeting place where teachers can let down their hair once a month, and have some good food. For the ones who are interested in activism, it's a chance to talk to principals when we hear complaints, work with organizations, lend videos, do curriculum work, have a booth at the San Francisco pride parade, or sponsor essay contests and events in the community." Sometimes the social and advocacy elements blend together. The program for one Saturday afternoon get-together included a potluck lunch, along with role-playing designed around all-too-familiar situations: gossipy colleagues, closeted principals, students with a crush on the teacher.

East Bay BANGLE draws fifteen to twenty teachers to each meeting. The paid membership numbers about fifty, though the mailing list has more than twice that many names. "Teachers don't have a lot of time, even on weekends," Mr. Backus noted. "But BANGLE is important to them. They need the chance to affirm that the gay or lesbian side of themselves is not being neglected." However, many gay East Bay teachers will have nothing to do with BANGLE. Even though the Bay Area is progressive and tolerant, teachers worry about coming out. There are plenty of places where the administration is still seen as unfriendly.

For that reason, one important area of activism is personal: tackling problems head-on. "At Skyline High School a social studies teacher took a half hour out of the lesson to rant and rave about homosexuals," Mr. Backus said. "One boy, who is not gay, felt uncomfortable. His mother heard about BANGLE through a lesbian friend, and called me. I talked to the principal, who was very supportive. He brought the teacher right in, and talked to him. I'm not sure anything would have happened if someone hadn't heard of the BANGLE name."

East Bay BANGLE has sponsored a talk by Karen Harbeck, author of *Coming Out of the Classroom Closet;* working informally with the Pacific Center speakers' bureau and East Bay GLAAD, they maintain a visible presence in the county, and in 1994 the group received a $2,000 grant from the Bay Area Career Women's "A Fund of Our Own." The money was used for partial scholarships to help send fifteen lesbian teachers to Equity Institute's Project Empowerment workshop.

The local chapter also sponsors an annual writing contest, with prize money coming from sale proceeds of the *Gay Youth* video and $15 annual dues. One year's theme was "A Gay Person I Admire." East Bay teachers – perhaps with BANGLE's influence – must be doing something right; much of the writing is stunning. Brent Calderwood, a senior at Livermore High School, won first prize and $125 in the essay category for his description of Leatha Jones, co-editor-in-chief of the monthly lesbian and gay youth newsletter *InsideOUT* and a health care worker at the Women's Needs Center in San Francisco.

"Her words are a callback to ancient tribal goddesses and African queens," Brent wrote. "Her work is reminiscent of Audre Lorde, Maya Angelou, Alice Walker, and countless other women who would no doubt welcome their phenomenal protégé." After describing his heroine's work and impressive "herstory," Brent concludes: "Although I have known what it is like to be poor and what it is like to be harassed in high school for being openly gay, Leatha has educated me to the certain privileges I have in this society as a white male. These are privileges I would gladly give up to bring social, political, and economic equality. The one privilege I would never surrender, however, is knowing Leatha Jones."

Second prize was won by a straight girl, Livermore's Yasmin Craig, who wrote about a classmate who was gay, while third place was shared by two girls. Nilaja A. Akalu of Albany High School discussed the woman she called the original lesbian: "I admire Sappho because she was a strong and intelligent person. She introduced society to the notion that women are worthy and equal to men ... Sappho said she would leave her mark on the world. She has left her mark on the world and me." Castro Valley High's Elizabeth McCracken selected English author E.M. Forster: "He did not focus on sex and violence, instead he concentrated on the spiritual needs of man ... Fundamentalists are always saying that homosexuality is sinful and wrong, yet Forster presents a love that is neither of these."

The poetry category produced two winners, one of whom – in a reminder that BANGLE still has work to do – wished to remain anonymous. He was an athlete at Fremont's Washington High whose poem "With Liberty and Justice for All..." eloquently – but namelessly – described his friendship with his gay teammate:

> I do not love you *because* of who you are.
> I do not hate you *because* of who you are.
> You are who you are.
> I admire you because of what you do and how you do it.

South of San Francisco, in the land of Stanford University and Silicon Valley, Ron Schmidt runs South Bay BANGLE. He has taught English and social studies for thirty years, most recently at Martin Murphy Middle School in south San Jose's Morgan Hill Unified School District, and has been out for the last seven. Working with BANGLE made him aware of the importance of being out in the classroom, he said, and aided him during his coming-out process.

Spurred by the comments of the mother of a gay child, South Bay BANGLE helped organize and run ten-hour training sessions for all staff members in the second largest school district in Santa Clara County. "The fundamentalists were absolutely irate," Mr. Schmidt said. "They've made a real impact here, but we're persisting. Now we're petitioning other districts for mandatory awareness workshops." BANGLE sent representatives to a Louisiana conference on adolescent issues; their "Family Life Education" awareness seminar was so successful, they were asked to return, and given twice as much time as before.

A teacher for thirty years, Ron Schmidt *(left)* leads South Bay BANGLE. Barbara Blinick *(right)*, who once chaired San Francisco's BANGLE, believes its biggest accomplishment was establishing an administrative position offering districtwide support services for lesbian and gay youth.

The workshops Ron and his chapter colleagues run include half an hour of informational statistics; stories told by lesbian and gay youths, teachers, and PFLAG members; and discussions that can, he said, become quite heated. Yet the reactions of participants have been overwhelmingly positive. "We often hear that this was 'the most important workshop I ever took in education.' Or they say, 'I had no idea of the magnitude of the problem.' To that I say, 'It's not a "problem"; it's an "issue." Society's reaction to gayness, that's a problem.'"

Mr. Schmidt, who has been involved in several gay controversies in his district (in one, fundamentalists objected to the inclusion of a gay hotline number on the back of student identification cards), said that South Bay BANGLE has three prongs: support for gay, lesbian, and bisexual educators; social networking; and advocacy. The latter is his passion.

"With all the advocacy we do, the major thrust is to break through the silence in the classroom, the faculty lunchroom, the faculty meeting, so that we can normalize the discussion of gay and lesbian issues," Mr. Schmidt said. "These gay and lesbian kids don't have a voice. BANGLE speaks for them. When I hear of little things, like the formation of a fully bona fide gay and lesbian club in the East Side School District, or that some teacher's job is saved or some teenager decides that life is worth living, then I know that what BANGLE is doing is worthwhile."

Sonoma BANGLE, nestled in the northern hills and vineyards, is the Bay Area's quietest chapter (after several zigzags between an informal, social focus and more visible political activity, it seems to have settled into a role as a quiet support group), but the fifth chapter – mother BANGLE, headquartered in San Francisco itself – is anything but low-key.

It too has undergone a number of permutations, from social to political and back to social; from small to large and back to smaller. It now boasts one hundred paid members, with triple that number on the mailing list. And even those figures don't tell the whole story: countless other teachers and administrators have passed in and out of the organization.

Former chairperson Barbara Blinick, a social studies teacher at elite Lowell High School, declared her group's biggest accomplishment to be the establishment of the position of "districtwide support services for gay and lesbian youth," currently filled by Kevin Gogin. He works with teachers, counselors, administrators, and health care and social workers in assisting gay and bisexual students and their families. "We agitated in meetings with the superintendent for two years for this position," Ms. Blinick said. "We worked with Democratic gay and lesbian clubs in the area, and they took this on with a vengeance. We brought huge support to bear. BANGLE was well placed politically, and we were able to help out. We couldn't have done it alone, but in conjunction with lots of other gay and lesbian community forces we did do it. Being part of a coalition really helps."

That success followed another: getting each high school to name a "gay-sensitive" staff member as a contact person for students questioning their sexuality. This important service costs the district nothing, beyond sending out monthly mailings. BANGLE members even provided in-service training for it on their own time.

BANGLE also worked with the United Educators of San Francisco to write the *Legal Guide for Lesbian/Gay Educators,* a valuable resource providing information on both professional and personal issues.

Barbara Blinick cited "stick-to-itiveness" as the reason for San Francisco BANGLE's "well-respected name" in the community. "We get called in a lot as the 'voice of authority' when educational issues are concerned. And people are not afraid to come to us when they're in trouble. We've written letters when schools do illegal things, we talk teachers through their problems, and generally we are here for whoever needs us – although individual issues don't come up nearly as often as

I thought they would. We're proactive and reactive, and that's exactly what I envisioned BANGLE doing when I first got involved."

Another BANGLE success, again as part of a communitywide coalition (this one involving the Delinquency Prevention Commission and Bay Area Sexual Minority Youth Network), was an Adopt-a-Book project. Sets of ten fiction and nonfiction works were donated to all nineteen San Francisco high schools, and two youth groups. Because gaining access to United Way funds is more difficult in the city than in Contra Costa County ("They've got like two gay groups, and we've got about two thousand," Ms. Blinick noted), San Francisco BANGLE solicited community donations via bookstores and news articles.

The chapter's scholarship, started by Rob Birle with $500, received a gigantic boost when Pacific Gas and Electric's Lesbian and Gay Employees Association kicked in $2,000 a year. Applications are solicited through high school and youth groups; as with other chapters' awards, the scholarships are not limited to gay, lesbian, or bisexual youths. However, references are requested, along with essays describing how the applicant supports the gay community. Recent winners included a closeted gay boy, an openly gay girl, a gay boy who moved to San Francisco on his own from the East in order to participate in the gay community, and a straight girl with gay friends who volunteered her time to secure domestic partnership legislation. A dinner held each June adds prestige to the scholarship awards.

The San Francisco chapter does hold monthly brunches, but, Ms. Blinick admitted, they're for fun more than anything else. "The gay community here is so strong, teachers don't need special events or outings. We're lucky that way, I know."

As are teachers, administrators, students, and parents everywhere in the vast San Francisco Bay Area who touch, or are touched by, any one of the five dynamic, focused, and proud BANGLE chapters.

———>◦◦<———

Not for All Lovers

For every uplifting BANGLE tale there is another – dozens of others – freighted with anxiety, filled with fear, ultimately serving as a reminder that the strides made in places like San Francisco have not been matched in many other parts of the country.

Consider Virginia. The state that calls itself the "Mother of Presidents" and whose rivers, fields, and mountains embody American history is no bastion of liberty and justice for all if the "all" includes gay and lesbian teachers. In fact, though much of the populous northern part of the state is filled with bedroom communities for Washington, D.C., spilling over with politicians, bureaucrats, lobbyists, and lawyers from around the country, the rest of the state is far more representative of the Old Dominion. Richmond, just 105 miles from Washington, was the capital of the Confederacy.

Judd Proctor lives in the Richmond area. He is an elementary school teacher, and a superb one at that: in 1986 he was one of forty teachers named to the National Association of Science and Technology Centers' Honor Roll. His speech, dripping with the soft accent of the northern part of the South, is quiet, measured, slow. His actions are deliberate too – but that can be deceptive. A man of few words, Mr. Proctor is one who acts on his convictions. He is the driving force behind the fledgling organization of gay and lesbian Virginia teachers, and while it is light-years away from BANGLE, it has moved some of the state's educators light-years beyond the closets in which they hid themselves for so long.

Like so many gay Virginians, Judd Proctor cowered in the closet for years. Tentatively, through his involvement with the National Education Association (NEA) Gay and Lesbian Caucus, he took his first steps out. He felt energized the year the national convention was held in New Orleans; Ryan White addressed the caucus, and the room was over-

Elementary school teacher Judd Proctor opened his home to give Virginia's gay and lesbian teachers a safe place to meet. The first meeting attracted a hundred educators.

flowing. (The young AIDS sufferer later addressed the entire Representative Assembly, and received a similarly warm reception.)

Gradually Mr. Proctor ventured further out of the closet, becoming regionally active as a member of the caucus's board of directors for the mid-Atlantic region. (Gay issues are one of the few areas in which it is easier for many individuals to get involved at the national level than locally.) For years he was the only teacher from the state to join the Gay and Lesbian Caucus. "Virginia teachers have been scared even to get on the mailing list," he explained. While he knew of no firings for joining the caucus, Mr. Proctor noted that teachers had been moved around. "You know, Pat Robertson and Jerry Falwell live here. This is where we had the Sharon Bottoms case [in which a lesbian mother was denied custody of her child], and the Fairfax library case [in which county libraries removed copies of the *Washington Blade,* a gay newspaper, because of its sexually explicit ads]. It's almost like Virginians are uneducated about accepting discrimination."

That is why Mr. Proctor has not come out in his school system. However, he is sure that people know. And recently he's taken steps that have increased the chance of everyone knowing.

At the statewide Virginia Education Association (VEA) Representative Assembly in 1993, a straight Richmond teacher brought an item to the floor. It involved disseminating information to teachers regarding "sexual minority youth." The woman felt that gay, lesbian, and bisexual youngsters needed more help than they were getting, and that teachers needed more resources to provide such help. On the floor, a teacher from a rural area moved that the item not be considered, and his motion passed with a two-thirds majority.

"I felt the fact that teachers didn't even want to hear about this meant that a lot of teachers were alarmed by 'sexual minority youth,'" Mr. Proctor said. "In fact, they didn't even know what the term meant – yet they voted on it!"

Later that year, driving to the March on Washington for Lesbian, Gay, and Bisexual Rights, he expressed his concern about the vote to Carol Watchler, co-chair of the NEA's Gay and Lesbian Caucus. He also made a silent vow never to be quiet on the issue again. Returning home, he phoned the president of the VEA, who admitted he was not happy with what had happened either. He told Judd that education was not about denying people information, and asked if the elementary school teacher would volunteer for the state issues committee, which advises VEA delegates how to vote at the NEA convention. Judd agreed to serve, and traveled to San Francisco for the '93 Representative Assembly (RA). When a new business item arose advocating the distribution of copies of the "Sexual Minority Youth: An At-Risk Population" report to all locals, Judd Proctor spoke forcefully in favor. He cited statistics, gave examples, and concluded, "Knowledge is power. In this case, knowledge can help save lives, and promote tolerance and better understanding. I urge your support."

In the past, Virginia delegates to the national RA had voted against every gay and lesbian issue introduced. In fact, Mr. Proctor knew gay and lesbian delegates who voted against such issues merely to avoid suspicion. But when he spoke in San Francisco, he recalled later, "every coffee cup and cheese Danish froze. Everyone listened intently. No one moved. You could have heard a pin drop." Mr. Proctor, who admitted he was a nervous wreck, explained in plain English what the term "sexual minority youth" meant: gay, lesbian, and bisexual students. The president of the VEA called for a vote supporting the item; there was a thundering chorus of ayes, and not a single nay. "It was such a resounding yes vote, anyone voting no would've felt conspicuous," Mr. Proctor said.

The Virginia delegation later voted unanimously to support another new business item, this one addressing gay and lesbian rights in Oregon. Again Mr. Proctor spoke publicly, urging its passage; this time he told real-life stories. The Virginia teachers accepted what he said; they knew him, and were able to relate what he said to their own classroom experiences.

Though he admits that, as a group, the teachers attending the national convention are more liberal than the VEA as a whole, he still felt good about what he had accomplished – and basked in its aftermath. "I was bowled over," he said. "Many teachers and staff people approached me to thank me for speaking to the issues. Some wanted more information, and others wanted to talk about gays and lesbians who had impacted their lives. I knew speaking to the issues had made a difference, and the feeling was totally euphoric."

But Judd Proctor's new level of activism did not stop in San Francisco. Returning to Richmond, he realized that teachers who had not gone to California needed information about gay youths and teachers. So he took the next bold step: he decided to hold a gathering for homosexual educators.

This was a good deal more difficult than speaking out three thousand miles from home. He chose a Saturday date in mid-September, and set a place: his home. "I wanted somewhere people could feel safe," he said. "I've got a fence around my backyard. I knew Virginia teachers wouldn't feel safe in any public building."

He mailed out five hundred invitations. "I thought I didn't know too many people, but then I started calling," he said, explaining how he found the names. "Almost everyone said they knew someone else, and they passed the word on." The invitations included a detailed map, and an offer for overnight housing for those traveling far.

Mr. Proctor recruited speakers: Jon Klein, executive director of the Richmond Organization for Sexual Minority Youth (ROSMY); Jim Testerman of Pennsylvania, the NEA Gay and Lesbian Caucus co-chair; a man from northern Virginia who wrote the NEA curriculum on sexual minority youth; a woman from Maryland.

One hundred strong – from the D.C. suburbs, the navy cities of Chesapeake Bay, the Cumberland Mountains of the south and west – these gay, lesbian, and bisexual teachers streamed into Richmond, a city filled with Baptist churches and lined with statues of Confederate heroes. They represented public, private, and parochial schools, as well as colleges and universities; they taught kindergarten and physics, physical education and special education; there were counselors and librarians too. Some came with partners; a few brought children.

They began gathering on Mr. Proctor's spacious, two-level deck at midafternoon; by five p.m. they started digging into the potluck feast (a hat was passed to cover other costs). After dinner the speakers spoke; Mr. Proctor gave out information he'd gathered at the NEA convention, along with handouts from ROSMY and data from a New York doctor who studied how disclosure or nondisclosure of a gay or lesbian teacher's sexual orientation influences his or her perception of job satisfaction and job stress.

Then came the videos, projected on a large screen, drive-in-movie style: *Speak Thy Name,* a short film about the NEA's participation in the AIDS Quilt NAMES Project, and *Who's Afraid of Project 10?* describing the Los Angeles–based program for gay and lesbian students. The meeting was scheduled to end at ten p.m., but a number of teachers stayed late to talk — and talk and talk.

The meeting was a tremendous success. "I got so many comments about it! People loved it!" Judd enthused. "It was such a positive thing. Nothing happened that was negative. It was very empowering for people. And the best thing is that it was the right thing to do."

The meeting accomplished several things beyond greater self-confidence, heightened self-esteem, and increased awareness of numbers, power, and pride. Three different mailing lists were generated: a confidential "what's happening next" list; a confidential "special purposes" list, and a nonconfidential list to be used for networking. Future plans were discussed, new projects initiated. Word spread quickly; within days, gay teachers from West Virginia and Texas called, looking for information about using the Virginia model in their states.

The only part that did not go according to plan, in fact, was out of Mr. Proctor's control. The meeting had been well promoted in the Virginia gay press, and the straight news media learned of it too. Newspapers, the statewide wire service, television, and radio all mentioned the upcoming event. That cut down on attendance; many already-hesitant possible attendees believed the press would be there, and decided the risk was too great. In fact, whenever he received a call from a media representative, Mr. Proctor emphasized that they could not come into his yard. They quickly agreed, having assumed the gathering was set for a school or hotel. Though his home is in what he calls a gay-friendly neighborhood, Mr. Proctor took the extra precaution of asking two people to patrol the area before and during the meeting. Yet he expected no problems, and none occurred.

A *Richmond Times-Dispatch* article by Peter Bacque the day before the event was long and even-handed. It ran in the business section; the subhead below "Gay teachers to meet here tomorrow" read, "Employment rights is probable topic." The piece included quotes from Brenton Lago, a gay special-education teacher from Chesterfield County, who said, "We're having a [gay] teachers' organization in the state. I think that's going to be a shock [for Virginia]."

The story continued, "The meeting tomorrow is almost a nightmare come to life for Virginia conservative and Christian right groups, which have been deeply opposed to any intrusion of gay concerns into school life." Mike Russell, of the Virginia Beach–based Christian Coalition, asserted that while his group is "not out to deny anybody their civil rights, we will be very interested in what sort of issues and agenda is produced by the first meeting. And if it does result in any sort of effort to teach homosexuality as an accepted, mainstream lifestyle, we will oppose that."

Anne Kincaid of Richmond's Family Foundation argued that the meeting would be "part of a national agenda to try to bring legitimacy and special rights to behavior that historically has been out of the moral order that keeps society stable. Once we validate this lifestyle, it will be the source of disorder ... and the demise of western civilization."

The article ended with a quote from a male teacher who disagreed that his high school serves all students as it claims it does. While no one in his building would tolerate the word "nigger," he said, "'fag' is used a lot, and nobody even questions it. That, to me, is teaching that derogatory, demeaning words are acceptable. There's a lot of education that has to go on."

Which is exactly why Mr. Proctor organized the first-ever statewide meeting of gay, lesbian, and bisexual Virginia teachers. And even though he declined to lead the budding organization – as national chairperson of a health group for gay and lesbian ostomates, and a board member of the Richmond Organization for Sexual Minority Youth, he's got more than enough volunteer work to fill his time – it blossomed under the leadership of others. A second statewide gathering in February 1994 drew seventy-five educators. A series of five Saturday workshops, exploring such topics as teachers' rights, coming out in school, and success stories, was sandwiched in between social events: a Friday evening cocktail party and Saturday night potluck dinner, followed by cards and board games. The next meeting was set for a new site: Virginia Beach, an area of the state arguably even more conservative than Richmond. And, hot on the heels of a resolution passed by the Virginia Education Association, Henrico County held its first workshop on understanding gay and lesbian youngsters, featuring Mr. Proctor and two counselors as presenters.

Judd Proctor is understandably proud of that presentation, as he is of all that his fledgling organization has accomplished – especially considering its quaking beginnings. "I didn't really have anything to go by," he said. "I just wanted to get something going. I can't believe what's come out of this." But, with typical Southern courtesy, he refuses to take special credit for bringing his state's gay educational community together.

"It was," he said, "just the right thing to do."

The State of
Washington State

Seattle sprawls southward from the center of the city, the landscape featuring mile after mile of Pizza Huts, Jack-in-the-Boxes, and Taco Bells. But suddenly, in Auburn, the cookie-cutter homes give way to farms and ponds; the suburban clutter hasn't reached here as badly, at least not yet. Ruth Frobe and D.J. Reed share a modest yet comfortable Auburn home — and there, one February afternoon, they and several friends sat around a fire, talking about their professional and personal lives as homosexual teachers and coaches.

There was plenty of easy banter; this group goes back a long, long way. Most of them met in college; they're roughly the same age, share many of the same experiences, frequent the same bars and clubs. They laughed, traded in-jokes, and gossiped about this teacher or that student — but they also grew quiet as they shared the pain of being lesbian and gay educators in school districts that range from extremely homophobic, to only somewhat so.

The words "conservative" and "redneck" came up often when the women (only one man was present) described their schools and communities. Ruth Frobe, for example, called 385-student Orting High School, where she teaches health and student leadership and serves as athletic director, "small, conservative, white with a capital W, racist, homophobic, and sexist." A woman who used the alias "Jody" (only Ruth and her housemate agreed to be quoted by name) said that those words were perfect for her own Puyallup School District, where she teaches junior high physical education and coaches volleyball, gymnastics, and track. "'Redneck' probably wouldn't be an insult to the residents," she added.

The lone man present, "Frank," also teaches in the Puyallup district, and has coached at the high school level. "We're five times the size of Orting," he said, "but still very, very conservative. It's a small, very white farming community that combines upper class and a trailer park. It's very family oriented – we've got second and third generations of students – and they don't welcome outsiders. They treat new kids like shit. It's a 'they're my cousins, and you're not' mentality – almost like inbreeding."

Frank's father was a teacher and principal; his sister and brother taught too. He was the smartest child, and was supposed to do something better. But he admired his father, and the only things he wanted to do were teach and coach. He chose women's sports for two reasons: they represent a long-denied opportunity for females (his older sister never had a chance to participate), and he is hesitant about coaching boys, a decision he recognizes as "personal paranoia." He relates well to all youngsters ("The boys *worship* him," Jody interjected). Frank takes students on golf and other outings, but is careful not to place himself in one-to-one situations. He feels badly about that, because it denies children a valuable personal contact with a trusted adult. He knows he should not worry, but feels nervous even when giving a student a ride home.

Ruth earned a master's degree in physical education at Pacific Lutheran University. For her major research project she surveyed parents of high school soccer players regarding the personal and professional characteristics they consider important in their daughters' coaches. She never expected to teach; now, however, she feels it is where she should be. She also never expected to end up in a place like Orting. "I took this job because I needed it; I could have papered my walls with my rejection letters. But I sure wouldn't stop in this place if I was just driving through." What she especially dislikes about Orting is that she is in the closet there. It is a particularly difficult circumstance for someone who in college was so out.

"I knew that would be the hardest part of the job," she admitted. "The principal who interviewed me had cowboy boots and a rodeo belt buckle, and he made comments to find out if I was a dyke. He beat around the bush, but I heard later he told people I sure walk with a swagger. He called my references. One professor said he didn't know whether I was gay or not – of course, he did – but he said I was good, and they hired me anyway."

As closeted as she is at Orting, Ruth did tell one person: her superintendent, on Coming Out Day in 1993. He was interested, and called back to talk about the ramifications. He told her he would be supportive, but that if she came out at school and the parental backlash was disruptive to the educational process, he probably would have to remove her. He said Ruth had shown she was competent, and that small towns can be quirky — they can accept "weirdos" if they're a known quantity — but added that is not always the case. She told him she wanted to be a resource person for anyone who needed it, but that she understood the need to go slowly.

Ruth has heard rumors about her lesbianism in school, and the topic of homosexuality has arisen often among the seven girls in her leadership class. "They talk about everything in there; they put their guts on the table. They want to know why I say I won't be married. I think they know, but I haven't told them yet. I said I'd tell them on graduation day."

In Frank's case, the subject of marriage came up even before he signed his first contract. "One of the first questions they asked was whether I was married. That's not legal, but they got around it by asking about things like would my wife be covered on the insurance plan. Fortunately or unfortunately, I was married once for three months — half my family doesn't even know — but now I have that as a 'great excuse.' Every kid and teacher in school knows I've been married."

He described his colleagues as older. "I'm the second youngest teacher, and I'm in my midthirties. Half of them don't know what a computer is, and we get religious mail-order catalogues in the staff room. And you want to know why I'm not out?" His laugh held a bitter undertone.

He covers at work. "People ask me about my friendship with Jody" — their schools are close together — "because we hug and call each other 'honey.' I work with real naive people, and I get set up with a lot of eligible women. Still, I think the kids know." However, Frank remains uncomfortable whenever a rumor surfaces. The most recent one made him paranoid all night. The school gets phone calls starting at six a.m., and he worried throughout the next day. But he heard nothing after that first whiff, and soon was able to relax and carry on with his work.

Frank's fears are well-founded. He knows a man in Tacoma — "a great, great teacher" — who was branded gay by a student in retaliation for giving the boy an F. "The principal called him in and asked him if it was true. The principal said he could answer in any way he wanted, but he said yes — and got fired. I saw him the other day; he looks like he's aged fifty years. That's the image I have of coming out."

Jody, who hugs men and women in school, wears pink triangles and has a lavender office door, said that she was told by both a state legislator and a discrimination lawyer that sexual orientation is no longer an issue – but, she immediately added, she has no desire to serve as a test case.

Jody's parents live in Seattle, less than an hour away; they do not know she is gay. Frank's father "basically disowned" his sister when she came out as a lesbian; his father told someone who called her a great teacher that she embarrassed him. So Frank never actually came out to his father, who said, "I guess I'll always wonder about you," and warned cryptically, "Be careful. You're a teacher."

Ruth's housemate, D.J. Reed, joined the group late that winter day, amid a boisterous welcome. "Sorry, guys," she apologized. "I had a problem. My senior gay female and my sophomore gay female were having a spat." She teaches in the Kent School District, the fourth largest in the state. "It's on the leading edge technologywise, and very redneck studentwise," the math and computer teacher and fast-pitch softball coach said.

The talk turned to coping. "We all support each other," Ruth said. "If I have a terrible day at work, I know I can call up these guys and get some support. They're my family."

"It's so important to have support," Jody emphasized. "You can't imagine the magnitude. We help each other on a personal level, and a professional one. I don't know how people without it – people who are completely closeted – survive."

When Frank has a bad day, he walks over to the nearby junior high and talks to Jody. They don't have to talk about anything serious; the mere thought of being with someone who knows his secret – and thus knows *him* – enables him to get through the day.

All four of the participants coach, so the discussion moved along to those stereotypes. The group laughed uproariously while reeling off the names of coaches they work with and against who are lesbian or gay. The list went on, and on, and on.

D.J., the math and computer teacher whose hair was cut extremely short, said, "I get called a P.E. teacher all the time." Part of the reason may have as much to do with her brassiness as her looks: when an anonymous phone caller tabbed her a lesbian and she was called to the principal's office ("Bring a union rep," they told her), she stood up to him. "I got a reputation of 'Don't fuck with me,'" she said. It helps that she has "a good following of computer-geek-hippies" at her school. "I get thirty kids for extra-help math sessions each Tuesday, and probably twelve of them are gay. I know they're not there for math; they're there because it's a safe place."

Still, there are limits to what she can do. "I have gay kids who know they're gay, and I have kids who have gay parents, but I can't reach out to them," she said with a combination of sorrow and anger. "I still can be fired for saying something inappropriate. All it would take is for some kid to take stuff I said the wrong way, repeat it, and I'm gone."

Parents of athletes react to D.J. in different ways. Some have told her she was among the best coaches their daughters ever had, and they don't care what she does on her personal time. But one father threatened to out her unless his girl played varsity. D.J. replied that the girl just wasn't good enough. And she also hears people say, "Of course she's not gay. She coaches, but she doesn't teach P.E."

At that point, two more women joined the group, again with much joviality, hugging, and high-fiving. "Robin" – the only one with even moderately long hair (and whose mother once said to feel free telling her anything except that she was a lesbian, because then her mother would kill herself) – teaches high school and coaches in the Kent School District. In seven years, no one has learned she is gay. "If they knew, that would be it for me," she said with calm certainty. "Kids and parents say such nasty things. If I were known, that would be my only identity; everything else I had to say would suddenly be discounted." Robin has seen gay and lesbian teachers who come out never be taken seriously again by staff members or students.

A few youngsters have come out at her school. "Girls are sympathetic, but boys get beat up," she said. "No one does anything about it, and eventually the kids leave school."

Robin lives with the second woman who arrived, "Suzanne." She teaches in one school, and coaches at two others, in the Kent district. "Some kids know we live together," Suzanne said. "And I know girls on my team speak freely with D.J.'s kids about both of us. They're more curious than anything, I think. They ask about dating, and I say, 'I don't have a *boy*friend.' They ask if I'm happy being single – how do you answer that? They know; they just want to hear me say it. But I won't. I don't want to jeopardize my job, or the respect I get from other teachers and parents. I'm able to sit here and feel very comfortable with my lesbian and gay friends, but I don't want to force it on other people. I'm very conscious of that, and of the choices I've made."

Part of being closeted in school means turning a deaf ear to words like "dyke" or "fag." Robin said, "It's so hard to control things in the hallway. You don't want to be known for disciplining a kid for it, and besides, kids today use it so loosely – 'This assignment is so gay.' But I *will* challenge what they say in the classroom. I ask whether their remark comes from their own experience, or are they repeating what their parents say. I want to get them to think about what they say. As a teacher you deal with many subjects, and get them to think about lots of different things, so with homophobia it's easy to do."

Still, Robin constantly feels on guard. Last year a player she cut started the rumor that she was a lesbian. The girls who liked Robin said, "No way." But it made her nervous, because so many high school kids are close-minded. She was sure if they knew she is a lesbian, her credibility with them would suffer. Robin said she worked too hard to get where she is to lose what she has.

School can be a place for discussing controversial topics, but even that has limits. A hot topic at the time of the interview was a right-wing attempt to pass two ballot initiatives prohibiting civil rights legislation for gays and lesbians. Several teachers discussed it in their classes, but all agreed they trod lightly. Some were even afraid to put a "Hands Off Washington" bumper sticker opposing the initiative on their cars, for fear they'd be seen as supporting gay rights.

Given the repressive environment they feel just a few miles south of Seattle – a cosmopolitan, progressive city with a thriving gay and lesbian community – why do these teachers continue?

Frank said it's in the hope that "later, down the road, kids will look back at me, their sixth-grade teacher, realize that I'm gay but that I did a really good job – they'll remember they had a great year – and maybe that will count for something."

He also likes getting his two cents in with kids. "We talk about AIDS, and other stuff I'm not supposed to, and maybe that little bit does something for someone. When you're twelve or thirteen years old, one little suggestion or influence might stay with you for the rest of your life. Something I say won't make them gay – but it might keep someone from killing himself, or from treating someone else poorly."

Heads nodded, and Jody said, "We all concur with that. We all want to help people reach their potential. For me, it's women in athletics. It has nothing to do with being gay; it has to do with helping kids live life the best way they can."

D.J. is buoyed by the thought that "seven years ago no one imagined talking to kids about this. Now it's out there; people are talking about lesbian and gay issues all the time, and they're using the right words. It's getting better, and I don't think the pendulum is going to swing back. People listen now, and that keeps me going."

Yet her ambivalence – echoed by the rest of the group – returned in her final words: "If we stay in the closet, things won't be perfect. There comes a time when we should all stand up and say, 'This is who I am.' But I'm sorry, I'm still not ready to stand up at a faculty meeting and tell the world."

An hour north of where Ruth Frobe, D.J. Reed, and their friends – twenty- and thirty-somethings all – live and work, Ed Lockett spends his retirement from teaching. He's in his sixties; his trailer, filled with computer equipment and artwork, sits in a park just a few yards away from a hazardous waste collection site, on Seattle's north border. The juxtaposition of his comfortable home with the surrounding industrial area is echoed in other ways: Mr. Lockett has lived in the Pacific Northwest for a quarter century, yet his speech retains the gentle drawl and slow rhythm of his native Knoxville, Tennessee. He has known he is gay as long as he can remember, yet he did not come out until the mid-1980s, when he was already in his fifties. And in the progressive-yet-laid-back city of Seattle, he calls himself a "conservative activist."

By that, Mr. Lockett means "I am not flamboyant. I'm not a flag-waver." He was shaped by his background: born into what he calls a very dysfunctional family, he knew from an early age that he was different. "I liked to do girl-type things," he explained. "I had difficult peer relationships." From the beginning, school was a disaster. On a playground segregated by gender, he was lost: "I liked to play with girls, because I was a 'sissy,' but I had to be with the boys." In junior high he was called "queer" and "faggot"; he had no idea what the words meant, but understood they were the worst things anyone could be. High school was just as bad, save for one art teacher – the first person who ever said his work was worthwhile.

At the University of Tennessee he escaped his pain by drinking heavily. "To be gay in the South around 1953 was unbearable," he said. "It was sort of equivalent to being a child molester, or a horrible deviant. Because I knew I was gay, and I was sure I couldn't change, I would drive to the top of Smoky Mountain, then drive down without brakes. But I never had the guts to miss the curves."

He came out to his older brother, a doctor, with fear and trepidation. His brother referred him to a psychoanalyst, who spent four years trying for a cure. His years at the University of Tennessee at Memphis Medical School were filled with heavy drug (amphetamine and barbiturate) and alcohol use; a brief psychotic episode resulted in hospitalization.

At an Alcoholics Anonymous meeting, he met someone who knew the Knox County superintendent of schools and who got him a job working with physically handicapped youngsters. After a year he began teaching what were then called "brain-damaged" children (today they're referred to as special-education, or learning-disabled, students).

Mr. Lockett thought he had two choices: live alone, or get married. He did not want a lonely life. He got married. He fathered a daughter. He stayed legally married for twenty years, although the marriage broke down after eight.

By 1968 Mr. Lockett wanted a change; he'd also grown distressed with the low teacher salaries in the South. He and his wife moved to Washington State. He got jobs in Aberdeen, Renton, and then the Shoreline School District, where he taught special education in a mainstream school. Shoreline is an upper-middle-class suburban district; Patty Murray, now a U.S. senator, was PTA president in a local school. Mr. Lockett stopped drinking, but suffered episodes of major depression in which he was "beyond suicidal." In 1986 he and his wife divorced – and Mr. Lockett came out of the closet.

"It was the middle of the AIDS crisis," he recalled. "My first friend, who was also my mentor, died shortly after I came out, on Valentine's Day. That was my introduction to the gay community."

Mr. Lockett was outed by a teaching assistant who also attended his gay fathers' group; soon everyone at school knew. He was generally accepted. Only two teachers avoided him; both, he believes, are closeted lesbians.

In 1988, while he was taking an in-service course on the prevention of adolescent suicide, the subject of AIDS arose. The instructor dismissed the disease, saying, "When you know what these people do to each other, it's surprising they don't get something worse." Mr. Lockett seethed, but said nothing; however, he wrote the teacher a letter. He never received a response. A similar note to the president of Seattle Pacific University, where the course was conducted, also went unanswered.

Undeterred, Mr. Lockett approached a guidance counselor at his school, asking the department to act on the problems of Shoreline's gay and lesbian students. There were four thousand boys and girls in the district, so he estimated that about four hundred were "indescribably lonely and isolated," with critical unmet needs. The first reaction, he said, was horror. "She told me to be quiet, that this stuff shouldn't be discussed. It was like I was suggesting we molest kids." The second person he talked to, whom he considered a good friend, reacted cautiously. Mr. Lockett wanted her to have literature in the guidance office that students could steal when no one was looking. Instead, she gave Mr. Lockett information on available resources. "I knew all that," he said dismissively. "I wanted to get direct information to the kids themselves." The implication, he said, was "Don't call us; we'll call you."

At a dead end with the guidance department, he went to the district administrator in charge of in-service training. "She listened politely and did nothing," he said. "It had no impact on her whatsoever."

The insults piled up. Teaching at what he called a million-dollar school on the waterfront, he heard three colleagues pass his open door telling "faggot" jokes loudly enough to hear. "It was repulsive. I was surprised, yet at the same time I wasn't. The school had scored low on an educators' report on our recognition of cultural differences and the needs of minority students. One day we spent an hour discussing that report in a faculty meeting, and the very next issue was kids on the playground getting hurt playing 'smear the queer.' The principal brought up the topic, and didn't say a word about the name of the game!" That time, Mr. Lockett had spoken up. However, no one had gotten excited. It was as if they didn't know what he was talking about, or else it made no difference to them. At Shoreline, gay and lesbian concerns were a non-issue.

The incidents reminded Mr. Lockett of his own feelings growing up in Tennessee. "One of the greatest disservices to any group of people is to pretend they don't exist," he said. "If you don't exist, you're not even worth worrying about."

He transferred to a new school, which had a complex phone setup integrated into the public address system. One day the principal's phone conversation was inadvertently broadcast to the entire building – and Mr. Lockett's name was slandered. Worried administrators asked him what it would take for him not to pursue legal action; he answered, "Getting involved in curriculum planning for sexual-orientation issues; making sexual orientation part of the drug and alcohol curriculum." He was moved out of the school, but not given curricular responsibilities. When the state legislature made it convenient for veteran, well-paid teachers like Mr. Lockett to take early retirement in 1992, he did.

How does the retired educator assess his career, including his late attempts to introduce gay and lesbian awareness into the schools? "Under the circumstances, given the environment I was working in, I don't know of anything I could have done differently," he said. "I faced a stone wall right from the beginning, and I wasn't willing to face that stone wall. I knew an 'attack' attitude would not have been appropriate, or well received. If anything at all was going to work, it would have to be done in a 'conservative activist' way. I could push, but only so far. A more aggressive move wouldn't have been productive."

What did he think he had accomplished? "Nothing," he said simply, "other than for myself." He hesitated, letting the harsh words fall in his quiet trailer, then spoke again. "Well, let me retract that. I think the first step in overcoming prejudice and bigotry is to make people aware that it exists. Maybe I made some people aware. In Memphis in 1955 or '56, if I had met a black person walking the opposite way, he would have crossed the street until he got past me, then walked back. Everybody took that for granted – the black person, I – and nobody thought about it; it was just the way it was. In order for Martin Luther King, Jr., or anyone to do anything, the first step was to make people see that that wasn't the way it had to be.

"Maybe I made some people see a problem existed," he concluded, "even if they were not willing to address the problem at all."

On the Private Side

The United States has a long love affair with public school education. One of our country's most basic principles – not written down with "life, liberty and the pursuit of happiness," to be sure, but ingrained in our consciousness nonetheless – has long been the right of every citizen to attend school. Our September-to-June calendar grew out of the rhythms of the land – youngsters were expected to help with the crops in the summer, but the rest of the time to be in school – and when we expanded west, a staple of frontier life was the one-room schoolhouse, complete with reader, bell, and school-marm or -master. Today, as we peer round the corner toward the twenty-first century, public school experiences – gym class, cafeteria food, hall passes – continue to be part of the glue that holds together our increasingly diverse society.

What, then, to make of private schools? With their haughty names, manicured campuses, and snobby stereotypes, they seem foreign to most Americans – a throwback to the British shackles we tossed off two centuries ago. George Bush went to private school, Bill Clinton to public school, and if that doesn't say something about America, nothing does.

But private schools today (and for the purposes of this chapter, the term encompasses both boarding and day independent schools, but excludes religious schools) are not the bastions of privilege they were. True, many cost upwards of $10,000 a year – but more and more students receive some sort of scholarship these days. Where once the only faces one saw were white and male, now diversity has made inroads, so that the yearbook pages are filled with females, and dotted with black, brown, yellow, and red skins. And of course, in the 1990s, gay people have come out of the dorm closets and into dorm suites, classes, locker rooms, even faculty apartments. In fact, it is at some of America's most elite private schools – those that spawned the Rockefellers, Roosevelts, and Kennedys – that the most intriguing lesbian and gay events are occurring.

One man whose finger rests firmly on the pulse of America's private schools – at least those that call themselves "independent boarding high schools" – is Al Chase. A young-looking, slow-speaking man who lives in an airy flat just one block from San Francisco's famous Castro Street, he seems an unlikely candidate to have such a broad overview of boarding school gay and lesbian issues. But, as is so often the case, things are not always what they seem.

Al – nobody, he says, calls him Mr. Chase – attended Phillips Exeter Academy, and after college returned to the boarding school environment he knew so well. He taught for nine years at two coed schools in Colorado and California, but realized he did not want to spend his life in the front of a classroom. "When I decided to try to help improve conditions for sexual minority youth, the boarding school arena was the obvious choice for me," he said. "I'm more familiar with boarding high schools than any other educational setting."

What he chose to do, however, was unfamiliar to most people, private school grads or not: he began a newsletter for administrators, teachers, students, alumni, parents, and trustees of independent boarding schools, and others actively involved with lesbian and gay issues in those schools. As Al wrote in the inaugural, sixteen-page issue of *Speaking Out,* its mission is "to serve as a forum for the exchange of information, opinions, and questions on sexual minority issues in order to increase understanding of the needs and contributions of sexual minority members of the boarding school family, and to help lift the burden of homophobia from everyone: gays, straights, those who are in the process of ascertaining their orientation, and those whose orientation has yet to unfold."

He has succeeded.

The first copy, mailed in the spring of 1993 to 370 individuals at 180 boarding schools (including heads, admissions officers, faculty advisers to gay-straight groups, and others who were referred or expressed interest), crackled with excitement. The writing was lively; the issues were cutting-edge; the information sounded crucial, exciting, and powerful. An important link between private school people was made.

The first story, fittingly, was Al's own. He described how his newsletter came to be. On a Friday afternoon the previous December,

he said, he felt the urge to write. What emerged was a fictitious letter
to boarding school admissions offices, in which he said he was the
father of an openly gay son ("Chris"), and was seeking a school that
would be affirming of him. The letter expressed his unequivocal
support for Chris as a gay person, and asked specific questions about
the school's support for their gay and lesbian students and teachers.

The letter went to admissions offices at 115 independent coed
boarding high schools. When the seventy-nine responses cascaded in,
he felt badly about having deceived the individual recipients – but at
the same time he learned so much he could not turn back.

Many responses, Al wrote in his first newsletter, "were very personal, often expressing deeply felt personal concern." That concern was
often evident even from respondents who felt that their school would
not provide an accepting environment for Chris.

Several notable themes recurred in the responses, which Al para-
phrased:

- Our school does not provide support systems or social opportunities for gay and lesbian students, and so would not be an appropriate place.

- Although our school does not have formal support systems, it is
  very caring and inclusive, and we believe (or know from experience) that we can provide an affirming environment for a gay
  student.

- We'd be very happy to have Chris apply for our sake, to help us
  pioneer the issues, but we question whether we could provide a
  supportive environment for him.

- Our school is caring, and we are very diverse and value differences in many ways, but we haven't yet addressed sexual minority
  issues.

- We honestly don't know how to answer some of your questions.
  No one has ever come out as gay here. The issues have never been
  discussed.

- This would not be a good place for gay students, because of our
  location in an area that is actively intolerant of homosexuality.

- There must be an undercurrent of homophobia here. Students are
  not comfortable identifying themselves as lesbian or gay.

- A gay alum came back to address the faculty (or entire school).
  The presentation was among the most moving and powerful we
  ever had.

- Your letter has sparked valuable discussion and will help us move closer to being an inclusive community.
- We are suspicious of your letter. (They wondered if they were being set up for a sting by an anti-gay group, or a lawsuit by a pro-gay organization.)
- Our faculty is ahead of our students on these issues (or) our students are ahead of our faculty.
- The head of our school is resistant (or) the trustees are resistant (or) many of our parents would be resistant.

Al did find that twelve schools had active support groups for gay, lesbian, bisexual, and questioning students (most often a gay-straight alliance, where students and often teachers could address issues such as homophobia, without necessarily identifying themselves as gay or straight). Some schools also had an additional group exclusively for gay, lesbian, bi, and questioning students. Seventeen schools reported having at least one openly bi, lesbian, or gay student; seventeen (not all the same ones) reported at least one such teacher. Three schools reported having an openly gay or lesbian faculty member living on campus with a partner; at one school, a same-gender couple served as dorm parents.

Twenty-nine, however, stated directly that they would not be an appropriate place for Chris, because of acknowledged intolerance or the absence of clear support for gay students. In most cases, Al wrote, this was made "in a tone of genuine regret and concern."

He concluded his review of responses to the letter with a personal reflection:

As an *openly* gay student applying for admission, 'Chris' was in a position to make choices. The closeted gay, lesbian, bisexual and questioning students currently applying to or enrolled in boarding schools are unable to make those choices. They aren't able to say to their parents, their friends or their school that they feel unsafe, unacknowledged, and alienated, that they want to be in a school which affirms them. I'm concerned about these students, particularly those who happen to be in the many schools which 'Chris' would have chosen to avoid. In an environment which is not already manifestly affirming, these kids can't speak up for their own needs without taking tremendous risks. They can't be expected to take the lead in making their schools safe for themselves.

Much of the rest of that first newsletter was filled with the individual stories of male and female educators at a variety of boarding schools. The words of coaches, dorm counselors, gay-straight alliance faculty advisers, a history teacher, a theater technical director, an admissions officer, and a multicultural education coordinator sizzled off the pages; their experiences – positive and negative, empowering and frightful, extraordinary and routine – were both unique and universal. A two-page resource list completed the first edition of *Speaking Out*.

The feedback he received was overwhelmingly positive. Virtually everyone who wrote back was "enthusiastic, encouraging, and appreciative." He received only two negative responses – both requests to be taken off the mailing list (and one woman changed her mind after Al wrote back, explaining why he felt that *Speaking Out* was so important). However, he emphasized, all the letters he received represented only a small percentage of copies mailed. He realizes that not everyone who received it was enthusiastic.

Subsequent issues of *Speaking Out* addressed other important private school topics. Al gave students a forum to write about what it was like to discover their orientation, question it, or live with lesbian and gay classmates as a straight person. He solicited articles by gay alumni, gay parents, and parents of gay students. Other stories covered lesbian and gay curriculums; concerns of heads and trustees; the roles of counselors; and homophobia and athletics. Producing such an exhaustive quarterly newsletter is exhausting work. Why does he do it?

"It was hard for me to come to terms with my own sexual orientation," he said. "I had picked up homophobic attitudes from my surroundings, and developed a rock-solid conviction that at my core I was a terrible person, and that I didn't have a legitimate place in the world. I came much too close to killing myself. Finally I realized that I'm *not* a terrible person, that I *do* have a place in the world, and that it's the damage caused by homophobia that isn't right. It isn't right for *anyone* to have to go through that. I decided to do something to try to make it better for others."

His newsletter has educated Al, as well as thousands of boarding school students and staff (the mailing list surged to twenty-three hundred within a year of the first issue). He learned that most of the boarding schools taking the most visible steps were in New England – "but that's where most boarding schools are," he noted. The political climate of a school's geographical location has some effect on the amount of attention paid to gay and lesbian issues, but is not always a deciding factor: one teacher at a school that has made big changes described his institution as being located in "not merely an intolerant state — many people feel it's a seek-and-destroy kind of state."

Another important factor is whether a school has more qualified applicants than it can accept. Schools in a tight financial situation are less apt to take risks — of any kind.

Boarding schools face a number of challenges that are of less concern to day schools. First, Al said, "While day students have access to their family and the resources of the surrounding community, a boarding school has almost sole responsibility for providing the parenting, nurturing, role models, social climate, and every other resource a student needs for every aspect of life — including their developing sexual and social identity."

Second, sexual interaction between students at school is of greater concern — and more of a reality — at boarding schools than at day schools. No school is in a position to condone student sex, and different schools work out details in different ways, but, he said, "all boarding schools build from the same first line of defense: there are separate boys' dorms and girls' dorms. But what about same-gender attractions and interactions? While a boy and a girl have to take at least some risk to have sex at school, same-gender lovers could be roommates." He is aware of just a very few schools that are facing this issue openly now, but foresees it becoming an important area in the evolution of boarding school policy. In the meantime, he said, "one of the challenges for a boarding school in acknowledging that it has students who are same-sex oriented is that in doing so it may also have to face awkward gaps in an area of policy which is already sensitive and fraught with difficulties."

Despite all those caveats, Al gives generally good marks to boarding schools for the way they've reacted once lesbian and gay issues have been raised. "The rate of progress is close to revolutionary in some areas," he said. "These issues are now in the public eye. People are much more aware of them than they used to be, and boarding schools are responding."

Thanks, in no small measure, to the work Al Chase does *Speaking Out*.

———

Al noted that one major difference between boarding and public schools is dorm life. Students who live in small rooms, sharing hallways and bathrooms with others their own age and gender, obviously have different experiences than adolescents who go to school together a few hours a day but eat and sleep (despite their best efforts to avoid it) in their own homes.

Dorm issues assume special importance for gay and lesbian faculty members. On the surface, the idea of homosexual teachers supervising living quarters might seem fraught with controversy – but, as with so many other lesbian and gay issues, reality is not always surface-deep.

Vicky Greenbaum knows. A violin teacher and symphony orchestra conductor ("Don't call me a 'music teacher,'" she requested), she is openly lesbian at Northfield Mt. Hermon, a century-old college preparatory independent school in rural Massachusetts, where tuition runs $17,000 for the thousand boys and girls in grades nine through twelve (approximately half the students are on scholarship). She is also a dorm parent – and one of the most popular ones on campus.

Like many prep school teachers, Ms. Greenbaum reached Mt. Hermon via a circuitous route. A Northridge, California, native who became a professional violinist, she went back to school for a master's degree in English. She had come out to herself and the music community while with the Houston Grand Opera, but then decided she'd rather teach than tour. Her first positions were in public schools on the West Coast, but she realized she did not like the "lockstep, large-class approach" to public education. Though students had always flocked to her – she was one of the few teachers who truly paid attention to them – many colleagues thought of her as weird. She was, she said, heavily closeted. She even made up names of boyfriends.

She began searching for a very good school where she could conduct a good youth orchestra. She spent two years in private schools in the East, waiting for the right job at Northfield Mt. Hermon to open up. When it did, she nailed it.

NMH, like most boarding schools, requires new faculty members to serve as dorm parents. She agreed, and spent her first year there in the closet. She was apprehensive about homophobia from students, faculty, and parents; she knew from experience that some closeted women have gone so far as to request assignment to boys' dorms.

Though not comfortable in her closet, she worried about the insecurity of leaving it. Nevertheless, in her second year she began coming out. The first people she told were some girls in her dorm and her orchestra – but it was they who forced the issue. "I was in a relationship, and they asked other adults if I was a lesbian," she recounted. "The teachers said they should ask me themselves, so they did. They said, 'So what about your sexuality?' I blushed – I was nervous about saying the l-word – so I said, 'Yeah, I like women.' It makes me laugh now to think about it."

The girls asked if they should keep it a secret. Ms. Greenbaum told them she planned to come out slowly, but that they could tell people if they wanted.

Were there repercussions? "None. Zero. Zip," said Ms. Greenbaum firmly. "Three years later I'm still waiting for something to happen." She later mentioned that a girl in her dorm once asked another if she were afraid of Ms. Greenbaum. "That girl was ostracized and scoffed at for saying that," she said. "That was probably the closest thing to anything negative that happened."

There were, however, benefits. "I don't have to hide my reading matter from kids anymore," she began. "And – this is a huge one – in slow dribs and drabs, a lot of kids started coming out to me. I was asked by one gay student and one bisexual to advise the new gay-straight alliance, and a lot of kids with bisexual feelings came by to talk to me. Four boys who were being harassed came to talk to me, and I spent a lot of time that year going to the deans with them. A lot of stuff was coming out of the woodwork." Some students were worried, apparently, about being seen talking with her, and telephoned with their questions.

The positive effects of being out continue, Ms. Greenbaum said. "The faculty support has been great. Lots of people give me clippings about gay and lesbian things – I've become sort of the homosexual information person. One colleague invited me over, and told me very casually to invite any 'significant other.' And I feel really good about myself. I didn't realize how constricting it had been to be closeted. Now I feel I can do something really good for the school community."

Among those good things are presentations made by the Homo/ Bi/Hetero (HBH) alliance. "Because I'm a music teacher, I made everyone rehearse what they were going to say," she laughed. "We gave our speeches twice, and both times we got applause and standing ovations. That felt especially great, because campus meetings are supposed to be boring."

And the visits to her apartment continue. "There are forty-five girls in the dorm, in all four grades, and I probably see about ten on a regular basis," Ms. Greenbaum reported. "Some others I see less regularly, and some never. I suspect my apartment has among the heaviest traffic of all the dorm parents at NMH. I think the girls feel welcome here – no, I know they do."

One who felt particularly welcome was Shula Kleinerman. She landed at Northfield Mt. Hermon after a bad experience at another private

Student Shula Kleinerman announced that she was a lesbian at a schoolwide assembly and found the reaction from other students "really, really positive."

school, and came out at the large meeting Ms. Greenbaum described above. She began her speech by relating an incident in Spanish class: the teacher assigned an essay on "your ideal man." Shula wrote it without gender, on her "ideal person." She then told the schoolwide assembly, "I'm Shula Kleinerman, and I'm a lesbian." She explained why she would no longer keep her mouth shut about her sexual orientation: "I'm not going to lie anymore when I'm discussing birth control methods with my friends!"

The reaction, she said, was "really, really positive. People I barely knew stopped me on campus. One guy came running up and said, 'That's so cool!' It was so odd to realize people all over school were talking about me." One student wrote a negative letter to the NMH paper, and was soundly answered by four others. "That person ended up looking really stupid," she said.

Vicky Greenbaum was, of course, an important and supportive link for Shula. "Before I came out, I had really long talks with her," the youngster said. "We kept talking about did I want to take this really big step in front of the whole world?" (Shula admitted that she was one of those students who first left messages on Ms. Greenbaum's answering machine. "I thought she was cool, and wanted to be part of HBH — I had a pretty good reason! I said that on the message, and then said, 'Talk to you later about it.' She was pretty amused.")

Shula said that Ms. Greenbaum plays an important role on the NMH campus. "She's very much — aside from her sexuality — seen and heard. The orchestra makes her visible, and it's obvious people in the orchestra like her a lot. She communicates well with people; she's just a good, representative person. There's no taint for anyone in talking with her."

Northfield Mt. Hermon is, Shula said, a very good place for a gay or lesbian student. "There's an accepting air among students," she said. "People don't put up with intolerance. It's hard to say why, but I think people coming out help. The more people come out, the more other people change the way they think about it."

Still, Shula wishes there were more openly gay students. "Vicky calls me 'the campus lesbian,'" she said, "and sometimes I feel a lot of pressure. It's like I have to represent an entire group of people, and that's totally unrealistic. But anything that opens people's eyes is okay, I guess." Together, Shula Kleinerman and Vicky Greenbaum are doing just that.

———⧫———

Still, even liberal Massachusetts is not yet ready for some things — like lesbian houseparents living together in a girls' private school dormitory.

Chris Huff discovered those limits in the spring of 1993, when she requested on-campus housing at Chapel Hill–Chauncy Hall (CHCH) in Waltham for herself and her life partner, Karen Keough. The school said no — even though living on campus was a requirement of Ms. Huff's many jobs (head houseparent, assistant dean of students, teacher, peer adviser, and coach). The school's refusal touched off a genteel — yet very personal, principled, and important — battle that continues to wend its way through the Bay State judicial system.

Chris Huff's request for on-campus housing with Karen Keough did not arise out of the blue. She had come out at CHCH — a coed school for 160 ninth through twelfth graders, many of whom have learning disabilities or otherwise need small classes and close staff attention — the previous fall, first to headmaster James Clements, then to the entire faculty at a meeting. Everyone, from the headmaster on down, was very supportive. She came out to her human sexuality and relations class soon afterward; by midyear, most of the school knew she was a lesbian, and no one seemed to care. Whatever remarks she heard from students had more to do with her job as assistant dean of students than anything else. She had to discipline them in the afternoon, then be friendly with them as a houseparent at night, and that was not easy. She described her dorm as very accepting. "Kids would come in when Karen was there and I was on duty, and she'd help them with their homework." The couple had met several months earlier; Ms. Keough taught physical education and health and coached lacrosse and junior varsity field hockey at Milton Academy, half an hour away, for seven years.

As the love between the two women grew, they discussed living together. It seemed natural to share housing at CHCH, Chris Huff said. "I couldn't move off campus; I had to be on school grounds so many hours each day, I would never have seen the inside of my house if it wasn't on campus."

So Chris asked Mr. Clements for permission to live there with Karen. He replied that he would not immediately say no; he needed time to talk with trustees, administrators, and other headmasters – and, Ms. Huff said, he did. He kept her informed about all the conversations he was having.

But in March, just before the couple left on spring break to visit relatives in Arizona and Nevada, Mr. Clements gave Ms. Huff his answer. "You're a great asset to the school," he said – in fact, he had rated her performance and professional conduct as excellent during her two years there – "but I'm sorry, you can't live together here."

"He said something else about the school not being in a position to have two openly gay women live in a dorm, but I can't recall how he said it," Chris said several months later. "It was such an emotional meeting for me. Part of me was ready for what he said, but another part felt all along he just had to say yes. I hadn't prepared myself as well as I should have. All I remember is getting the basic idea that the school was not ready to be the first – or second, or third – to have two openly gay teachers living in a dorm." So far as either of them knew, no other boarding school in New England allowed a homosexual couple to share dormitory housing.

Mr. Clements's decision meant that Chris Huff had to make "an impossible choice" between her partner and her career. She was offered a contract with the proviso that she not live with Ms. Keough; she could not accept those terms and so, she says, she was forced out of her job.

The next decision was equally difficult. "I'm not the type to run off and hire a lawyer," Ms. Huff said. "I think there are too many lawsuits already in the world. I really didn't want to take legal action. But I talked with Karen and lots of friends, and finally I decided to contact GLAD." The Boston-based organization – Gay and Lesbian Advocates and Defenders – is a fifteen-year-old nonprofit law firm representing gay men, lesbians, and HIV-infected people throughout New England.

After much discussion, GLAD decided to take the case. Ms. Huff met with three lawyers: Mary L. Bonauto, who ultimately handled the matter, and John Ward and Gary Buseck, who worked as cooperating attorneys. "The legal issues went way over my head," she admitted,

Chris Huff *(right)*, a teacher at a Massachusetts private school, filed a complaint with the state after her headmaster refused on-campus housing to Huff and her partner, Karen Keough *(left)*.

"but they gave me two options. I could file a complaint with MCAD (Massachusetts Commission Against Discrimination), or I could sue the school. We went over the pros and cons, and two or three weeks later I decided to go with MCAD."

Her reasons, Chris said, were many. "For me, this wasn't an aggressive move. I didn't want to shove it down the school's face, like I'm right and they're wrong. I just wanted to get the policies changed, so everyone – not just gay and lesbian people – could benefit. I wasn't out to sue the pants off the school and make a pile of money; I didn't want to put them on the defensive. I love the school. I have a lot of respect for the kids and the faculty; they're great. It was not my intention to shut them down – but I did want them to change things, so kids there and at private schools everywhere could have access to all different kinds of role models."

GLAD filed a complaint on Ms. Huff's behalf; CHCH responded, and the legal wrangling began. The school denied that it discriminated based on her sexual orientation, citing in its defense an exception in the 1989 state lesbian and gay civil rights legislation that provides that the law not be interpreted "to provide health insurance or related employee benefits to a 'homosexual spouse,' so-called." (Ms. Huff and Ms. Keough formalized their partnership in a Unitarian-Universalist commitment ceremony a few months after filing their complaint. The rite and reception were held at the Milton Academy chapel.)

Ms. Bonauto countered, "The defense in this case boils down to 'Yes, we're discriminating, but we're allowed to.' That won't work. Living on campus was a job requirement, not a fringe benefit. If CHCH can provide housing for married teachers, it should certainly be able to provide housing for gay and lesbian teachers who can't marry under state law. CHCH is not required to mimic the discriminatory marriage laws."

Mr. Ward added, "This case highlights the costs of discrimination. CHCH has lost a valuable employee. The students have lost a dedicated teacher, adviser, and the one open lesbian role model at the school."

MCAD found probable cause for sexual discrimination, and in late December 1993 the lawyers for the two sides tried to settle. Chris asked that she be allowed back to teach; that she and Karen live together in a campus dorm; that the policy prohibiting such an arrangement be changed; and that she begin receiving her salary again. But, she said, the school was not interested in settling, so both sides prepared for a long legal process.

In September 1994, just after the school year began, MCAD chairman Michael Duffy – an openly gay man – ruled that the private school's refusal to allow Chris and Karen to live together on campus did not violate a state law prohibiting employment discrimination on the basis of sexual orientation. The ruling was based on what Ms. Bonauto called "an unfair exception to the civil rights law": a provision that the law cannot be used to "validate or legitimize (a) homosexual marriage, so-called." Chris and Karen vowed to appeal the ruling to the full, three-person commission. However, that process could take up to two years.

Ms. Huff called the ruling a disappointment, especially in terms of students' rights to positive role models. "Kids need to see adults in committed, loving relationships," she said. "They see that so seldom, especially with gays and lesbians. This will just perpetuate the stereotype of one-night stands. Once again, kids are being told it's not okay for gay and lesbian people to live together – in essence, to love each other."

Ms. Huff has been buoyed by the positive reactions to her fight. "To be honest, I have yet to hear anything majorly negative – I'm sure it's out there, but I haven't felt it or heard it." She does not visit CHCH often, but when she does she is greeted warmly. "I was told that when the headmaster presented the case to the faculty at the beginning, it was in a very positive light," she said. "He doesn't hold a grudge. He said he felt I was doing what had to be done. And I wouldn't hold it against him if he was mad. The school was put in this situation, but it could have been any other school in New England."

In the year prior to Mr. Duffy's ruling, Ms. Keough continued to teach at Milton, but Ms. Huff's road was rougher. She left CHCH and picked up several small Milton jobs: coaching, driving the community service van, and supervising gym programs six nights a week. She also worked as a bagel cook. After hearing the MCAD ruling, the couple sought work elsewhere in Massachusetts. Ms. Keough got a job teaching public school health and physical education; Ms. Huff was named activities coordinator at a school for emotionally disturbed boys. They also started looking for a new house together.

Their fight continues, but Chris makes clear that future battles need not be fought on the same grounds they chose. "The MCAD decision does not mean that a school can't change its policy to permit same-sex couples to live together," she pointed out. "Schools don't have to mimic the state's marriage laws. This isn't law; it's policy. Well, any school can change its policy whenever it wants to."

Although she chose the woman she loved over the career she loved, she regretted being forced to make such a decision. "No one should have to do that," she noted. "It's time for employers to work with the gay and lesbian population, and recognize that a committed partnership is the same regardless of sexual orientation."

Was her decision to leave teaching and pursue legal action the correct one? "Oh yes," she said without hesitation. "Definitely. It's not like we're starving to death. Once in a while we get a little emotional, but that's part of what sharing a life together is all about, isn't it?"

Public schools don't have to dorms – and they certainly don't have religion. But church sponsorship is one major difference between some private and all public schools, and you don't have to look farther than the chaplain's office to see how the presence of a cleric – and his or her attitude toward homosexuality – can affect the attitudes of students, teachers, administrators, parents, and trustees.

Oregon Episcopal School (OES) is said to be, at age 125, the oldest boarding school west of the Mississippi River. Seven hundred mostly middle- and upper-class students attend grades kindergarten through twelve on the southwest Portland campus; though only 30 percent are actually Episcopalian, and the school has no formal diocesan affiliation, it maintains what middle-school chaplain Mike Devenney calls "an Episcopal tradition." That means that he conducts weekly chapel services, in conjunction with students; it means too that he exposes youngsters to the Episcopal faith, while challenging them to explore their own beliefs and ideas. And it also means that he challenges the entire school to confront the issue of homosexuality head-on.

"We discuss gay and lesbian issues a lot," he said candidly. "School can be a very homophobic atmosphere. Middle- and upper-school kids are in the throes of puberty, trying to work a lot of things out. They have so many issues. Our main thrust is to let kids who are struggling know that the chaplains have an open door. We won't tell them this will 'go away.' Our message is they'll be accepted for who they are." He hangs posters for the local Phoenix Rising support group on his walls, and stacks lesbian and gay books on his shelves. "When kids see those they realize the chaplain is willing to talk to them without saying they'll be sent to hell," he said. "That's a real fear in kids with a religious background."

Sometimes a youngster will approach Mr. Devenney with concerns about a friend or relative. "Those kids need a forum to talk and ask questions too," he noted. "I'll talk in my office, at Hot Lips Pizza – wherever they feel comfortable."

Mr. Devenney also challenges the student body as a whole to confront stereotypes. "That means recognizing that being a loving, caring person means loving and caring about *everyone,* not 'everyone except gays.' It's *not* okay to make people the butt of jokes, because you never know who's suffering."

Mr. Devenney and his fellow chaplains do plenty of educational outreach. They bring in speakers; they monitor the atmosphere on campus, and in their classes (all teach academic courses) they raise the subject of homosexuality whenever and wherever they feel it's appropriate.

Mr. Devenney teaches health, and makes sure gay issues arise often. His classroom has a "question box," through which youngsters can anonymously ask anything they want. "I give the best answer I can, and then we open it up for discussion," he said. "Inevitably, questions come up about homosexuality – and if they don't, I spice the box so it does." Each year, a handful of boys react with disgust to these discussions, but for the most part, he finds kids open to discussing it. "They see gay and lesbian kids as just others in the school."

It is rare, he added, for an eighth grader to say to him, "I think I'm gay, and I want to talk." More often, he gets quick questions about something that was on TV, or kids request another question box session. "That's a real safe space for them. I think it's important to be open at whatever level individual students are open. They have to set the agenda. I can only create an open atmosphere, and then be there for whatever they want."

However, he admitted, with only one openly gay OES student – an upper-school girl – for most of the students this is just theory. They haven't actually met anyone they know is gay. The chaplain sees his job as laying the seeds in eighth grade, so later in life they will have something to fall back on. The students who have come out to him after graduation explained that because OES is so small, they felt that revealing their sexual orientation would dominate their entire lives for the rest of their time there. They didn't want to deal with the expected negative reaction from a few classmates.

Mr. Devenney organizes visits from outside groups, such as the Seattle-based Growth and Prevention (GAP) theater, which focuses on issues of gender and homophobia. Their presentation included an assembly, a play for faculty and staff, and a follow-up forum. "This school does not believe in silence," the chaplain said emphatically. "If kids see that the staff is not panicking, then they can deal with this on a serious, mature level."

Another important project, Mr. Devenney said, is an annual retreat for eighth graders. "They call it the 'Sex Trip,'" he chuckled. "We prep for it for four weeks. First I take care of the 'plumbing'; they think they know it all, but they really listen closely. When we go away we talk about everything: birth control, date rape, loving relationships, marriage – the whole range of sexuality issues. The kids can't slough it off. And they know we'll be there for them and their questions when we come back."

The sexuality workshop can provide dramatic moments. One youngster found out right before it began that the reason his mother was trying to prevent him from seeing his divorced father was that he was gay. "It was incredibly painful," Mr. Devenney said. "We talked about it, and the boy made the decision that he'd tell his classmates about it during the weekend, and say that he didn't believe his mom's message that it's not okay to love a gay person." That was one of the most uplifting moments of any retreat.

Mr. Devenney praised the OES faculty as fully supportive of his work. "They're real open," he noted. "They come to me and the other chaplains and counselors with concerns about particular students – things they've heard or observed." The administration has also reacted strongly, to the point of sending six staff members on a school day to a homosexuality awareness workshop three hours away in Washington State.

When the anti-gay ballot measure 9 was a hot topic in Oregon, some parents felt it was inappropriate for faculty to wear "No on 9" buttons. "The headmaster said it was okay with him," the chaplain said. "Parents were concerned about role modeling, but the headmaster said it was incredibly important for kids to see teachers being politically active. And we aligned ourselves with the Church diocese statement, which was 'Vote no on 9.'"

There have been a few other murmurs. Some parents kept their fifth graders home rather than go to the GAP theater presentation. "We let it slide," Mr. Devenney said. "But in middle school we make it clear that gay issues are part of the curriculum. We're not *promoting* a gay or lesbian lifestyle; we're showing our kids the world as it is. We always have a parent meeting before the sexuality workshop, so they can air their concerns. Six years ago there were a lot of questions; as time goes on and they talk to other parents, there's less and less of that. They're becoming much more comfortable with it."

Through conferences and workshops, Mr. Devenney believes that the situation at OES is "very much in line with what's happening at other Episcopal schools. And around here there's also strong support among chaplains and counselors at Catholic schools for gay and lesbian teenagers, even though there's no word about it from principals." He contrasted that with the situation at area public schools, which he called "devastating. In Portland they did an entire AIDS presentation without ever mentioning homosexuality or condoms. I could see what was going on; the school could have been deluged, and been a prime target of the OCA (Oregon Citizens Alliance). Their hands were tied. Fortunately, that's not the case in private schools."

Three thousand miles across the country, in Wallingford, Connecticut, sits another very old, very established, independent private school with an Episcopal tradition: Choate Rosemary Hall. Founded in 1892, and boasting a list of alumni that includes John F. Kennedy, Adlai Stevenson, Edward Albee, Glenn Close, and Michael Douglas, Choate has fallen away from its religious roots. Chapel meeting was dropped in the late 1970s; the crucifix was removed from the altar, and the music department moved in. But Choate still has a chaplain. And even though

Rev. Joseph Devlin, S.J., chaplain at Connecticut's prestigious Choate Rosemary Hall, is one of the school's best-known, most respected, and well-loved figures.

he has been on campus for only a couple of years, one of the best-known, most respected, and well-loved figures at Choate is Rev. Joseph Devlin, S.J.

Most of the 975 students call him "Father Joe"; to some he is just "Joe," while others greet him as "Padre" or "Fag Face." The Jesuit priest laughed as he rattled off his nicknames; he laughs frequently, for he finds much of life amusing, or at least quirky.

Father Joe arrived at Choate via a typically circuitous Jesuit route. He was ordained in 1966, after working for several years with a variety of Boston-area campus ministry groups. He was one of the earliest protesters against the Vietnam War, and got ensnared in a St. Patrick's Day parade issue two dozen years before the current controversy surrounding lesbian and gay marchers. "That one was about race," he said.

After ordainment, he worked with the Reverend Dr. Martin Luther King, Jr., and Ralph Abernathy on civil rights issues, and in Chicago with community organizer Saul Alinsky. He picketed the National Rifle Association in Washington, D.C., grew more involved in the peace movement, and was arrested and imprisoned a number of times. Those experiences created, he said, "a peculiar outlook on what is important, and not important, in life."

Asked by his provincial to serve on the Jesuit staff in New England, he spent eight years "raising hell." His mandate, he said, was to create change. In 1976 he headed off to Dartmouth College, three years after the first females were admitted. It was quite an eye-opener. He saw the terrible way fraternities treated them, and that led to many social justice projects involving women. He also worked with gay groups, noting wryly, "There had never been anything like that before – no gays at Dartmouth for two hundred years! It was still an outdoorsy, beer-drinking, jock school, and I found it exciting to try to create change. My whole approach to God and the Church is social action. Jesus set us on fire to challenge cherished beliefs. I saw kids at Dartmouth start to set the school on fire – figuratively, of course! – and I thought I would stay there the rest of my life."

But in 1984 he was appointed rector of Fairfield University, a Jesuit school in Connecticut. He dealt primarily with the priests who ran the college, but also spent time with the affiliated prep school. After six years at Fairfield, he became head chaplain at the University of Connecticut, a post he likened to being "head chaplain of Beijing. It was gigantic: 18,000 students. I had two other priests, but I was over-whelmed. There was so much to do – questions every day about premarital sex, birth control, sexuality. There was never a question about dogma, though; my dogma got a bit rusty there."

Just when he felt he was getting a handle on UConn he received a call from Ed Shanahan, Dartmouth's former dean of students who had recently been named president and head at Choate. He needed someone to help him deal with the private school's diverse population (students hailed from thirty-two countries, and practiced more than thirty different religions). Mr. Shanahan asked Father Joe to develop an ecumenical, interfaith worship program for the entire Choate community.

"In a private boarding school, people need to make links with one another," the priest said. "Kids constantly question themselves and their lives: 'My mother's getting divorced; what do I say to her?' 'I'm a Muslim and I'm in love with a Jew; what do I do?' 'I think I'm gay; what's going to happen to me?' My whole job here is to help people with those questions, and help them link everything together."

Father Joe has become deeply involved with SMAC (Sexual Minorities Awareness at Choate), which he described as a safe place for kids and staff to speak about gay, lesbian, and straight concerns. His job is to listen, support, talk, give resources, and meet in greater depth with smaller, private groups. Some of his SMAC work is pastoral: "Kids always begin, 'You're a priest, right? So all this is confidential, right?' – but a lot of it has nothing to do with religion. Anything kids think about, they talk to me about. Themselves, their brothers and sisters, parents, uncles, aunts, cousins – sometimes it seems everyone in their lives is touched by homosexuality. The language changes, depending upon where they're from – the kids who grew up in San Francisco or New York or Boston or Chicago are a lot more aware than the ones from

Des Moines – but a lot of the questions revolve around growing up. They want to know, 'Who am I? Will you love and accept me if I'm gay? And if you do, will my parents, or my brothers and sisters?'"

Father Joe has heard horror stories from friends and colleagues at other schools. "I just say, Thank God I'm not at a place run by a monsignor, with a bishop and archbishop over him, and the Pope on top of that, and over all of them, God. How do you begin making changes there? Thank God I'm at Choate!"

Choate students feel so at ease about homosexuality that, he said, it is simply not an issue. They're curious, of course, and they ask questions – "When did you first find out you were gay?" "If I get a hard-on when I look at a guy, does that mean I'm gay?" – and he responds as best he can. He is proud that the school has created an atmosphere in which the biggest jock in the school could respond during a visit home to a homophobic comment from his father: "Dad, don't talk like that. At Choate they teach us to respect everyone. Gay men are looking for love, just like you and Mom."

Of course, he noted, Choate is not perfect. There is no gay alumni group there (Andover has one with over 150 people). But the support he has received from the head, the board, and parents for his work on gay and lesbian issues – along with many related social justice projects – has encouraged him, and the dozen or so staff members who are also openly gay. "There's a freedom here," he said. "No one's afraid. At Choate, being gay or lesbian is just not a big deal anymore. And those ten or twelve people who are out are absolutely wonderful human beings. They're free, honest, lovely, and crazy. They love the kids, and the kids love them."

Just as they respect, confide in, and love Father Joe Devlin, S.J.

———————

Private schools are different from public schools in many ways beyond housing arrangements and chaplains, of course. One major difference is what occurs after graduation. Most public school graduates don't particularly care about the place once they leave – they'll attend reunions to see friends, although anecdotal evidence suggests that for many lesbian and gay adults, reunions are the last place they want to be – but private schools are another story. Because so much of their financial support comes from alumni, they nurture school ties forever. Most private schools have administrators whose sole job is to solicit contributions from loyal alums.

Now gay and lesbian graduates are trying to raise something from their private schools in return: awareness.

GALAN – the Gay and Lesbian Alumni Network – began, like so many organizations, as the simultaneous brainchild of several people. Henry Schniewind and a few of his friends from GLSTN (then the Gay and Lesbian School Teachers Network; now the Gay, Lesbian, and Straight Teachers Network) decided that, as a corollary to their efforts, homosexual alumni of private schools should band together. They envisioned a loose group of educators with common backgrounds, getting together to trade tales and network.

Then Sue Phillips got involved, and the focus changed.

Ms. Phillips "prepped" at the all-girls Madeira School in McLean, Virginia. She received her undergraduate degree in women's studies and sociology at Colgate University in New York, and earned a master's of divinity (with a concentration in feminist ethics) from an Episcopal seminary. She moved into the nonprofit sector, doing policy and demographic analysis in rural, low-income housing for the Housing Assistance Council in Washington, D.C. Interested in effecting change in all areas, including lesbian and gay affairs, she leapt at the chance to tackle the nascent GALAN project.

"When I do social justice, it's important that I do it in my own community," she explained. "I come from an upper-class background, so I have access to private schools that a lot of people don't have. It's important to me that I use that access in positive ways, to try to help make things happen that haven't happened before."

In other words, she wants to let private schools know a little bit more about some graduates' private lives, in the hope that life will be easier for every private school student who follows.

Working with Steve Dew, a graduate student at Johns Hopkins University, Sue spent six months surveying private school alumni (the mailing list came from intense networking) and developing a mission statement for GALAN.

"We found that alumni develop a real identity, a real connection, to their schools, gay or straight," she said. "Many people knew they carried some weight as alumni, and they wanted to work with their schools on gay and lesbian issues, but they didn't know how – by writing letters? Coming back to speak? Acting as mentors? So we realized that GALAN would work best as a resource for lesbian and gay alumni to tap into." That's how GALAN functions now: it is an umbrella for people who want to do anything along the lesbian and gay continuum. When lesbian and gay alumni talk, private schools listen, in part because the money they represent is as green as straight folks'.

Responses to the initial mailing were excellent. "People said, 'Wow! I'm so glad this exists! How can I help?'" Ms. Phillips said. Replies came primarily from three areas: Boston, California, and Washington, D.C. A majority were men, not surprising since the original list was overwhelmingly male; what was not expected was that the most enthusiastic respondents were thirty-five or older. "They grew up in a different political point in time, and I think this organization really speaks to a need of theirs," Ms. Phillips said.

Alumni interests vary according to age, however. "Older people are more inclined to want to meet with the headmistress or director of admissions, with the idea of getting them interested in discussing concerns or just learning about the issues. Younger people are into pressuring schools to do more – not confrontationally, but in a proactive way. They're more likely to go back to schools in person, to run workshops or give schoolwide assemblies, and put pressure on for workshops or courses." Younger alumni are also more likely to call themselves "queers" or "dykes," rather than "gays" or "homosexuals," she added.

Although a few alumni have had difficult times when they returned to campus, most report overwhelmingly positive responses. And the visits were positive for administrators, faculty, and students as well as for the gay alumni themselves, as Sue Phillips's own visit illustrates.

"I went back just to say the word 'lesbian' in public," she said, "and succeeded in getting a broad-based discussion going. It didn't go totally smoothly, and not everyone was nice, but it initiated a dialogue that didn't exist before. There was tentativeness on the part of the administration, and angry parental phone calls, but I managed to do workshops, and that was the first time they'd been done there. Nothing changed overnight, but it was an important event in the life of the school."

GALAN has begun work on several different fronts. Members are contacting existing gay, lesbian, and bisexual groups on school campuses, offering whatever assistance they need and GALAN can provide. A mailing prior to the 1994–95 academic year alerted school officials to GALAN's existence, and let heads know that gay and lesbian alumni were willing to help alumni offices, administrations, and counseling services better address the needs of homosexual students and graduates. An advisory board, consisting of alumni, a school counselor, and at least one gay student, was formed to help GALAN with fund-raising.

Future projects include developing a speakers' bureau; collecting bibliographic and curricular resources to share with schools; and organizing a conference for gay, lesbian, and bisexual independent school alumni. Further ahead, Sue hopes GALAN can collect accounts of how alums have worked with their schools, including letters to campus newspapers and alumni publications, anti-homophobia workshops, and informal organizing.

GALAN's mailing list quadrupled in two months and now nears three hundred; it spans eleven states and four decades of independent school attendance. Some alumni remain hesitant – "an overwhelming number were not out when they were in school, and so there's always a bit of worry when we contact someone for the first time," Ms. Phillips said – but many more express delight at joining a network that recognizes them both as private school graduates and as gay people.

"It's wonderful to be able to address those two important aspects of my background," she concluded. "And to be able to effect change at the same time makes me feel really, really proud."

But perhaps she shouldn't be surprised. After all, isn't reaching people and effecting change what education – whether in public school or private – is really all about?

Out in the Wilds
of Montana

Montana abounds with contradictions. It sprawls across the northern U.S., the fourth largest of all fifty states, yet it is one of the least populated. Its forests are filled with Ponderosa pines, its fields with bitterroot, grain, wheat, and barley, its mountains with copper, lead, zinc, silver, and coal. But for all its natural beauty and natural resources, much of the Treasure State has an unnatural look. Entire hillsides have been strip-mined, then abandoned; whole forests have been denuded. Folks in Montana tend to do what they want, when they want to; they ask questions later.

Billings, population 85,000, is the largest city in Montana – the largest, in fact, in the entire vast region between Minneapolis to the east and Spokane to the west, and from Denver in the south to Calgary way up north. It is a professional city, with an economy dominated by the medical and banking industries. Still, it is in many ways a small town. Billings does not take kindly to homosexuals.

That's the view of Doyle Forister, who teaches world history at Skyview High School, one of three public high schools in the city. The son of a man who worked for Pan American World Airways, he claims he's "not from anyplace." But Mr. Forister has lived and worked in Billings ever since 1969, when he left the military, and he has as good a grasp on gay and lesbian issues there as anyone.

Mr. Forister spent most of his life in the closet. "I didn't even accept being gay myself until I was thirty," he said. "I had always been taught that bad persons called 'fairies' molested children. I wasn't interested in children, so that couldn't have been me. And as a kid I was told that little boys do like boys, so I thought it was something I would grow out of."

When he was twenty-six, his wife died, and Doyle realized that life does not always work out the way it should. One day while visiting friends – a couple who were no longer having sexual relations – he got into a playful wrestling match with the husband. It felt great to be physical with a man, Mr. Forister recalled; bit by bit, he recognized he was bisexual. After having "a phenomenal set of experiences" in the early 1980s, he realized he was not bisexual, but gay.

Mr. Forister, an avid traveler, was in California in 1988 when the *San Francisco Examiner* ran a series of stories on being gay in America. He read the statistics on teenage suicide and was incensed; he had been a teacher for twenty years, but had never heard or read anything about that at all.

A year later, on the first day of school, the Billings school board chairman gave his annual districtwide address. He noted that the problems heading into the 1990s were vastly different from those of the fifties – suicide, guns, dysfunctional families, teenage pregnancy, as opposed to gum chewing, tardiness, running in the halls, and forgetting gym clothes – and added that education is not working. He pleaded for every educator's help.

Mr. Forister had been brooding over the suicide statistics for a year. He screwed up his courage, went in, and told his principal he was gay. He presented the statistics on teen suicide, and asked whether what he had just heard from the chairman was all rhetoric, or if the district was indeed willing to do something.

The principal replied that there were no gays in Montana: "Out here we have cowboys and truckers." Mr. Forister's response was "Please. I've danced with those cowboys and truckers." But the principal passed Mr. Forister's request on to the district superintendent, who met with both of them.

At that meeting, Mr. Forister had a lot to say. He reminded the administrators of an incident from a couple of years before, when he had caught a student cheating, then lying about it. If the boy were to fail the course, he would have been ineligible for athletics. His father demanded a transfer out of the class and a clean slate; otherwise, he said, he would continue to pass along the rumor his son was already spreading: Mr. Forister was gay. "The principal went along with the transfer, and that was that," the history teacher said.

A similar incident, Doyle noted at the meeting, happened to a friend in Great Falls, 220 miles to the northwest. However, in that case the man asphyxiated himself. "I was angry about that, and I was angry about the statistics on kids killing themselves too," Mr. Forister said. "No one deserves to have that happen to him."

Nothing came directly out of that meeting, but a year later the superintendent asked Mr. Forister, "How do you teach kids to be homosexual?" "You don't," the Skyview teacher replied. "You either are or you aren't. The issue isn't teaching how to be gay or straight; the issue is dealing with the staff. Every staff member needs to know everyone is different; everyone has flaws and attributes, but I don't think we are dealing very well with that at all." Mr. Forister used the analogy of a blind student he'd known. "A teacher once said about her, 'She's lucky. She knows what her disability is.' Well, all of us have disabilities; the difference is that most of us don't know what ours are."

About that time, Mr. Forister heard that the National Education Association (NEA) was running a training program to help teachers counsel gay, lesbian, bisexual, and questioning students. "I asked how to get Montana involved," he said. "They were happy to have us, but there was one catch: there had to be two people from the state. I phoned all over Montana trying to find someone else. I called the NEA and the AFT (the American Federation of Teachers, a rival union). The AFT asked someone to go. He said, 'They'll know I'm gay.' The AFT said, 'But you are. Kids yell, "Fag," when you walk down the hall. This will be good for you.' He decided not to go.

Finally Mr. Forister found Mac Swan, a straight teacher from the northern part of the state – four hundred miles away – who was interested. In 1992 the two traveled together to Washington, D.C., for the "Affording Equal Opportunity to Gay and Lesbian Students through Teaching and Counseling" workshop. It was an inspiring weekend, and when he came back, Mr. Forister wanted to start something locally. He addressed a districtwide meeting of guidance counselors from Billings's Yellowstone County. About fifty people, representing all levels, attended. One or two, with strong religious-right inclinations, walked out; others went home and called their churches, inciting a barrage of phone calls to the superintendent. "This was so much easier when just you and I knew," the superintendent told Mr. Forister. Doyle replied, "I spent forty years by myself. I'm not going to do that again."

To appease the fundamentalists, the superintendent invited a doctor to address the staff. The man said that the average gay male has five hundred sexual contacts in his life and dies at forty-two; he also claimed that there were very few gays in Montana. "It was all slander and lies – no facts," Doyle said. "I wrote him up for spewing religious dogma as medical fact." The case is under review, he said, by the state board of medical advisers.

Stymied by the district in his quest to speak about homosexuality, Mr. Forister turned to nearby Rocky Mountain College. He asked about the possibility of teaching a night course on sexual diversity and homophobia, and followed up with the state office of curriculum instruction. They offered to give in-service credit to teachers for the course. However, the superintendent warned Mr. Forister that no one would get "step-up credit" (leading toward higher pay) for taking it. "That's the first time I ever heard of people not getting credit for learning something that would help them become better teachers," the instructor said dryly. Though the district did not publicize the course, as it usually does with teacher education offerings, six counselors and teachers enrolled.

Mr. Forister received a letter from Eastern Montana College, asking him to be a presenter at a "Children at Risk" conference in the spring of 1993. He warned them that the district opposed his speaking, but signed on. "There were 125 people at my session," Mr. Forister said proudly. "Nobody was forced into it. It was the most heavily attended session of all. I was told it was the first choice of everyone who attended."

At the conference he was approached by a television reporter.

"I talked about children being at risk, and said that everyone has the right to know they're not alone, no matter what their sexual orientation is. I did not discuss my own sexuality at all." The night the report aired, however, the news anchor made a presumption about Mr. Forister, and in introducing the interview announced that the station's reporter had spoken to a local teacher who is gay.

If that had happened five or six years earlier, Doyle said, he probably would have used up all his sick leave remaining home for the rest of the year. He would have felt emotionally unable to walk into the building again. Yet although he had been coming out more and more in school, and was feeling more secure about himself than he had at any previous time in his twenty years at Skyview, the television report — broadcast all over the eastern half of the state, and northern Wyoming — still stunned him.

The phone calls to the superintendent and principal began immediately. "He admitted he's a fag; fire him!" many said. The superintendent assumed Mr. Forister had outed himself. The television reporter, mortified, sent letters of apology to Mr. Forister and the school district, but the damage had been done.

However, Mr. Forister said, he was able to find some good in the controversy. "What's the worst anyone could threaten me with after that?" he asked rhetorically. "That they'll tell the superintendent I'm gay?!"

The incident spurred him to further activism. In the spring he planned to a trip to Washington, D.C., to coincide with the march for gay, lesbian, and bisexual rights. As a world history teacher, he welcomed the chance to visit the show on Renaissance history at the Library of Congress, and to attend the opening of the Holocaust Museum. At the same time, a colleague was headed to the nation's capital on another program. "The district paid for his substitute," Mr. Forister said. "I sent a check to cover the cost of my substitute. Still, at first they told me I couldn't go, and the superintendent told me I was obsessed with this. Ultimately they docked me three full days' pay for going to Washington, yet meanwhile they gave my colleague all sorts of leads for his own trip. I was punished, just because I went to Washington the weekend of the march."

Doyle Forister denies an obsession with the gay issue; he is, however, far more open at Skyview than ever before. He wears a gold earring to class; he is open about his sexuality in discussions with adults, and although he said he does not talk about being gay much with students – he has not come out to them – he will answer any questions "clinically."

He pointed to the NEA workshop as a turning point in his life, professionally and personally. "I know they've helped a lot of people, and in my case it gave me all the ammunition and clarity I needed to confront people. It's been a blessing, because it allowed me to confront stereotypes, my own as well as others'. I've always studied the Bible, and this gave me a lot of information I never had access to." The workshop was also exciting because it drew together educators of all areas and backgrounds. They heard speakers from scientific perspectives, as well as lesbian and gay teenagers, and straight students with homosexual parents.

It was important for him, too, because it occurred at a time Mr. Forister was still coming to terms with accepting his sexuality in an open setting. One attendee from a fundamentalist background told the group, "What you people are doing is wrong, but we're here to help kids." He did not necessarily like that comment, but he felt free to discuss it at length. "No one was put down, or put anyone else down," Mr. Forister said. "Everyone was treated professionally. It gave us a broad perspective, and plenty of energy."

After returning from Washington, conducting his Yellowstone County workshop, and instructing his college course, Mr. Forister joined the fledgling Billings Human Rights Network. He led a session at the state human rights convention in Great Falls. And he has had some interesting discussions with his principal.

"He really is a gem of a man," Mr. Forister said. "He disagrees with homosexuality as a lifestyle, but he also disagrees with other teachers about abortion and birth control. And he emphasizes that we're in school not to meet my needs, but the needs of the kids. He's told me he admires the way I separate my personal and professional lives."

The fall after the Washington trip, Mr. Forister's principal asked about his "agenda" for the upcoming school year. "I told him I wasn't pushing any particular platform," Mr. Forister said. "But I also said I was going to be free to talk about Alexander the Great or Peter the Great, or anyone else with my orientation. I said that just being there, in school and open, is a major accomplishment." And then, a few days later, Mr. Forister marched a boy down to the principal's office for using the word "faggot," just as he'd promised he would.

———————

Just as interesting as Doyle Forister's story is that of Malcolm (Mac) Swan, the Polson High School teacher who Mr. Forister finally found, after a long and difficult search, to join him as the second Montana teacher to attend the NEA's Washington conference on working with gay and lesbian students.

Mr. Swan would certainly not top the list of teachers expected to travel to such an event. A straight man, he teaches English and language arts in a 450-student high school on Flathead Lake, fifty miles from Kalispell and four hundred miles from Billings. About 20 percent of the youngsters live on a Native American (Salish and Kootenai) reservation. "There's an enormous amount of deep-seated racial tension around here," Mr. Swan explained. "It's a really conservative area, with a big Christian Coalition element. There's a lot of euphemisms, but it's really anti-Indian. Because of all that, things are ripe for homophobic rhetoric initiated by right-wing Christian extremists. Things are fairly polarized along race lines, and homophobia just throws a real nice froth onto the boiling pot." Mr. Swan, a native of western Montana, added that there are no openly gay students or teachers at Polson High.

However, when Mr. Forister called – he'd gotten Mr. Swan's name from a mutual acquaintance, a straight female attorney who'd moved from Polson to Billings – and said that funding was available to go to Washington, Mr. Swan asked for more details. "She thought we'd make a good match," he said of his lawyer friend. "She was right."

Mr. Swan belies the image of the typical Polson resident he's just drawn. "When Doyle called and asked me to go, I'd already had experiences that had led me to think about things," he said. "I had a roommate in college one year who was gay. I never knew, but I found out later. He died of lymphoma, and I'm pretty sure it was AIDS. Plus, my wife and I have people we like in our lives who are homosexual. So I went."

The workshop came up quickly, on a tight deadline. To avoid problems with his superintendent, Mr. Swan said he couched the title in much more covert language. He used euphemisms, to make it sound more innocuous. He had no idea what would have happened if he had applied for professional leave for a workshop that had "gay and lesbian" in the title, and no desire to find out. So he used buzzwords like "human rights" and "gender equity." His trip was approved.

After he returned, he said, "the superintendent received notification from the NEA that I had completed this training, and of course the words were much more direct. My sources told me he held up the letter like a dirty diaper, between two fingers, and dropped it in the waste-basket." The superintendent has never spoken directly to Mr. Swan about the conference, even though the teacher has since presented workshops on homophobia in western Montana. "It's not like I've been quiet," Mr. Swan noted. "I don't know whether he can actually say the word 'homosexual.' He is, let's say, real religious and conservative."

For Mr. Swan, the most important part of the weekend was listening to gay people raising children talk personally about their difficulties. He connected with the common problems and joys of parenthood. He knew it is a tough job to begin with; what he had not realized was how difficult the stigma of homosexuality makes it for gay men and women. His compassion deepened.

He also appreciated receiving factual information on sexuality. He had considered himself widely read, and liberal in his experience, but when he heard about such things as hermaphrodites and the conflict-ing causation theories of homosexuality, he was struck by his own ignorance.

He found the diversity of attendees interesting. He never learned the percentage of straight and gay people at the conference, but that did not matter; he felt excited to be part of the mix. He learned a great deal just from being around so many different people – folks he seldom has a chance to meet in Montana.

Upon returning to Polson, he felt an obligation to run workshops. He spoke to the counseling staff for grades five through twelve. "Their reaction was 'This is a huge, terrible problem and we need to do more – but it will be very, very tough to do,'" he reported. "Remember, this is an area under attack from the Christian right. They already censored Pumsy the Dragon (a self-esteem program for children), and this is a lot deeper than that. The guidance people are right: they do have a lot to do, and they will help the kids who come to them, but to take a political stand on this issue around here right now would be suicide. Triage works best."

Still, Mr. Swan made a presentation with Mr. Forister in Great Falls, midway between their two schools, and a statewide NEA newsletter announced that he'd been trained to present gay, lesbian, and bisexual workshops.

That prompted, he said, "zero responses. Absolutely none. That tells me there's lots of people in the same situation I'm in. They're in areas that have real conservative agendas."

Yet, he said, he knows there are people in Montana who are discussing the issues, and are concerned about them. "After the Great Falls workshop, someone real interested and motivated came up to me. She said what I'd done was great, and she talked about my coming to Helena to do something. I gave her my name, and never heard back. My guess, and it's only a guess, is that she went back to Helena, and people told her she was crazy. I can easily visualize that happening."

Mr. Swan is unsure what's ahead for lesbian and gay education issues in Montana. "I really don't know where we're going," he admitted. "On a personal level, for me, I've got a lot more knowledge now, and I can create a climate in class that's a lot more accepting – no more homophobic comments, things like that.

"I've gone directly to the superintendent and principal, and told them I've been trained. They say, Yeah, we'll put you on the agenda – but I've been moved back twice now, and never had a chance to share this information with the rest of the staff. It's a very conservative community, and teachers are members of this community. There are plenty of people here who feel homosexuality is a choice, an abnormality, an aberration."

But Mr. Swan also sees signs of hope. He believes Montana is trying to be progressive. At a human rights conference in Great Falls he saw a PFLAG-type organization; the next weekend they appeared at a community fair not far from Polson. He called that a positive sign. "It's very slowly becoming part of the dialogue. The first step is saying the word 'homosexuality.' After that, anything could be possible. I think we're slowly seeing people pulling the blinders off their eyes."

Still, Mr. Swan knows that Montana is not San Francisco, Los Angeles, or New York. And although he has not heard any direct criticism of his trip to Washington and subsequent commitment to anti-homophobia education, he knows it lurks out there. "I think the fact that I have a wife and two kids deflects some of the comments," he said. "I'm pretty sure there would be some talk about me if I was a single guy. Folks are pretty quick to judge others around here. There's still a frontier mentality in Montana: shoot first, and ask questions later."

Even if you have no idea why you're aiming at a particular target.

NEBRASKA

Open Hearts in the Heartland

Smack in the center of the country lies Nebraska. It's flat. It's best known for growing grain, and raising cattle and hogs. It's gay.

A comedian once joked that the reason there are no homosexuals in the Midwest is because when God created the world, He looked down on the United States and commanded, "You people – get to the sides!" But, of course, all gays and lesbians do not huddle together on the East or West Coast; they inhabit every city, town, and village in America. Many gays prefer the friendliness of an Omaha to the falseness of a Los Angeles, or the easygoing rhythms of life in a Grand Island to the hectic lifestyle of a commuter in Hackensack. Some flee their small, constricting hometowns as soon as they can, lusting for life in the gay ghettoes of Greenwich Village or the Castro – but a good number eventually return to their roots, seeking the familiar sights, sounds, and smells of the land they once could barely wait to leave.

Homosexuals live in Nebraska, as they do in every state in the union, and many live there by choice. But that doesn't mean it's easy to grow up gay there.

One woman with a good perspective on lesbian and gay teenagers is D. Moritz. In her 25-year career as a public school counselor in Omaha she's met plenty of them; as an educator with a special interest in gay and lesbian issues, she's traveled throughout the state and heard many more stories about them.

Ms. Moritz is proud of her state. "It's a good place," she said with feeling. "There's lots of set values. There's a whole gamut of churches, synagogues, and good schools, particularly in the big cities like

Omaha and Lincoln. There are lots of entertainment choices." And there are boys and girls grappling with difficult questions of sexual orientation. For them, obtaining accurate, helpful information is a major concern. "From what I've seen, only in the last five years has the gay community been visible, with singing groups, choruses, plays, and entertainment," Ms. Moritz said. "Only in the last five years have adolescents been able to see healthy role models. Even healthy publications haven't been available until the last five years. And as you move out of the big cities, it's even harder finding people in the state with helpful information or resources."

It is only within the past five years, too, that Ms. Moritz has heard requests from lesbian and gay students for a school service to address their needs – but those requests have come through loud and clear. Students began asking, "What do I do? I'm sitting in the cafeteria and kids are calling me names. How do I talk to my parents about this? Are there any organizations I can join?"

To answer those questions, she and a colleague organized a support group. It is not just a social setting, she emphasized; it's educational too. Like any other support group, members talk about special concerns. Discussions include family problems, current events, and the gay culture (it affords many students their first opportunity to learn that the gay world actually has a history), but the talk often veers back to survival techniques. Someone asks, "What should I do when somebody yells, 'Hey, queer!'?" The group debates whether the student should report the harassment, and, if so, what are the consequences?

Ms. Moritz and her co-facilitator also show videotapes, and bring in guest speakers to serve as role models. She sees her job as providing positive, healthy information, to boost students' self-esteem. She wants them to know that they can grow up to be whoever and whatever they want to be.

She relates stunning success stories. One girl identified herself as a lesbian in eighth grade; entering high school very despondent, with nonsupportive parents, she talked about dropping out, even committing suicide. Other students told her it was safe to talk with Ms. Moritz; the girl soon joined the support group, and eventually brought her mother to meet the counselor.

Ms. Moritz spent ninety minutes with her that first time. She gave the mother resources – books, information on PFLAG (Parents, Families and Friends of Lesbians and Gays). That grew into a solid, three-year relationship with both the girl and her mother. The three talked in school, and at the student's home. The mother became active

D. Moritz *(left)* is a public school counselor in Omaha, with a special interest in gay and lesbian issues. Lois Hansen *(right)* began teaching high school students about homosexuality in 1969, in psychology classes at Lincoln East High.

in PFLAG; the girl ended up graduating early – and now works in a nursing home, taking care of Ms. Moritz's own mother. "She's just blossomed," the educator reported. "She always knew who she was. She just didn't know how to express herself."

A young man spent three months gathering information from D. Moritz for his "cousin." The counselor told him the same three things she says to every youngster: it doesn't matter if you are gay; it doesn't matter if you aren't; it doesn't matter if you don't know. She repeated it often – she's learned the importance of patience – and eventually, of course, he said, "It's not for my cousin. It's for me." He told his mother, who said how proud she was that he admitted the truth. He's since graduated, but while he was in school he became an advocate for himself, for gay rights, and for all human rights.

Some students have gained the courage to serve on panels, recounting their stories at colleges and in front of other groups, which heightens their self-worth. Ms. Moritz gains particular pleasure from watching these students grow into "teachers" themselves.

Every staff member knows about the support group. However, the time and location are not announced; those are obtainable only through the school counselors, in order to protect privacy and weed out curiosity-seekers. The group meets irregularly – sometimes once a week, sometimes once a month – as determined by the participants.

While Ms. Moritz is proud that the group has affected the lives of its members, she recognizes it does not reach everyone it should. "As we all know, there are tons and tons of kids who lack the confidence even to come to a group like this," she said. "And unfortunately, this is happening only in a place like Omaha. I've gone into western Nebraska to do workshops for teachers and counselors, and it's a different story out there."

However, that situation is changing. After years of confronting blank faces in her audiences, she now hears feedback — sometimes weeks, even months later. No matter; the calls and letters come from people seeking help. "They're suddenly realizing now that they *do* have gay and lesbian students in their schools, and they *need* information and resources," she said. "Until recently, they never even realized that."

Ms. Moritz feels that the surge in national publicity about homosexual issues has helped. "I think a lot of Nebraska kids never even saw the words 'gay,' 'lesbian,' or 'bisexual' in a newspaper before the last couple of years. Now they're seeing them, hearing them, and they're able to ask for help. I think that's kind of great."

Another Nebraska educator who recognized that students needed to know more about such issues is Lois Hansen — but her reach extended beyond lesbian and gay youngsters. Mrs. Hansen taught psychology and English for twenty-two years at Lincoln East High, an upper-middle-class school in the state capital's suburbs. She did not begin teaching until after the oldest of her four children started college, but that did not stop her from addressing one of the most potent subjects around.

It was 1969, and the sixties had had a big impact — even in Nebraska. Individual teachers were discussing sex, mainly in health classes, but little was organized. Mrs. Hansen knew the students in her psychology classes needed a unit on sexuality. "They have more interest in psychosexual development than just about any other subject in school, so I figured we ought to talk about it. This is information they absolutely want to know, and need to know. It's so important to talk about those issues that are so important in everyone's lives."

She structured her psychology class so that students spent one or two days bringing in speakers or films, or working on other activities of their own choice. This enabled youngsters interested in homosexuality to search for resources on their own — in the context of a classroom project. She soon began to see that that brief time span was inadequate; however, she found no information available in high school textbooks to supplement what her students were doing. So, bit by bit, she developed an entire unit on sexuality.

The unit examined the biological changes associated with adolescence, but the bulk of the time was spent on social ramifications, from a psychological perspective. However, she still had trouble unearthing information on homosexuality. Eventually she found a college text. Using that as a base, she broadened the discussions to include the consequences on personal development when people do things they feel good, and badly, about. Discussions swirled around behavioral choices.

Soon her classes spent four or five days on homosexuality. The unit came near the end of the semester, after students had developed a level of trust with their teacher. They had to know how she operated before they grew comfortable talking about such serious issues.

Lois Hansen broached the topic by asking students how they felt when their point of view about something differed from their friends'. "This had nothing to do with sexuality," she noted. "But it took the whole period to go around the room with everybody, and it was very revealing. I never set it up saying 'felt bad,' but more than ninety percent of the time people talked about feeling bad, not good, because they were different. Most of the comments were about being new to a school, or divorce; sometimes it was not having the same clothes as everyone else." The comments almost never concerned sexuality, although Mrs. Hansen is certain some of them thought about that.

Next, the teacher introduced same-sex attraction as a difference. Students brainstormed words involving homosexuality, and discussed whether those terms were positive, negative, or neutral; that led to more discussion about feelings in general. "One of my major agendas was not to teach the words themselves, but to sensitize the kids that most of the common insults around school have to do with sexual orientation – and that those insults are hurtful to 10 percent of the kids," she said. Then the class listed facts they knew about homosexuality – mighty few, according to Mrs. Hansen. "They had a high level of interest, and a low level of knowledge."

The rest of the unit was filled with speakers from the gay and lesbian community, handouts, and audiovisuals (including a filmstrip, *An Invisible Minority,* made by the Unitarian Church in 1969, when, she said, almost nothing else was available).

Initially, the students reacted either with antagonism, ignorance, or fear. By the end of the unit, after hearing the speakers, the students saw that homosexuals are just people. They realized they could ask questions, and get answers. She saw plenty of changed attitudes.

The unit proceeded without fanfare until the mid-1970s, when Mrs. Hansen began to hear complaints from religious Christians. She started sending letters home to parents prior to the first day; signed by the teacher and principal, they explained the unit's purpose. She never received more than three or four calls a year – out of up to a hundred sets of parents – asking that a son or daughter be excused.

But she gained a certain notoriety when other people without children in her classes joined together to paint her as a villain. Some wrote letters to the newspaper, demanding access to her classroom because she was "debauching children." During that period, she said, her principal was wonderful. He made decisions based on what was best for students, not on which person yelled the loudest.

The superintendent of schools was also fair, she said, but the associate superintendent for curriculum was nervous about homosexuality. The two administrators visited her every semester, for two or three years. Each time they met with her principal; each time they asked her to stop inviting a gay person into her classroom. Before the first visit Mrs. Hansen called her state association lawyer. He advised her not to say yes or no, but that if she was ordered to stop, to do so immediately – and start thinking about academic freedom issues. The order never came, and eventually the superintendent quit coming. The associate superintendent and Mrs. Hansen continued to spar, but eventually became¡ good friends. When he left Lincoln for a job in Madison, Wisconsin, he told his former antagonist that he had learned things from her that probably would be helpful in his new, liberal community.

But before he went, the associate superintendent did tell Mrs. Hansen to bring in a speaker who would say that homosexuality is a sin. She resented that, and worried about its impact – but, she said, "It worked out better than I ever expected it to. A few kids liked what he said, but most of them hated it. Kids don't like being lectured to. They did like hearing the gay speakers talk about the lives of gay folks in a nonjudgmental, nonoffensive way. And of course an enormous majority of the kids understood the religious speaker to be a violation of church and state separation, which led to a lot of good discussion too." On balance, Ms. Hansen said, "a lot of good came out of the religious speaker – except I had to sit there and listen to it!"

The students came to enjoy the controversies that occasionally erupted in the newspaper's letters-to-the-editor column, but to protect herself and the integrity of the class Mrs. Hansen began videotaping the presentations of each gay or lesbian speaker. When the associate superintendent convened a special districtwide curriculum committee of teachers, administrators, and parents to examine the unit ("That committee never met before or after to look at any other curriculum," she noted wryly), they examined the tapes. Two committee members voted that the speakers were inappropriate for students; the other twelve committee members deemed them entirely appropriate.

Another time a student's mother tried to turn public opinion against Mrs. Hansen. Only one other mother signed on, but the school's parent advisory group – which, the teacher said, had supported her all along

– agreed to view the videotapes with the two women. "We looked at them, argued with each other, went home, and that was that," she said. "Fortunately this wasn't very fertile ground for getting a vendetta going based on prejudice."

Commotion swelled once more when the minister of "a large, Bible-thumping church" preached against Mrs. Hansen from the pulpit. She had never talked to him; the student he got his information from was never even in her class. But then a youngster who *was* in her class let the minister know what was true and what was not, and that was the end of that.

After each sexuality unit, Mrs. Hansen asked students for anonymous feedback. Many reported it was the most valuable thing they'd done in the class; some said it was the most valuable thing they'd ever done in school. Virtually all told her to keep doing it.

In the middle of everything, Mrs. Hansen learned that her youngest son – who back in junior high had written an extensive report on homosexuality – was gay. She did not talk about it in school because too much controversy was already raging, and she did not want to confuse the issue. But on her roster of classroom speakers at the time was a gay man who had married a woman and had children, and had strong religious feelings that homosexuality was not acceptable. "He was open enough with the students that they understood he was a person who made a life choice based not on his most natural feelings," Mrs. Hansen said carefully. "He was much better as a religious speaker than the ministers, because he didn't bash people."

The man invited Mrs. Hansen to breakfast, where he demanded to know how, as the mother of a gay child, she could objectively teach a unit on homosexuality. "He thought he was dropping a bombshell, that this would blackmail me," she said. "But I just looked at him and said that I don't want my heterosexual children – or anyone else – to be bigots, and that I thought education was the most important way of going about it. So that was the end of that."

Mrs. Hansen retired from teaching recently, but continues to be active in education. She now works on staff development for the Lincoln public schools. Her project should come as no surprise: she is teaching teachers how to teach lesbian and gay issues.

Of course, most Nebraskans live in places far smaller than Omaha (population: 335,000) or Lincoln (191,000). Some live in communities like Grand Island, a farming town of 40,000 in the southeastern part of the state. Many Grand Islanders have German backgrounds; many also believe, said Nita Lechner Danklesen, that "we just don't have any gay or lesbian people here." And then she chuckled, an ironic laugh. Ms. Danklesen's brother was diagnosed with AIDS in 1983, early in the epidemic; however, she knew he was gay long before that. Her first reaction to his homosexuality was, "How could this person who is so cool and loving go to hell?" However, she began reading about homosexuality, and when he grew ill she became active in AIDS issues around the state.

Since 1984 she has been an AIDS educator throughout Nebraska, and has talked about gay and lesbian issues in her physical education and health classroom at Walnut Middle School. She observes all the precautions – sending slips of paper home with students, letting parents know that if they or their children object to explicit talks they can be excused – but very few students have opted out.

In 1993, as the March on Washington neared, three parents called the principal. They said that Ms. Danklesen was promoting homosexuality ("I wouldn't even know how to do that!" she protested). They claimed too that she was out of line inviting a gay man with AIDS to talk to her classes ("It would have been okay if he was an IV drug user," she said). However, her principal stood behind her. "She's very open to having kids educated. I'm very fortunate, in that respect," Ms. Danklesen said.

The speaker, Jerry Murphy, received his AIDS diagnosis in December 1992, one day before his partner died of AIDS. Ironically, Mr. Murphy's job was giving in-home care to AIDS patients. He had served eleven different patients, in California and Arizona, before he found out he himself was infected. After the twin blows he decided to move back to Grand Island, his boyhood home.

"Nita heard I was willing to speak about AIDS to kids," he said. "We had coffee, we hit it off, and so I went to her junior high. I spent the whole day there, talking to six P.E. classes."

Jerry had spoken to college groups before, but found the junior high boys and girls much more receptive. He told them there was no such thing as a stupid question, that they could ask him anything. They did, and he answered right back. Because he recognized that many students might be afraid to ask things in front of their peers that they truly wanted and needed to know, he passed out paper and pencils.

"You know how parents are – they hem and haw around issues, especially sexuality issues," Mr. Murphy said. "Well, this was one of the first times an adult was open and candid with these kids, and they really responded."

The youngsters wanted to know what it was like to be sick, and what it was like to be dying ("I told them we're all dying – I just know what's going to cause my death," he said). They were very curious about his friends, the gay lifestyle, how he had been treated when he was their age, and what it was like to be teased in school.

"You get preconceived notions of gay people hanging out in dark bars. A lot of people think being gay is just about sex," Jerry admitted. "But of course it's a lot more than that. It's who you're attracted to, not what you do. I'm not an effeminate person. I'm a masculine male. Being gay is a combination of what I was born with and what I've been exposed to; that's my personal opinion, and I let the kids know it. I just tried to be honest and open with them all day."

The students responded well. "Several walked up to me afterward," he recounted. "I knew they were going through exactly what I went through at their age. It was such a relief for them to know they're okay, that they're not bad people, and to find out that other gay people have morals and values just like them."

One boy told Mr. Murphy that he thought it was okay to be gay. "It looked to me like he was dealing with the issue right then," the speaker said. "There are a lot more kids out there dealing with this than we realize."

When those youngsters came up to him he smiled, and tried to be there for them. He did not know what profound words to say that would make things easier. It's not easy being gay, and he told them that. But the second part of his message sank in too: gay people can be active, positive members of their communities.

One parent was upset that Nita Danklesen and Jerry Murphy did not stress abstinence. The call was fielded by a male phys. ed. teacher, who defended Mr. Murphy's presentation – and that was a victory in itself. Described by Ms. Danklesen as "a football coach – you know the type," he was formerly extremely homophobic. But he was so taken by Mr. Murphy's words that he called his college-age son, and brought him in that afternoon to hear the talk.

"That teacher is really compassionate now," Ms. Danklesen added. "He says, 'I really don't understand all this, but I do understand that they're people too.' He's completely flip-flopped, and I think education has been the key."

The day took a lot out of Mr. Murphy, but he was buoyed by the responses – which continued long after he left the school. He still sees the youngsters around town. They remain supportive, always stopping what they're doing to walk over and ask how he feels.

He hopes to address more classes. "I really want to do this," he emphasized. "I figure it's all I can do at this point — to help not only younger gays, but anyone thinking of becoming sexually active. I don't want anyone to end up in my shoes. And I want to be a positive role model too — to let younger gays know they can stand up and be proud of who they are, whoever they are."

After Jerry's talk, Nita surveyed everyone who heard him — all eight hundred students. "It was a pretty explicit survey," she said. "When I asked, 'What did you learn about gay people?' maybe six put, 'It's gross.' Most of them wrote things like, 'They're people too,' 'They have feelings,' 'They don't deserve names.' Several of the kids said they knew gay people. They're junior high kids, and you know how open they are — they say whatever's on their minds. So I really think they were helped by this."

Ms. Danklesen is, obviously, a firm believer in education. "I don't tolerate any name-calling," she said. "When I hear the word 'fag,' I stop the class and ask, 'What is it that causes you to have a problem?'" At Walnut Middle School she has become recognized as a teacher students feel free to seek out. "At least they know I'll be sympathetic," she said. "I'm known as someone who will stand up for those who can't stand up for themselves." For that, she said, "I'm so grateful to my brother. I went from the point of praying he'd change, to standing up with him in the gay community." She also works with AIDS patients as an agency counselor, and has earned a degree in massage therapy in order to work with people with AIDS.

But Nita Danklesen does not confine her activism to her school and the gay community. She has taken the issue of homosexuality into her own children's sixth-grade classrooms, bringing in the book *One Teenager in Ten* and other materials. She has never had negative feedback. "I believe the younger our kids start hearing about this, the less homophobic and prejudiced they'll be, and the more understanding and open. They're going to get this information somewhere; the question is whether what they'll hear will be valid and true, or rumors and false innuendoes."

While admitting that all is not perfect in Grand Island — "If people around here found out a teacher was gay, all hell would break loose. We're out in the country, and pretty far behind. It's not like Omaha and Lincoln, where they've got support groups for kids" — she is certain that "addressing the myths and the stereotypes has helped so much. My belief is, God didn't screw up; He had a plan. So I take that angle, but in a nonthreatening way: What if...? Maybe...? It's all food for thought.

"I believe in education," she concluded. "It's out of fear and ignorance that people have problems. If I can address your inner fear, and say it's okay to have that fear, that you're not a bad person, I think people will become way more compassionate. And schools are where you hit the most number of people to make that happen."

Many Nebraska communities make even Grand Island look like a teeming metropolis. Take Holdrege, a small farming town of 5,000 souls in the south-central part of the state, thirty miles north of Kansas. Kathy Tschabrun was born in Holdrege, and though she grew up in a nearby town, they were similar places: very sheltered. She feels she was not exposed to the real world. But two years after her daughter Dawn graduated from college, Mrs. Tschabrun asked her whether she was gay. That day, her sheltered life came to an end.

"Holdrege is a very, very closed town," she said. "It's what you would call a fundamentalist community – very judgmental." Just how judgmental became obvious a year and a half after Mrs. Tschabrun and Dawn talked.

She decided to tell the people she was directly involved with at the local hospital, where she works as director of materials management. "It was essentially selfish, because I wanted to protect me and not hear things behind my back. But it's one thing to *say* you're supportive of me, and another to *act* supportive." Most colleagues failed to act supportively; even the director of surgery ranted and raved one day about a lesbian couple, who happen to be her neighbors.

When Dawn and her partner come home to Holdrege and visit Mrs. Tschabrun at work, she said, "A lot of people can't handle it. You really find out who your friends are when you divulge that your child is gay – or different in any way, really. A lot of our friends have fallen by the wayside. Our true friends are still with us, but it's been painful."

Kathy Tschabrun belongs to the Episcopal Church, and she interprets the liturgy as saying, "Love your gay neighbor as yourself." "When I was in church I seriously thought about this," she said. "I thought there are not a whole lot of parents willing to talk about their gay children to others. I can't say the path I've chosen has not been painful, and it has not been painless for my daughter, but I realized there was a great need to speak out. I felt I had betrayed Dawn by not being there for her when she was younger – I was raised in my church, my school, and my community to feel that homosexuality was wrong, although I couldn't tell you why. I wrestled with God and myself, and finally I realized no one has to know the reason. I didn't choose my sexuality, and neither did Dawn."

The more Mrs. Tschabrun anguished, the more she realized she needed to go into schools to talk about her daughter and homosexuality. Then she met Jean Durgand-Clinchard, a PFLAG (Parents, Families and Friends of Lesbians and Gays) speaker, and the two women spoke together on a college panel. Ms. Tschabrun recalls it as the most uplifting thing she had ever done:

Since that day, in conjunction with PFLAG, she has helped run fifty sessions, each lasting two to three hours, for professionals needing to renew their certifications. She has spoken to teachers, guidance counselors, and school nurses, along with businesses and other groups. Some attendees are very positive. Others, she realizes, are there because they have to be; they're the ones with their arms folded across their chests.

Few, however, leave unaffected.

In Minden, a small town east of Holdrege, a man kept staring at the photos of Dawn and her partner that Mrs. Tschabrun had placed on the table. After her talk he shook her hand, and told her he'd had Dawn in his English class when she was seventeen. "I never knew," he said.

"She and all the others are very good at hiding their pain, because they have no one to talk to," Mrs. Tschabrun replied. "There's no one in school who wouldn't be nonjudgmental, or wouldn't make fun of them." The man had tears in his eyes.

In Kearney she noticed a young man having difficulty listening to her. Afterward, he came up and enveloped her in a big hug. "I'm so glad you said what you did," he told her.

"I don't know how many people we touch," she said later, "but until you see their expressions you don't realize how difficult it is to be a gay individual, or the parent of one."

Her most difficult talk was in her hometown of Holdrege. "I was so frightened," she admitted. "I expected to come out and see my car egged. I did the talk with a gay man from Bertrand, about fifteen miles away. He had relatives in the audience, and we agreed it was probably the poorest one we did – but also one of the best, because we were both so in touch with our feelings."

One of Mrs. Kathy's fears was that the school nurse, a good friend, might be there – and she was. Mrs. Tschabrun had no idea how she would react, but during a break after telling her story, she felt an arm around her waist. With tears rolling down her face, the nurse said, "Kathy, this must be very difficult for you."

"This was a joy," Mrs. Tschabrun replied. "Getting here was the hard part."

She spoke at a high school 150 miles east of Holdrege, with a woman who believes her son is gay. "As soon as we walked in we were placed in the library," she reported. "Out of sight, out of mind! And I think the teachers were trying to ascertain if we both were gay ourselves."

The invitation came through the persistence of a high school senior, who kept calling Mrs. Tschabrun. The speaker told the girl her principal had to okay it; finally he did. Most of the attendees were seniors. The boys giggled and acted immaturely, so Mrs. Tschabrun set them down in their chairs and told them it was not a laughing matter. The girls asked many good questions, such as what causes homosexuality, and how to react if a friend is gay.

The superintendent and principal both sat onstage while Mrs. Tschabrun and the other woman talked. Neither administrator said a word, and when it was over neither shook the speakers' hands. Later the women had lunch with the girl who arranged the talk. Mrs. Tschabrun commended her for being so persistent.

The Holdrege mother's effectiveness is measured by the repeated calls to return to the same schools. She also appreciates the anonymous evaluations that participants fill out, which are invariably very positive. Professional educators write that they never realized the pain young people go through, and how hard it must feel to be different on top of everything else young people feel. They add that they have been forced to think about how those feelings affect how students in school manage to learn – or not learn.

Does that mean things are better now for gay students in south-central Nebraska than they were when Mrs. Tschabrun's daughter was growing up? She thought a long while, then answered, "I'd like to say yes, but I honestly don't think things are a whole lot different. There might be a greater realization that there *are* gays and lesbians here, that they're not all in Los Angeles or New York, but that's probably about it."

However, she believes her message is sinking in, if slowly. Her telephone number is listed in local lesbian and gay publications and by PFLAG, so she fields plenty of calls about all kinds of gay issues. "It's wonderful," she concludes. "Some of my best friends now are in the gay and lesbian community. I just cannot imagine what my life would be like if I'd said to my daughter, 'I don't want any part of your life.' And I hope that comes across to the teachers and counselors I talk to, and that they take some of that back to their schools. I really hope they do."

PART 3

Programs

Get with the Programs

American education is awash in a sea of programs and policy. Long gone are the days when a schoolteacher could whip out a primer and ruler to train obedient pupils how to read and write, add and subtract, and love their country to boot. In today's world federal guidelines, state mandates, and local laws regulate not only what can and cannot be taught, but when, where, and how it should be done. Schools are in the business not just of readin', writin', and 'rithmetic, but of computer education, physical education, nutrition education, substance abuse education, and a dozen other types of instruction – including, from time to time, sex education.

Opening up our classrooms to sex education has led, finally, to the recognition in many places that homosexuality is a topic fit for discussion. And now that the subject has at long last been broached, there's no telling where gay and lesbian issues will next appear.

They pop up, with increasing frequency, in the pages of the high school press. They are talked about on auditorium stages by gay, lesbian, and bisexual speakers, some of whom are students themselves. They are discussed in gay-straight alliances, read about in libraries, and studied by teachers searching for curricular materials that will engage their students' minds in classes ranging from English and history to psychology and biology. They are the topics of laws passed by state legislators, and signed by the governor. They are even the raison d'être for two full-fledged schools.

Lesbian and gay issues, in other words, have traveled well beyond the simple declaration of a student or teacher who says, "I am gay." They are no longer theory, and far more than fact; they actually drive curricula and courses. They have drawn the rapt attention not only of teachers and students, but of researchers, union leaders, and high-level education bureaucrats. Lesbian and gay issues have moved from the shadowy fringes of education – from the days when, if they were considered at all, they were whispered about furtively, in the far corners of faculty rooms or principals' offices – onto center stage. The full spotlight of curriculum committees, faculty workshops, and boards of education now shines on the subject of gay and lesbian topics.

In Los Angeles, the board of education gave grudging approval to something called Project 10 – an in-school program aimed at building the self-esteem of lesbian and gay youngsters. Founder Dr. Virginia Uribe devised it not as a "homosexual" project (that would not have flown in the Reagan-Bush era), but as a dropout-prevention program. It worked; Project 10 is now a shining (but inexpensive) jewel in the L.A. school system crown, and the model has been imitated in other places as diverse as Santa Rosa, California, and Cambridge, Massachusetts.

Another program, Project 21, has focused on books, not people – the idea is to get gay-themed readings onto library shelves and into curriculums – but the aim is the same as Project 10: to raise the self-esteem of gay and lesbian youngsters. If homosexual students can read about, hear, and see positive role models, founder Rob Birle believes, then perhaps the hours they spend in school will not be as bleak as so many others' have been, for so long.

In New York, the Harvey Milk School has served for ten years as a beacon for lesbian and gay students and teachers everywhere. Its premise is at once simple and revolutionary: if the homophobia of regular schools makes it impossible for lesbian and gay youths to attend classes there, then give them their own, homo-friendly building. The physical site of the Harvey Milk School has moved often in the past decade, but the caring, compassionate people behind it have never wavered in their commitment to the cause of giving a couple dozen boys and girls each year the educational opportunity they so richly deserve.

Around the country, gay educators and their straight allies are making a difference in tens of thousands of students' lives. They're doing it in places like Massachusetts and Minnesota by serving as faculty advisers to gay-straight alliances that illuminate the dark nooks and crannies that fill so many schools; they're doing it nationally and regionally by forming gay and lesbian organizations – including union caucuses – that educate colleagues, supervisors, and school boards about homosexual concerns and issues; they're doing it by walking across the state of Washington, knocking on principals' office doors to let them know that, even in bucolic wheat- and apple-growing communities, there are boys who like boys, girls who like girls, and what is anyone there doing to help them?

Individual educators are making individual efforts, too. Psychology, biology, and social studies teachers are introducing homosexuality units into their curriculums; health and phys. ed. teachers are bringing gay folks in to talk to their classes; librarians are recognizing that when they design a book display honoring "families," they should include titles like *Heather Has Two Mommies*.

And, of course, students are rallying behind the banner of gay and lesbian rights. They're the ones forming gay-straight alliances; they're the ones writing editorials, feature articles, and letters for their school newspapers; they're the ones asking the intelligent questions of guest speakers (occasionally even coming out to classmates in the middle of a presentation).

Some of the gay and lesbian steps being taken in schools today are major; some are tiny and tentative. Most demand courage. Many engender furious debate, and the discourse does not always end on a positive note. But men and women involved in education – teachers, administrators, parents, policy makers, students themselves, and everyone else with an interest in the future – no longer shy away from facing a topic that concerns each and every American today: not only every gay, lesbian, bisexual, and questioning student, but every heterosexual (and questioning) classmate, their countless gay family members and friends, plus their numberless homosexual teachers (and all their straight allies).

America's schools can only be healthier for it.

———➤●◄———

Extra, Extra,
Read All about It

J ust about everything in high school has changed in the past couple of decades. Dress codes – for teachers as well as students – are out; McDonald's, Pizza Hut, and Taco Bell have invaded the cafeteria. And high school newspapers are no longer the grimy, grainy, poorly written, and badly designed purveyors of administrative pabulum that seemed their fate for so many years.

Gone are the puff pieces on cheerleading tryouts; in their place are investigative stories probing gender equity in extracurricular athletics. The fawning interview with Mr. Blivet that tried (and failed) to show that typing teachers have personal lives too has been supplanted by a hard question-and-answer session with the assistant superintendent for curriculum affairs, zeroing in on the school district's inability to keep current in computer technology. And the "inquiring photographer" no longer asks students whether the Bald Eagles will whip the Whippets in the Big Game Friday night; now she seeks responses to questions like, "What would you do if your best friend told you he's gay?"

Homosexuality has come to the high school press.

"As recently as the early eighties, there were no gay or lesbian stories in high school papers at all. Today it's so common, you're almost wrong to call it a trend," said Tom Rolnicki. He should know: as the longtime executive director of the National Scholastic Press Association (NSPA), a nonprofit organization providing evaluation services, advice, contests, competitions, and other support to high school journalism advisers and student writers, he scans hundreds of high school papers each week. They come in all sizes and every conceivable style. They pour in daily from fifty states, their pages filled with a bewildering array of local

Tom Rolnicki, executive director of the National Scholastic Press Association, which provides services and support to high school journalism advisers and student writers.

controversies and concerns. But in many ways, they're all the same: the social currents that ripple across MTV, *Sassy* magazine, and Blockbuster Video bind teenagers together from Point Barrow to Key Largo. The jungle telegraph transmits, with faxlike speed, news of fashions and fads – and gay issues are part of today's messages.

"It's common practice now to do one story or more a year about gay and lesbian students, accompanied by sidebars on support groups, and maybe an editorial or opinion column," said Mr. Rolnicki at NSPA's Minneapolis headquarters. As a gay man, he is both pleased with and intrigued by what he reads.

"I've been thinking about this for a long time," he said. "I think the main reason for the shift is AIDS – not because it affects gay men, but because it afforded student journalists the opportunity to write candidly about a serious topic, and use correct adult language in reporting."

In the 1970s, Mr. Rolnicki said, the high school press got serious. Stories about drugs, divorce, and other personal issues first crept, then swept onto the pages of high school papers. Yet teenage writers still tiptoed around lots of stories. "They might do a teen pregnancy piece, but they wouldn't write the word 'penis' or 'vagina.' But then in the early eighties came AIDS, and they had to use both clinical medical terms and also street language. It would have been hard for a principal to tell a high school reporter not to cover AIDS, when everyone from the Surgeon General on down (not up, unfortunately) was saying that students *needed* that information. And the student press was a great way to get that information across." That led, Mr. Rolnicki said, to peripheral stories on gay men, which in turn sparked stories on gay students, homophobia, and other related topics.

A female reporter for a high school paper in Georgia wrote a column titled, "Keep Uncle Sam Out of Our Bedrooms"; it was an explicit response to a Supreme Court decision about invasion-of-privacy laws. "That was a landmark story for the high school press," Mr. Rolnicki remembered. "It took the subject of sodomy laws and made it real." He also was impressed by an editorial in a school paper commending a college for allowing a lesbian organization on campus. That too was a real breakthrough, the NSPA director said, because it showed that stories about lesbians were important too. Up to that time it was easier for the high school press to talk about gay men.

School papers deal with homosexuality in a host of ways. There are opinion pieces – occasionally penned by a self-identified gay or lesbian student – as well as feature stories, editorials, and hard news pieces concerning homophobia or curricular issues. "Student writers sometimes still have difficulty with terminology, and sometimes the stories lack the polish of the commercial press," Mr. Rolnicki said. "Some of them read like a high school theme – they cite *Seventeen* magazine or *Newsweek* as sources, rather than firsthand information – but these writers make up for all that with candor. They deal in depth with difficult issues; they devote a couple of pages to it, and they are doing more and more interviews with actual kids."

Because he is not in the schools when the papers come out, Mr. Rolnicki finds it hard to judge reactions to lesbian and gay stories. "My sense from follow-up stories, letters to the editor, and phone calls to us is that there are occasional slaps on the hands and a few complaints. But because I've seen these types of stories for several years now, and all across the country – Wyoming, Montana, Wisconsin, Iowa, not just California and New York – it says to me that schools are more enlightened than they used to be. And they should be. These really are student topics, even if some teachers and parents don't like their kids to be thinking about them."

One highlight of each school journalism year is NSPA's national convention and workshop. Hundreds of teachers, advisers, and students exchange ideas, papers, and addresses; attend seminars; and listen to professional writers and editors. For the first time recently a speaker was identified as a member of the National Lesbian and Gay Journalists Association. He did not speak on a gay topic, but afterward a number of students went up to him, and identified themselves as gay or lesbian. The NSPA did not seek him out as a speaker because he was gay, but the organization is very conscious of the need to provide role models – whether female, African-American, Hispanic, or homosexual.

As the visibility of gays and lesbians in schools increases, student press coverage won't fade into the background. But, Mr. Rolnicki said, the *type* of stories might change. "I think we'll see more 'normal' coverage of student activities," he predicted. "Stories about a kid who's involved in a gay youth group, or sewing a quilt panel, or going to Washington for the march, rather than survey-type pieces on gay rights or homophobia."

That kind of coverage of gay issues – any kind, actually – amazes Mr. Rolnicki. "I think back to when I was in high school, and this stuff was not even covered in the mainstream press, let alone high school papers. It's so valuable to everyone, especially gay and lesbian kids in high school who have no other access to information. And these sidebars that include addresses and phone numbers for support groups – that's real important, informational journalism. It's what high school papers are all about."

As Mr. Rolnicki noted, lesbian and gay coverage in the high school press takes many forms. The one most talked about is the feature or editorial-page column that brings lesbian and gay issues directly into the classroom, by talking about homosexuality as it exists in a particular school. These stories are exceptionally powerful, because they force students to face up to what previously was only joked about or rumored: that someone they know is gay.

Not that real names are used. In fact, a review of scores of student newspapers provided by the NSPA did not unearth even one story in which a teenager revealed his or her sexual orientation by name at that student's school. But many came close.

The centerpiece of a two-page spread on homosexuality in the *Charger Account* (Leland High School, San Jose, California) was headlined, "Teenager divulges true identity." The unbylined story began:

I have no idea what kind of rumors are floating around Leland right now, but I would like to set some stuff straight. Please read this with an open mind and read the whole thing. You might want to save this article.

It was always hard for me to be accepted by people and I always felt out of place. The one thing I hated most was lying to people and friends about myself. But here is the truth: I am gay.

Shock? Maybe not. Many people in my life have asked me if I was gay. And of course, I always answered no. I felt that if I had said yes, I would be insulted and in danger of physical harm. I guess the only reason I am "coming out" now is because I will not be attending Leland any longer.

The author went on to describe despair at always knowing he was different, yet never receiving any support; loneliness that led to his contemplation of suicide; the importance of first accepting, then admiring oneself. The writer concluded with a schoolwide plea:

People should accept others for who they are, not what they are. Be who you want to be and most important, be who you are. Remember, you're not alone and there are people who care.

Live your life the way you want to live it. Don't be pushed around by peers, parents or any other adults. You have the choice in what you want to do and become.

Be yourself, go ahead, wear that outfit you thought nobody would like. Use your imagination and wear weird clothes. Don't let society brainwash you and turn you into a bunch of Kens and Barbies. Express yourself and be open to what the world has to offer. Peace.

At the end of the piece was a cryptic editor's note: "This article came to the *Charger Account* with a signature. In consideration for all concerned, the *Charger Account* staff withheld the name. The author fully intended and endorsed the release of his identity."

In a separate story, staff writer Anthony Corchero appended his own thoughts. "I have met many people, seen many things, but I have never experienced anything to match such a display of courage and compassion ... such dignity and self-respect. And [the author] did so without tangible compensation, for he is to receive no grade, and most certainly no great boost amidst the social circles." After praising principal Don Bell and vice principal Pat Dewey for their personal support of the article, Anthony wrote, "I regret that before the student left Leland, I never had the opportunity to make his acquaintance, and what is more, I regret that this community has lost the privilege to claim so remarkable a human being as one of its own." (Anthony revealed in another article on the facing page that a close relative of his is gay, and excoriated himself for formerly laughing at anti-gay jokes and spouting homophobic opinions.)

The rest of the two pages were filled with a variety of gay-related stories, including an examination of stereotypes at Leland (all gays at Leland do not have AIDS, act "feminine," or dress a certain way, writer Kim Mok said); information on mandatory meetings on homosexuality for all district administrators; and listings of support services and hotline numbers for gay youths.

———

A large special section headlined, "Homophobia and High School" appeared in the Newton (Massachusetts) South High School *Denebola*. Numerous articles approached the issue from a variety of viewpoints — "Educators tackle homophobia at school"; "Teens' own uncertainties can fuel discrimination"; "Parents request education on homosexuality" — but two in particular stood out, both for their crackling writing and for their willingness to examine several sides of a complex story.

Matt Baker's piece, "South students attribute homophobia to insecurity and environment," began by noting the responses of most of the students queried: cruel jokes, followed by "No, wait. Don't quote me on that!" But beneath the superficial reaction, Matt discovered many thoughtful responses.

"In light of the Magic Johnson story, I have become more aware of the existence of homophobia at South," sophomore Jamie Horowitz said. The morning after the basketball star's startling announcement, many students assumed that because he had AIDS, he was gay; some said they did not admire him as much because of that.

Another student, who said he might be bisexual, remarked:

In a school where I think there is still uneasiness about interracial romances, how well would I be treated if I announced that I was sexually attracted to both sexes? There's a lot of pressure here to hide every freaky side of your personality, take your tests, go to the keg party, and if you're gonna put on Mommy's high heels, do it in the closet. I personally think there are a lot more bizarre sexual attitudes swirling around in this school than ever get dealt with.

A second *Denebola* piece described interviews with two (relatively) old South graduates, one from the class of 1970, the other from that of '79. Each provided a unique look back at their former high school, interesting to gay and straight readers alike. The younger alum, who at the time of the story was a graduate student in anthropology and medicine at Harvard, offered advice that could be heeded by many students:

If you think you're gay, odds are you probably are and congratulations. It's wonderful for many reasons. To discover yourself sexually and to be gay ... allows you to totally reinvent yourself. In Newton there's very little sense of "What do I want?" Being gay challenges presuppositions. Once you begin challenging simple things, everything is up for grabs. Coming out for me was tied to moving away from a standard career path. Don't be despairing; you're lucky. Approach it with a sense of excitement.

The editors of the Lincoln Southeast *Clarion* – "The Official Newspaper of Southeast High School" in Lincoln, Nebraska – placed a potentially volatile story in an obscure, middle-of-page-five location, then stuck this headline on it: "Homosexual students do exist at Southeast." However, according to reporter Wendey Heitmann's piece, the existence of those students is not exactly welcomed. "Last year junior Steve Launer admitted he was gay and quit hiding his homosexuality," she wrote. "While he did not pursue relationships with other males at Southeast, he was harassed to the point where he later moved to Los Angeles to get away from the prejudice he experienced here."

"I couldn't take it anymore," Launer was quoted as saying. "I always heard all these people say that they didn't care if someone was gay, as long as they didn't hit on them. Well, I didn't hit on them and I was harassed terribly." He went on to describe his parents' reactions (they sent him to a "Christian counselor" who told him that if he didn't change, God would punish him) and his reaction to that (he contemplated suicide). But the article did not explain the type of harassment he endured at Southeast, what his teachers and administrators did about it, and whether any classmates supported him. The rest of the piece meandered through such topics as the movie *Basic Instinct,* a church that will marry homosexuals (the marriages "are not legal in the sense of taxes, however"), and the introduction of a gay superhero by Marvel Comics.

The Liberty High School (Issaquah, Washington) *Patriot Press* hyped its two-page gay and lesbian feature with a front-page cartoon of a jail door covered by the word "unacceptable." Under the headline "Gay and in high school – Liberty students try to make it work," Debra Cunningham profiled several anonymous classmates and recent graduates who attend a community support group. "When I was there, there were a lot of gay people at Liberty, and they still are there," one lesbian said. A companion article featured an eighteen-year-old who was out at his nearby high school. "One of approximately 15,000 gay teenagers now living in King County" (and a 4.0 student), Perry Brooks established the first organized group of homosexuals at the University of Washington.

Another gay young man in the Pacific Northwest, Jason Saffir, was prominently mentioned in the West Albany (Oregon) High School *Whirlwind.* Jason, who at the time the article appeared was a junior at Seattle Pacific University, never mentioned any connection to West Albany, but his supportive parents were quoted extensively ("We encourage Jason to bring home his companions. It seems that it is much harder on Jason and his friends than it is on us," his mother said). That issue of *Whirlwind* is impressive for its wide-ranging coverage of gay issues: in addition to the Jason story, there was a page-one piece on high school homophobia in general; an article linking homosexual stereotypes to teenage anxieties; a long, fact-filled, and fair piece on the upcoming Oregon ballot initiative that sought to declare homosexual activity "abnormal"; and a box with telephone numbers offering information, counseling, and support.

One issue of the Bakersfield (California) High School *Blue & White* was filled with nineties controversies: condom distribution, racism, and neo-Nazism. Homosexuality was included too, in a story titled, "Teen confession of sexuality raises awareness of issues." "Lloyd," a pseudonymous local student who was going out with another local male, talked about his relationships, a subject rarely explored in other school papers. Lloyd admitted he was not ready for his relationship with "Jim," but noted, "We were both lonely. It's hard to find a good relationship with another teenager because of society and people who think that love shouldn't be shared between two males."

It's exceedingly rare that real names are used – but when they are, the impact is thunderous. Consider the page-one story that appeared in the Robert E. Lee High School (Springfield, Virginia) newspaper *Lance.* It reported on a speech Wayne Steward, a student at nearby Thomas Jefferson High School of Science and Technology, made before the Fairfax County School Board, urging the body to retain "sexual preference" in their verbal-abuse policy despite an outcry from religious organizations and parents. (A compromise later changed the wording to "matters pertaining to sexuality." Steward realized that "sexual preference" is a politically incorrect phrase, but felt that fighting for half a loaf was better than none.)

The straightforward news account described Steward's realization of his sexual orientation (he saw an episode of *Phil Donahue* when he was ten or eleven, and it occurred to him then that he was gay); his coming-out process (he left a copy of his school board speech on the dinner table, with a note telling his father to read it); and the reactions to the speech at school (some classmates and teachers congratulated him).

It's also exceedingly rare to see a story as candid as "Hatred fuels teenage 'fag-bashing,'" Jyll Stettler's contribution to a two-page spread in the La Cueva High School (Albuquerque, New Mexico) *Edition*. Printed in white letters on a black background – the better to highlight its strong subject matter – the piece was especially powerful because an actual La Cueva student spoke about beating up homosexuals.

"Why do I go fag-bashing? Because I don't like fags," one senior told Jyll. "We go fag-bashing a lot. A bunch of us will hang out (at the gay bars) and we'll pretend we are fags. We bring bats and just beat the s**t out of them. Either singly or in groups (of homosexuals), we've done both, it doesn't matter."

He continued:

I've been hit on, but that's not why I hate fags. As soon as I became aware that there was a difference in some people, I was against it. My parents weren't a big influence. My friends feel the same way. If I had a friend or hung out with someone who I found out was gay, I would stop hanging with them. If people ask how I feel about fags, I tell them I hate 'em.

Jyll included information about gay advocacy and support groups, but concluded her piece with some more thoughts from her informant:

We go bashing because they are homosexual, no other reason. I don't think that's wrong. My opinions aren't going to change. If I had a son that was gay, I would disown him. I know [my opinions] are prejudiced, but I believe in some sort of segregation between homos and regular people. Maybe a different school. They should just stay by themselves. You make your own decisions, take your own chances, and you make your own life.

The Edition devoted the rest of its two pages to other sides of the gay issue: a column by Jennifer Wall explaining her reaction when a friend told her he was gay (she learned courage, understanding, and acceptance from him); the story of a pseudonymous gay student, Dave, whose mother drove to his school, broke into his locker, took the keys to his drawer at home, unlocked it, and read his poems; a piece headlined, "History of homosexuals stretches back to Renaissance"; and a box of four biblical quotations (all interpretable as condemning homosexuality).

Though gay and lesbian stories now proliferate in the high school press, virtually all focus on the student angle. "I haven't seen any stories about gay or lesbian teachers," the NSPA's Mr. Rolnicki said. "I may have missed them, but my guess is that gay and lesbian teachers are quieter about their lives than their students are today."

Mr. Rolnicki would have had to have been an exceptionally eagle-eyed reader to catch the few gay-teacher references an exhaustive search of the student press turned up. One mention came deep in a page-five story in the Redwood High School (Larkspur, California) *Redwood Bark,* dealing primarily with an attempt by the Novato Unified School District to add the phrase "homosexual, bisexual and heterosexual" to its nondiscrimination hiring practices. That in turn sparked a local debate over whether or not gays should be allowed to teach in public schools.

Near the end of the article, writer Chris Debo mentioned that earlier that month Chuck Smith, a social studies teacher at nearby Tamalpais High School, told his classes that he was gay and had AIDS. He died the next night of a heart attack that may have been induced by his weakened state. The article added that the Tamalpais administration fully supported his decision to continue teaching despite his illness; the story then discussed other gay-related issues.

Another gay teacher in the high school press was vocal-music teacher Phil Carey of North Central High School in an Indianapolis suburb, who nearly came out in his school newspaper, *Northern Lights.* In an interview, he revealed his homosexuality; he then told the superintendent about it, as a courtesy. The superintendent told Mr. Carey not to do the interview at all, and definitely not to mention his sexual orientation if he did. Mr. Carey replied that the interview had already taken place.

The superintendent countered by calling the sponsor of *Northern Lights* to say, in Mr. Carey's words, "what could and could not be written." The next move was Mr. Carey's, and it was a beauty: he came out in the local Sunday newspaper – photo and all. The school newspaper, defying the wishes of the superintendent, printed the original article around the same time.

The result, according to Mr. Carey (who died soon after, of cancer), was worth it. He received so many notes and comments of support from parents, colleagues, current students, and past students that he couldn't remember why he had ever been apprehensive. The power of the press had worked. The pen – or, this being the nineties, the desktop publishing program – once again proved to be far mightier than the sword.

A third article was penned by openly gay Stratford (Connecticut) High School teacher John Anderson. Asked by student editors to write in *The Trident,* the newspaper of Amity Regional Senior High in nearby Woodbridge, Mr. Anderson confronted students head-on.

"When you see the word 'homosexual,' what are the first five words that come to mind?" he asked. "My guess is that none of the words are kind, complimentary, or supportive."

He asked them what Amity Regional says about the subject.

Did your principals greet you last September with a statement against discrimination and include gays and lesbians? Do you have posters on the walls of your school supporting your approximately 85 gay and lesbian students? Do you have openly gay and lesbian teachers and administrators? Has your school library ever had an exhibit for Gay Pride Month in June? ... Does your American history teacher tell you about the gay rights movement when he or she teaches you about the civil rights movement in this century? Does your English teacher tell you that Walt Whitman was gay? Does your music teacher tell you that Tchaikovsky was gay? Does your coach tell you that Dave Pallone, former major league umpire, was gay, or that Martina Navratilova, world-class tennis pro, is a lesbian?

The fact that not many of these questions have a yes answer "doesn't mean that Amity is full of bad people," Mr. Anderson wrote. What it does mean, he told the students in conclusion, is that

maybe you need to think about the world as it is and as it exists in microcosm in your school. Maybe you need to remember that ten percent of the population is gay or lesbian. Maybe you need to be more sensitive when you call someone a faggot. There are gay and lesbian students who hear you. They are hiding and hurting. Please don't add to their pain.

————◆◆◆————

Another teacher, Andrew Watson, used *The Log* to inform the Loomis-Chaffee community that he — an English instructor at the Windsor, Connecticut, private school — is gay. His "Open Letter to the Community: Gay Like Me" began:

In truth, I don't fit all the stereotypes. I played soccer throughout high school. Twice a week, I study Tae Kwon Do from a 7th level black belt. I'm an active Republican — even, God help me, a CONSERVATIVE Republican.

But stereotype or no stereotype, the ugly truth is, I'm gay.

What a funny way to put that. The ugly truth is, Bosnians starve to death as you read this. The ugly truth is, heroin use is on the rise in the United States. The ugly truth is, we had a cancer scare in my family just weeks ago. The ugly truth is, I'm gay. How strange it is to wake up every day, feeling a little bit like a statistic about heroin addiction.

The rest of the piece expressed the wish that, now that the school knew "a little bit more about me, that's all," students and colleagues would reconsider things they have felt, said, and done. "Maybe it will help to know that gay people are just people, like me," Mr. Watson ended.

The reaction, in both the editorial and the letters-to-the-editor columns, was swift and sure. Most students adopted a ho-hum, so-what attitude, tinged with respect for his honesty and courage. One writer pointed out that "From Socrates to Yves St. Laurent, homosexuals have made many contributions to culture and society." Another, after quoting an upper-class friend as saying, "Dude, Mr. Watson is the best English teacher I've ever had," noted, "I'm sure Mr. Watson knows his participles and gerund phrases just as well as the straight members of the English department." And life at Loomis-Chaffee went on.

There was, however, a bit stronger reaction at Boston Latin School when Latin teacher Owen O'Malley vented his spleen in a letter to the *Argo Forum* editor headlined, "No to Gay Rights." (The paper had already carried several articles on the subject.) He scathingly attacked Gov. William Weld for "promoting homosexual propaganda in the public schools" by supporting a gay student rights bill, labeled homosexuality "a great weakness and sickness," and hinted that those who "deliberately engage in ... perverse and wicked and extremely dangerous (acts)" can, if they want, "rise from the depths of evil" and change their behavior. The same page of the *Argo Forum* included two letters from students criticizing Mr. O'Malley's comments.

A firestorm of debate enveloped the school, with classrooms blazing into discussions over a variety of issues: the teacher's opinion specifically, what it said about the state of gay issues at Boston Latin generally, and the newspaper's overall responsibility in printing such strong words. Editor Hilary Krieger said that while she strongly disagreed with Mr. O'Malley's statements, she believed publication of the letter would further the discussion of gay rights, an issue she thought a large majority of students support. Then the local media – print and electronic – got hold of the schoolwide debate, and inflamed passions even further.

But, true to editor Krieger's words, some good things arose from Mr. O'Malley's diatribe. David LaFontaine, head of the Governor's Commission on Gay and Lesbian Youth, named Mr. O'Malley as one of the first violators of Massachusetts's new state law banning anti-gay discrimination in public education. Parents, faculty members, and homosexual alumni began speaking out. Students talked of forming a gay-straight alliance. And barely a month after the letter appeared, Boston Public Schools – which previously had reacted coolly to the state Department of Education's safe-schools training – decided to get moving.

Where did the Boston School Committee decide to hold its first day-long workshop? At Boston Latin, of course.

A nasty controversy also arose when the *Westlake Featherduster,* the student newspaper of Westlake High School in Austin, Texas, devoted five pages to gay issues. There was a full-page interview with an unnamed gay student, and other stories bearing such headlines as "Sects vs. Sex" and "The Struggle Within." Naturally, the paper caught the attention of a Christian call-in show, causing complaints to administrators and journalism teacher Deanne Kunz. As a result, Eames Independent School District officials would not allow Ms. Kunz or Westlake principal John Matysek to respond to reporters on the record.

Religious groups were not upset with certain angles: "We are all created in the image of God and to be homosexual would be to be detestable to him," Oakhill Church of Christ youth minister Bobby Gober was quoted as saying, and student Sarah Sunukjian claimed in an opinion piece that homosexuality is "an unsatisfying lifestyle, incapable of giving happiness." However, they deplored the sentiments of student Katie Shotwell, who wrote, "Let us take this opportunity to bow our heads in shame at government, religion and family. All three have helped condemn a part of society that just cannot be ignored any longer."

And they certainly did not care for the interview with the anonymous gay senior, even though the picture he painted of life at Westlake was bleak. "I get tormented daily by half the guys at our school," he told the *Featherduster.* "I'm used to people verbally attacking me. I've learned to block it out and get on with my life." The student, who revealed his name – Maverick Shaw – to the *Texas Triangle,* a statewide gay newspaper, said the principal would not allow him to identify himself in the school paper. "Straight people are able to use their names along with their opinions, but I wasn't able to use mine," Maverick told the *Triangle.*

Interestingly, the journalism class got its idea for the issue from the Eames District's own theme for the year: "Celebrating Diversity."

One of the broadest, deepest spreads anywhere appeared in *The Shield,* the monthly paper of Pleasant Valley (Iowa) Community High School. A quick glance at page one of the twenty-page tabloid paper seems to confirm that Pleasant Valley is aptly named: a photo showed a student struggling humorously with messy hair, and headlines informed readers about a variety show and the boys' swim team's fourteenth-place state meet finish. A story and photo on Gov. Terry Branstad's visit to present an award for excellence in education was relegated to page two.

But wedged in on the bottom of page one was this: "Student body discusses homosexuality in Features." Those inside two pages were filled with articles, graphs, surveys, and information about gays and lesbians, complete with a two-page, triangle-draped banner reading, "Battling fear and ignorance: The fight for gay rights."

Features co-editor Megan Rocker's lead story began by asking why, "with all the discrimination and persecution placed upon them ... so many millions of people choose" to be gay. Megan quickly revealed that homosexuality is not, in fact, a choice, but rather "an inborn trait and an hereditary issue." However, a *Shield* poll showed that 45 percent of students at PVCHS believed homosexuality to be a "controlled decision."

The lead article discussed other results from the survey, including student views on gay marriage (53 percent were in favor) and adoption of a child by a homosexual couple (31 percent felt comfortable). Strong quotes were sprinkled throughout, ranging from "Love is love, no matter which way you look at it" to "I think (homosexuality) is wrong, no ifs, ands, or buts." All students were named.

Three other stories surrounded the main one. "Churches give insight into their perspective about homosexuality" contrasted the views of Pleasant Valley's Unitarian and Baptist ministers, with Megan Rocker and *Shield* editor-in-chief Geoff Mulvihill drawing these quotes from Pleasant View Baptist Church youth pastor Mike Fendley:

> I've never had anyone come to me and say, "Can you help me? I'm heterosexual." But I have had people ask for help because they felt they were homosexual. I think this shows that people have an inherent sense that something is wrong ... The jury is still out on (the issue of causality), but just because it's in your genes does that make it okay? They are saying now that alcoholism may be hereditary,

but does that justify it when someone becomes an alcoholic and drinks and drives and injures someone? We are all predisposed to be sinners. We choose to commit the sins.

Fendley told his interviewers that he has witnessed several homosexuals turn to heterosexuality through counseling and spiritual guidance.

"Gays and lesbians battle for additional legal liberties" proved to be an evenhanded analysis of gay rights issues (including the information that "only during the time of crisis are homosexuals invited into the military"). A "Dialogue" interview elicited a senior boy's opinion that "the military is for defending the country, not a haven for sodomizers," while "Mattson shares advice and information on gay teens" turned out to be an interview with a guidance counselor on the subject. (According to the newspaper's poll of 158 students, only 16 percent know any homosexual peers.) One main reason for "the incomprehension" of a gay PVCHS student's situation, Jean Mattson said, was the school's lack of diversity. "There are not a lot of differences in our school," she noted. "It is very homogeneous. There are so few minorities, whether ethnic, racial, religious, or disabled, that we as a school have very little tolerance and are prejudiced against many things." She advocated the formation of a school peer support group, if it could be assured that members would not be persecuted.

Not far away in Davenport, Iowa, the Central High School *Blackhawk* highlighted gay issues in a story headlined, "Homosexuality not taught." Ryan Harvey reported that the Davenport Community Schools' health curriculum does not deal at all with homosexuality – although, according to junior high health teacher Steve Knoche, "If a student has a question about it, then we are more than happy to give him information. That's what we are here for." Two other instructors were also quoted: junior high health teacher Jay Ryan said, "Usually there isn't enough time throughout the semester for this to be taught," while Banks Swan, coordinator of the health department, opined, "In heavily populated areas, the issue is much more evident. It doesn't show up around here as much. It is like that with most controversial issues."

That did not sit well with *Blackhawk* reporter Kait Allebach, who submitted an opinion piece titled, "Health forgets about homosexuality." The column began with the example of a little boy yelling, "Fag!" as if it was

the worst insult anyone could ever be called ... The fact that he had already developed negative feelings about something he was completely uneducated about, should be a warning to the parents of our society. The only education he'd had about homosexuality was from what he had heard and learned from other kids at school. Is this how the children of our society should be educated?

Homosexuality is a fact of life, Kait concluded six paragraphs later. "When the seventh grade health class learns about the birds and bees, homosexuality should be taught right along beside it."

One of the most forthright two-page spreads on homosexuality appeared elsewhere in the Midwest, in Naperville (Illinois) Central High School's *Central Times*. The main story, featured under an arresting "Homophobia" banner, was titled, "Fear of homosexuals causes discrimination." It led with this quote, from junior Kevin Brunson: "My friend and I went on a vacation and a couple gay people were on a bus we were riding in. They were giving us looks and scared us, and we thought they were going to jump us or something." Brunson noted that he could not be friends with a homosexual ("I would be afraid that he'd try something gayish"), adding that he would "not even want to sit next to one in class."

According to sophomore Kelly McCreary, fear of homosexuals and their civil rights was a common item of discussion at NCHS. Writer Betsy Wille showed this to be so by recounting the story of humanities teacher Dave Dillon, whose policy of inviting gay guest speakers during his sociology class unit on homosexuality had led to controversy. Local fundamentalists protested, and Mr. Dillon was called in by his superiors who were concerned that the unit would become a national issue. The problem was resolved by having gays address the class via speakerphone.

Alongside that story were student answers to the question "Should homosexuals be allowed in the military?" Four students answered yes, including freshman Adam Lawson, who said, "Someday on the front lines it could very well be a gay who saves your life, and then it wouldn't matter." On the other side were three male students (all using aliases) who thought not. "Put them out on the front lines and let them be killed," said one senior. "I would be disgusted having to live in the same quarters," added a sophomore.

But columnist Aaron Burns weighed in with a strong opinion piece supporting the rights of gays to serve in the armed forces ("We should be proud that there are still people out there who actually want to join and defend the very country that persecutes them"), and page two's lead editorial counseled tolerance and justice for gays. An editor's note at the end read, "The *Central Times* voted 21–2 on this issue," presumably referring to the editorial stance.

Another two-page special section on homosexuality appeared in *Miner Detail,* the monthly paper at parochial Bishop Manogue High School in Reno, Nevada. Pages four and five caught readers' eyes with a cartoon of a boy, his finger to his lips in a "don't tell" pose, surrounded by the male and female symbols, and question marks. A hard news story by Courtney Fagan on Amendment 2 began, "Colorado has made history. But the kind of history the state has made may not be something to proudly pass on to future generations." A pie chart showed that 64 percent of the 185 Manogue students surveyed disagreed with Colorado's anti-gay Amendment 2. Other stories examined the issues of gays in the military and work force. A pair of rational, well-researched editorials discussed in greater detail the controversy over gays in the armed forces; Laura Clark supported the idea on the basis of equal opportunity for all, while Tom Wainscoat used quotes from a Nevada Air Guard general (and Manogue graduate) to oppose it because of its potential disruptive effect on military discipline.

A more personal view appeared in Walt Whitman High School's *Black & White,* in Bethesda, Maryland. On the page facing the obituary of a former English teacher who died of AIDS at age forty-eight, Christina Kim and Alex Robbins told the stories of "Scott," a gay Whitman senior; "Rick," a recent graduate; and "Tim," a former Whitman student who transferred to a Virginia high school.

Scott, who came out at sixteen to family and friends, described the humiliations he endured, such as students who laughed in the halls, "Look at that fag." "It's really hard to live as a gay in a small society like Whitman where most of the people are not comfortable with homosexuality," he said. His family, too, was unaccepting: after "only a couple of long talks," his older sister told him, "I can't accept that you're gay, and I don't want you to be my brother anymore."

Rick also experienced family problems, noting, "It's tough to be any type of minority to begin with. However, if you belong to a racial or ethnic minority, you can go home to a supportive family. But if you're gay, you don't go home to a gay family."

Tim spoke candidly about finding out who his true friends were after he came out. "Everyone at school knows that I am gay," he told the paper. "And so a lot of people are uncomfortable when we are all changing in the locker room. My closest friends will come up to me and talk to me even though they are half-naked, while others will shy away." He also described the way he once tried to gain acceptance from his peers: "I dated fifteen girls in a two-year span and tried to force myself to like them. It didn't work, and I was depressed. Now, I can find girls attractive, but I am never attracted to them." The *Black & White* article included information about Washington, D.C.'s Sexual Minority Youth Assistance League (SMYAL), including its phone number, statistics on gay youths, and quotes from school psychologist Penny Peterson. It was illustrated with a clever cartoon of a scared youth peering out of a closet door.

Sharp graphics, an eye-catching vertical banner ("Homophobia"), and solid, no-nonsense writing helped make "Homosexuality triggers uneasiness" an interesting, full-page feature in Shaker Heights (Ohio) High School's *Shakerite*. Staff reporter Emily Troia opened her story this way:

"I'd kill him."

"Be serious."

"I am being serious. I'd kill him."

. As they listened to the class discussion about homosexuality, a chill went down a few students' backs when they realized just how serious he was. He would kill his parent, even his own child, based solely on one piece of information: they were gay.

Using as her hook a *Shakerite* survey of two hundred students (which found that 35 percent were personally or religiously opposed to homosexuality), Emily quoted schoolmates, psychiatrists, and social workers in her comprehensive piece. The survey revealed that only 18 percent of male students would feel comfortable discovering a friend was gay, compared with 35 percent of girls. Nearly three-quarters of the students said that discussions of homosexuality have been avoided in their classrooms, though "personal social responsibilities" teacher Allan Slawson was cited for giving students an opportunity to debate how they felt about gays and lesbians. The class made senior Quinn Chambers realize that homosexuals "are humans like everyone else," Emily wrote.

———

Of course, some lesbian and gay issues never make it into school newspapers. As executive director of the Washington, D.C.–based Student Press Law Center (SPLC), Mark Goodman fields calls from student journalists facing censorship or other legal problems. In the case of homosexual issues, this often involves censorship of advertising for support groups for adolescents concerned about their sexual orientation.

For example, according to the *SPLC Report,* an ad offering counseling for gay, lesbian, and bisexual students was cut from the *Pirate's Hook* at Riverside High School in Durham, North Carolina, after parents protested to the principal. The ad had already appeared in several other local student and commercial newspapers.

The *Pirate's Hook* staff voted 10–2 to run the ad the first time they saw it; principal William Batchelor and the adviser met separately, and also agreed it could be printed. However, when the parents protested, Mr. Batchelor requested it be run in a "less visible" location. The high school staff moved the ad, but the parents were not satisfied. After the second printing, the principal decided to cut the ad entirely.

The controversy soon surfaced in the local *Herald-Sun* newspaper. Two Riverside students wrote an article conceding the principal's right to slice the ad, but attacking his basis for doing so (he said that running the ad condoned its message, which had upset "many parents"). The principal added that he was advised by a local mental health professional that the ad could be damaging to students, because "high school males particularly are confused about their sexuality." Mr. Batchelor said that he was told the content of the ad could lead these students "to go one way instead of the other."

Erin Iannacchione, editor-in-chief of the *Pirate's Hook* and co-author of the *Herald-Sun* piece, said that there were letters to the editor supporting both sides of the debate every day for about a month. "All this came from one little ad that wants to help people," she observed. "There are still people out there that need that service. These people shouldn't have to think that they are doing something wrong."

A similar situation arose in the Virginia suburbs when Annandale High School principal Ray Watson refused to allow the student newspaper the *A Blast* to run an ad from Washington's SMYAL. The ad, which provided information on gatherings for gay, lesbian, and bisexual youngsters, along with a helpline number for information and counseling, was submitted to seventy-nine Washington-area high schools; only fifteen initially published it.

The problem began when the *A Blast* student business manager Matt McGuire and editor Margie Brown argued over whether to accept the ad. A majority of staffers favored publication, but Mr. Watson refused to allow it. The principal based his decision, Matt told the *SPLC Report,* on conservative community standards, personal beliefs, and a court decision. Matt resigned his position after the incident, and told the *Washington Post* that he felt community advertisers would shy away from a paper with the gay advertisement. "What sort of position do we want to have in the community?" he asked. "The idea of being associated with gays and lesbians, it bothers me."

But Margie, the editor, disagreed, saying, "You can't allow some ads to run and not others. It's censorship. The ad was not inappropriate by any standards ... The original decision was based on homophobic attitudes."

An appeal to school superintendent E. Wayne Harris worked, and the advertisement appeared in a subsequent *A Blast* issue.

A stronger reaction occurred in Williams Bay, Wisconsin, when students published a series of articles on homosexuality in the *Bulldog Barker*. The two-page spread included an interview with a gay man, a report on community counseling for gays, and a general information piece. Twelve residents complained, after which community members protested, the administration considered discontinuing the paper, the faculty adviser's job was reviewed, and editor Jennifer Knight became something of a hero in the gay press.

The protests cascaded in from all sides, ranging from members of local religious groups to those who felt that AIDS was insufficiently discussed. Others believed the articles' sources, including the American Psychiatric Association, were not reliable or relevant. (The community became involved because the *Bulldog Barker* is distributed with a local paper, and thus reaches beyond the student body.)

Principal Patrick Byrnes, who told the *SPLC Report* that he had mixed emotions about the article, felt that the controversy was caused not by the administration, but by the appearance of a local church group at a school board meeting. "Williams Bay is a very conservative town," he said. "Although we have another, more liberal religious group, the conservative church that complained about the articles is very active."

Editor Knight said the articles were "burning topics" for many students, and were handled responsibly. "I think it's a shame to have to diminish the quality of a newspaper in order to avoid controversy," she said. While she eventually felt a sense of support from the community, students, and school board, and was quoted in several gay papers, she believed the self-censorship of the staff that resulted damaged everyone.

A school principal in Fort Worth, Texas, also got into the act when students working on the Arlington Heights High School *Jacket Journal* attempted to distribute an anonymous survey to four hundred students about their attitudes toward homosexuality, including their exposure to it through family, friends, or personal experience. The idea arose after twelve men at nearby Carswell Air Force Base were discharged because of their sexual orientation.

Homosexuality hung heavily on students' minds, stated faculty adviser Donya Witherspoon. "Some of these students even live on the air force base. They'd been asking to run this survey on homosexuality to find out just what the attitudes of their peers were about a sensitive subject." She called the survey "bland" compared to similar (and permissible) student surveys concerning drugs, child abuse, date rape, and teenage drinking.

Principal Winifred Taylor felt that the survey was offensive, and likely to cause emotional problems in those who participated. Ms. Witherspoon disagreed, noting that previous surveys had not "promoted" drugs or drinking. "Distribution of a survey does not mean that students feel any certain way about an issue," she said. "They were not trying to promote homosexuality. That's not a survey's function."

Forbidden to hand out the surveys, the *Jacket Journal* published instead a copy of the survey itself, along with a related editorial. When the school board met to discuss the subject nearly one hundred parents, faculty members, and students showed up to support the staff's right to conduct the survey; the incident was covered on three local television stations, and in the *Fort Worth Star-Telegram*. Eventually the students reached a compromise: the principal won the right to review all surveys within classrooms, but students are now allowed to distribute surveys before and after school, and during lunch, without administrative approval. While pleased with what was termed a victory, the students nevertheless had one final complaint: managing editor Angela Sweeney called the principal's three-day survey review period "ridiculous."

Finally, one story proves that not all high school papers treat lesbian and gay issues as Very Serious Stuff. In the May 1993 issue of the Mountlake Terrace (Washington) High School *Hawkeye*, Bryan Theiss dove into the debate "Do you decide to be gay?" with a delicious parody. His dry wit would have impressed Oscar Wilde.

"I can still remember it like it was yesterday: the day I made one of the most important decisions of my life," he began. He met the Sexuality Fairy, who visits "everyone when they must decide who and what they will be sexually attracted to later in life." The fairy gave Bryan three choices – "hetero, homo or bi" – and then elaborated. If he chose to be homosexual, Bryan said the fairy told him, he would be treated as an outcast, blamed for the spread of the HIV virus, never allowed to marry the one he loved, barred from jobs in certain fields, castigated for asking for "special privileges," urged to change, assaulted, perhaps even killed. If he decided to be bisexual, the fairy continued, Bryan would be treated with much the same misunderstanding. If, however, he chose to be heterosexual, he would be "considered by most to be normal ... [and would] better appreciate a lot of the jokes on *In Living Color.*"

Well! "The pressure was on. So many choices – and they all sounded so good! The same sex down one road, along with a large segment of society hating me because of my attraction. Both sexes down another road, with the same hatred. And the opposite sex down the third road, with no drawbacks. How could I possibly decide?" Bryan wrote.

"Oh, I don't know," he told the fairy. "How about ... uh ... hetero? Yeah. I'll be hetero, I guess."

"Hetero it is!" the fairy replied. And with the wave of a magic wand Bryan ran off to the other side of the playground, "to throw dirt bombs at girls in hopes they would notice me.

"It was hard to believe that such a tough decision could be made in so little time," he admitted. "But I made the decision, so I felt the attraction.

"It wasn't until later in life that I met the Physical Attributes Fairy, who made me decide whether the girls I was attracted to should be blonde, brunette, or bald with no teeth," he concluded. "But that's another fairy tale."

The Harvey Milk School
Makes Its Mark

Not all of the thirty or so students at the Harvey Milk School know who their eponymous hero was. But everyone in New York City's education community knows of the Harvey Milk School – the first and, for nearly a decade, only high school in the country established solely to serve lesbian, gay, and bisexual youth. Since its founding in 1985 it has made remarkable progress; where once it was an object of curiosity and derision (one early newspaper headline called it "The High School Where Every Senior is a Homecoming Queen"), today the institution draws admiring visitors from around the globe.

The Harvey Milk School, named for the openly gay San Francisco supervisor assassinated in 1978, has racked up some impressive successes since first opening its doors in donated church space. In early 1994 it abandoned its cramped, drafty, and dilapidated quarters on Manhattan's outermost edge – an area infested by bars, sex shops, and porn theaters that, one spokesperson observed, sent a cruel message to students: "This is what you deserve." The school now occupies an expansive, renovated Greenwich Village loft, just a couple of blocks north of New York University. It has overcome a number of difficult challenges – its unique mandate to teach homosexuals; bureaucratic wrangles between the New York City Board of Education and the collaborating agency that helps run the school, the Hetrick-Martin Institute; constant battles for funds, respect, even lunch – to reach a population that for decades has been ill-served by mainstream schools (and as a result developed learning and behavioral problems that were often misdiagnosed, unappreciated, or ignored). The graduation rate is good; many other youngsters return before graduating to their former neighborhood schools, buoyed by the academic skills they have gained in the tiny school with its dedicated staff of two full-time teachers, two paraprofessionals, and a few dedicated volunteers.

But wherever they go, virtually every student leaves Harvey Milk with heightened confidence and self-esteem. For perhaps the first time in their lives they have met men and women who care about their progress, both as students and as human beings; men and women who discuss with them math, science, English, history, sex, and AIDS – men and women who, like them, are gay.

Of course, all this did not happen overnight. The Harvey Milk saga began when staff members at the Hetrick-Martin Institute, a social service agency for lesbian, gay, and bisexual youth founded in 1979, recognized that many of the youngsters they were counseling and treating – some just fourteen years old – were not attending school. The reasons varied – verbal harassment, physical violence, even (in the case of homeless youngsters) lack of a school to attend – but all were related, in some way, to their homosexuality.

The institute seized upon a board of education policy that provides for a teacher to be assigned to any social service agency with at least twenty-two clients who are not attending school. The difficult path to accreditation wound through the New York City Public Schools' Alternative High Schools and Programs division, which administers three dozen small schools as safe, supportive atmospheres for youngsters who, for a panoply of reasons ranging from drug addiction and criminal behavior to hospitalization, cannot make it in mainstream schools. However, it took the threat of a class-action suit from the Hetrick-Martin staff before the board of education approved the idea of a school for gay and lesbian youth.

But they did, and on April 15, 1985, Fred Goldhaber faced twenty-two youngsters from the altar of the Washington Square United Methodist Church. For perhaps the first time in the history of education, an entire high school classroom was filled with openly gay students.

"I didn't know I was gay until I was twenty-four," Mr. Goldhaber – a big-framed, somewhat rumpled-looking New York native – said. "And I was very furious at the board of education for not teaching me there were such things as gay and lesbian people. When I became a teacher I hoped someday to help other gay kids in schools so they wouldn't have to grow up ignorant, as I did." A colleague at the Brooklyn high school he'd taught at for seventeen years told him that the board of education was planning to open a school for homosexual youngsters, and Mr. Goldhaber applied for a transfer. He was accepted for the Harvey Milk faculty – in fact, he became its *only* faculty member. "It was like the answer to a dream," he recalled. "I guess I'm pretty lucky. I had a lot of personal problems with self-esteem – but I do have a lot of confidence in my ability to teach, so I must have said the right things to the right people."

Mr. Goldhaber had plenty of preconceptions about what his new school would be – and, he laughed, "they were totally wrong. I thought all my students would be like little T.S. Eliots and Gertrude Steins. I expected to find kids who were pretty much like me – not particularly gay, not easily identifiable as gay. I was surprised that many of the boys were effeminate, and many of the girls were somewhat masculine." For what he called, self-mockingly, "that great revelation" – and which first appeared in a newspaper article early in the school's history – he was given one of *Esquire* magazine's "Dubious Achievement Awards."

Mr. Goldhaber was appalled that most of his new students had the same learning disabilities and problems as those in his Brooklyn high school – and many had behavioral problems as well. But he also learned that they were not willing to give up on their education. "Originally the board of ed. talked about a GED (general equivalency diploma) program, with me basically teaching six subjects to help the kids pass the test. Much to my horror, the kids said they didn't want that; they wanted to go the whole forty-credit route. They wanted the same education anyone else would get; the only thing is, it had to be in a safe place. So we changed the structure of the school, to make it into a full academic program." However, for two years he remained the only teacher.

In that first term, Harvey Milk students took two English courses, math, global studies, and music – all together, all in the same room. When a few complained that they'd covered some of the material already, Mr. Goldhaber realized he had to develop courses in which students could do their own work, at their own pace. Over the next two years he created nearly forty classes to accommodate the needs of thirty students, who by then ranged in age from fourteen to twenty-one. Mirroring the New York City school population, the majority were – and still are – Latino or black. "The minorities," Mr. Goldhaber pointed out, "are really a majority here now."

The other Harvey Milk faculty member is English teacher Donna Farnum. When she arrived in February 1993 to replace Monica Fishof, who had been hired in 1987, she had her own image of who she would be teaching. The young African-American's preconceptions were also wrong, but in a very different way from Mr. Goldhaber's. "I thought the kids would be hanging out, or jumping out, windows," Ms. Farnum said. "I guess I fed into the whole notion of stereotypes, especially of kids with behavioral and adjustment problems. When I came here, I really got to understand that all that clinical stuff that had been written about gay kids really wasn't the case."

The arrival of Ms. Farnum coincided with the evolution of Harvey Milk into a more diverse school. The board added a pair of paraprofessionals to the staff; members of New York's gay and lesbian community – men and women who did not hold teaching certificates, but wanted to be part of the exciting school – got involved too. A registered nurse came on board; a Hetrick-Martin volunteer talked about tax forms; an assistant district attorney taught a course on the judicial system; and NYU students instructed students on "street law." A special "community" class, dealing with emotions, relationships, and conflict resolution, was initiated.

As the school changed, so did the two teachers. "I came here wet behind the ears – literally knowing nothing," Ms. Farnum admitted. "These kids have taught me a lot; I'm still growing and learning every day. They taught me how to teach, and how to live as a human being. I've grown so much in terms of how I see the world, and my place in it. I don't think enough has been said about our kids as people, but I know they've brought a lot of their world here, and they help make this school what it is." To illustrate her point, she led a visitor into her English classroom, its walls decorated with Valentine's Day poems and essays. The writing was strong indeed, but what struck a reader more were the content and depth of expression. Ms. Farnum's youngsters had written about love – winning at love, losing at love, wanting love, and wanting to forget about love – in its starkest, boldest terms. And it was same-sex love, a topic that seldom appears on classroom bulletin boards anywhere.

"Working at the school has made me realize what awful lives many of our kids have had as gay and lesbian youths," Mr. Goldhaber noted. "More than half of them come to us absolutely closed. They're unwilling to trust, unwilling to believe in themselves or that anyone could give a damn about them without trying to use them. We've had major success in opening up these kids, resensitizing them to the concerns of others, teaching them to work together and care about each other.

"I didn't have these problems in high school. I had a good family support system behind me, but many of our kids don't," he continued.

"They come in angry, frightened, and incredibly hostile; even when we're gentle to them, they're suspicious. We give a lot of respect to the kids; we work very hard to make them feel good about themselves. I do a lot of 'unteaching' – trying to let the kids know that if they're math-phobic (and most of them are), it's not that they're stupid. They probably had attendance problems at their other school, maybe because they didn't want to be harassed anymore, and so they probably missed some of this stuff along the way. We take them back as far as we need to, even if it means teaching them how to add and subtract. Gradually the hostility subsides, and we build their self-confidence. Eventually they learn math – but just as importantly, they learn to care about themselves, and about each other."

A sense of gayness is never far from the Harvey Milk School surface. During breaks, students tell staff members about their weekends; everyone knows Mr. Goldhaber has a lover, because he proudly shows photos. Classroom discussions are occasionally interrupted by a question about safe sex, and Hetrick-Martin counselors are always available for any topic the teachers feel they cannot handle. Students have access to the institute's extensive counseling and advocacy services, and are encouraged to participate in other Hetrick-Martin programs as well. That's not hard to do – as soon as the three p.m. bell rings the school transforms itself into a drop-in center, with attractions including computer, video, theater, and photography workshops.

"Basically, our defenses are down here," Mr. Goldhaber explained when asked how "gay" a lesbian and gay school could be. "Donna and I are gay human beings who happen to teach here, so our discussions can be as frank – or general – as we want them to be. That might not be the case in any other high school in New York City. It's normal here to bring up lesbian and gay issues, and we deal with them in a normal way."

That's especially true in Ms. Farnum's English classes, which Mr. Goldhaber called "incredible." If her students were in a traditional high school, he said, "they could never write their true feelings or beliefs in their journals. They'd have to change pronouns, or couch everything in heterosexual terms. In Donna's classes they can respond completely honestly to a poem, or express their thoughts without fear of ridicule or having to go through self-censorship."

The teachers' sense of pride is palpable throughout the Harvey Milk School. They are proud of the students (of their personal growth as well as of their academic work), proud of the school, and proud of their own contributions as educators to the lesbian and gay community. "I think we have something special going on here," Mr. Goldhaber said. "We stress responsibility, self-empowerment, commitment to self-learning, and the development of social skills. I really think we do the impossible here, given all our limitations. We can, and do, provide overlooked kids, who otherwise might never receive one, an education." However, he noted, there is plenty of praise to pass around. "The Hetrick-Martin Institute pulls this all together, along with the board of education. Without the support of an agency like this, it would be incredibly difficult – probably impossible – to have a Harvey Milk School. The institute and the board have locked horns, but both of them have been crucial to what we've been able to accomplish."

The Harvey Milk School has not gone unnoticed. The Los Angeles Unified School District has fashioned its EAGLES School in West Hollywood after the New York program. Harvey Milk plays host to flocks of frequent high-level guests, ranging from education professionals like city schools chancellor Ramon Cortines to reporters from *Time* and *Newsweek*. Closer to its spiritual home, it is a tremendous source of pride in the lesbian and gay community. "All you have to do is mention our name and people applaud," Mr. Goldhaber said.

Yet for all its fame (and, he noted, no more infamy; the "crazy, off-the-wall attacks have dwindled to almost nothing"), the Harvey Milk School remains unique. Despite all the dignitaries who troop through, none return to their home districts to initiate their own version of the school. Mr. Goldhaber, who had been able to answer every other question about his institution, was stumped when asked why the Harvey Milk School was still, at the time the question was asked, the only one of its kind in the world.

"I have no idea," he said finally. "People from other cities say their gay and lesbian kids are well integrated into their own school systems, but I don't believe that at all. Gay and lesbian kids are at incredible risk, for all kinds of reasons. Many of them are just not being served by their community schools. They don't have positive role models, or peers who treat them as equals. They need schools where they can get support, and learn about self-confidence and self-esteem, along with math and science and English too."

Yet it is only in New York City that, every year since 1985, a lucky thirty youngsters get that chance.

Speaking Their Minds
to Open Up Eyes

Of the many emotions a gay man or woman feels, perhaps the most powerfully pervasive is fear. The fear of being found out is real enough, but the worry does not end there: beyond it lurks the fear of being called names, being assaulted, perhaps even being killed. For adults, those fears are horrible enough; for lesbian and gay teenagers, who lack experience and life skills to cope with them, such fears can become overwhelming.

In San Francisco, one organization is doing something to allay those fears. And, in an ironic twist, the work of that group's dozens of volunteers brings them almost daily into the very place where those fears are not only strongest, but where they are actively fomented: the schools.

Community United Against Violence (CUAV) occupies a suite of offices on Market Street, San Francisco's main drag. The reception area is decorated with posters that assail gay-bashing, at the same time warning men and women to protect themselves against baseball bats, bricks, even bullets. One large, typical sign screams, "4 Kids Jump Lesbian Near Dolores Park." The message is both clear and frighteningly true: high school youngsters commit hate crimes.

CUAV's mandate is to combat homophobia, and it does so in many ways: letter-writing campaigns, monitoring police, even contests. But one of the most effective methods is its speakers' bureau. Whenever any of the nearly one hundred men and women on their roster enter a classroom, they actually fulfill two missions. They're educating youngsters about homophobic violence, hopefully stopping hate crimes before they occur, and they're also providing important role models to homosexual, bisexual, and questioning boys and girls who, even in a city as gay oriented as San Francisco, may not feel good about themselves or have access to accurate information.

CUAV's official statement describes the speakers' mission since the organization's founding in 1979, in the wake of the riots following the assassinations of Mayor George Moscone and openly gay supervisor Harvey Milk: "By providing students with an opportunity (often their first) to meet open lesbians, gay men and bisexuals, we allow them to question values, destroy myths and explore feelings." Added Sylvia Weisenberg, speakers' bureau coordinator: "We're a group of volunteers who talk about our personal lives in order to break down stereotypes. Some of us have been actual victims of gay-bashing, and want to speak to potential or actual perpetrators; more of us talk because we knew we were gay in high school but were closeted and struggling. No one told us it was okay, or that we could have happy, productive jobs and good relationships. And some of our speakers are gay and lesbian parents who want to assure their own kids' safety in school. We think we can reduce violence against gays by reducing fear, because fear is based on ignorance. If kids have a chance to meet us and hear our stories, we're not as scary to them."

All speakers undergo an eight-hour training session, and are handed a voluminous, 67-page manual. They learn how to introduce themselves and describe CUAV; they also learn to start off each talk with a disclaimer of what they are *not* in the classroom to do. "We're not there to recruit students into being gay," Ms. Weisenberg said. "We're not there representing all gays and lesbians, because every person is different. We're not suggesting they try anything we say. We're not there to lecture. And we tell them there's no question that's too dumb or too personal." In fact, after brief biographies, the bulk of each class session – thirty minutes, in most cases – is filled with a flurry of not dumb, but often very personal, questions and answers.

The speakers represent San Francisco's diversity: they're evenly split between men and women, and more than half are people of color. Some talk in Spanish; others use sign language. A representative sample appeared in CUAV's spacious conference room one winter weekday to discuss their presentations; although no women were available that morning, all three men acknowledged the importance of having both a male and a female appear in each classroom.

The three were Robert Morgan, a white man with graying hair and a soft Southern accent, whose tweed jacket fairly shouted "businessman" (he is, in fact, an insurance manager); Joseph Clark, a twentyish

black man; and Richard Carrazza, a twentyish white Massachusetts
native with an intense manner. They began by discussing their personal
motivations for speaking to students.

Richard Carrazza saw a newspaper article about the speakers'
group, and realized that gay youngsters need role models. "My perception growing up was of transvestites – and I didn't want to wear
dresses!" he said. "Also, most violence is done by males in their teens
to midtwenties. I thought if they met us, and saw us as people, they'd
get a better attitude and that would mitigate violence against us. And
maybe girls could stop the boys, by letting them know it's not okay to
say 'faggot,' or beat us up."

"For me, the AIDS crisis was the final straw," said Robert Morgan.
"That, and the far right."

Joseph Clark felt an urgent need to show young African-Americans
that there are happy, successful gay blacks in the world. Although he
first felt trepidation about speaking at inner-city schools, he has found
that the worst high schools are the best to go to, because those students
ask the best questions. At Lowell, one of the city's most prestigious
schools, they seem hesitant to ask anything.

Richard Carrazza overcame his initial fears when he realized "how
obedient the kids were, and so small." He finds his talks satisfying. "I
get such a charge out of it. I'm never nervous. If I were to talk to a gay
group, I'd be much more nervous. I'm very confident with kids – I
think because they're so interested in what we say. We're much more
interesting to listen to than their teachers."

Robert Morgan, who attended private schools while growing up in
North Carolina, had very little knowledge of public schools. From the
beginning, however, he realized "the kids want us there. They're
inquisitive. It may start slow, but things pick up quickly." He said that
"the rougher kids ask rougher questions. That's okay, but the school
board has made us be circumspect about what we say."

"We can't talk about our own sexual experiences," Richard explained. "We have to talk in a more general sense."

But that does not inhibit the questioners. They want to know about
anything – and everything. "Kids love you to be frank. They don't
want b.s.," Robert said.

"'Honesty' is the most universal thing we get back on the comment
cards," Richard agreed.

The most direct questions come from younger boys – "with a little
smirk," Robert noted. "They can be very specific. It's not unusual to
be asked, 'How do you like taking it up the ass?'"

"And religion," Joseph added. "'Aren't you going to hell?' I address it as 'God preaches love, not hate. That's how I live my life.'"

Richard talks about freedom of religion. "Everyone chooses his or her religion, and that includes the right of others to choose their own religion – or no religion at all. And that sort of leads into a discussion about choices. I say, 'You wouldn't want your parents to choose who you date, would you?'"

"Religion really gets me going," Robert admitted. "Two-thirds of the way through, someone usually raises it. I tell them I was raised a Christian, the same way some of them were. But I didn't think for myself until I was out of college, and as long as people can think for themselves, and not accept dogma, that's good. Then I drop it as fast as I can!"

"When they quote the Bible to me, I talk about the sins of eating shellfish," Joseph said. "With African-American kids, I tell them the Bible used to justify slavery."

Other popular questions include the age at which the speakers first knew they were gay, why they "chose" to be homosexual, whether they would change their sexual orientation if they could, how their parents reacted, the age of their first experience, whether they've had encounters with the opposite sex, if they want to have children, and whether they were abused when they were young.

Many speakers find it less inhibiting to have students write questions anonymously on index cards, program coordinator Sylvia Weisenberg said. Youngsters often word their queries negatively: "How many friends did you lose?" not "What were your friends' reactions?" Stereotypes arise quickly in the questions. Teenagers find it surprising that Mr. Morgan has good female friends, both straight and lesbian.

Some students ask what kind of partner the speakers like. Joseph Clark anticipates that, so he brings in photos of his boyfriend. "He's Asian, and that really gets them going – especially the Asian kids," he laughed. "And when a lesbian brings in pictures of her kids, that really gets the girls going!"

Joseph once stunned a particularly tough group by introducing his sister, who had come simply to hear him talk. "She's a lesbian, and they were amazed," he said. "And when I told them I have another brother who's gay, they asked if we had sex together."

Sprinkled among the questions are supportive comments. "I've had students turn to their classmates and say, 'It's okay to be gay; it's just a choice,'" Richard said.

But much of the support comes after class, when boys and girls linger. "One boy just wanted to talk, but I didn't know what I could do for him," said Richard. "I mentioned some resources he might be interested in, but I didn't want to scare him away by implying that I thought he was gay." To ease students' reluctance to ask for help, speakers put resource phone numbers on the board, advising them to call if they have further questions.

The men are aware that the slightest gesture or remark carries significance. Richard explained, "Sometimes kids will look away from me at the beginning, so later I say, 'Think about the way you didn't look at me.' Then they all look right at me!"

"But eye contact is dangerous too," Robert Morgan noted. "When a guy asks a question, you want to connect with him, but you don't want to embarrass him by looking right at him the whole time.

"It constantly amazes me that here in San Francisco, where kids are constantly exposed to gay stories and gay controversies, some kids are not aware of gay life," he continued, shaking his head. "Still the worst thing you can call someone in the halls, even in San Francisco, is 'faggot' or 'queer.'" When Richard asks students what would happen if one of them came out at school, the answer is usually the same: harassment, teasing, possibly violence. "That's why I try to talk about suicide statistics," he said. "I tell them they can help do something about that."

The periods fly by, Robert marveled. "All you want to do is make one impact they can take away. I feel for these kids – I would never want to be fifteen again. That's why I so admire the kids who speak up, especially the ones who talk about having a gay family member or a gay friend. That's such an age of ridicule. Peer pressure is so great; you just see it in their eyes. They're so interested in what we're talking about, but they're so terrified of being identified with us."

"I see kids trying to act tough, and yet they're only boys – they're fourteen, sixteen years old," Richard added. "That's how kids that age survive – they act tough, so no one will mess with them. What a shame they can't act more naturally."

Robert said the real satisfaction from speaking in schools comes when they read the anonymous comment cards that students and teachers fill out. Sylvia Weisenberg concurred: "The faculty is one hundred percent positive. A lot of them say they think kids are less likely to be prejudiced after hearing the talk. The students are about ninety-five percent positive. They overwhelmingly say they like us, and that they learned things. They appreciate our honesty – and they're honest in return. They write things like, 'I used to think the gays were monsters, but now I think they're okay.' And when we get an evaluation back that says, 'Thanks. I'm gay. Now I can tell someone' – that makes it all worthwhile."

One day, she noted, a student pulled his hood over his head when the speakers walked into the room, to show his contempt and disgust. At the end of the hour he walked up, shook the man's hand, and hugged the woman.

And then there was the student who wrote a poem after hearing the CUAV speakers. She submitted it to a citywide poetry contest – and when it won a $50 prize, she invited Ms. Weisenberg and the speakers to the awards ceremony. "Talk about making an impact!" Sylvia Weisenberg laughed.

————————

Burlington, Vermont, can – with a bit of imagination – be thought of as a New England version of San Francisco. Both cities take much of their identity from nearby bodies of water; both are ringed by hills; both attract hordes of outdoors-oriented young men and women. True, Burlington does not boast the ethnic diversity of San Francisco – although many of the white suburbanites who came to town to attend the University of Vermont and then stayed on to ski, wait tables, or just hang out have made it the reggae capital of northern New England – but it goes San Francisco one better in the politics department: it's where Bernie Saunders, now the only Independent member of the U.S. House of Representatives, got his start; he was the Socialist mayor.

As the state's largest city, home to a whopping 40,000 souls, Burlington is a magnet for freethinkers, wanderers, footloose adventurers – anyone who feels different, strange, or otherwise unable to fit in in the straitlaced towns and villages that dot Vermont and the neighboring "North Country" of New York.

Which is why Outright Vermont thrives there. The organization attracts gay, lesbian, bisexual, and questioning youths with a drop-in center and educational projects; it also operates an outreach program extending throughout the state. In the center of all the action, working long days and sometimes longer nights, sits executive director Karin Eade. She is justifiably proud of the many activities she helps develop, organize, and staff, but one of the most satisfying is the speaking she does. "Gay and Lesbian Studies 101," she calls it jokingly, but it is obvious that for some who listen, it is the most important class they will ever take.

"I do it for a very personal reason," she said. "I think if one person had talked to me about gay, lesbian, and bisexual people in a healthy – even just a nonderogatory – way when I was growing up, it would

have made my life a lot easier. So I do it almost as a healing process."
Her life story includes being kicked out of her New York house when
she came out to her parents ("and basically they've lived up to that
pledge"), followed by a five-year period filled with drugs, alcohol, and
battered self-esteem. But she discovered she had a gift for working with
young people, and when she landed in Burlington, she found it the
perfect place to do that. Her volunteer work at Outright Vermont led
to a work-study position, followed by paid administrative posts. One
of the first tasks she tackled was educational outreach; in Vermont that
means heading into the hinterlands to talk to students.

There are approximately 112 high schools in Vermont; Karin has
spoken at nearly one-quarter of them, along with some middle schools
and one elementary school. She tailors her talk to the particular school
or area — the poverty-stricken towns of the elegantly named Northeast
Kingdom are far different places from the ski resort towns of central
and southern Vermont — and is also aware of whether a course is
introductory or advanced. But she often utilizes one specific activity to
determine the level of homophobia in the room.

"I ask the kids to stand in one of three areas that best describes the
atmosphere in their school," she explained. "I'll call one side of the
room 'very homophobic,' another side 'totally safe,' and the third area
'someplace in between.' I emphasize that they should stand where they
do based on what they hear in the halls, not their own experiences.
Then we talk about why they stood where they did, and what that says
about the attitudes of their teachers and everyone else in the school."

If the class seems to have little knowledge of homosexuality, Karin
tells her story (she often brings one or two youngsters with her; they
talk too, then answer questions). If the group is more advanced, she
breaks them into small discussion groups and challenges them with
three questions: What were the first three descriptions you heard of
gays and lesbians? What were the first three stereotypes you heard
about them? What do you know to be important to all teenagers
everywhere?

After each group reports back, they try to link everything together.
The most common responses to question three include issues involving
peers, independence, families, and school. "We talk about how those
kinds of things relate to homophobia," Karin said, "and suddenly
people 'get it.' You can almost hear a gasp of recognition when people
suddenly recognize that *all* young people deal with this stuff — independence, relationships. That sudden knowledge makes gay, lesbian,
and bisexual youth the same as everyone else." Her talks end either

with questions or with more group work to brainstorm ideas about breaking down homophobic barriers in that school.

Sixty to seventy percent of the time, young people and adults feel free to ask challenging questions. Many of the attendees want to know about families ("Is it a good choice for gays to bring up children?") and – not surprisingly for a very Christian state like Vermont – religion ("Don't you feel bad being a sinner?"). There is such a thing as being too polite, Karin noted. "I tell them I *want* tough questions. I begin by saying the only way we can have a dialogue is by talking about our fears, but that doesn't always happen. I think kids want to ask tough questions, because they don't always get a chance to, but very few people in school ever allow them to think, or challenge them to ask about difficult subjects. This gives them a right to think and ask – and it's about a subject they're incredibly interested in!"

There has been no organized opposition to her talks, although sometimes parents attend in lieu of their children. "I think they walk away surprised that it's not as threatening a subject as they thought," Karin said. She has received one or two letters against her presentation – and an overwhelming amount of positive feedback. "We get lots of calls from kids who are questioning their sexuality, thanking us for helping them focus on things a little better. I get calls from parents who heard we were in their kids' school; they think their child is questioning his or her sexuality, and want more information. And we hear from teachers who were unsure about what we were going to say, but who now want to do something – make a change – in their schools."

Karin thought that talking to high school groups would be harder than it is. "Kids are supposed to be so brutal. But I've been pleasantly surprised at how little I've been harassed. And I'm definitely impressed by how receptive kids have been to their peers. I was hesitant at first to bring kids with me, but they've been very, very well received. They get the respect of their peers just by being there, and then when the kids in the schools hear what they have to say, that respect just increases."

After one presentation, half a dozen students organized a lesbian and gay youth group that continues to meet weekly. "They banded together because they realized they had a *right* to meet together – and not in secret either," Karin said proudly.

One of her most successful talks came in a rural community, where several students suffered homophobic harassment. Forty youngsters and three teachers showed up for a voluntary meeting. The youths being harassed beamed when they realized they had allies in the school.

The session ended with the students writing letters to their teachers and board of education members.

Why have Karin Eade's talks for Outright Vermont been so successful? She believes it is because "kids don't get a chance to talk about sex, and the issues surrounding sex – communication, relationships, honesty – very much in school. Schools are so nervous about touching it, even approaching it. But kids are really eager to talk about these things. They're among the most important things they want to hear about, and learn. Then I come in, and I don't talk about sex either – I talk about sexuality – but kids realize that that's what they need to learn about. Homosexuality is just part of sexuality, but the discussion ends up being very helpful for everyone."

If anyone should feel comfortable speaking in front of a classroom, it's Jennifer DiMarco. A Seattle native who holds positive memories of that city's alternative schools, she's also an accomplished writer who penned her first novel at age ten, finished a dozen more in the next decade, and has few qualms expressing her most personal thoughts in conversation as well as on paper. In addition, she is a lesbian who revels in her sexuality – and who was raised by lesbian parents (her "mama" is a construction worker, her "moo moo" a psychotherapist).

Yet her experiences as a speaker have not always been positive.

While still in high school – the Summit School, which she terms "great for the creative heart and soul, because there's an underlying thread of respect through everything" – she gave a talk at a larger public school. She felt as if she had walked into a prison. Summit had six hundred students, prekindergarten through twelfth grade; the larger school had over a thousand high school boys and girls. There were few windows, and fewer smiles.

In the middle of her talk a boy called her a "filthy dyke." She left the stage, went to the end of his row, and said, "If you're angry at me, let's get you excused from class and we'll talk later." They did. She found out that three weeks earlier his father had died of AIDS. He was angry, but had no one to talk to. Jennifer learned that such lack of support is common in public schools.

She also was followed into the parking lot by boys who swore at her and broke her car window. "I told them they were proud of being straight, and I was proud of being gay – but I wondered, what kind of behavior do our schools allow?" she said.

However, she's also had positive experiences: two girls hung around after her talk, then shyly asked her to autograph a book and

Already a prolific author, Jennifer DiMarco wrote her first novel when she was ten years old. Now in her twenties, this out and articulate lesbian-raised-by-lesbians is often invited to speak at high schools, sometimes about lesbian and gay issues, other times about creative writing.

explained how much her lesbian-themed writing has meant to them; a group of gay students leapt to her defense when a boy shouted homophobic remarks.

Not all her speaking is on lesbian and gay issues. Some schools specifically ask that she not talk about sexuality; they want her to focus only on creative writing. She complies reluctantly, but the mentality that underlies those requests disturbs her. "School is such an essential part of your upbringing," she said. "Any school that carries books by Judy Blume or Stephen King should also have a gay and lesbian section in the library. Any classroom that has *Sports Illustrated* or *Time* or *Teen* magazine – or a Boy Scout magazine, I see that a lot – should also have *The Advocate* or *something* that tells gay and lesbian students that that's okay too.

"At the very least, every guidance counselor must be educated to feel sympathetic talking to kids. Part of everyone's teaching degree should be a course in diversity. Teachers have to be able to recognize the difference between when Susie dumps John, and when Susie dumps Sally, and how kids and friends react differently to those two situations. But the more schools I go into, and the more I see and hear about kids getting the heck beat out of them..." She paused, suddenly at a loss for words.

"I just wish schools would be more open, and not just with seminars," she resumed. "For a kid who lives in the shadows, shame always lingers. I can do a little bit to help them, and battle the ignorance of everyone else in the school, but one speaker can't do it all. It's got to come from the entire school, as a whole, and everyone has to be involved."

———

Jennifer DiMarco helped blaze the way for a younger generation of Seattle gays and lesbians. Many now hang out at a dilapidated wooden building in the middle of the city's chic gay mecca, Capitol Hill. Lambert House serves as a drop-in center, a safe haven – and sometimes the only home they know – for lesbian and gay youngsters from across the Pacific Northwest.

Several social service agencies operate programs out of Lambert House, among them the American Friends Service Committee (AFSC). Loren Smith founded that organization's Gay and Lesbian Youth Program, of which one major focus is education. That entails, among other things, organizing panels of young people to talk to students, teachers, counselors, nurses, administrators, businesspeople – in short, anyone and everyone who needs his or her consciousness raised.

Loren Smith has done her homework. On any afternoon Lambert House is filled with lesbian and gay youths of every size, shape, color, and clique. They range from a girl with a nose ring to a boy in a tennis sweater. Many of them appear, at least periodically, on one of her panels.

Typical (if that is the right word) of her speakers is Isaiah Brokenleg. A sixteen-year-old part–Native American youngster who attends the Indian Heritage alternative high school in Seattle, he spoke quietly, yet eloquently, about his presentations.

"I do it because I really don't like homophobia," he said simply. "I think it's a product of ignorance. People have had it drilled into their heads that gay people are perverts, and we're not."

Like most speakers, he was extremely nervous before his first talk. He was worried he would have nothing to say, and that people would stare at him. But Ms. Smith prepared Isaiah well – she makes sure first-timers know in advance the types of questions they'll hear – and his fears proved groundless. The audience responded with understanding and respect.

Over time, he has come to enjoy speaking. He now knows what to expect; for example, "in the beginning everyone sits there with their hands folded, judging us. And they're all as far back as they can be. So we have them all move to the front. By the end we can see they're more relaxed."

They often want to know how gay people have sex. But, Isaiah noted, "they're usually scared to ask that in the beginning, so they wait until the end." He and his fellow panelists answer that by asking the class to list on the board the various ways straight people have sex. "We tell them it's all the same, except for one. Then the next question is about lesbian sex," he laughed.

Other popular queries reveal similarly limited knowledge about homosexuality. Students want to know why gay males hate women, and why they wear dresses. Isaiah has learned that those questions stem not from malice, but from ignorance. Sometimes they wonder whether the speakers themselves have AIDS. "We just say that's a very personal question," he said.

Isaiah continues to speak because he believes it helps combat homophobia. In addition, he appreciates being able to spread the word about Lambert House to youngsters who might need its services but do not know it exists. And, he said, he never can tell who is listening closely. "One kid spent the whole period with his head down. The teacher was bugging him, 'cause she thought he wasn't paying attention. But then at the end he handed the facilitator a note that said how much he understood what we were trying to say. That made us feel great."

Occasionally, Isaiah will be questioned about the Native American attitude toward homosexuality. He seizes that opportunity too to educate, telling students, "In my culture, it's accepted. Gays are seen as counselors, because they know 'both sides.' They've got both female and male qualities, and that is seen as special."

Rebecca Hover, a junior at Nova (another alternative high school), echoed Isaiah's feelings. "I think the main reason people have problems with lesbian and gay people is that they don't know any," she said. "They think we're scary monsters. Well, I'm not a scary monster."

A self-described "not terribly shy person," she never worried about being hurt or taunted by students when she spoke. Besides, she noted, "the kids have always been prepped the day before not to insult us. They're polite." Still, the questions can be pointed: Why did you choose to be a lesbian? Why do you hate men? Have you ever had sex with a guy?

Rebecca sees those types of queries as opportunities to educate. She tells the audience that homosexuality is not a choice; she didn't wake up one morning and decide to be gay, nor did Satan help her "choose." The tough questions usually come from boys in the back of the room; she doesn't mind, as long as they're asked without spite. Middle school guidelines prohibit explicit explanations of how lesbians have sex, but she'll answer such questions as "How does it feel to be gay?" "The same as it feels to be straight," she replies. "We just like different people."

Teachers often encourage students to hang around after the presentation, offering to write late passes, but most don't stay. There are few deep conversations, although sometimes audience members commend the panelists for their bravery. Rebecca is never sure if her words stick or not, since she seldom has a chance to return to the same classroom. However, she has heard that the panels open up people's minds, and cause conversations.

She concluded by saying that although her message remains the same, one thing has changed in the years she has been speaking. "When I first started I thought it was so cool to be able to get up and talk about myself. I did it for personal reasons. Now I see that I'm not the one who's so important. It's the kids who are listening that really count."

William Balgobin shares the same hopes, dreams, and fears as the Seattle speakers. He does the same sort of work, too; the major difference is his slight New York accent. William serves as a peer educator for the Hetrick-Martin Institute, the city's premier education and advocacy organization for lesbian, gay, and bisexual youth. Chunky, goateed, earringed, and earnestly articulate, by the time he was an eighteen-year-old senior at the Harvey Milk School for gay and lesbian students he had already addressed over fifty groups, reaching more than a thousand students, teachers, and social service providers. It is work he loves.

"I got involved the first time I heard there was this group *about* gay, lesbian, bisexual, and transgendered youth that was also *of* them," he said, the all-inclusive description rolling easily off his tongue. "Everything else I'd ever seen was done by adults. I never saw gay youth speaking about themselves in an honest context. When I heard about the peer education program here, I was just amazed. It's so great to be able to speak for yourself, uncensored and using all the proper communication skills. I realized I was in a safe position – my mother is accepting of me. Most gay youths don't have that opportunity. Since it was there, I wanted to use it."

He underwent a comprehensive training program. Hetrick-Martin makes sure its student speakers are well versed not only in what to say, but in how to say it. They learn about conflict resolution, dealing with difficult situations, and how to refer students to appropriate resources without making them feel threatened or singled out. For instance, he said, "We don't just walk in and say, 'Hello, we're gay, you have to accept us.' A lot of times we don't even say we're gay; we just say we're from Hetrick-Martin, and explain what that is. People sort of assume we're just supportive of gay and lesbian issues. Our main job is to get a discussion going, and then go on from there. If someone has a problem with homosexuality, fine; the whole idea is to get a dialogue going, and then break down the homophobia."

William has learned not to judge reactions as either positive or negative. "*Any* reaction is positive," he said, "because it opens the doors to communication, and that's our goal: to communicate. So it's fine to have a student who's very hostile against homosexuals, just so long as that person is willing to sit down with us and talk." The only rule is that all comments be framed in a personal context: "*I* believe...," rather than "*Everyone* thinks..."

Students are eager to learn things they don't know through TV or their parents. Questions can become very personal – "How do two guys do it?" "What's it feel like to get fucked?" – and, William noted, "It's up to us to decide whether to answer or not. My opinion is it's best to answer as much as possible, because the more answers people have, the better. They really want to know about our lives." Occasionally a youngster will come out to the peer educators, though this is more likely afterward, when one or two students linger. "If it happens in the middle then we have to stop everything and deal with that person," he described. "It can get pretty emotional, when everyone turns around and says, 'Oh my God, you're gay!'"

The toughest questions deal with sexual identity, transsexuality, transgender, and transvestism. "Those things are really confusing for most people," he noted. "They don't know the differences. It's hard to explain the different parts of sexuality, and how they don't always intertwine. How someone can be homosexual and not have sex is just like how someone can be heterosexual and abstain from sex, but those concepts seem especially difficult for most people to understand."

Because all-male groups are particularly hard to deal with – "with the macho attitude, you really have to get guys comfortable talking about sexuality," William said – peer educators often begin with a word association exercise aimed at breaking down stereotypes. They write "homosexual" on the board, and ask the audience to shout out everything they know. That produces plenty of stereotypes, generalizations, and misinformation, which in turn allows the panelists to ask, "Why are we getting so much sexual stuff? Why are we getting words like 'flamboyant' and 'hairdresser'?"

William's most memorable talk came in a decrepit South Bronx building. There were holes in the ceiling and graffiti on the walls; the students strode in hostile and cursing. To get them to respect first each other, and then William, took time. But when he showed them he wasn't going to tell them what to think or do, they calmed down. "I don't think anyone had ever done that with them before: showed them respect, and listened to what they had to say," he analyzed.

He learned how to do that through the Hetrick-Martin training and at the Harvey Milk School, a tiny (thirty students) alternative school that emphasizes confidence and self-esteem. By contrast, William said, the urban high schools he talks in are "usually very big and very scary places to the thousands of students in them, straight or gay. You have to fit in with a group, or you're an outcast. To be gay and think you're the only one, or know that there are only a few of you and you don't know who the others are, makes it even scarier. And then to know there are teachers who are homophobic, and staff people who aren't going to support you – it's really horrible. And then the weapons, and the gangs ... That's the high school experience these days, to be scared shitless."

One of the main reasons William is a peer educator is to be able to help break the isolation and fear felt by the thousands of lesbian and gay youngsters cowering in New York schools. He receives little feedback after he speaks – he heads immediately back to Harvey Milk, or off to another talk. Yet that's okay, he explained. "Our goal is to get communication going. So if anyone's spoken to us during our time, that's a good thing. We know we've gotten through when that quiet kid in the corner, who didn't say anything and pretended to be asleep, suddenly starts talking to us or to people around him, or looks us in the eye or asks a really good question."

Communication – that's what it's all about. "In a sense, I'm speaking not only for myself, but for other gay youths who don't have the opportunity to speak," he concluded. "Because I very rarely see young out gay politically aware youths who speak about their lives, the gratification comes when I can share my information with other people, and get information back. It's great to be networking with other people, gay and straight. We share stories; I never got to do that before. I've learned an incredible amount by doing this."

Confident, poised, well-spoken, William Balgobin might go into community service – or politics, or perhaps photography – after college (an option he never would have thought about before enrolling in Harvey Milk). Still, he said, even after dozens of peer education sessions, it's not easy talking about himself and his life as a gay youth. A certain amount of trepidation is present every time he enters a new classroom, auditorium, or gymnasium. "It's always there," he admitted.

"You don't get over that. I don't know if I ever will. I just try to remember I'm there not only for myself, but to connect with other people. That really keeps me going."

———————

Of course, it's not only gays and lesbians who speak in schools. PFLAG (Parents, Families and Friends of Lesbians and Gays) is a support organization whose members swell the ranks of speakers from coast to coast. Typical of the men and women who bring their stories to students year after year, whenever and wherever they're asked, are Gerald and Cherie Garland. He's a former high school English teacher who, with his wife, later owned a chain of school supply stores in Arizona and California; they're no strangers to the insides of classrooms. Yet until their daughter came out to them at the age of twenty-seven, over fifteen years ago, they were ignorant about homosexuality. "PFLAG was our salvation," Mrs. Garland said, and with the fervor of souls who have been saved, they began spreading the word. In this case the word is that homosexuality, far from being a sin, is an orientation about which the entire country can stand to learn a bit more.

In Southern California, where they then lived, the requests to speak came primarily from churches, Mr. Garland said. "We had gotten very smart about this phenomenon (homosexuality)," he said. "People were interested in knowing how we felt about it as parents, and we were willing to share. Cherie and I had always been interested in minority groups, so we were naturals, you might say."

But although Mr. Garland had been a teacher for twenty-four years, he was ignorant of the pain lesbian and gay students endure. Mrs. Garland had a similarly unenlightened background: "I grew up in Oklahoma, so I was used to seeing colored drinking fountains and segregated swimming pools. As I got to be an adult I questioned my parents as to how they allowed this to happen. They said it was just the way things were. I vowed I never would let it happen. But after our son came out to us I looked back, and I realized that when I was in high school, the littlest things would get us going – if you wore green or yellow on Thursday, that meant you were queer."

In 1990 the Garlands moved to Ashland, Oregon, a town twenty miles north of the California border that boasts the world's largest Shakespeare Festival and with which they had fallen in love. They thought they were moving to a very progressive state, but were shocked to find bigotry and small-mindedness. Quickly they organized a local PFLAG chapter and the Human Rights Coalition of Jackson

County; soon thereafter they formed a small speakers' bureau of relatives of gay men and women, and gays themselves. It blossomed to forty-five members.

"We go into the schools by invitation, which is hard to obtain sometimes," Mrs. Garland said. "We always try to go in with an openly gay person to show that gay people don't have two heads, but are actually quite normal." The speakers' goal is not to preach, she said, but rather "to expose the children to an unbiased view of things. We're guests of that high school, and we have to be sensitive to that. It's very important to us that we be asked back. And of course, it's not mandatory. Students can stay away if they want. I get the feeling some kids are told by their parents not to come, but that's okay. The school has to allow that."

When he first started speaking, Mr. Garland thought most students would reject what he said. For the most part, however, he has found them to be open, friendly, and accepting. At Ashland High School he debated several representatives of what he called "hate groups," during the time Oregon was wrestling with a ballot initiative to prohibit municipalities from passing gay rights legislation. When he was finished, two dozen students came onstage to hug him. "I thought it was interesting they were so accepting," he said. "They've experienced homophobia only marginally, but they know it's affected others out there. That's wonderful to see." They receive other, more personal feedback, including gay and lesbian youngsters who tell them, "I thought I was the only one in the world!"

The Garlands begin their talks by telling the students they can ask anything. Sometimes they ask about methodology, which is fine. No one has yet abused the privilege of asking tough questions. One query that always arises is how the Garlands reacted as parents when their son came out to them. "I tell them, as close as we were to our son, he didn't know what we'd say. He wondered whether we'd put him out on the street, as some of his friends' parents had done," Mrs. Garland related. (At that time the family belonged to a fundamentalist church, some of whose pronouncements, Mr. Garland admitted, "could have been frightening.")

Many of the questions reveal the need for "help with the mythology and misconceptions about homosexuality," Mr. Garland said. "There are so many myths, in the biological, social, and biblical areas. We shy away from religion – it's such an incendiary topic – but it's frustrating to have to avoid religion, because that's where so much hatred comes from."

Some of the most vituperative comments come from youngsters who later reveal themselves to be gay. "Plenty of gay and lesbian kids are more homophobic than straight people," Mr. Garland said. "They need affirmation, and they've never had any." The speakers always bring literature to their talks, and it always gets picked up without qualms.

Students are not the only ones who welcome the Garlands' presentations. "At Crater Lake High School, the teachers were so grateful to us, they fell all over themselves thanking us for coming," she said. At that school the couple spoke as part of a human rights unit, not a sexuality or health unit. "That helps us get into schools," Mrs. Garland noted. "It's easier to be announced as human rights speakers than as part of a 'queer issue.'"

Their talks in Oregon are very different from those they gave in Southern California, Mr. Garland said. "In California we grew accustomed to having the issue of homosexuality discussed openly, even though some people on the religious right objected. But in Oregon we see much more opposition, although Ashland is an oasis." However, he noted, "the OCA (the anti-gay rights Oregon Citizens Alliance) has really done us a favor. They've galvanized those of us who have an interest in this issue, and the result is we're going out, talking, and addressing all the ignorance."

When Mr. Garland debated in Ashland, one man began derogating lesbians. A student leaped to her feet, yelling, "You can't say that! It's not true!" Afterward, in the parking lot, she hugged Mr. Garland and said, "That man was talking about my mother." The students surrounding her were supportive, Mr. Garland observed. "They knew her, and they knew her mother. They were both human beings to them. Those are the kinds of things we see and hear that makes this all worthwhile."

And if not all speakers are gay men and women, not all PFLAG speakers are mothers and fathers. Ede Denenberg, at age seventy-five, is a regular speaker in southern Maryland. She realized, after spending a morning talking to health and child development students at Paint Branch High School in Montgomery County, that "there's something about a grandmother speaking to kids about homosexuality that's a bit different."

She was well received. She talked about her daughter, a middle-aged lesbian who is the mother of a son, and how important it is for family members to stay close. She discussed the reasons parents get upset when they learn about a child's homosexuality: the specter of AIDS, the fear that all of a sudden they face a different person, the possible loss of grandchildren. But, she counseled, most parents love their kids before they know they're gay, and continue to love them afterward. Mrs. Denenberg talked too about the reasons youngsters should talk to their parents if they feel it is wise. "How awful it is for a young person to live a lie," she said.

She encountered a bit of hostility when a few youngsters spoke of homosexuality as a sin, but other classmates quickly refuted them. "I hardly had to say anything, and there was nothing raucous," she recounted. "It was just wonderful to see other kids stand up and speak out." The morning ended with many boys and girls thanking Mrs. Denenberg, saying they had learned something. She later received appreciative notes from students, though she said wryly, "The teacher probably suggested it."

Mrs. Denenberg approached her talk with no trepidation, although she did worry about being boring. "I wasn't!" she said happily. "They asked plenty of questions that evoked thoughtful answers, and they found it interesting." Among the queries: Are homosexuals born that way, or do they become gay? How do you tell your parents you're a lesbian? What do you do if you suspect a friend is gay? What exactly is bisexuality? Her answers to most such questions were the same: find a trusted adult; call a youth hotline; get in touch with PFLAG; talk to a friend.

"They were enthralled," she said, adding quickly, "I don't know whether it was prurient or genuine interest. But they did seem intent on listening. They were very introspective, very subjective about my life, my daughter's life, and their own lives. I talked to them frankly, which I think was a shock coming from a grandma. I guess most grandmothers aren't that open with their grandchildren. But I told them, don't sell your parents short. They're educated, they read, they have ideas. Most parents are pretty accepting about anything you want to talk about."

Just as most listeners everywhere simply want to learn. All they have to do is hear the facts, the stories, the words, from someone who's been there, and knows. Fortunately, there are plenty who have been there, and do know. Better yet, many of them are willing – even eager – to talk.

Out in the Country

Gay youths in big Pacific Northwest cities like Seattle or Portland are no different from their counterparts anywhere else; they're often frightened, confused, and upset. Fortunately, they have access to resources galore: in-school speakers, sympathetic teachers, counselors who can point them to the support groups, and services that help them connect with dozens of youngsters who feel just as they do. Gay youths in other parts of the Northwest – the smaller cities of Spokane and Eugene, the suburbs up and down Interstate 5 – have fewer options, but seldom feel completely alone. Their schools, too, make a concerted effort to make sure they get the guidance they need.

But lesbian and gay adolescents growing up in rural America – and in the Pacific Northwest, that means vast stretches of mountains, desert, and farmland in Washington, Oregon, and Idaho, in microscopic towns and crossroads villages with names like Soap Lake, Dusty, and Rufus – often have nowhere to turn. To come out to anyone in their tiny, often conservative schools is to commit social suicide; even to hunt down resources in the local library is to invite suspicion and rumors that may never die.

That's why the blandly named Outreach to Rural Youth Project is so important to so many boys and girls.

For over two years Scott Thiemann has traveled the "outback" of eastern Washington, often on foot. He has knocked on school doors, walked into principals' offices, distributed information packets, and spoken on radio, in churches, and at community meetings, all in the hopes of opening small-town eyes to the existence of lesbian and gay youngsters, right there in River City. Starting in October of 1992 the former landscaper, teacher, and community activist has directly reached several thousand people – no small feat in areas where a large population is one that reaches triple figures. When over a hundred people attended conferences in Wenatchee and the Tri-Cities of Richland, Pasco, and Kennewick, he congratulated himself on a major accomplishment.

Scott's Outreach Project has touched more than 3500 counselors, principals, teachers, students, and agency staff through more than a hundred presentations. That does not include his presence, in a small booth, at three county fairs, but it does include the many educators he met during two "Walk Across Washington" treks.

Scott's route through the wilds of the Northwest began several years earlier in the small, dying logging town of Falls City, Oregon, a place he describes as backwoods – "like God lifted an Ozark community and dropped it in the foothills of Oregon." He taught sixth grade there for three years, before finally being driven out by "the warped education system and rampant sexism." He was closeted, but says if he were teaching there today he would not be.

In 1988 he joined the gay and lesbian subcommittee of the Seattle Commission for Children and Youth. He discovered that city's Parents, Families and Friends of Lesbians and Gays (PFLAG) organization, and AGLYA – the Association of Gay and Lesbian Youth Advocates. "I never understood why gay and lesbian people didn't get involved with youth issues," he said. "I know there's an inherent fear of being tied in with the sexual abuse of young people, but that's stupid. It didn't apply to my own reality. If you as a teacher can't be open and honest about who you are, it affects your relationship with everybody, and you can't be very good at your job."

His AGLYA connection led to activism in suburban schools. Scott talked to librarians about the materials they were ordering and displaying, and met with faculty representatives of school newspapers after they rejected ads for a phone line he also worked with. "The farther we got from Seattle, the more important it became to get information to young people, because these issues weren't being talked about openly in school," he noted. "There are always stories under the surface – people who divorced under suspicious circumstances, someone who left quietly never to return, or someone who was rumored to have AIDS – but in these smaller schools no one was talking about it."

After ending a dysfunctional relationship with a military man that he likened to *Fatal Attraction,* Scott decided to turn all his energy toward rural lesbian and gay youth. He approached AGLYA, Portland's Meyer Memorial Trust, and the gay-friendly Chicago Resource Center, proposing a project that would provide informational resources to rural youngsters and the professionals who work with them. Enough funding came through to allow Scott to get started – but at such a low level that he earned only $7,000 that first year. His Outreach to Rural Youth had four separate components. One involved face-to-face meetings with guidance counselors, to inform them of the prevalence and problems of lesbian and gay youth. (He knew enough not to ask to speak to actual students.) He soon learned that to get to the counselors he first had to go through the principals, who control the climate of a building. (In some tiny schools, principals also serve as counselors.) Most principals and counselors, he found, were fairly receptive to his pitch. "They knew they had kids who were dealing with these issues," he said. "They knew there were gay and lesbian kids whose brothers and sisters were beating up on them, or who picked on them. They knew they had kids whose parents were divorcing and were acting out sexually. They knew they had teachers who didn't know how to deal with same-sex crushes, and with teasing in classrooms and halls. I think the counselors were happy to get this information, especially because there's so much misinformation and fear surrounding it."

Not all were glad to see him, of course. One Idaho counselor booted Scott out of his office. "It seemed like he couldn't hear anything else I had to say after he found out I was gay. You can imagine how much help a kid might get in that situation," he said ruefully.

Counselor Dennis Greene rebutted that charge, in a story carried by the Associated Press. He said he did not kick Scott out of Prairie High School in Cottonwood, but thought the issue was sensitive enough to refer him to the principal's office. Principal Darrel Pantalone stated that Scott should have contacted him prior to his arrival, adding, "I said, 'If you feel what you are representing is so right, then why didn't you call and make an appointment?' He said because then people won't talk to him. I told him, 'Well, that should tell you something about the sensitivity of the issue, and how unacceptable it is.'"

The three other parts of his project involved presentations to college classes, the creation of regional consciousness-raising conferences, and networking with social service organizations to provide leads into schools.

In the fall of 1991 Scott took another step by organizing his first "Walk Across Washington." He and four like-minded individuals traveled from school to school, from Spokane near the Idaho border to Seattle, spreading the word about gay youth.

In the eastern Washington plains, where farming communities lie a day's walk apart, the word spread rapidly. "There were lots of preconceptions," he said. "In Reardan, the very first town, the sheriff was put on patrol by the city council because they heard that 'hundreds of militant homosexuals' were descending on them. That was a great example of rumor-mongering. They thought we'd take over the streets, and have wild sex in the park. And then all the sheriff saw was three walkers, and me with my dog. I told him to go off and play golf, and he did."

Three days later, outside Wilson Creek, another sheriff suggested the group leave town by 5:30. This was Redneck Night, he told them, a time for people to drink beer and throw horseshoes. "Talk about tar and feathers!" Scott said. "But the sheriff said we didn't look too threatening to him. We had a good talk. He told us some parents had kept their kids home from school because they'd heard we were coming, and a minister had blessed the school to keep it safe from the 'encroaching sinners.' When we got there the principal, who had not wanted us around, ended up inviting us in. It was so anticlimactic. We so often draw conclusions about people, especially rural folks. Eight months later I returned and talked to the health teacher. I found out he'd been talking about sexual-orientation issues in his classes for three years."

Scott found that once most people saw his group face-to-face, they re-examined their own beliefs. He in turn was forced to confront his own misconceptions about rural schools. Although many are indeed white and homogeneous, others have high percentages of Hispanic or Native American students. He noted, though, that "discovering you have a different orientation can be difficult, even terrifying, in any of those settings. There's nothing for you socially. The expectation is that you're heterosexual. In that environment, people know each other's business. There's less discussion of differences than in other places, more religion. Often, no agency comes near to touching, or even being sensitive to, homosexual issues. These kids' lives are basically on hold until they get out of high school."

Scott understands how difficult it must be to grow up gay or lesbian in such a setting. "It was hard enough for me in a suburban, liberal school of two thousand kids," he said. "I didn't know anyone there. The library was the only place to get information. And in these small schools, they don't have a lot of books dealing with sexual orientation. They may have to order them – and not many kids are going to ask the librarian to do that." In fact, he said, he has been to libraries that do not even have the words "homosexual" or "gay" in their card catalogs. As he talked with principals and counselors on his walks through Washington, Scott also listened to their stories. People talked about friends and family members who are gay. They'd always felt unable to bring it up in their communities; it was quietly swept under the rug. He found that administrators appreciated him, as almost a bridge to cross the gap between what they don't know, and what they know they need to know.

He heard about suicides, too: in one town, the manager of the girls' swim team and two athletes all killed themselves. Another tale involved two football players: after one boy drowned, his friend shot himself. "How many heterosexual people would do that?" he asked. "There's such a tremendous sense of fear and isolation. You've met the only person in the world you can connect with, and then this happens. You think your world has ended." Some of the youngsters who have the hardest time dealing with gay issues are athletes. "They see absolutely nothing that reflects the reality of who they are. Everything they get is from the religious right; there's nothing from the other side that tells them they're okay, that there are other kids, even athletes, like them."

The closer Scott got to Seattle on his walks, the less publicity he received. But he did not mind; his walk, after all, was part of the Outreach to *Rural* Youth Project. "Part of the reason I like working in rural areas is that the people there have a sense of honesty and straightforwardness that's refreshing," he said. "You don't always find that in urban areas." Just as you don't always find adequate resources for gay and lesbian teens out in the country. Thanks to Scott Thiemann, though, that is beginning to change.

Of course, Scott can't cover the entire Pacific Northwest by himself. Help arrived in late 1993 in the form of Dave Swartout, who signed on as Outreach's Washington State director. Previously, he had been a crisis and HIV counselor in what he calls "the boondocks," so he knew what he was getting into. Sort of.

"I grew up in the early eighties in a town like these, population about forty-five hundred," he recounted. "I was pretty much out. Growing up gay really wasn't that terrible, because I had such a supportive family. But now I think around here things have taken a turn for the worse, with all these ballot initiatives (to limit gay civil rights). I don't know if I could do now what I did then."

One of his first contacts as Washington director was with a guidance counselor in a tiny town of fewer than a thousand people. She was working with fourteen youngsters who had identified themselves as lesbian or gay to her – but everything was underground. She could do nothing publicly, so she used him as a resource, and still does. "I go into her town on other business, and sneak away and talk to her. I get materials to her, and she passes them on very quietly to the kids, without the extreme right finding out. She's the strongest counselor I know."

However, he said, "She's constantly on pins and needles that the kids will be found out. All the kids' burdens and woes are on her shoulders. She has no public support whatsoever." He finds it ironic that this straight counselor is now experiencing how difficult it is to be in the closet.

While most school administrators approve of his talking to counselors, Dave said that the process stops there. He can talk directly to students through the juvenile justice system and the alternative schools, but not in the mainstream public schools. There, the far right watches everything that happens with gay and lesbian youth.

At the same time, he noted, "The big difficulty I've found with counselors – and my training is in guidance and counseling – is that we're not trained to deal with gay and lesbian youth issues. *Maybe* once a semester some gay guy comes in and gives a speech or runs a training session. So even those counselors who are *willing* to talk to kids don't have the resources to do so. They need information, studies, pamphlets, you name it. We provide those, and if we have to do it quietly, that's okay too."

Gaining the ears of recalcitrant or unaware counselors is not easy. "One of the horrible things I have to do to get their attention is what I call 'pimping on pathology,'" he said. "I talk about the high rate of gay and lesbian youth suicides, and I tell them that 40 percent of the street youth in Seattle engage in unsafe sex to survive – and some of them come from towns just like theirs. The down side of talking like that is it doesn't leave a whole lot of room for them to think that kids can be empowered, or feel like they're good, fine people."

Since starting his work as state director, Dave's greatest frustration has been that there is so much willingness on the part of counselors to help and listen, yet it is tempered with so much fear about the loud reaction from the small, extreme right. He is constantly amazed to find people who are actually willing to put youngsters at risk.

As Scott Thiemann concentrates his energy on Oregon, Dave is working to build as many coalitions and safety nets as possible in Washington. Some of his staunchest support has come from religious groups: the Washington Association of Churches, consisting of 1700 congregations ranging from Methodist to Roman Catholic and Baptist, has endorsed the Outreach to Rural Youth Project. "In today's climate, that's a very powerful thing to have," he said (noting ruefully that the Assemblies of God – "in Washington, the loudest voices of the extreme right" – were not among the endorsees). Other groups that have lent their names to the project include the League of Women Voters, American Friends Service Committee, Mothers Against Drunk Driving, and the Association of University Women. The National Education Association, through its Washington Education Association affiliate, provides one-third of the Outreach Project budget.

Frustration comes almost daily: when Dave learns about a youngster who is kicked out of his or her home and ends up on the streets of Seattle, or when he hears of teachers or counselors making homophobic or ignorant remarks and recognizes that for another youngster the path down the road to low self-esteem (and possibly the streets) has just begun.

But plenty of joys counterbalance those teeth-gnashing times. "Little things – finding a safe counselor, or having someone donate stamps or a copier to keep us going," he said. "And I've met some great kids! We've got thirty or forty meeting regularly in the Tri-Cities, and a good group of fifteen or twenty in Yakima. We see the improvement from when they first clandestinely call the Outreach number, to then finding others, to coming out to their parents and seeing – if they're lucky – that that's not a disaster, to seeing they're not alone in school.

"And then I see that there's so much willingness to help on the part of teachers and counselors in schools, even if it's not necessarily with a big public splash. That's the great thing – it doesn't have to be loud. Just so long as something gets done."

In the Pacific Northwest, slowly but very, very surely, something very important is indeed getting done.

Gay-Straight Groups Grow

To a casual observer, Brookline High School, just outside Boston, might seem an ordinary school in an ordinary town — except for one thing. Every Wednesday at 2:30 p.m., on the fourth floor of the Unified Arts building, where just minutes earlier students studied automotive mechanics, construction electricity, architectural design, and desktop publishing, Brookline High School's Gay/Straight Alliance meets.

In the winter of 1994, most of the seventeen hundred Brookline students leaving the building wore baggy pants and backward-pointing baseball caps, and carried backpacks in that very uncomfortable-looking, single-strap way. But the girls (and, with one late-arriving exception, they were all female) who wandered into room 48 for an early February GSA meeting were a bit more individualistic than their peers: a nose ring here, an all-black outfit there, even a long granny skirt. Two were Asian-Americans; all the rest were white.

They greeted each other casually, picking up conversations where they had ended a class, a day, perhaps even a week before. A visitor wandered over to the bulletin board — not the one that advised proper safety precautions when operating equipment, but the one the Gay/Straight Alliance uses for its notices. There was plenty to read: a message from a faculty member announcing her availability to talk with any student wanting to chat about gay and lesbian issues; a letter from an instructional aide expressing regret at missing meetings because of work; newspaper clippings, brochures, flyers from other gay-straight groups; AIDS information; and several notes of thanks, encouragement, or support from individuals and groups.

When the chatter subsided, the meeting began. Announcements centered on an anti-homophobia program scheduled for the following month; speakers would include an openly gay teacher from another school, a politician addressing gay rights legislation, and a Boston police officer working in the hate crimes division. The final word was directed at the visitor: he was expected, one of the two teachers in charge said, to participate fully in the GSA session that was about to begin.

However, the meeting never really got started. One girl mentioned Valentine's Day; a Brookline tradition, it seemed, was to send messages to loved ones via the school paper. This put lesbian and gay students in a quandary, so the girl who raised the subject suggested the GSA buy an ad reading, "For all you '1 in 10s' who feel lonely: you're not alone." There was a murmur of approval.

The talk soon degenerated into what different people had done the previous weekend, with much laughter. Some students had seen the recently released AIDS movie *Philadelphia;* they chattered about that for a while, then moved on to *Schindler's List* and a *Murphy Brown* TV episode involving a gay bar. But the talk petered out after a few minutes; two girls got up to leave, and the meeting soon dissolved.

The mere fact that Brookline, the town in which John F. Kennedy was born, has a high school gay-straight alliance might have been front-page news several years ago — for that matter, such a group at *any* school would have warranted publicity. In 1995, however, Brookline's GSA is one of at least three dozen such organizations at public and private schools across Massachusetts. It was not the first; it is not the biggest; it is, simply, typical of similar groups around the Bay State.

The Brookline GSA was formed midway through the 1992–93 school year. Three girls did most of the organizing: they hung posters, invited friends, found faculty sponsors — and then waited nervously for the first meeting.

A dozen students attended that initial session. They talked about why they were there and what they hoped to accomplish. They decided they wanted to support and celebrate all sexual orientations, purposely *not* including the word "tolerance" because they sought more than that. They also discussed ways they could educate the school and community about the dangers of homophobia.

It did not take long before they came up with several rules: no assumptions were to be made about any member's sexuality (in other words, no one was to assume anyone was either gay or straight); all meetings were to be confidential (attendees were not to tell anyone else who was there, although they could repeat in general terms what was said); and teachers and students were to participate as equal members.

All members of the school, including support staff, secretaries, and custodians, were welcome.

By 1994, Brookline's GSA boasted a core group of thirty people, with up to a hundred attending the parties it occasionally sponsored. Throughout the school year a total of about 120 students and teachers came to room 48 for meetings, making it one of the largest clubs on campus. As the group evolved, it focused on two areas: political-educational and personal. Included in the political and eduational realm were lobbying for the statewide gay rights bill for students (nearly forty-five members were involved); participating in the March on Washington; developing a health education curriculum; getting information into school and local newspapers; and decorating the halls with posters (one explained the meaning of pink triangles; another listed famous gays and lesbians in history).

On the personal side, GSA members shared stories and discussed problems, such as how to react when friends or parents made homophobic remarks. And, said one faculty leader, "We have a regular old good time. That's important, because talking about gay and lesbian issues can be so serious." (Food, she noted, is very important for a successful meeting.)

Of all the activities, the March on Washington in April 1993 drew the biggest raves. "It was awesome!" one participant said. Twenty-five students and five teachers traveled to the nation's capital; the feeling, one said, was like the Celtics winning the playoffs. The GSA members strode behind a large banner identifying both Brookline High and their organization. "The cheering didn't stop," one marcher marveled. "It was overwhelming. People kept coming up to us – a lot of graduates from Brookline, including one from the Class of '46, and a lot of people who said they were in the PTA at their school." Many spectators could not believe Brookline was a public high school.

One marcher was not a Brookline student; she attended a different school in a nearby town, where she had been harassed. "This was her first positive experience as a lesbian," a faculty member said. "Two weeks later she was gay-bashed when she got off her bus. That's what this group is all about – being persistent about making change. The students' gay rights bill was passed in Massachusetts, but our posters are being defaced again. That's the nature of homophobia; civil rights don't instantly happen. We have to keep pushing, pushing, pushing for them."

The teacher, who asked not to be identified by name, said that the GSA has had an effect on Brookline High simply by raising lesbian and gay issues. Her colleagues now tell her that previously they had no idea of homophobia's reach. "We've also brought out a number of straight allies," she said. "But I don't know if we've made the school any safer for gay or lesbian teachers. I think perhaps we've also raised some people's hatreds."

The administration, she noted, has been great. "The principal has made it very clear that gay and lesbian youth must be supported. He's said that homophobia is right up there with racism and sexism." He attends occasional GSA meetings, and because of the rule that everyone present must participate as equals, the students make sure he contributes.

The teacher said the best times for her come when she sees students realize they're not the only ones who have questions. She feels as comfortable as they do raising issues and seeking answers. She said she has experienced no frustrations – only "challenges, and that's what education is all about. Helping kids figure out the best way to get their message across; helping them balance the good feelings about being out with the realities of gay-bashing – those are important things that schools have not done much of in the past. I'm glad we're doing it here at Brookline."

GSA co-founder Sarah Lonberg-Lew agreed. She noted that while no specific incident fueled her desire to organize the group, "there doesn't have to be blatant homophobia for there to be a need for a gay-straight alliance. Just the fact that everyone *assumes* everyone else in a school is straight is a good enough reason. It leads to isolation and fear, and students need to know they're not alone."

Sarah emphasized that straight students need the organization as much as gay students. "*Everyone* in school is dealing with sexuality in some way. It might be a friend who came out to them, or they might think somebody has a same-sex crush on them. Or they just want to talk, and bring up questions they might not have a chance to have answered any other place." She is proud that at Brookline, the GSA serves that function.

And, apart from occasional scribbled-over signs and nasty newspaper articles, there have not been many obstacles to the group's existence. However, there have been misconceptions. "At first everyone thought we were a gay and lesbian alliance. They didn't realize we include straight people too," Sarah noted. "People worried about being stigmatized. I think we've gotten over that, even though some people probably don't come to the meetings because of it."

How has Brookline's Gay/Straight Alliance managed to get its message across – the message that it welcomes heterosexuals as well as homosexuals, so long as they want to help educate schoolmates and have a good time? "We just kept going," she said simply. "At first people thought maybe we were a freak group, meeting in an out-of-the-way place. Now they see our signs all over the place, and they know that we're just another part of Brookline High School."

But Brookline and several other Massachusetts public schools are not the only ones where gay-straight alliances meet as openly and proudly as the chess club or Young Republicans. Halfway across the state, on the remote campus of Deerfield Academy, a few hardy students fight the difficult battle against homophobia at one of America's oldest, and most conservative, private boarding schools.

Deerfield traces its origins to 1797, and many of its attitudes seem stuck in another century. It is not a place where students or faculty members easily discuss emotions, or even feel free to hug one another or show affection. It is, said Bradley T. Bowers, a "very safe, secure place, with a strong sense of community – but there's not much individuality. Most of us come from the same kind of background: middle class or upper class. People are generally accepting, although if I walked in tomorrow with a Mohawk, I don't know how people would react." And, because Deerfield is so isolated (the closest store is three miles away), "we're pretty sheltered from the rest of the world. World War III could happen, and we wouldn't know it."

In a school filled with bright, articulate youngsters, Brad Bowers stood out. A musician, actor (he played the emcee in *Cabaret*), and honor student (he won a major prize for his English "declamation"), the easily-smiling-despite-his-braces, relatively long-haired senior was, everyone agreed, a real personality. At Deerfield, it took a Brad Bowers to plant – and keep from being trampled – GROH!

GROH! (the exclamation point "keeps it positive," Brad said) stands for Get Rid of Homophobia! He and his friend Allyson Mount formed the group at the end of eleventh grade, a year after a classmate came out to the school (to primarily negative reaction; she subsequently transferred away), and several months after two gay graduates gave a talk about their experiences there. Brad had been active in social awareness organizations; for him, this seemed a natural progression.

The summer before their senior year, he and Allyson discussed the future of the group. "We had to figure out whether to be small and quiet, or outward and vocal," Brad recalled several months later, not long before graduation. "Was our aim going to be support, or education?" The answer they settled on was "low-key, educational"; that, they believed, would work best at Deerfield.

On a campus of 660 students, GROH! attracted a core of about five students to their weekly meetings; a few others became irregular members. But its impact went beyond its small numbers. For one early project, members took a photo of graffiti scrawled on a student's door – "AIDS Kills Fags" – and made it into an anti-homophobia poster. Then they secured a permanent bulletin board near the entrance of the main building, and plastered it with a constantly changing barrage of news clippings, flyers, and other information. They arranged for speakers at a schoolwide Diversity Day, participated in a New England conference of gay-lesbian-straight alliances at Northfield Mt. Hermon School, and passed out colorful buttons (worn only once a week, in order to not weaken the impact).

But just as important as their visible activities, Brad said, was the opportunity GROH! gave members of the Deerfield community to start talking about gay issues. "People know that if someone wears one of our buttons, they can feel comfortable discussing certain things with that person," he explained. "It's opened up some dialogue here."

However, he was under no illusion that his organization created massive, campuswide change. "Certainly, there are people who actively dislike us," he said. "And there are lots of people who don't want to hear about it, whether they support us or not – 'Don't talk to us about it,' that sort of thing." But Brad – who, like some others in the group, did not discuss his own sexual orientation – is pleased with what he's accomplished. Personally, he said, "I've learned to stick with an idea that goes somewhat against the grain. I've forced myself to express my beliefs; I own myself now. This group is a constant reminder to myself that I can do something meaningful now, and not have to wait until I'm in college."

Despite his self-confidence and poise, Brad noted that the decision to start GROH! was not an easy one. "I thought it would be social suicide," he admitted. "I had to talk with a lot of people at other schools before I was sure I wanted to go through with it."

Three female members of GROH! – only Allyson agreed to be quoted by name – echoed Brad's feelings. Lacking Brad's special cachet on campus, they found their affiliation with the group to be, in varying degrees, more difficult. "It's been hell – sheer hell," admitted one girl, who identified herself as straight. "My parents say the initials should stand for Get Rid of Homosexuals, and I've gotten so much stuff from everyone around me." Another girl said that people look at her differently after they learn she belongs to GROH! Only Allyson claimed that it was not hard walking into the first meeting. "It was something I knew I had to do," the co-founder said. "It was the first time I was excited about anything at Deerfield."

But she too experienced negative reactions – most of them subtle and insidious. "People say things under their breath," one girl explained. "Or people exclude you from things. Or they disregard what you say in class, or talk over you. You know it's because of GROH!, but it's not overt so you can't put your finger on it." Allyson, who came out at a GROH! session, had a door slammed on her by a friend of someone who had attended that meeting.

Why such resistance? The answers varied: the organization is upsetting the status quo; people feel threatened; homosexuality represents a "real, physical, actual something" students fear or know nothing about. "This is a conservative, traditional school," one member said. "People are unwilling to open themselves up to new ideas. They came to Deerfield thinking they'd have a secure boat, and we're rocking it."

Some students don't even think about why they don't like GROH! – they just do – but others flaunt it. "It's almost become a cool thing for people to say, 'Dude, I am *so* homophobic,'" Brad noted.

"Yeah," one girl agreed. "And people support each other and say, 'Great! So am I!'"

"I think that's the same reason so many people have Confederate flags in their rooms," another added. "It's cool to be anti-p.c. – to be racist or sexist or homophobic. So there's this huge barrier we have to break through, not just normal opposition."

The GROH! members get some help from the faculty – at least, from the younger, more liberal teachers. "A lot of them are great; they're tolerant, they wear our buttons," a student said. But the older, more established and remote staff says nothing, and their silence allows homophobia to fester. "There are language teachers who, if someone uses the feminine form instead of the masculine one, they'll start mimicking the word, lisping and effeminate," one girl reported. "That's pretty ridiculous. We look at them and they stop, but we feel like we're the 'p.c. police,' and that shouldn't be the way we have to feel." The administration, she said, is of little use; it operates as an "old boys' network."

But the GROH! students did not need much prodding to come up with positive stories as well. The girl who had been through "sheer hell" at Deerfield noted with pride that a woman on the counseling staff called her "a real role model. She told me I'd made a big impact on the school, that she was glad there were people like me who stood up, that all the younger kids looked up to me, and that the faculty members had so much respect for me. That made me feel real good, because no one had ever said that before."

Some of the strokes they mentioned were personal. "I feel a lot better about myself," one girl said. "I'm not guilt-ridden about sitting back and letting things happen without expressing myself. I really feel I'm making a positive contribution to the school. There's negative things – I know people talk behind my back, so I feel intimidated and insecure, even though I try not to let it show – but I'm glad I've opened people's eyes. They don't always admit it, but I know I have."

"I'm more willing to question people, ask them why they say certain things," another added.

And, Allyson noted, "I was so nervous the first time I had to stand up in front of the school and make an announcement about GROH! Now I do it without even thinking, in a real confident voice."

But the most intriguing analysis of GROH! came from the straight girl whose Deerfield life has been made miserable by her participation in it. "I've traded my social life for my views," she began. "There are times I've cried because I can't deal with it anymore. People automatically assume I'm a lesbian – there's nothing wrong with that, but they look down on me. I'm in classes where you have to work closely with other people, and they've made it hard for me. I've been very discriminated against. It's hard for me to stay here sometimes, because I'm defined by being part of GROH! It's made me realize you have to be very careful about how much of yourself you let on to other people."

Knowing all this now, does she ever regret walking into that first GROH! meeting earlier in the year?

"Definitely not!" she answered firmly. "I'm not the kind of person who can see something wrong, and not do something about it. It's like the line I heard – I think it was in Brad's play, *Cabaret*. It goes something like, 'If you're not part of the solution, you're part of the problem.' Well, I want to be part of the solution. And I think with GROH!, I am."

Of course, Massachusetts does not have a monopoly on gay-straight alliances. A similar group exists in North Carolina. It may be the only one in the state – but it thrives. And the tale of how it came to be is at least as interesting as the story of what it does.

With two thousand ninth through twelfth graders, Chapel Hill High is overcrowded (the city's second high school opens in 1996). But CHHS is by no means a typical large school. Veteran English teacher David Bruton describes it in his soft drawl as "filled with a lot of kids who are ambitious and work hard. Chapel Hill's got a pretty high percentage of well-educated, upwardly mobile folks"; it is, after all, home to the University of North Carolina, and sits on the edge of the famed Research Triangle. In 1994 *Redbook* named CHHS the top high school in the Tar Heel State, and if that isn't exactly true, Mr. Bruton allowed, "I think most people wouldn't hesitate to call it at least one of the best."

He and his partner, middle school teacher Duff Coburn, have been together for nearly twenty-five years. They met at UNC, and have always taught in the same school system – first Raleigh, now Chapel Hill. For a while they were even in the same building where, Mr. Bruton said, "You couldn't *not* notice our distinctive rings. Our relationship was never secret, even the first year. We always used the words 'we' and 'our,' and parents always invited us into their homes. As a couple we did couple things, so for a long time we had more straight friends than gay friends. And we never had a problem with administrators or colleagues. Never."

But at the outset they commuted more than twenty miles from Chapel Hill to Raleigh, because they thought it would be difficult to teach in the same community as they lived. In Raleigh, Mr. Bruton said, "I saw kids going through the kind of anguish most gay people go through when they're young. I heard the word 'faggot.'" But as out as he was to adults, he felt he could not say anything to his students; in his classroom, he remained in the closet. "I stewed about it. I was frustrated," he admitted. "But I felt if I was out to kids, my job would be in jeopardy. It wouldn't have been, of course. That was just my own pure internalized, institutionalized homophobia."

In 1986 he transferred to Chapel Hill High. Things went well until 1989. "We started talking about the importance of multiculturalism, but we never *did* anything about it. I teach mostly American literature, so I finally said to myself, 'What can I include?'" He worked up a multicultural unit, based on collaborative learning. Small groups would explore what made various groups – Native Americans, Hispanic-Americans, African-Americans, Asian-Americans, Jewish-Americans, females – different from, and similar to, white Anglo-Saxon Protestant males. His department chair and his assistant principal both okayed the inclusion of gays and lesbians as a multicultural group. In the summer of 1991 Mr. Bruton began assembling book lists; they soon grew to more than two thousand titles.

He stressed that he did not assign students to groups they did not want to be in. During the year-long independent study project, each group of three to five students read sixteen to twenty books. It was a tremendous success, he said; their faces beamed with delight.

In the winter of 1992 a faculty committee received a letter from a CHHS junior, who complained that the school was not addressing gay and lesbian issues. Had it done so, he wrote, he would not have attempted suicide the previous year. Many staff members felt that homosexuality was an inappropriate subject for school discussion, but an optional schoolwide meeting was set. It was announced the same way as other talks: through posters, bulletins, and memos. Mr. Bruton's name was included in every announcement.

The discussion – which included a mother from Parents, Families and Friends of Lesbians and Gays, and a representative of the Outright organization – went well. But around that same time the English teacher's classroom windows were shot out; bricks were hurled through, and a dead opossum landed on his floor. The vandalism escalated: one night "Bruton's a Fag" and "Fire Bruton" were painted on nearly a dozen school buses. They rolled through Chapel Hill the next morning with those words emblazoned on the sides.

David Bruton was crushed. He had done nothing to hurt anyone; he thought most students liked him. He still had not told any classes that he was gay. (He learned later that one of the vandals was a boy who went along with the crowd to hide confusion about his own sexuality.)

No one at school knew what to do. At a well-attended voluntary faculty meeting, a colleague suggested an "old-fashioned, sixties-type demonstration." A number of staff members agreed to show solidarity by holding hands in the school courtyard during lunch. "No sooner had we done that than students poured out," Mr. Bruton described. "They all wanted to join in. There was even a little scuffle when kids tried to get next to me." The circle grew so large that another one formed inside. Students apologized all day to Mr. Bruton for the graffiti; some of them he did not even know. He was flattered and honored by their concern.

The teacher soon noticed a new group of students hanging around his classroom. "A sizable number were from the lacrosse team," he said. "They decided they'd take care of me. 'Liberating' is a cliche, but I don't know a better word to describe how I felt. Kids started asking me stuff about everything – including homosexuality. The word started getting around school that I don't judge anyone harshly." He felt as if he had gotten a new family.

The next year a former student committed suicide, just a few days after asking to talk with Mr. Bruton about an unspecified problem. Soon thereafter he and his partner traveled to Washington, D.C., to see the AIDS Quilt. "I wasn't prepared for the vastness of it," he recounted. "But what really got me was seeing very young guys squatting on the soggy ground weeping uncontrollably, and being hugged by total strangers just so they wouldn't feel alone. I saw those people doing more just by hugging than anything I'd ever done for anyone."

Mr. Bruton returned to Chapel Hill convinced he must do something. He asked a guidance counselor if she would be willing to co-sponsor a support group for gay and lesbian students. Coincidentally, she had also been thinking of the desperate need for such a group. They decided to move slowly, spending the rest of the school year writing schools around the country to find out how to begin such a project. But when a student approached the counselor seeking support, the need became more urgent.

At the same time, the group that had caused such an uproar the previous year with its schoolwide discussion on homosexuality announced plans for a mandatory assembly on oppression. Student organizers asked Mr. Bruton to speak. He did – and announced the formation of the gay and lesbian support group. The first meeting was set for mid-December.

By the end of 1993 a Gay/Straight Alliance of about twenty-five people, in all four grades, had developed. Thirteen teachers signed on as faculty advisers. They soon discovered that some self-identified lesbian and gay youngsters wanted an even more comfortable group, so during the 1993–94 school year Mr. Bruton started a separate support organization for homosexual students – and teachers. The principal, new to CHHS, has been very supportive of both groups, he noted.

The Gay/Straight Alliance meets weekly during lunch period, in Mr. Bruton's classroom. (The gay-only support group gathers in the less-open counseling center.) Alliance meetings are wide-ranging affairs. Sometimes members talk about frustrations students are having with peers or teachers; other times they just laugh and tell jokes, and homosexuality never comes up. They also try to generate school publicity about homosexuality, aimed at getting people to go a step or two beyond "tolerance." Meetings are "times for kids to get together, feel comfortable, and not have to keep masks up in front of their faces. We want kids to feel safe, and we also want to educate the school community." However, David Bruton added, "a lot of kids not in the group don't understand why their friends want to participate. They keep asking, 'Are you gay?' 'Are you lesbian?' But on the other hand, I'm still amazed at the number of kids who want to stand up for the rights of other kids in the school."

Individual stories abound about the group's impact on the CHHS campus. One boy asked Mr. Bruton many questions prior to a social studies discussion on homosexuality. Later, he proudly announced he won the debate. Now he goes out of his way to speak with Mr. Bruton – and even joined the group. Other students walk past the room during Gay/Straight Alliance meetings, but do not enter. "That's okay," he said. "So long as they know the room is there, that's fine. Eventually they'll come in, or at least talk."

In the spring the alliance organized a prom party. Members met at a student's home, then attended the dance together. The group also sponsored a day-long conference for students, teachers, and parents. There were four main topics, with participants rotating through different rooms. It was a community outreach effort, and teachers who attended were rewarded with continuing education credits.

However, Mr. Bruton said he does not want to do too many activities with students outside of school. "I don't have time!" he laughed. "Besides, this is a university community, so a lot of kids do things on their own with the UNC and Duke gay alliances – and those are very active organizations."

David Bruton did not reveal his own homosexuality to students until November 1993, when "a radical-right group used one girl to try to get me fired, and the multicultural program thrown out." (The organization, called Putting Children First, alleged that Mr. Bruton was attempting to "sensitize" students to gay lifestyles. Three hundred students, he said, knew the girl was not telling the truth about the way he conducted his class.) At that point he decided the time was right to come out, and sentiment was in his favor. There were no negative repercussions.

Mr. Bruton looks back with satisfaction on what he and Chapel Hill High School have created. "When we first started, we didn't know if we'd get one single kid. We didn't even know if the boy who spoke to the counselor that day would come. But just by existing, we thought we'd accomplish someting – and we did."

He is uncertain what lies ahead. "From here, who knows? There's no formula I'm aware of for dealing with these groups. We may have one or two years when we might have just one or two kids, and then other years it might be the cool thing on campus. We have to be ready for anything."

A gay-straight alliance is risky, he concluded. "But the rewards far, far outweigh the risks and the hassles. The time was right, and something had to be done. I'm just very, very glad we did it."

Teachers' Unions Tackle Gay and Lesbian Concerns

To teachers and other educators, the National Education Association (NEA) and American Federation of Teachers (AFT) are important professional organizations. From their Washington headquarters they track national education issues, keep abreast of state and local concerns, and make certain that all 535 members of Congress know their stands on upcoming legislation.

To teachers' detractors, the NEA and AFT are unions, hell-bent on picking the pockets of taxpayers by negotiating outrageous contracts with helpless school boards.

To gay people in America's schools – teachers and students alike – the importance of the NEA and AFT has nothing at all to do with salary scales, and little to do with pedagogic trends of the day like "outcome-based education." The best thing about the two large organizations, homosexually speaking, is that they actively support gay and lesbian caucuses – and those small groups have had enormous impacts on the entire memberships.

With more than two million members, primarily in suburban and rural districts, the NEA is the larger of the two teachers' unions (the AFT's 900,000 members are concentrated in urban areas). The NEA's gay and lesbian history dates back to the 1970s, when resolutions were first introduced in support of human rights issues. Yet no formal structure existed until 1987, when a group of teachers set up an information table at the national convention in Los Angeles. That nascent Gay and Lesbian Caucus (GLC) brought a motion to the floor supporting the upcoming March on Washington, which was referred back to the executive committee. The body was not quite ready to take on the issue – but the next year they were.

The next year the caucus prepared resolutions supporting equal opportunity for every man, woman, and child involved in public education, regardless of sexual orientation, and backing the rights of counselors to answer the questions of students concerned about their own orientation. The full membership supported the resolutions at the annual convention, which spurred the NEA/GLC to do even more.

By 1991 the group had developed a two-and-a-half-day training workshop called "Affording Equal Opportunity to Gay and Lesbian Students through Teaching and Counseling." The ponderously named session is offered in Washington to interested participants from anywhere in the nation. The hope is that attendees will return home inspired to make things happen, then create similar workshops on the state and local levels. Each Washington workshop, coordinated by the NEA's human and civil rights division staff members (with the help of a professional trainer), draws thirty to sixty teachers. Carol Watchler, the caucus's first chairperson, said participants were gay, lesbian, and straight. "They're people with real concerns, ready to take on this challenge. They come because of professional concerns and because they care about students, and they leave very moved and receptive to the work that needs to be done. They want to make their schools positive places for everyone. The feedback is great. People say, 'This is a breakthrough.' A number of people go back to their states and present the first substantive workshop ever offered to members on a gay and lesbian topic."

Ms. Watchler, a feminist activist and high school science and math teacher for nearly thirty years who now serves as coordinator for an experiential learning program in central New Jersey, has been involved in the NEA/GLC since its inception. During that time she has learned the importance of educating educators about gay issues. Too often, teachers have no clue what's going on in the lives of their most intimate colleagues, or their best (or quietest, or most troubled) students.

Yet the NEA's Gay and Lesbian Caucus's work goes beyond seminars and education. The group has become an important force on the convention floor. At the San Francisco meeting in 1993, for example, where many members wore pink "Straight but not narrow" buttons, delegates passed a resolution directing the organization to publicize existing research which shows the damage that sexual orientation discrimination does to institutions, and the threat it poses to the civil rights of all citizens. The caucus also established the Ryan White Memorial HIV Education Fund, which will be used to educate the nation's school employees about AIDS.

At the same meeting, members beat back challenges to two existing resolutions. One urges every school district to provide counseling for students concerned about sexual orientation questions; the other includes among recommended sex education topics "information on diversity of sexual orientation." And the caucus prodded the NEA to move several meetings from Colorado, in protest against its anti-gay Amendment 2.

But as an offshoot of a union, the GLC recognizes that one of its primary purposes is to support teachers' rights. "If a member is discriminated against, or senses discrimination because of sexual orientation, he or she needs the same job protection as anyone else," Carol Watchler noted. She cited Meridian, Idaho, where teachers brought lesbian parents into their classrooms as speakers. The teachers were reprimanded, and threatened with letters in their permanent files. The local NEA affiliate, along with the statewide Idaho Education Association, went to work to ensure that inappropriate letters were not written, and to deflect criticism of the teachers in the community.

Local and state leaders are not always willing to get involved in such issues, Ms. Watchler observed. "But they can't be afraid of them; they have to be willing to support academic freedom issues, especially because they'll occur more and more. There will be attacks on curriculum, and on individual teachers. We try to make sure the local and state associations know how to handle those."

They also involve themselves in a typical union battle: contracts. "Every leader must be prepared to make sure that contracts are inclusive – that nondiscrimination clauses include sexual orientation, and that any benefits packages for domestic partners are included in the bargaining process," Carol said. She harbors no illusions that enormous changes will suddenly occur; boards of education will not suddenly sit up, slap their foreheads, and say, "Holy mackerel, we've been missing the boat! We've got to start giving domestic partner benefits to all our gay and lesbian staff members! Let's do it today!"

However, the caucus feels it is vital to begin planting the idea of such benefits in local labor leaders' minds, so that they can first introduce them, then fight for them, during contract discussions. It is from such small steps that major progress comes.

Major progress has already been made in certain areas, such as membership. While the NEA/GLC has not conducted a full-fledged membership or publicity drive, it has attracted hundreds of members through word of mouth.

Of course, the parent NEA counts over two million members, and Ms. Watchler admitted that one obstacle the caucus faces is invisibility. "It's a matter of getting our information into the right hands. People are ignorant about what gay and lesbian people face, especially in some parts of the country. There is fear in some areas, and strident reactions toward homosexuality. In Idaho there was plenty of concern about how the community would respond to the local NEA affiliate's involvement in the Meridian case. Even in New Jersey, when people began to talk and make gay and lesbian issues visible, a lot of educators and administrators got afraid."

Ms. Watchler holds lesbian and gay teachers in great admiration, while any educator who does not take a stand against discrimination suffers her scorn. "If gay teachers are willing to go out on a limb, you would think straight teachers and administrators would at least have enough courage to follow their lead," she said. While the national leadership has been very supportive – despite intense competition for their resources and time – the level of support varies from one state leader to another. The challenge in the years ahead, said Ms. Watchler (who stepped down as co-chair in 1994), is to convince every state president that the work of the caucus is important beyond what it does for lesbian and gay teachers. "We're a professional organization," she stated, "with two main purposes. We want to promote the recognition of the special needs and rights of gay, lesbian, and bisexual students, making sure that every student has a safe space to learn in, and we want to advance the understanding and acceptance of gay, lesbian, and bisexual people in all areas of society. Those aren't teacher issues, really; they're education issues, society issues. They're issues that affect everyone in America today."

But of course they're individual issues too. "On a personal level, my work with the caucus has been one of the most positive experiences of my life," Ms. Watchler said. "I've gotten the opportunity to work with tremendous people of incredible courage. Knowing gay and lesbian people all across the country, and being able to support them, has been incredibly empowering to me. It's one of the best things I've ever done, as a teacher and a person."

Her co-chair, Jim Testerman, agrees. "Personally, the caucus has done a lot for me," the York, Pennsylvania, seventh-grade life science teacher said. "It's made me more comfortable as a teacher and a human being; I found I'm not alone, and developed pride in myself. Through the workshops and networking I've come to the realization that I'm at least an above-average teacher, and with the state education is in today, my district needs me more than I need it. So the worst thing they can do is fire me, and that's not so bad."

That hardly seems likely. Mr. Testerman is president of his Central York School District union; when he led the local through a bitter month-long strike, his sexuality never became an issue.

As co-chair, Mr. Testerman keeps an eye on the NEA. He makes sure they take care of lesbian and gay concerns, as well as all civil rights issues. Sometimes he has to do a bit of teaching to his colleagues. "Even people with the best of intentions need to be educated," he noted: "When someone asks why the NEA should be involved in the gays-in-the-military controversy, I point out that there are junior ROTC clubs in many schools, and that we represent teachers on military bases overseas. Then people say, 'Oh, you're right, these *are* educational issues too."

Mr. Testerman has gained statewide fame with his workshops for teachers, student teachers, and interested others, presented in conjunction with a Christian fundamentalist who works on the staff of the Pennsylvania Education Association. "She goes first, and explains that in her heart she believes homosexuality is a sin, but she realizes students are hurting, killing themselves," Mr. Testerman explained. "She says she feels that doing these workshops is where God wants her to be. A lot of people buy into that. Then I get up and say I'm everything she isn't: I'm not a woman, not a heterosexual, not Christian."

The rest of the time is spent sensitizing attendees to the fact that gay and lesbian students *are* in classrooms, and that they have special problems and concerns. The workshop includes an eleven-minute clip from Brian McNaught's *On Being Gay* video, in which he talks about what the world would be like if a majority of the population were homosexual, and only a minority were straight. "That initiates intense discussion," Mr. Testerman said. The session ends with him reading a letter his father sent him, throwing him out of the house when he was young. There is dead silence when Mr. Testerman says, "I hope this workshop will help prevent a little bit more of this."

"There's never enough time to cover everything, but I think we're helping make our schools a bit safer," he added. "There's always great feedback, but the best for me is the most simple. When someone says, 'I never knew my classroom was a place for gay and lesbian kids, and now I do' — that to me is what it's all about."

And the NEA/GLC is what Jim Testerman is all about. He credits it with helping him come out of the classroom closet — but it's also had

Jim Testerman teaches life science to seventh graders in York, Pennsylvania, and is co-chair of the Gay and Lesbian Caucus of the National Education Association.

an effect on his colleagues. When he ran for the national Gay and Lesbian Caucus co-chair, he had plenty of support from people in Pennsylvania. A number of straight people – including the state president – joined the caucus just so they could vote for him.

Mike Chiumento is a typical – if such a thing exists – NEA Gay and Lesbian Caucus member. The band teacher from Michigan's Plymouth-Canton School District got involved purely by accident in 1990 when he attended his first NEA Representative Assembly (annual meeting) in Kansas City. He was a substitute delegate, angry at his union over a previous, nongay issue. Wandering through the exhibit hall in search of freebies, he saw the group's pink banner and was mesmerized. "I said, 'We have a caucus?!' – and before I knew it I was signing a check, joining up, and learning about the political fight to get sexual orientation into the nondiscrimination clause. I suddenly gained new insight not only into the union, but that a professional organization existed for teachers. It was like someone had breathed new life into me."

He felt some initial hesitancy hanging around the booth, but purchased an NEA/GLC t-shirt. He attended caucus meetings, but said little. Yet when leaders asked members to wear their pink shirts for a floor fight the following day, he figured it was time to act. To Mike's relief, no one commented on his attire.

The following summer, at the Representative Assembly in Miami, he spoke with a fellow caucus member from Port Huron about forming a statewide group, and in November 1991 the Michigan Education Association Gay and Lesbian Caucus was born. As chairperson, Mike

Chiumento sent formal letters to members of the state hierarchy; he received no acknowledgment, except for a congratulatory note from one vice president. An article about the organization soon appeared in the *MEA Voice,* and Mr. Chiumento fielded a call from his local president. "The superintendent will see this," he was told. "That's okay," he replied. His principal told him she had received a couple of phone calls from teachers elsewhere in the district about "the fag" in her building, but she supported him firmly.

Mr. Chiumento played an active role in attempting to include sexual orientation in his local union contract's nondiscrimination clause ("There's no cost, except the ink to print it," he pointed out with the savvy of a union negotiator), but takes greater pride in his work at the twice-yearly State Representative Assemblies. "We have a colorful table with a big sign, and all sorts of great brochures," he said. "We've got material from PFLAG, and a booklet we put together filled with information on bargaining language from around the U.S., and why sexual orientation should be included in every contract. We've got information on teenage suicide – people are amazed when they hear the statistics on gay suicides. Everything goes like hotcakes; the response is phenomenal. Some people wait till no one's around, and then pick it up for 'a friend.' Some people say they're picking it up for their school counselors. We get teachers, custodians, everyone coming by. The important thing is, it gets picked up – and passed along."

In several years, Mr. Chiumento has heard only one negative comment. "A woman took all the stuff, then said she didn't agree with us and asked if I knew Jesus. I said I had twelve years of Catholic school so yes, I did. She handed everything back, and said she didn't want it. I said, 'That's fine, because there are plenty of people who do.'"

———

One teacher who believed the focus of the NEA Gay and Lesbian Caucus should be on student – not teacher – concerns was Phillip Carey, a high school music teacher in Indiana's Metropolitan School District of Washington Township prior to his death in 1994. He was impressed with the organization's desire to create a healthy educational atmosphere. He interpreted the caucus as saying, "Here's a group of students, and our curriculum, our extracurricular activities, and our social environment is not serving them. So how do we do it?"

One way, he said, is by helping create an atmosphere, beginning in kindergarten, that says diversity is good. "If Tommy has two daddies, or if Tommy likes playing with dolls, it's part of the school's job to say that's okay," Mr. Carey said. "Or – this happened at my high school

– when a boy asks why they skipped over the section on homosexuality in health class and the teacher said, 'Don't worry, they'll all die anyway,' that shouldn't be subject to discussion; that should get your butt fired."

The NEA/GLC helped "empower" Mr. Carey. "It directed my desire to direct the kids. It gave me resource material, and tied me in to other teachers across the country. It gave me access to research, so when I talked to other teachers or students I was not just talking off the top of my head. The caucus empowered me to go back to my school and empower students, teachers, and anyone else who was interested and willing to listen."

The caucus's camaraderie helped bring Mr. Carey out of the closet a decade earlier. At his first meeting in Washington he went to the annual caucus dinner, located off the beaten track so that people who did not feel completely comfortable could relax. He found a group of three hundred bright, articulate, passionate, professional men and women, chosen by their colleagues, who had the courage and commitment to take important issues to the floor, and get them passed by a group of eight thousand teachers. It was very impressive. He was hooked.

"Every teacher is committed to kids," Phillip Carey said. "But to see these people who are *so* committed to kids, and to making their schools better and safer places for everyone – against fairly formidable odds – made me feel so very, very proud."

———•◦•———

The NEA Gay and Lesbian Caucus is not limited to gay teachers, of course. Proof can be found in rural Vermont where Barbara Barbour, a straight woman, teaches seventh- and eighth-grade math at Windsor Junior High School, serves as secretary-treasurer of the Vermont Education Association, is active on the NEA human and civil rights committee, and has thrown herself into the GLC's work with a passion many lesbian and gay teachers lack, or are afraid to show.

Mrs. Barbour joined the caucus after meeting Carol Watchler through the civil rights committee. A few conversations with the GLC chair convinced Mrs. Barbour that there should be an organized support system for lesbian and gay teachers in the Green Mountain State. But when she tried to get a group going, she found it more difficult than she had ever imagined. "They didn't want to come out," she explained. "And I didn't know how far to push, because I wasn't sure whose feet I was stepping on. It was hard." Her next thought was to organize a gay-straight teachers' caucus, but that did not work either.

Barbara Barbour, a straight junior high math teacher in Vermont, has added membership in the NEA Gay and Lesbian Caucus to her civil rights activities.

Yet that did not stop Mrs. Barbour. She asked the NEA to list her as one of Vermont's gay and lesbian contacts, and soon began getting phone calls – some from people who knew her number but called Mrs. Watchler in New Jersey instead (she referred them back to Mrs. Barbour in Vermont). Many callers were hesitant to reveal their names, which at first surprised Mrs. Barbour. Now, however, she understands. "As I meet and become friends with more and more gays and lesbians, I realize how deep and intensely personal their issues are," she said. "I know now that being in the closet is okay; people learn to deal with it. After talking with lesbians and gays, I've eased up. I no longer try to get everyone to come out and be a positive role model, because I see there are more parts to gay teachers' lives than that."

Mrs. Barbour calls herself a resource person, providing caucus information to interested teachers, assisting guidance counselors in dealing with questioning youngsters, and helping plan workshops for educators. "When I first started doing this several years ago Carol was so good to me, filling me in on my ignorance," Mrs. Barbour said. "Now I'm trying to extend that comfort level to others, so they can understand what gay teachers and students go through. I can help teachers understand what their students are experiencing, and I can also help them give support to their colleagues who may need it." Some of the work takes place behind the scenes, some up front – but all is very fulfilling.

She pointed proudly to a situation in which the children of a gay single parent were having difficulty dealing with the noncustodial parent; they were also being teased by youngsters in school. The guidance counselor, who normally would have been involved, hesitated because of rumors concerning the counselor's own alleged homosexuality. Mrs. Barbour got someone else to handle the situation, and soon the counselor felt comfortable enough to step in. "At times like that I sometimes ask myself, 'Who am I that I should get involved?'" she said. "But I do. People appreciate it, and I in turn appreciate that."

Mrs. Barbour appreciates too the opportunities she's had for involvement with the gay community. "I've found gay people to be very special – far more loving than many of the straight people I know," she said with feeling. "The more I see of them the more comforted I am, to know that they're here and part of our world. This has been a very rewarding and enriching experience for me. I wouldn't trade it for anything."

Despite her activism, she calls herself a neophyte who just keeps plugging away. "I see the pressures on gay and lesbian kids as far more difficult and painful than I ever imagined them to be. So I keep working. And I keep hoping that someday we will have a gay and lesbian caucus here, because that would benefit everyone in Vermont."

The AFT, the NEA's putative rival, has a similar, two-pronged approach to gay issues. Dr. Paul Thomas, founder of the national Gay and Lesbian Caucus, has boiled that approach down to five words: "labor equity and educational equity." Like the NEA, the AFT group focuses on matters of concern both to individual teachers (contracts, benefits, disciplinary hearings) and to the larger school community as a whole (making buildings safe and comfortable for all students, teachers, and staff, no matter what their sexual orientation).

Dr. Thomas, a former elementary school teacher in Pennsylvania who left the classroom after twenty-three years to take a full-time staff position with the union, founded the AFT Gay and Lesbian Caucus in 1988. He corralled five colleagues to be officers, got the go-ahead from the Philadelphia local, and headed to San Francisco for the national convention (powerful national president Albert Shanker had already lent his support, too). Dr. Thomas asked the executive board to give its okay, saying, "I know I represent a lot of teachers. Now I've just got to find out who they are."

It wasn't hard. The fledgling caucus signed up two hundred members at that convention; the same weekend it got the AFT to reaffirm, in strong terms, its stand against discrimination based on sexual orientation. The group grew rapidly; within half a decade over a thousand names were added to its mailing list. Two years after San Francisco, at the Boston convention, the caucus was instrumental in the full organization's passage of several important resolutions: the AFT went on record backing bereavement leave for domestic partners as a legitimate item for contract discussion, it urged that union contracts include sexual orientation among the list of reasons for which employees may not be subject to discrimination, and it decreed that discrimination on the basis of sexual orientation by any local could result in the loss of charter. More recently the caucus has spurred the AFT to support the idea of domestic partner benefits as a legitimate contract item, and is producing for the union a binder on contract equity that will be available to all locals.

The AFT has put its money where its often contentious mouth is. With the full support of Mr. Shanker and several powerful city local presidents, the executive board sent Dr. Thomas and three fellow caucus members around the nation to conduct conferences and workshops. They've been eye-opening experiences for presenters and attendees alike.

"We did a two-hour session for two hundred people on educational equity for lesbian, gay, and bisexual children in Broward County, Florida," Dr. Thomas said. "I never heard the words 'anal sex' mentioned so much in my life. I thought the teachers would fall off their chairs. But at the end, every one of them but four gave us A's for our presentation."

Nonetheless, Paul Thomas knows there remains a long way to go. "We don't exactly have to overcome obstacles; it's more like helping the union see where and how they can be of service to our gay and lesbian members, and the kids that all of us teach. More and more I'm finding people coming to me with a problem they haven't faced before. They don't know how to handle it, so we help them work it out."

For example, a California teacher incurred the wrath of the religious right for handing out student identification cards that on the back contained support service information, including a lesbian and gay youth group. Board of education hearings ensued, but the local AFT chapter hesitated to get involved. Dr. Thomas got wind, called Washington headquarters, and with a little goosing from the national office, the local soon stood behind its member.

The situation arose, Dr. Thomas said, because the local was unaware of the importance of gay and lesbian issues. That's why he attends as many AFT conventions and meetings as possible, never passing up a chance to spread the GLC word. The word – that gay and lesbian issues are labor equity and educational equity issues of concern to all AFT members – finally seems to be filtering down. "There was one conference where I was the only one manning the GLC table," he said. "So what happened? A number of straight people came over and helped. They had no fears that people would think they were gay – and they shouldn't have. They just saw a need to help out with something important."

Dr. Thomas claimed, however, that he is not an activist. "Activists, in my mind, stand outside the system saying, 'This is the way it should be.' Don't get me wrong, we need that type of people, but I'm what I call an 'intramechanist.' I find out the ways in which the system works and try to help it work better, from the inside out."

Dr. Thomas is pleased that the union feels comfortable dealing with issues of discrimination, but feels that when it comes to affirmation, they shy away. He explained the difference. "It's one thing to stop a kid from being beaten up for being gay; I think any of our members would do that. It's another to tell him it's okay – in fact, it's fine – to be gay. That's an entirely different message to send, and I'm not sure everyone is comfortable sending that message yet. It's not so much a question of resistance as it is getting that message to everyone. Our job is to get that message through."

The most important way of sending that message, Dr. Thomas noted, is via union leaders in Washington. "Through them, we can get the word out to everyone about how important it is to be out, visible, proud, and professional. And that's important to everyone in every school community: teachers, administrators, kids, parents, everyone else."

However, Paul Thomas said, that does not mean that the Gay and Lesbian Caucus relies on the top leadership to do all the work. The real impetus for action, he concluded, must well up from the bottom. "We need to get our sexual minority people to be out, open, and pressing for equity. The union can take a stand on something – and they've done it, plenty of times – but only the locals can put it on the table, speak for it, vote on it, get action on it. Gay and lesbian issues have to come from the membership. If our members know our issues, and know how important those issues are to us, they'll be more likely to support us and stand behind us. And that's where the real strength of a union lies."

What the Research Shows

For as long as he's served as a college instructor of teacher education, Anthony Costa has been interested in homosexuality and the high school classroom. His awareness was heightened several years ago when a former student, coincidentally a teacher in his wife's school, died of AIDS.

"It struck me like a blow," he said. "Here I am in the field of teacher education, teaching young men and women how to be good, effective teachers, sending them into classrooms filled with youngsters trying to find out who they themselves are. And in those classrooms are a certain number of kids who feel that they're not 'normal'; they go to school in an atmosphere of prejudice and hostility, and nothing's done about it. We don't know anything at all about homosexuality in schools. That's a terrifying thought."

His first step was to invite openly gay high school teacher John Anderson and Lea Dickson, a health educator who conducts workshops for universities and professional groups on gay and lesbian issues, to present a seminar to Mr. Costa's students. The two-hour session focused on working with students who may be gay.

Mr. Anderson and Ms. Dickson's talk made him realize that theory was one thing, facts another – and, as an academic type, he had no facts to support his theories. Mr. Costa decided to find some hard data, but soon found the only way to get it was to unearth it himself. Aided by a grant from his school, Fairfield University, Mr. Costa designed a research project to measure how Connecticut high schools deal with homosexuality. Specifically, he wanted to know what they are doing to combat homophobia, how they perceive the problem, and how well or poorly they include homosexuality in the curriculum.

Mr. Costa mailed two virtually identical questionnaires. One was sent to 130 high school principals throughout the state; the other to 800 teachers at nine urban, suburban, and rural high schools. Neither survey was coded, to assure complete confidentiality. Forty percent of the principals returned their surveys; the teachers' return rate was 36 percent. Of the 289 teachers responding, 12 – or 5 percent – indicated that they were homosexual; of the 52 principals, none did.

The first survey statement read, "Our school promotes a climate of tolerance and acceptance of the lesbian and gay student population." While 62 percent of the principals agreed with the statement, only 45 percent of the teachers agreed. Of the gay and lesbian teachers, only 8 percent felt their school provided a safe environment for homosexual teens. Invited to comment further, one teacher wrote, "The problem has not come up." "Not much discussion occurs," another said.

Asked to react to the statement "Our school makes it easy for the lesbian and gay students to discuss their feelings with a resource person or persons on staff," 62 percent of the principals agreed, while only 34 percent of the teachers did. Every gay teacher disagreed. "No one on the counseling staff understands their feelings," one wrote.

Mr. Costa asked teachers, "Does your school have an explicit policy regarding the harassment, name calling, and verbal or physical abuse of the lesbian and gay student population in your school?" Federal law mandates that each school must have a harassment policy, though it need not include specific types of harassment (for example, gender, racial, or sexual orientation). However, only 18 percent of the teachers responded that their schools had one.

Educators were asked whether they believed their school should have "an explicit policy stating that we do not tolerate harassment, name calling, and verbal and physical abuse" of lesbian and gay students. Despite the federal law, 30 percent of the principals and 28 percent of the teachers disagreed that schools should have such a written statement, at least as it relates to homosexuals.

Respondents were then invited to reply to the statement "The counselors in our school are able, willing and open to the discussion of homosexuality with all of the student population, but in particular with the lesbian and gay student population." Principals overwhelmingly endorsed their counselors' effectiveness – 72 percent agreed with the quote – but teachers held a very different view. Only 46 percent agreed, including just 18 percent of the self-identified gay teachers. A teacher commented, "One guidance counselor is on the fence about the issue; the rest are homophobic."

The next statement dealt with teachers themselves: "The teachers in our school are able, willing and open to the discussion of homosexuality with all the student population, but in particular with the lesbian and gay student population." Teachers – those with the closest, most ongoing, and intimate contact with students – were perceived by all participants in the survey as being the least ready to discuss homosexuality. Sixty-five percent of the teachers, 70 percent of the principals – and 100 percent of the homosexual teachers – felt that teachers were not able, willing, and open to the discussion of homosexuality, even with gay students. One teacher said of his or her colleagues, "Most are homophobic."

Yet asked the same question with regard to the administrative staff, principals perceived themselves in a positive light. Seventy-eight percent felt they were the ones in their school most open to the discussion of homosexual issues. In sharp contrast, only 39 percent of the teachers (and a quarter of the gay teachers) agreed that was the case.

Other survey questions delved into the openness of schools to the hiring of lesbian and gay teachers to serve as role models (most principals and teachers agreed it is a worthy goal); the adequacy of the school library as a source of books, journals, and other materials dealing with homosexuality (most respondents called library resources inadequate); and the curricular preference for dealing with gay and lesbian issues (the majority of principals preferred "across the curriculum," while teachers opted for sex education classes, guidance counselors, and health classes).

There were two important areas of agreement. Asked how their school curriculum deals with issues affecting the lesbian and gay adolescent, most principals and all teachers said "slightly" or "not at all." A whopping 64 percent of all principals felt that their school's curriculum dealt with them only slightly. And questioned about the number of workshops their school has held in the last five years to help develop "skills, strategies and consciousness raising on the topic of homophobia in education," most principals and teachers indicated that their school had had either none, one, or two.

Having amassed this data, what does Anthony Costa make of it? "Schools in Connecticut have a lot of work to do," he said. "And I'm not so sure they're willing to do it. The commitment doesn't seem to be there. And even though you've got people pushing systems to do more, I'm afraid they could find themselves up to their ears in trouble.

Uneducated parents will begin to make noise, and once that turmoil begins, teachers can be let go. Not because they're gay – that's illegal – but because their effectiveness as a teacher has been compromised. Once a teacher's effectiveness is questioned, he's looked at with more scrutiny. And that starts a process that is hard to contain."

Mr. Costa, who has spent his career in teacher training, believes that this survey has important implications for his field. "It's made me more aware of how much I have to include information on homosexuality in everything I do – and how we train counselors and administrators, too. I include information in all my ed. psych. and methods courses, and in my seminars on student teaching. I don't make a special unit of it, but I mention it throughout each course whenever it applies. Kids have to be knowledgeable about homosexuality and have their fears eased; the only way to do that is to keep them informed. And the only way to keep them informed is to have informed teachers."

The reactions of student teachers to information on homosexuality has been very positive, according to Anthony. "They sit open-mouthed when John and Lea make their presentation," he noted. "They look at the vast amount of material John and Lea show them they can use in the classroom, and they're amazed." That encourages Mr. Costa. "The undergrad and graduate students here at Fairfield are intelligent. They have their biases, yes, but they're more open-minded toward homosexuality than a lot of teachers in the field now. That's so important, when you realize that 5 to 10 percent of their future students will be struggling with all kinds of worrisome, quote-unquote not normal feelings."

Of course, he added, the process of bringing homosexuality into the classroom – raising the issue during lectures and discussions; encouraging students to feel confident enough to ask a trusted educator about it; eliminating homophobic references, jokes, and taunts from the hallways and locker rooms – is a long one. "It's not about a flash of intuition or a revelation," Mr. Costa said. "It's more like a slow process of understanding. But that's our job as educators. Before a teacher can deal honestly with homosexuality in the school, that person has to deal with it himself or herself. And that's what we're trying to do here and now."

Dr. Thomas P. Juul knows all about the pressures a gay educator faces, inside the classroom and out: he's one himself. A high school librarian on Long Island with a doctorate in administrative studies from New York University, he had one of his most memorable brushes with homophobia when he worked for a principal who doubled as a fundamentalist minister. As soon as Dr. Juul received tenure at that school, he stopped hiding his homosexuality. There were immediate repercussions — he was transferred to the central office, away from students — but things worked out just as well, he said: "I had the time and the computers to do my dissertation proposal." His topic, ironically, was the extent to which disclosure or nondisclosure of a lesbian, gay, or bisexual teacher's sexual orientation influences his or her perceptions of job satisfaction and job stress.

With the help of the late Paul Savino, who edited a newsletter for New York's gay and lesbian teachers, Dr. Juul conducted a massive survey. He mailed questionnaires to over fourteen hundred members of eighteen gay and lesbian teacher groups throughout the United States; each contact was asked to give a second survey to another lesbian, gay, or bisexual colleague who was not a member of that organization. Over nine hundred surveys were returned, from forty-one states and the District of Columbia.

The work, he said, was groundbreaking. "There was plenty of information on gay teachers and the workplace, but no large studies had ever been done. Everything we knew came from small groups, with generalized results." The themes of "paranoia, the fear of being fired, and the relief of coming out" ran through all previous surveys; Dr. Juul hoped to replicate those results on a wider scale. Ultimately, he amassed sixty-eight tables of data, in a report of over three hundred pages ("a queen who couldn't stop writing," he calls himself).

When he presented his data at the 1993 annual meeting of the American Educational Research Association in Atlanta, Dr. Juul prefaced his remarks by saying that the research might be viewed by gay people in the audience as self-evident, though probably not so by the heterosexuals there. As African-Americans knew from experience, he said, discrimination hurts. "And we as gay people know that release from oppression and secrecy allows for individual growth and happiness."

Indeed, Dr. Juul did find that people who were closeted at work were less satisfied in their interpersonal relations there and far more stressed by sexual orientation issues. (Measuring "openness" is not easy, he admitted: "No one knows what 'out' is. It's self-interpretive. We had to rely on whatever people decided to tell us about their degree of openness.")

Dr. Juul also found that teachers who were more open about their sexual orientation displayed much greater job satisfaction than their more closeted colleagues. The reasons included expanded social interactions with staff and students, and lessened sense of isolation. It appeared too that teachers who were more open with administrators received more satisfaction from their role within the building than those who were not fully out. These teachers also seemed more willing to be noticed for their achievements, another element relating to job satisfaction.

The main lesson of the study, according to Dr. Juul, is that coming out in school doesn't have the social ramifications it once did. "It's less dangerous to come out now; in fact, there are *benefits* to coming out. I wasn't sure at first, but the more I look at these results, the more I'm convinced it's beneficial for teachers to be out in the school workplace."

Teachers hiding in closets, he noted, are under the constant threat of exposure. Once they're out, that threat ends, and they can be the people they really are, which leads to greater relaxation and more job satisfaction.

Regarding teachers' openness with administrators, Dr. Juul explained that "those who took the bull by the horns showed they were willing to become self-actualized people, getting on with their lives without excess baggage. They were much more involved with their school, and accepted more public recognition, which caused them to be more satisfied with their jobs. Closeted people always risk exposure, even when they've accepted awards."

Dr. Juul found significant differences between lesbians and gay men. Lesbian teachers were more satisfied with their jobs than men. The reason, he surmised, is cultural: it is more acceptable for a female schoolteacher to be perceived as a lesbian than it is for a male educator to be seen as gay.

The study also included a small number of bisexuals – 71 of the 892 usable surveys carried that self-description. "No one's ever looked at that group before in education," Dr. Juul said. "No one wants to hear about them." Bisexuals showed the most negative results in every area: they were the most stressed at work, they suffered the most identity crises, and they were most in need of recognition and acceptance.

While Dr. Juul assumed that achieving tenure would be a defining event in their lives – allowing gay teachers to be more open about themselves – the opposite result appeared. Tenured teachers were generally less satisfied; they experienced higher levels of emotional exhaustion and lower levels of personal accomplishment than nontenured teachers. Tenured teachers did, however, experience significantly less stress related to their sexual identity.

Another factor surveyed was age. While younger teachers were the most open about their homosexuality, those between thirty-eight and forty-four experienced greater satisfaction and diminished stress from teaching, and showed a compassion for students that neither younger nor older teachers displayed.

Teachers who had dealt with AIDS in their personal lives were more satisfied in their jobs, as well as more out in their schools. "When a close friend dies, you're morose and you cry," Dr. Juul said. "You can't do that in school if you're closeted. And dealing with AIDS gives you a different perspective on life, which comes through in the work you do. AIDS people are a lot more committed to civil rights, more satisfied with teaching and less stressed overall. That puts to rest the 'post-traumatic syndrome' we saw in the mideighties."

Dr. Juul noted that his survey measured job satisfaction and job stress only; no questions dealt with sexual practices. "That's not what our lives are about," he said emphatically. "Sex is only a piece of our lives. Gay research now emphasizes the *quality* of the life we're leading." And, according to his own studies, the quality of that life – for gay and lesbian teachers, at least – is surprisingly high.

GLSTN Shines Its Light

If Kevin Jennings is not the last person you'd expect to find teaching at a prestigious New England boarding school, he certainly is down near the bottom of the list. A native of rural North Carolina, he was the first person in his "poor Southern family" descended from Confederate veterans to go to college (and not just any college: Harvard). His father, now dead, was a fundamentalist minister; his uncles and cousins joined the Ku Klux Klan. As a child, Mr. Jennings said, he was "exposed to every 'ism' there is: racism, sexism, classism." And as a gay male in that constricting environment, he also suffered firsthand the stings and slaps of homophobia.

It was not an easy upbringing – along the way, the high school valedictorian used drugs and alcohol to dull the pain – but once out of college, he did not slide into a comfortable job, nor did he move over to law or business school (he thought of politics, but eventually realized he "couldn't stomach that kind of life").

Instead, Mr. Jennings entered the rarefied world of boarding schools. Less than a decade later, teachers at schools throughout the nation – public as well as private – are benefiting from the trails this young history instructor has blazed.

It was in his senior year at Harvard – not long before he was selected to give the commencement address – that Mr. Jennings decided to become a teacher. "I always wanted to do something to fight the forces of hatred I'd felt growing up," he explained. "I thought that because teachers reach kids when they're young, they can help make a better tomorrow." Deciding relatively late on a teaching career meant he had no time to get public school certification; that's how he ended up at Moses Brown School in Providence, Rhode Island.

"I had been very out in college, but very in during my interviews," he recalled. "I couldn't imagine being hired as an openly gay teacher." Yet he hadn't thought through the repercussions of one of his first seemingly innocuous acts: showing up at the first faculty meeting with an earring. He was told that if he wore it the next day he might as well not show up for work.

That scared him. "I was twenty-two, and very alone. I didn't know any other gay teachers. So I shut up, and removed the earring." That little incident rankled him, yet Mr. Jennings kept quiet again when, at a faculty meeting, the staff was discussing a student's nickname, "Veg" (for "vegetable"). Someone remarked, "Better 'Veg' than 'Fruit.'" The slur went uncommented upon, but it stayed with Mr. Jennings. "This was a Quaker school!" he noted.

"I'd had such a tough time coming to terms with being gay myself – I tried to commit suicide when I was seventeen – and being in the closet again was killing me," he continued. In his second year he knew he had to leave Moses Brown. He'd heard about Concord Academy, and when he was hired at the more progressive high school, he vowed never again to closet himself around colleagues.

"I think I brought my boyfriend to the first faculty party," he said. "I know I wore a ring I'd exchanged with him. The kids asked me if I was married, and the headmaster said, 'Tell them it's a gift from someone you love.' I asked him, 'Is that what you say about your wedding ring? That it's "a gift from someone you love"?!'"

That brief comment initiated a process by which a year later he came out to the entire school. His vehicle was the daily fifteen-minute chapel talk, a ritual during which any member of the Concord community can discuss any topic he or she wishes, without fear of censorship or punishment.

Mr. Jennings had come out to his history classes at the end of his first year, but he wanted to make a schoolwide declaration as well. "I thought it would be unhealthy if it was going around as a whispered rumor – 'Mr. Jennings is gay, Mr. Jennings is gay,'" he said. However, the headmaster was reluctant to have him make that speech. In addition, Kevin said, "This was 1988, a year before Massachusetts passed the gay rights law, and I didn't have tenure yet. I was aware I was taking my career in my hands."

The battles, both within Kevin Jennings's soul and with the administration, went on. The headmaster told him his announcement could drive the venerable school out of business. He even received a visit from "a closeted older teacher," who tried to talk him out of his chapel talk.

But the key moment came when another faculty member told him, "If you don't do this, you won't be able to look yourself in the mirror again."

So, on November 10, 1988, two days after George Bush was elected president of the United States, Kevin Jennings looked not in the mirror but at a sea of faces, and opened the closet door. "The place was packed," he recalled with pride. "Every faculty member was there, even people who always skipped. A former teacher, a legendary man who had AIDS, came almost directly from the hospital. There were maintenance people, secretaries. My best friend, a woman, flew in from California for my speech. It was really a moment of high drama."

The theme of Kevin's talk was "the power of the word 'faggot' to shape a life." He told the multitude, "I found I could have a happy life only when I was happy with who I am." At the close of a typical chapel talk, a few friends linger to congratulate the speaker. This time, he said, "there was a mob scene. Kids were hugging me; kids I didn't even know were crying. It was such a vindication of the power of truth."

He arrived ten minutes late to class, and noticed that the blackboard was covered with chalk. His first thought was that the class had scrawled epithets like "Fag" all over the board, but as he looked closer he realized his students had written messages like "We love you" and "We're proud of you." It was then, he said, that he realized he'd achieved "an incredible victory."

The good feelings continued. Two weeks later he was granted tenure. He suddenly realized that being out was, in fact, a smart career move; it would have been harder to deny tenure to an openly gay teacher than to one cowering in the closet. In 1992 he was named one of Massachusetts's Fifty Terrific Teachers Making a Difference by the Edward Calesa Foundation. And, contrary to the headmaster's fears, Concord Academy did not go out of business – in fact, applications increased each year.

"I don't get any credit for that, but I'm sure if they went down I'd get the blame," Mr. Jennings mused. One year a reporting error indicated that applications were falling; the next faculty meeting featured a discussion about Concord's "overrepresentation of gays." "But when they found the mistake, there wasn't a retraction," he said. "And when they set a new application record, there weren't any comments about the number of gay kids."

He didn't know it at the time, but Kevin Jennings's chapel talk did not represent the end of his journey. In fact, it was just the start of the next phase of his career.

Shortly after he came out, the trade journal *Independent School* asked him to write an article on being an openly gay teacher. "They told me I was the only one they knew," he said (there were a few others, he later learned). When he penned "Opening Closets and Minds" in early 1989, the reaction was phenomenal. He received invitations to speak at schools, conferences, and workshops around the country. "It just snowballed," he said. "I never planned to become the Homosexual Spokesperson of the World." But he was. And after each event, closeted teachers would come up to him and talk.

The more that happened, the more Mr. Jennings realized there was a desperate need, both professional and personal, for gay and lesbian teachers to connect. He approached the Independent School Association of Massachusetts (ISAM) and asked them to sponsor a gay and lesbian group, as they did for teachers of color and other minorities. He received an almost immediate "Of course!" from executive director Richard Barbieri. Though Mr. Jennings is full of praise for him, the executive director of ISAM downplays his own role, preferring instead to laud the heads of each school who went along with the proposal as soon as they understood its importance. Even parochial schools signed on and have encouraged staff members to become involved although, Mr. Barbieri noted, "they oppose the occasional Catholic-bashing."

Mr. Jennings asked Katherine Henderson, assistant director of athletics at Phillips Andover Academy and one of the few open lesbian teachers he knew, to become co-chair. The Gay and Lesbian Independent School Teachers Network (GLISTN, pronounced "glisten") was born.

Their first conference, in May 1991, attracted a hundred people. "That stunned everyone," Mr. Jennings said. "The only advertising we did was a blind mailing to independent schools. We expected maybe fifty. ISAM was blown away." The response indicated a much bigger need than anyone had realized.

Four precepts emerged from that inaugural conference. GLISTN's two goals were to support lesbian and gay teachers, and to fight homophobia; its two rules were that anyone could join, regardless of sexual orientation, and that public school teachers were also welcome. "I'd gone to public schools, and my partner taught in them," Mr. Jennings explained. "I knew they had the same needs we did."

GLISTN grew quickly. The following year's conference attracted 300 attendees, gay and straight; by 1993 there were 350, and in 1994, 400. The organization initiated an annual retreat, limited to forty

Kevin Jennings helped found the
Gay and Lesbian Independent School
Teachers Network (now GLSTN) after an
Independent School article he wrote on
being an openly gay teacher sparked
interest throughout the country.

CYNTHIA KATZ

lesbian and gay teachers. They inaugurated a newsletter; the mailing list ballooned beyond a thousand. They traveled to Washington, D.C., in April 1993 to participate in the march for gay and lesbian rights, striding behind a large banner (and were filmed by the Christian Coalition, which uses the group as "the embodiment of evil," Mr. Jennings said with a hint of glee). They developed two catchy slogans ("Coming Out Soon at a School Near You" and "Together, for a Change"), and marched in Boston's pride parade carrying large photos of famous gays and lesbians.

And they did it for five years without a full-time director. Grassroots organizing by passionate, committed men and women was the key to early success. It should be noted that the network's founder had even less free time than others: Mr. Jennings also co-chaired the Education Committee of the Governor's Commission on Gay and Lesbian Youth, headed Concord Academy's history department, and coached boys' and girls' volleyball and ultimate Frisbee. He spent the 1993–94 school year away from school, however, as one of twelve Columbia University Klingenstein Fellows. The award – the highest an independent school teacher can achieve – is used to develop a project beneficial to education. Mr. Jennings spent his time working on two books on gay and lesbian issues.

Surprisingly, GLSTN (the acronym evolved, and now stands for Gay, Lesbian, and Straight Teachers Network; the pronunciation remains the same) faced no organizational obstacles, Mr. Jennings said. "Dick (Barbieri) was always completely behind it; it was a nonnegotiable issue with him. Having ISAM was really helpful – it gave us instant legitimacy, like the blessing of the pope." ISAM itself changed; the group metamorphosed into the Association of Independent Schools in New England (AISNE). By the late spring of 1994 GLSTN had outgrown AISNE's sponsorship, which consisted primarily of sending out mailings, conducting conferences, and providing tactical advice.

As GLSTN's mission matured and membership skyrocketed, it became clear that the organization had to branch out on its own. Seeking to become the only national coalition of gay and straight teachers devoted to fighting homophobia through broad-based programming and networking, while offering its resources and conferences to individuals and schools across the country, the GLSTN steering committee asked Mr. Jennings to become the group's first executive director. He agreed, reducing his teaching load at Concord to a one-quarter position beginning in the 1994–95 school year.

The change was presaged a year or so earlier, when GLSTN began receiving letters from beyond the Northeast – as far away as Europe and Asia, in fact. For the first time in 1993, their lesbian and gay teacher retreat included educators from outside New England (two came from California). "It's incredibly gratifying to see a teacher take this issue and run with it," Mr. Jennings said. "GLSTN has been effective because we empower teachers, who then empower their students, faculty, and parents to come forward. It's an incredible story – almost like a fairy tale. It's been a mind-blowing series of events."

Yet he noticed that, while gay and lesbian teacher groups were springing up all over the nation, most operated in isolation. "We have to get together," he said. "We have to share ideas. I realize no one likes to be told what to do, but I think GLSTN can serve a purpose by sharing ideas and helping other groups devise strategies. There's lots of duplication of thought and energy going on now, and with the tremendous amount of work that needs to be done – curriculum development, empowerment, that sort of thing – there's not a lot to be said for continually reinventing the wheel."

GLSTN can help other groups frame what they're doing as educational issues, he said. "If people understand that our work is about helping kids succeed in school, then they're very, very receptive and supportive. But we can't hold back. We as gay people have to be willing to take this fight to the fundamentalist right's turf and say, 'Yeah, we do want your kids – we want them to be safe, and healthy, and unwilling to kill themselves.'" The coming battle with the Christian Coalition, Mr. Jennings believes, will be fought over schoolchildren – and he relishes that fight. "Too many gay and lesbian teachers see themselves as threats to kids. There are a lot of terrified teachers out there. They need a national organization to turn to for help." He thinks GLSTN can be that group. In the 1994–95 school year, GLSTN organized several first-time events: a Gay and Lesbian History Month celebration; conferences for mid-Atlantic, Midwest, and West Coast teachers; a West Coast retreat for lesbian and gay educators; and a summer institute for students and teachers.

"I joke that I started GLSTN because I was lonely," he concluded. "Well, one of the biggest pleasures for me has been meeting so many people. I'm sure not lonely anymore, and I'm glad others aren't lonely too."

For ten years, Mr. Jennings shared his home and life with another history teacher, Bob Parlin of Newton South High School. Mr. Parlin now serves as GLSTN's co-chair (founding co-chair Kathy Henderson, of Phillips Andover Academy, stepped down at the end of the 1993–94 school year, and was honored with the first GLSTN Pathfinder Award). He brings an important public school perspective to the organization, and in the midnineties is helping the group develop its national profile. He wants to help expand membership to every major urban network, and plan a rotating national conference.

Ultimately, the group hopes to develop ways to help teachers come out. "The more that happens, the easier it is to change schools," he said. "Being out is important for every teacher's self-esteem. Since Kevin came out, about thirty others have come out in the Boston area. Most of them are still in private schools, but every day more and more come closer to coming out. My personal goal is to have several openly gay and lesbian teachers in every school in the country – just as we should have people of color in every school."

To that end Mr. Parlin spends countless hours on the phone, making and fielding calls (his number is listed in gay newspapers). "One teacher's shrink counseled him to call," he said. "This man was forty, and terrified – he'd just realized he was gay. I had to explain, very patiently, that there *are* gay teachers who are out, and that it's not a devastating thing. He just couldn't believe there was such a thing."

Mr. Parlin spends ten to fifteen hours a week on GLSTN issues, plus another twenty to thirty working on the Department of Education's Safe Schools anti-homophobia program – in addition to teaching a regular class load. "I have no life right now," he laughed. "The only thing that keeps me going is the excitement of all this."

That excitement comes from events like the GLSTN retreat, when forty lesbian and gay teachers spend a weekend discussing such intensely personal topics as body image, oppression, and fear. "These aren't professionally led," Mr. Parlin emphasized. "It's purely peer support. But it's so great to see the incredible change that comes over people in just a couple of days, and then hear about the action they take after they leave. Everyone doesn't necessarily come out at school – but they all do something, even if it's just approaching the principal to add sexual orientation to the nondiscrimination clause.

"I think GLSTN has had a dramatic impact on many people, and many schools," he noted. "Even with Kevin out, I was very uncertain about coming out myself. I never would have done it without the support of friends and colleagues. My coming out has dramatically changed my school – its policies and attitudes – and I know that's true for other schools too."

———

Many of those other schools were among the hundred-plus represented at GLSTN's fourth annual conference, held in April 1994. Four hundred participants descended on Milton Academy in Massachusetts. They came from private schools in New England, New York, and Washington, D.C.; public schools as far away as North Carolina; and colleges and universities throughout the East. One man was from California; a woman flew in from Japan. Some of the attendees looked like teachers (whatever that looks like), others did not; some looked gay (whateve. that looks like), others did not. What they all shared was a desire to feel good about themselves, their schools, and the lives they were leading, both inside and outside their buildings. The theme of the conference was "Building Bridges" – to their heterosexual allies, administrators, and communities, and to everyone battling the evils of sexism, racism, classism, and homophobia – but it was the concerns and needs of their students that were foremost in most GLSTN teachers' and speakers' minds.

Mr. Jennings made the first substantive reference to lesbian and gay youngsters. "Contemporary battles over civil rights for homosexuals are not about us," he said in his welcoming speech. "They're about the lives of our children." He then announced GLSTN's incorporation as a nonprofit organization. Its purpose, he said, will be to help create change for students everywhere.

Plenary speaker Margaret Cerullo, a lesbian activist and professor of sociology at Hampshire College, enlarged upon Mr. Jennings's theme. Speaking both of the newly visible and often quoted gay power brokers in Washington and of the newly visible and often quoted out teachers in schools across the country, she said, "Don't confuse the access and influence of a few with the safety and security of all. The center of the gay and lesbian agenda must be saving the youth of our country." It is a mission made more difficult by the cloud of homophobia that still swirls around many education issues, from congressional proposals to cut off funding to schools that present homosexuality without bias, to administrators and teachers who tolerate the physical and verbal harassment that make so many schools such unsafe and uncomfortable environments for so many gay youths.

Co-chair Bob Parlin noted that GLSTN's work serves all students in a school, straight as well as gay, and that students can be gay and lesbian teachers' best allies in building bridges and creating change. When he came out at Newton South High School, he said, "I had far fewer problems with kids than with teachers or parents. The kids were fine. I think we constantly underestimate the capacity of kids to understand and deal with the issue."

He made those comments during a workshop titled "First Steps in Getting Started," which presented two working models for schools beginning to address gay and lesbian issues. That session, and twenty others, enlarged upon the "Building Bridges" theme. A panel discussion called "Straight but Not Narrow" was targeted toward the small but powerful band of heterosexual allies who attended the conference. A session on "Addressing Homophobia in Catholic Schools" examined the frustrations, fears, and hopes of everyone working in such settings. "But They're Too Young!" explored how one elementary school answers questions and concerns about its work on gay and lesbian issues. Other workshops dealt with gay-straight alliances, curricula, and the roles of guidance counselors. There was even a lively panel on gay students and the college admission process, covering such controversial and important topics as whether to be out when applying to schools – and if out, how out is *too* out in a college essay?

It was, in many ways, a typical teachers' conference. In between sessions participants gathered in small groups. They complained about administrative interference, petty and grand; compared notes about what works in the classroom, and what doesn't; dispensed advice on dealing with difficult students and tricky parents; and spent a lot of time simply trading war stories.

But what made this "Building Bridges" conference different from most educators' seminars – and what makes GLSTN different from most teachers' organizations – is this: it empowered people. It emboldened them. It encouraged them to return to their schools filled with energy, then harness that energy to reach out and create change in students, faculty, parents, and themselves. The Gay, Lesbian, and Straight Teachers Network is indeed, in co-founder Kevin Jennings's words, "almost like a fairy tale." And as it moves forward to assume a larger, more national role, a new chapter in that story is being written.

Lesbian Teachers' Network Reaches Far and Wide

The Michigan Womyn's Music Festival is Jesse Helms's worst nightmare. Each summer nine thousand women gather; in addition to making and listening to music, they socialize, plan political action, and re-energize their spiritual souls.

A significant number of attendees are teachers. In recent years they've used the occasion first to find each other, now to hook up in a loose confederation dubbed the Lesbian Teachers' Network (LTN). The low-key organization, whose main focuses are a newsletter and series of festival workshops, boasts about six hundred members from North America and beyond. The mailing list is filled with teachers, counselors, and other women in education; there is little organization or hierarchy beyond a couple of directors and fifteen or so regional contacts. But what it lacks in structure it makes up for in energy. In half a dozen years, the LTN has established itself as a vital, affirming group for hundreds of women. For some, it is their only professional link with other lesbian teachers; for a few living and working in small towns or villages, it is their only social outlet, period.

"What women are looking for, basically, is support," said organizer Judy Moxley, a high school teacher in the Midwest. "We're not a politically active organization; we're just here for lesbian teachers. A lot of our members are very closeted; they teach in small, rural areas where they don't feel safe. They want a connection, and through us they're able to get information they wouldn't have access to otherwise." This includes, via the newsletter, notices and reviews of periodicals and publications that other education journals never mention; letters through which women share their personal experiences in and out of the classroom; and (for those who are able to take more risks) curricular ideas. The LTN is, one member said, "just like a big lesbian bulletin board."

One active member, a woman whose first involvement came through Ms. Moxley, is Mary-Ellen Nuzzo. A therapeutic educator with the Connecticut Department of Children and Youth Services who teaches teenage psychiatric inpatients at a large institution, she volunteers as one of the network's regional contacts. For her, much of the gratification comes from empowering lesbian teachers. "Coming to terms with yourself leads outward, to dealing with the contradictions of your school system. Once a woman does that, she can use curriculum to reduce homophobia or even be in the forefront of her district, helping to make policy. It's not an easy process, but once you start building alliances, a lot can happen." However, Ms. Nuzzo warned, alliance building can also be slow: "Some people are able to find just one confidante a year in their school."

The degree to which a teacher is out often depends on how long she has been teaching – in an inverse way. "We see student teachers already grappling with the issue, wondering whether to ask in interviews what the district's policy is on lesbian teachers and domestic benefits. Then at the other end there are women nearing retirement, who vow to themselves they'll come out to at least one person before they leave. And that's a very big step for them."

Personally, Mary-Ellen Nuzzo said, "Connecticut has made it easy for me. My union has fought hard to make inclusion a reality, and the state has a hate crimes bill. Of course, I know people in every state don't enjoy what I have, and I hear the horror stories all the time." One recent tragedy: a veteran high school math teacher who came out was the immediate target of a strong effort to force her out of her job, with a loss of benefits, by people who felt it was inappropriate for a math teacher to also be a lesbian. "Letters were put in her files, and she really had to defend herself as to why she should be allowed to continue teaching. There's no way she should have had to expend all that energy and emotion on something so basic," Ms. Nuzzo said.

Women hear about the LTN in a variety of ways: through an ad in the *Lesbian Connection,* at festival workshops, and by word of mouth. Each woman, said Mary-Ellen, is in a different stage. "In Northampton, they might as well have 'Dyke' stamped on their forehead; in Connecticut, they're usually somewhat out; in Vermont, New Hampshire, or Maine, it's a whole different ball game. One woman called us who wasn't out to a soul – not in her community and not in her workplace, which was many miles away. Her connection with the LTN, and at an occasional festival, constitutes her entire connection with the lesbian community. And I don't think that's unusual in the Bible Belt either, or some parts of the Midwest."

The women's festivals Ms. Nuzzo mentioned have grown into an important part of what the LTN offers its members. The organization runs three types of workshops: minisessions, lasting about two hours, where teachers network and share anecdotes; half-day sessions, devoted to specific ideas; and day-long sessions. The latter, she said, are intensive; they deal with such topics as curriculum planning or dealing with school board homophobia that have broad ramifications and cannot be covered quickly. The average attendance at most workshops is twenty-five to thirty, though up to fifty women have come to certain day sessions. The reactions, Mary-Ellen noted, range from "Oh my God, I can't believe this exists!" to "It's about time you started talking about this subject." Though the LTN currently sponsors workshops only at the Michigan Womyn's Music Festival, discussions are under way to offer them at other women's gatherings around the country.

Why, Ms. Nuzzo was asked, is there a need for an organization devoted solely to lesbian teachers? She paused, then said, "That's a good question. I don't really know. If anything, I think gay male teachers probably have it harder than women – the 'recruitment' charges probably hit them harder. The basic issues are pretty much the same for men and women: we want to feel safe, not get harassed; we want inclusion with the rest of the faculty; and we want to varying degrees to be role models for our students. I guess what it comes down to is that we started as an outgrowth of a women's festival, and we've just stayed that way."

The reasons she has remained involved have changed over the years, Ms. Nuzzo noted. "At the beginning it was more personal for me. I got a lot of reinforcement from the network for what I knew was right. I wasn't very out then – just to a few faculty members – and the LTN gave me the courage, the additional ego strength, to use the system as a friend, not a foe. So eventually I was able to come out to all my co-workers and administrators.

"As I worked through these issues, I was able to move on and take on other responsibilities, for other people. That was very empowering. Now I do a lot of work face-to-face, and a lot of letter writing and phone calls. I enjoy being able to help other lesbian teachers. For some women, contact with us may be only in brown, unmarked envelopes – but it's contact, and that's what's important.

"We're not a radical, in-your-face group," Ms. Nuzzo emphasized. "We love kids, but we also are people who have to earn paychecks, and we don't encourage people to be reckless. If a member is in a district where there's precedent to be fired for moral issues, we tell them to be careful about who they take on as a confidante. But then there's the feedback — the women who say, 'I'm so glad you're there,' or, 'It's so great just to have the phone number of someone to talk to' — and that just makes it all worthwhile."

Library Shelves
Are Opening Up

A library is a library is a library, right?
Wrong.

The school libraries of yesterday are now called library media centers. Card catalogs – those little brown file boxes stuffed with white index cards – have been replaced by on-line databases. And information is as likely to be read from – sorry, "accessed off" – a CD-ROM disk as a book or periodical.

But some things never change. Uncertain students still use libraries as a vital source of information about homosexuality. Nervous teenagers still curl up on the floor at far ends of the stacks, furtively scanning the indexes of health books for the words "gay" and "lesbian" while praying no one notices. And petrified youngsters still hesitate to ask librarians for any information on the forbidden topic.

For students questioning their sexuality, school librarians play perhaps the most pivotal role of any staff member. Yet librarians don't always trumpet that fact; as a result, administrators, parents, and even most teachers fail to recognize how valuable they and their libraries can be for youths thrashing through the brambles of sexual identity. But many librarians know.

Their efforts show up in countless, though often subtle, ways. The books they buy (or don't buy); the magazines they subscribe to (or don't); the manner in which they catalog their acquisitions; the way they place materials; the style in which they announce what they've got; even the tone of voice they use when a student says he "needs information *for a report I have to do*" (his emphasis, of course, is deliberate) on homosexuality – all send crucial messages to youngsters at one of the most crucial junctures of their lives.

Fortunately, most librarians recognize the power they hold. The librarians she knows are fairly sensitive to gay and lesbian issues, said Christine Jenkins, a faculty member of the University of Illinois Graduate School of Library and Information Science. Library school instills the idea that a library should reflect wide points of view, offer a broad spectrum of materials, and point users toward that information – no matter what a librarian's personal beliefs may be. The American Library Association, a 118-year-old, 58,000-member group which in 1970 became the first professional organization to form its own Gay and Lesbian Task Force, has adopted a Library Bill of Rights that unequivocally affirms the importance of materials that include lesbian and gay lifestyles, the works of homosexual authors, and the products of gay presses.

Libraries often deal with issues of inclusion, noted Ms. Jenkins. This takes many forms, depending upon the age of the school population. At the elementary level it means purchasing books that include stories about kids with gay parents; at the middle school it involves buying a book like *When Someone You Know Is Gay;* in senior high it is about including Sandra Scoppettone's *Trying Hard to Hear You* or *Happy Endings Are All Alike* in the display headed "Novels about Teenagers Who Fight Discrimination."

However, simply owning gay-sensitive materials is not enough. Making sure every student has access to them is equally important – but sometimes overlooked. Many students are invisible library users; they walk in, browse through the card catalog or do an on-line search, find a couple of books or pamphlets, hesitate a long while before carrying them facedown to a carrel or corner, read them hurriedly, stash them somewhere nearby to avoid the risk of being seen putting them back (librarians constantly find gay material misfiled or dumped under tables), then leave – all without ever asking a professional media specialist for advice.

That is why card catalogs have been such a critical resource. "A kid could come into the library and look in the 'G' drawer for books on 'Gay,'" Ms. Jenkins explained. "But if the librarian filed them only under 'H,' for 'Homosexual,' the kid would find nothing there." As a result, computers – with their awesome capacity to run searches based on key words (not to mention cross-references such as "Gay" and "Teenager" and "Coming Out") – have been a tremendous boon to library users. There is a down side, though: computer screens are highly visible. Anyone walking by can see the information a seeker is seeking. In that respect, card catalogs were much more private.

Because many students are hesitant about asking librarians for help if it involves the *g* word, Christine Jenkins said, "It's important to figure out how to get materials into kids' hands in other ways." The more cross-references – in both the card catalog and the vertical (pamphlet) file – she can think of, the better; this enables youngsters who don't find enough material in one category to shift easily to another (for example: "See also: Sexuality" or "Related subjects include: bisexuality, human sexuality, transgendered issues..."). A vertical file can include not just general information on subjects such as AIDS or homosexuality, but also the latest brochures from local health and social service organizations. And, of course, videotapes find prominent places on library media center shelves these days; many good ones include gay themes or content, ranging from the 1993 March on Washington to dramas broadcast originally on TV.

But even in the midnineties the centerpiece of a library remains books, and that is still what most librarians know best. Many have no trouble finding good gay-related nonfiction, but come up short in the search for fiction. "It's a vicious circle, with plenty of blame to pass around," Ms. Jenkins analyzed. "There's not one big roadblock, and I think most people are well-intentioned. It's just that publishers [of young-adult novels] are worried about the bottom line, and fear that if they publish gay- or lesbian-related fiction people might not buy it. So there's very little out there, and then authors become hesitant to write something that may not get published, and then people think there's no call for it."

However, she noted, the situation is slowly changing, and as more and more young-adult novels get written and reviewed, more and more will be published. "It's a drip, drip, drip effect. Look at teen pregnancy. That never used to be dealt with, and now there are lots of books around." She cited two novels as particularly popular with young readers: Ron Koertge's *The Arizona Kid,* about a straight boy who spends a summer with his gay uncle, and *Annie on My Mind* by Nancy Garden, a book with positive lesbian characters first published in 1982 and never out of print. But, Ms. Jenkins said, "It's a shame that almost all the characters in almost all the popular books are white. That's an inclusion issue too."

Shari Barnhart, learning resources coordinator for public schools in New Canaan, Connecticut, said that youngsters looking for gay-related material have a better chance of finding it in the nonfiction section than under fiction; by tradition, nonfiction books have been grouped under subject, while novels are shelved according to author. However, she added, "With on-line connections, subject headings are accessible in ways they never were before. Most fiction books published now come with thematic subject headings listed, so a kid on a terminal can now type in 'gay' or 'lesbian' or 'homosexual,' and pull up not only nonfiction but fiction too."

Of course, not everyone agrees that information on homosexuality, whether fiction or nonfiction, should be readily available in school libraries. Battles abound, and the stories cover the gamut.

Candace McGovern, media specialist at Staples High School in Westport, Connecticut, told of a student's mother who hangs out there for hours. "She leaves prayer cards in the books. She has a real problem with things like the lesbianism and masturbation sections of *Our Bodies, Ourselves*. And what she's really upset at is that these things are all over the library; they're not confined to one section you could just put a glass cage around and restrict access to. I explained to her that's because homosexuality is all over life, but I don't think that went over too well either."

Ms. McGovern is hardly alone. The American Library Association's Office for Intellectual Freedom (OIF) has recorded more than two hundred challenges to lesbian and gay material in children's books since it began keeping records in September 1990, with the number of incidents rising each year. And, noted OIF director Judith Krug, those are only the challenges that are reported to the Chicago office. She estimates that her statistics represent only a fifth to a quarter of all cases.

Three of 1993's five most challenged books featured homosexual themes, with *Daddy's Roommate* by Michael Willhoite heading the list. That book "tries to make the point that nontraditional families are loving, too," Ms. Krug said. "But because the father is gay, the book has engendered a storm of controversy nationwide in school districts and public libraries." Also among the top five were *Heather Has Two Mommies* by Lesléa Newman (a story about lesbian parents), and *The New Joy of Gay Sex* by Charles Silverstein. (Number two was Madonna's *Sex.*)

Ms. Krug attributed the rise in gay- and lesbian-themed book challenges to their increasing visibility. "This genre of literature is really new," she said. "It's like the family member who used to be identified as lesbian or gay; she or he was put in the bedroom until company left. Homosexuality has not been a topic of conversation in polite society until very recently. In the past these materials have been nonexistent, so there was no need to censor them. Now they're out there, and they're being challenged."

While many controversies swirl around issues of "appropriateness" for young readers, Ms. Krug feels it is censorship itself that is wrong. "Personally, I think *any* material is appropriate for particular people," she said. "You don't know how appropriate something is until people have a chance to select it, or not. I think young people have the ability to ferret out what is appropriate for them, and what is not."

The specific issue with homosexuality, she continued, is that "people believe if the materials are available, then young readers will feel this lifestyle is acceptable and permissible, and then they will become homosexuals themselves. Well, if they read about witchcraft, does that mean they become witches?"

Ms. Krug said she has been fighting "the same damn fight" against censorship since 1977, yet does not see the battle over lesbian and gay books abating soon. In fact, she believes the number of challenges will continue to soar. "When the Iron Curtain came down, and the 'Evil Empire' became our new best friend, Americans needed a new enemy. Homosexuals are the new scapegoat. A number of recent complaints have smacked of 'We need something or someone to blame our problems on. If you teach this, you'll turn my kid into a homosexual.'"

———

But, of course, problems with lesbian and gay materials do not always arise from the patrons' side of the circulation desk. Some censorship comes from librarians themselves, and that is harder to detect. As Ms. Krug noted, "When someone removes material from their shelves, they don't call me to tell me they're violating basic professional tenets."

And sometimes the material is simply never ordered. Ms. Krug recounted that while the ALA urges each library to develop its own collection based upon the purposes for which that library was established and the needs and desires of its particular users, she has heard of stories such as a school librarian who explained why she did not purchase *Daddy's Roommate:* "You wouldn't understand my community."

Ms. Krug countered, "That's unacceptable. I told her I could condone that answer only if she could say there were no kids in the population she serves who come from same-sex families, and no kids whatsoever with any curiosity about homosexuality. If she could say that, then I could admit she really knew her community. But of course she could never say that.

"Every kid growing up thinks that in some way he or she is a freak," Ms. Krug continued. "One of the things we do as librarians is to help kids over the hard times in their lives. If we can give them books that make their world easier to understand, or more palatable, then we've done our jobs. I'm not saying we've got to shove books down kids' throats. What I am saying is we've got to make books available, so kids can take solace however they can. That's so important. It's one thing we can do to make growing up a little easier. Books won't solve everyone's problems, but they certainly can help. Whether it comes from outside or within, censorship is very frightening, because it removes information from people who need it, and need access to it."

Carol Bloom, a New York City public high school teacher, was appalled to find just three books under the heading of "homosexuality" in her library's card catalog (one was titled *Overcoming Homosexuality*). She requested the librarian to order more; he asked noncommittally for a bibliography to consider. She supplied one, and after repeated prodding he agreed to buy a few titles. Months later he reported back – "with evident satisfaction," she said – that none of the books was available from suppliers. When, at the beginning of the next term, Ms. Bloom suggested that the librarian give her the money he would have spent on the books so she could order them directly, he informed her that the funds had dried up.

Undaunted, she took up a collection among sympathetic colleagues. With $120 from twenty-two teachers, she bought eighteen books, including two in Spanish. The librarian "was less than thrilled with the gift, and began to stall on making the books available to students," she wrote in the *Interracial Books for Children Bulletin*. Among his complaints were that they were "not written for children." He sent them to the chair of the physical education department to review, who, in turn, gave them to a hygiene teacher, who passed them on to students for book reports. "Not surprising to me," Ms. Bloom continued, "the kids loved them, reviewed them enthusiastically, and returned them to the library. His delaying tactics exhausted, the librarian reluctantly processed the books and placed them on the back shelves, alongside the books on VD and abortion."

There, despite their out-of-the-way location, students found them. One boy borrowed *Happy Endings Are All Alike*, a lesbian-themed book, then returned it, asking the assistant librarian for one "about boys." She gave him *Reflections of a Rock Lobster*, the true story of a high school boy's battle to take a male date to his high school prom.

Encouraged by that happy ending, Ms. Bloom prepared for the next step: approaching the librarian "with a forceful suggestion that he place one or two of them in the glass case in the corridor where new books are displayed."

Fortunately, such stories do not appear often. Most librarians seem to believe that the library is a place where, in Ms. McGovern's words, "absolutely everyone can feel free to come to find information. No one ever wants to feel isolated. This is a place, especially, where no one should."

Project 10 Provides Hope

In 1984, a black gay youth named Chris transferred to Los Angeles's Fairfax High. The school, with approximately twenty-five hundred students of many racial and ethnic backgrounds, is just two blocks south of West Hollywood (nicknamed, appropriately, "Boys' Town") on Melrose Avenue, a street lined with New Wave and punk specialty shops. But Fairfax was not much different from schools anywhere else: from his first day there Chris was physically abused by his peers and verbally bashed by both teachers and students.

That was not unusual either; he had been harassed for years, simply because he was gay. His parents forcibly ejected him from home when he was fourteen; he lived on the streets for a year before landing first in a juvenile detention center, then a group residential home. His teachers and counselors described him as "sweet" – but that did not halt the abuse. And it came not only from fellow students, but from administrators and staff members too. One school, in fact, responded to an incident of gay-bashing by transferring Chris – not his tormentor – to another school.

So it was no surprise when Chris dropped out of Fairfax High. What happened next, however, was unusual: someone did something about it.

What separates this incident from the thousands of others like them that occur each year is that Dr. Virginia Uribe did not let Chris's story go unnoticed. An earth science teacher at Fairfax since 1959 – and a closeted lesbian who as a married mother of two had painfully come to grips with her own homosexuality in her midthirties – Dr. Uribe initiated an informal lunchtime rap group with a few lesbian and gay students. "I kept asking about that student, why he was no longer in school, why he was pushed out other than the fact that he was gay,"

In the mid-1980s, Dr. Virginia Uribe, an earth science teacher in a Los Angeles high school, founded the groundbreaking Project 10, a dropout prevention program aimed at gay teens.

she said. "It just so upset me. Our commitment to equality should extend to all children."

It did not take long for the group to mushroom to twenty-five regulars. They discussed common problems, and quickly realized that Chris's plight was hardly unique. Dr. Uribe – who looks as if she just stepped out of a Norman Rockwell painting entitled *The Grandmother* (which she is), and who in 1988 earned a Ph.D. in psychology with an emphasis in adolescent homosexuality – noticed that although most of the students were intelligent, few of their school records showed that. Instead their feelings of low self-esteem, isolation, alienation, and inadequacy manifested themselves in self-destructive behavior, including substance abuse and attempted suicide. Several were on the verge of dropping out. And nearly every one of them felt alone: they had no adults to talk to, no traditional support structure to lean on, no young people to socialize with. When she researched major school districts in California and elsewhere, she found no services anywhere for homosexual students in public education. "It was outright bigotry," she said.

Dr. Uribe sprang into action. "After a couple of months I realized this was getting bigger than me," she said. "I knew I had to talk to the principal, Warren Steinberg. I was very nervous – it was almost like a coming out for me. I screwed up my courage, told him about our meetings, and held my breath."

Mr. Steinberg's reaction surprised and elated Dr. Uribe. "He was very supportive," she recalled. "He said we were public educators, that educators needed to serve all kids, and that it was our job to help every kid no matter who he or she was, or what their problems were. He encouraged me to go forward."

She certainly did. Heeding his advice to seek allies on the board of education (to head off problems before they blew out of control), she contacted Alan Gershman, the member in charge of her district. He understood the problem, and saw that the principal was behind it. So he got behind it too, Dr. Uribe recalled.

She also enlisted the support of Jackie Goldberg, a lesbian who was serving as president of the board of education. "She was the pivotal person on the board," the teacher said. "She was very protective of this right from the start, and got other board members on line. She was kind of my angel."

The support Virginia Uribe garnered was for a program she dubbed Project 10 (the number stands for the oft-cited statistic that one in every ten persons is homosexual). Its office – Dr. Uribe's own classroom, room 308 – is stocked with brochures about coping with homosexuality (there for the taking, no questions asked), and features an eye-catching wall display of AIDS-related obituaries of men, women, and children.

From the outset, however, she emphasized that Project 10 is not a gay and lesbian program; she calls it a dropout-prevention program aimed at gay, lesbian, and bisexual teenagers. It operates on the school campus; its centerpiece is nonjudgmental counseling aimed at the needs of gay adolescents that are otherwise unaddressed in the educational system. Students meet together in a schoolroom without windows (to guarantee privacy), where they discuss such issues as coming out, safe sex, AIDS, condoms, parents, and friends, and vent their feelings and frustrations.

Project 10 also focuses on education, verbal and physical abuse, suicide, and sexually transmitted diseases. Services include workshops and training sessions for administrators and staff personnel; informal drop-in counseling for students at Fairfax and other school sites; outreach programs to parents and significant others; liaisons with peer counseling, substance abuse, and suicide prevention programs; and coordination with health education programs that encourage sexual responsibility and risk-reduction behavior among gay youth. The program has also sponsored a youth conference that drew two hundred participants; it was followed by a dance so successful and poignant that it brought tears to Dr. Uribe's eyes. Project 10 is, in her succinct words, "simply committed to keeping students in school, off drugs, and sexually responsible."

Yet despite the founder's attempts to keep the focus on dropout prevention, Project 10 has been attacked. The first controversy arose four years after its inception, when a Republican ally of fundamentalist Rev. Lou Sheldon in the State Assembly proposed that all funding for the entire Los Angeles Unified School District be halted unless Project 10 was discontinued.

"Give me a break," Dr. Uribe said in exasperation. "This is the second largest school district in the country, and Project 10 is an incredibly minor part of it." (In fact, the only cost to the district is the release time she receives to work on the program. She teaches three morning periods, then spends afternoons counseling gay students and consulting with officials at other schools about Project 10. She also leads sensitivity workshops for teachers, administrators, nurses, school psychologists, librarians, and counselors.) "They could never have gotten that passed – but it got lots of publicity."

Reverend Sheldon hired a telemarketing firm to raise money by attacking Project 10 as a gay recruitment program. "Someone at the firm was gay, and leaked the script they were using," Dr. Uribe recounted. "I got hold of it and gave it to Jackie Goldberg on the board of education. She threw a fit, and the next time Reverend Sheldon came before the board, she really let him have it." Nevertheless, the board had to hold an open hearing. When it was over, they reaffirmed their support for Project 10.

"I don't know how I got through that period," Dr. Uribe said. "The phone rang off the hook. I was on all the TV stations, talking about the needs of students. The tide flowed with me, not against me, but there were some scary moments. Today I just consider this and other right-wing attacks part of doing business. There's been a groundswell of support, with letters and a major *L.A. Times* editorial in favor of Project 10, but back then I didn't know what was going to happen. So I just told the truth. I told people that I started Project 10 because there was a desperate need to help gay and lesbian kids, and it obviously filled a need."

Since its inception, Project 10 has helped hundreds of Fairfax students. Boys and girls have talked to Dr. Uribe, and been referred to appropriate resources. They've learned they're not alone, and discovered friends right on the school campus. Most importantly, they have stayed in school – and both their grades and their self-esteem have risen.

Fairfax High boasts a display case dedicated to gay and lesbian issues, maintained by Dr. Uribe. "It's never been defaced, and there are always people looking at it," she said proudly. Her colleagues invite her to speak to their classes about gay and lesbian topics. Dr.

Uribe gives credit to the school's administration, saying, "They react swiftly whenever there's a problem. They're very sensitive about 'fag-bashing.'"

But that does not mean that Fairfax has become an ideal school. "We have our share of homophobia," she admitted. "It's pervasive, just as it is in schools everywhere. But I think Project 10 has performed an important role by opening up the area of homosexuality for discussion. People are talking about the issues, and once they do that then any kind of change is possible."

She knows, through her contacts in Los Angeles and around the country, that much work remains to be done. "It's terrible that we still have people on our staffs who are saying things like 'These kids are going to hell' or 'They're sinners.' Of course, we hear that from our legislators; that's bad enough. No wonder the kids commit suicide. I'm surprised that they don't all kill themselves. If they really were aware of how much hatred there is, they probably would."

She also vilifies some school board members as "spineless, cowardly, gutless individuals who at the slightest criticism fall apart at the seams. If they could just get it into their heads that public education serves all children, then they'd want to protect all children."

But Virginia Uribe is proud that her program is seen as a model for other districts. Schools across America have taken the basic premise of Project 10 and adapted it to their own special needs and considerations. Whether they name it Project 10 or not is of little concern to the founder; what *is* important is that administrators and teachers call, ask questions, then develop their own dropout-prevention program for underserved lesbian and gay students.

Though Project 10 has spread from coast to coast (primarily in urban centers more used to dealing with diverse groups), Dr. Uribe warned that many challenges lie ahead. "We have to broaden our visibility on this issue. Lots of districts simply don't want to face the fact that there are gay, lesbian, and bisexual students in their schools. We have to implement something like this in every school at every level, to make each and every faculty member sensitive. And once they admit the existence of a problem, then we have to get them to understand that they have to provide services for this population. Just acknowledging their existence isn't enough."

Dr. Uribe laughed as she recalled some of the roadblocks Project 10 has overcome. "I was so insistent we not call this a gay and lesbian program," she said. "I wanted the focus to be on dropout prevention, or education and support. But then in San Francisco they had to fight a major battle to have a program, and the superintendent was insistent that they not call it Project 10. So they called it a gay and lesbian program! But it doesn't matter what you call it – the important thing is to get something going, so that the needs of gay and lesbian kids somehow get met."

She recalled one typical boy who, long before high school, thought he was the only person who was gay. At Fairfax he disguised his sexual orientation by dating girls. He smoked large amounts of marijuana, spent weekends away from home with men he met at bars, and wanted to drop out of school. He did not come out at Fairfax – his closest female friends covered for him by being his dates at school dances – but he found a safe haven with Project 10. "Dr. Uribe didn't think I was crazy or weird," he said. "She saved me from suicide."

But Virginia Uribe downplayed the praise, saying he saved himself. "I hope that's why we're here," she concluded. "Not only to keep kids in the classroom, but to keep them alive and claiming their right to be who they are."

A few hundred miles from Los Angeles, in the heart of Sonoma County, sits Santa Rosa, where Santa Rosa High School became one of the first in the country to do exactly what Dr. Uribe wants: adapt Project 10 to fit the particular needs and nuances of a school and community.

With a population of just over 100,000, Santa Rosa is not Los Angeles – nor is it San Francisco, an hour to the south. There has been resistance to Santa Rosa High's Project 10, and no other school in the city has followed its lead, but that has not deterred its backers. They are led by Sheila Horowitz, a psychotherapist who moved north from Los Angeles a few years ago and, in the midst of writing her dissertation on the relationship between homophobia and self-esteem in the high school setting, discerned a need for a school-based support group for gay, lesbian, bisexual, and questioning students. The principal agreed; he noted that in the previous graduating class, students had named homophobia as one of the school's five biggest unaddressed issues. Through a newspaper article, a co-director was found.

Ms. Horowitz presented information about the group to administrators, staff, and students, after which a straight youngster stood up and suggested that any effort at the high school be placed in the hands of students, not adults. She agreed, and the result was a gay-straight youth group called US (United Sexualities). Within two weeks it had attracted thirty-five teenagers.

Santa Rosa High's Project 10 grew out of that group. It focuses, Ms. Horowitz said, more on education and less on counseling than its Los Angeles counterpart. Santa Rosa teachers do no counseling in school; they do, however, listen to students, and offer appropriate resources. Twelve staff members have been named "gay- and lesbian-sensitive adults," men and women who will speak nonjudgmentally to students with concerns about sexuality.

The educational component of Santa Rosa's Project 10 involves introducing lesbian and gay themes into the school curriculum. "We want kids to have gay role models, whether they're historical figures or contemporary men and women," Ms. Horowitz said. "And we want the general population to see this too, and be educated about the normalcy of gay and lesbian people." The Project 10 group also sends speakers into classrooms, in conjunction with PFLAG (Parents, Families and Friends of Lesbians and Gays), and the city's Positive Images youth group.

Santa Rosa's Project 10 did not escape controversy. First, Sheila Horowitz noted, high school administrators "had to decide whether they were ready to 'come out,' as it were, and be the first in the area to tackle homosexuality head-on. They did, and they've been very supportive." However, the support stops short of funding. "We realize schools are dealing with a lot these days: gangs, racial stuff, basic city problems," she said. "This certainly isn't their biggest issue. We know schools today have no money, and we wouldn't imagine they'd direct it our way if they did. So we haven't asked for anything in terms of dollars." Project 10 members and advocates raise their own funds to buy library materials and curricular resources.

But a bigger obstacle arose in the form of an opposition group, the Project 10 Research Committee. That organization follows Project 10 around, offering speakers to rebut their presentations. The Research Committee also sends observers to board of education meetings – with a chilling effect on some teachers. "They're not always comfortable expressing their interest in Project 10 publicly," Sheila said. "They don't know who's listening, or what might happen to them. So whatever gets done happens quietly, at school, not openly at public meetings." Ms. Horowitz wears the opposition of the Research Committee proudly: "We've stimulated them, so I guess that means we're making progress."

The feedback to Project 10 has been ninety percent positive, she said – even though Santa Rosa High School remains the only one in the district with such a program. "A lot of teachers and principals we've met have been sympathetic. But they don't have the resources or the energy to follow this through, and maybe take flak from the community. So right now we're out there alone."

Yet that has not stopped Sheila Horowitz from thinking ahead. "We believe this would be very valuable for the junior highs too," she said. "But that might come later. We're not ready to push it that far. If parents around here don't think something like this is appropriate for high school kids, just think what would happen if we tried to introduce it at a younger age."

Project 10 founder Dr. Uribe spends much of each day fielding phone calls from people she's never heard of, at schools she never knew existed. One such call came in 1989, when a photography teacher named Al Ferreira asked if a group of students at his Cambridge (Massachusetts) Rindge and Latin School (CRLS) could retitle their already existing, yet nameless, gay and lesbian group "Project 10 East." Intrigued, she asked for details. "We've got this idea of a transcontinental railroad," he said. "You're starting from the West Coast, we're here on the East, and hopefully one day there will be Project 10s everywhere in between."

She asked how Mr. Ferreira and his students heard about Project 10. The best way possible, they said: straight from the source. Dr. Uribe had delivered a speech at Harvard University – literally two blocks from the CRLS campus – that influenced many members of Al's group. They were inspired by what she'd done, and motivated by her vision of what she still hoped to accomplish.

Dr. Uribe warned them that by wrapping themselves in the Project 10 mantle they would open themselves to criticism from outsiders; it was a proud name, she said, but one that invited controversy. Cambridge is not Kansas – no one has ever confused Harvard Square with Topeka, home of the homophobic Rev. Fred Phelps – but neither is Cambridge all Harvard and MIT. It is a working-class city of nearly 100,000 whose social, economic, and ethnic diversity is reflected in the halls of CRLS, the city's only public high school. A majority of the 2,000-plus ninth through twelfth graders are nonwhite; they hail from sixty-four different countries. The school's courses range from vocational education to college preparation, and it pays more than lip service to its mission of breaking down the barriers thrown up by gender, race, and economic differences. (In Al's photography class, all equipment – film, developing paper, even cameras – is provided, affording every student an equal shot at success.) But Cambridge is sometimes not as open-minded and progressive as it seems when viewed only through the Harvard lens; many students, for example, come from homes where homosexuality is declared a sin — if it is talked about at all.

"I told Dr. Uribe that we understood the risks," Al said. "I told her we wanted to use the Project 10 name because we admired what she was doing and how she integrated it into the school as a whole."

Up to that point Al's group was tiny. It began two years earlier in 1987, Al Ferreira's fifteenth year at CRLS. The precipitating event was a homophobic remark a teacher made about a gay colleague. When the superintendent mediated the ensuing conflict, one result was a series of staff development workshops on homosexuality. Al had been "discreetly" out to a few students (urged on by a straight colleague, following the attempted suicide of a gay youngster), but at the end of a faculty panel he came out to all three hundred teachers at once. He spoke about how hurt he felt when he heard homophobic comments from fellow educators — and how his pain was as much for the lesbian and gay students at CRLS as for himself.

After he came out, two students inquired about a gay and lesbian group. He asked his principal for permission to form a discussion group; there was concern about confidentiality but the group got under way, very quietly. After hearing Dr. Uribe speak, they realized they could involve more students if they publicized what they were doing.

But it was not until Mr. Ferreira heard about a group at nearby Concord Academy, and learned that they called themselves a gay-straight alliance, that he spotted a better way to appeal to a much broader range of students. "As soon as we let people know that straight kids were welcome, we instantly got more numbers," he said. "That made it safe for questioning kids to come. We have plenty of kids who are straight, and who come because they're interested in these issues — they see it in social justice or civil rights terms — and it's wonderful to have them as allies. But there are also kids who have come to our meetings for two years, and I don't know their orientation. If they don't identify themselves, that's fine. Project 10 East exists for all Cambridge Rindge and Latin students."

He defined the group's focus in three ways: political, educational, and social. Politically, Project 10 East was a leader in the long battle to pass a state civil rights law for lesbian and gay students; in fact, both Mr. Ferreira and student Jessica Byers were members of the Governor's Commission on Gay and Lesbian Youth (Al served as co-chair). They also march each year in gay pride events. The first time they were the only school represented in Boston's parade; three years later, there were fourteen others.

Their education efforts involve the entire school. They maintain a display in the trophy case outside the main office; a typical exhibit includes books, posters, and notices of meetings. They run a peer educator program that trains high school youngsters to go into classrooms after homophobic incidents, where they help teachers and students talk about homophobia. They organized a National Coming Out Day assembly at which two prominent local citizens spoke about being gay: Mayor Ken Reeves and Randy Price, the top-rated news anchor for WBZ-TV. That was followed by a youth panel, moderated by Karen Harbeck, educator and author of *Coming Out of the Classroom Closet*. At the end of the event, a CRLS student came out as bisexual.

Every October, they set up an information table at Freshman Club Day – and every year, Al noted, "Our membership increases after that. Freshmen look on it as natural; they think every school has a support group for gay and lesbian kids right next to the Alpine Ski Club and the French Club." Each spring, when the ninth-grade health classes focus on sexuality, Mr. Ferreira and his Project 10 East students talk about lesbian and gay issues. That serves two purposes: it puts a human face on homosexuality, and it takes the burden of speaking about it off teachers who might be embarrassed or uncomfortable.

Socially, the group sponsors dances, inviting all gay-straight alliances in the Boston area. Those are special events, he said, because "no one sits. Everyone has a great time. And believe it or not, there's plenty of gender mixing."

Three years ago the yearbook editors wanted to include Project 10 East in the club section. Mr. Ferreira asked which students would agree to be photographed; none raised their hands. "Fine," he told them. "I'll sit on a stool surrounded by ten empty chairs, and there'll be a caption underneath saying that the fact that no one wanted to have their picture in the yearbook says something about the school."

That did it. "This is ridiculous," Jessica Byers said. "I'll go." Several others soon agreed, and that year a dozen Project 10 East students had their photos and names in the yearbook. Now, Al said, taking the picture is routine – and that shift in attitude speaks volumes. "It's just one of the ways that, whenever I can, I try to institutionalize the group as part of the school community."

The number of participants varies throughout the year, based on other activities and the vagaries of adolescent life, but Project 10 East has clearly become an important part of CRLS. However, even in a city like Cambridge, the group must weather vicious attacks – some of which have been sharply personal. A few teachers Al described as "religious fundamentalists" leafleted the faculty one morning; the flyer claimed that Al was creating a new Sodom and Gomorrah. "Fortunately," he said, "it was also very anti-Semitic, so the Jewish staff members registered their disgust before I even saw it. The administration dealt with it, and dealt with it well."

A local minister complained that Mr. Ferreira was forcing students to wear pink triangles. "He was given a hearing at an Administrative Cabinet meeting. They pointed out his errors, and told him this was a public high school at which every student was entitled to feel safe and secure, and get whatever support they need." Al did not hear about the incident until it was over; when he asked the principal why he was not informed of it, the principal said, "You don't have to justify your existence."

Al counts many supporters at CRLS. Some he expected; others have surprised him. All, he said, are important to Project 10 East's success – but straight allies are particularly crucial. "They come from positions of power in school," he explained. "And their words carry a lot of weight. Just as when I, as a white male, advocate for more faculty of color, it's also important for me to build coalitions with heterosexuals, so they can advocate for us." He added that straight allies include administrators and students, as well as teachers.

The result, he said, is that Project 10 East enjoys an excellent reputation on campus. Yet that does not mean that every gay, lesbian, and bisexual student and teacher at Rindge participates in the group. "A lot of gay kids don't come, and a lot of faculty members still aren't out," he said matter-of-factly. "There's still a lot of internalized homophobia here, even in the face of what looks like so much support."

As proof – but proof too of Project 10 East's intangible impact – he cited two experiences with recent graduates. One girl sent him a letter; she wrote that while she was not comfortable with her own sexuality while in high school, merely knowing that Al was open and that the organization existed meant a lot to her. "She never came to a meeting – but we had an influence," Al said.

The second contact came in a phone call from a Vietnamese boy. "He said if he ever came out, his grandfather would forbid his name to ever be mentioned in that family again, and every picture of him would be destroyed," Al said. "That's a cultural thing. But this boy had always known he was gay, and he told me that it was a great thing for him to know me and realize I am in an open, loving relationship. I've learned that everyone doesn't have to be out, or even come to our meetings. It was important for this boy just to have a role model."

Much of Al's work takes place at odd hours. He's called on for crisis intervention, or to meet in the evening with families of students who are exploring their sexuality; he has organized meetings with lesbian and gay parents of area youngsters; he runs workshops in other Cambridge schools. (The one for sixth through eighth graders is called, in typical middle school–speak, "That's So Gay.") Sitting in a lavender chair in his tiny, windowless office, its walls plastered with newspaper clippings, bumper stickers, and photos of lesbian couples, his attention one afternoon was directed three ways: fielding telephone calls about a fourteen-year-old runaway, organizing student speakers for a Harvard sociology class, and arranging for a transgendered student to have access to a unisex bathroom in the Teen Health Center, no questions asked. "Can you imagine – he hasn't been going to the bathroom at all here," Al said in wonderment. "What kind of school experience is it when you spend your whole day worrying about the bathroom?"

To give him time to do everything, the Cambridge school system cut his teaching load to one class in the 1993–94 school year – and none in '94–95. That frees him up to do the myriad tasks associated with running Project 10: counseling frightened students, dealing with press inquiries, speaking on lesbian and gay issues across the nation. (He has appeared on the *NBC Nightly News* and *Larry King Live,* among other shows.) It might seem that the Cambridge taxpayers are paying a lot of money to a teacher who spends little time in a classroom, yet Al noted that his work reaches an enormous number of students, and his influence stretches far beyond the city. "I think I'm sending a great message about Cambridge," he said. "When people hear me talk, they get the idea that this is a school district that really and truly cares about all of its students."

But the centerpiece of Project 10 East remains the weekly Monday afternoon group meetings. An interesting cross section of students, ranging from a sullen boy with a beard and several earrings to a girl looking preppily peppy, assembled in a classroom next to Mr. Ferreira's office one typical late-winter day. They were representative of the diversity both at CRLS and in the gay youth community, though the majority were female ("Maybe because the macho myth is so strong, but that's just a guess," Al said). There was, of course, food (the peanut butter cookies were baked by a young African-American student teacher); warm greetings and hugs were offered by some, while one or two shyer students stood off to the side, quietly observing.

The meeting opened with a discussion of the court decision, late the previous week, to allow gays and lesbians to march in Boston's upcoming St. Patrick's Day parade. The students discussed the pros and cons of the extensive publicity, including whether it was a battle that should even have been waged, then turned their attention to a VCR when Al popped in a cartridge of the group's latest television appearance. The Lifetime cable network segment explored the "controversy" over schools limited to gay and lesbian youths. The show's producers apparently got Al and the CRLS students to appear by claiming they were covering gay teens in general; Project 10 East is certainly not an exclusionary group. The students' reactions varied from disinterest to displeasure; most felt that, as TV shows about them went, this was one of the weaker efforts.

One visitor, a girl who attended private school in New York, moved the discussion away from the video and toward her own school. She described her difficulties in getting a group like Project 10 East started. Another visitor, playing devil's advocate, asked whether such an organization was needed at all. "It feels really good to come here," responded one girl. "It's so good to know you're doing something about homophobia. I'm straight, but I feel really comfortable here. It's very important to me to have this group here."

Had the group made any difference at Cambridge Rindge and Latin School? the visitor wondered. "Of course," one student replied, amazed at the question. "The fact that we exist legitimizes the fact that we have power. And if you're in this school and are breathing, you have to know about Project 10 East. Then, once you know about us you have to think about us. And then you can't be uneducated. Of course we make a difference."

Toward the Twenty-first Century

Robert Birle remembers growing up in Philadelphia. He knew he was gay, but like many people he believed the stereotypes about homosexuals. So he dated girls, even though he had no interest in heterosexual relationships, at the same time furtively scouring the library for books on homosexuality. With a touch of sadness he said, "I kind of felt because of these experiences that I had my youth taken away from me."

Two decades later, Mr. Birle knows that gay and lesbian teenagers are living the same lies, looking for the same information, and losing the same years. When the twenty-first century rolls around, he hopes that is no longer true.

That's one reason he quit his job as an Antioch, California, art teacher – where he kept a photo of his lover on his desk, and received a faculty wedding gift after participating in a commitment ceremony during the 1987 March on Washington – and moved to Kansas City. He serves there as director of the mid-American region for Project 21, an informal alliance of organizations and individuals working to ensure that fair, accurate information regarding the nature and diversity of sexual orientation is available and presented to youngsters through libraries, counselors' offices, and curricula.

Project 21 was launched in 1990, a joint effort of Jessea Greenman of the San Francisco Bay Area Chapter of the Gay and Lesbian Alliance Against Defamation, Hank Wilson of the Gay and Lesbian Youth Advocacy Council of San Francisco, and Mr. Birle of the Bay Area Network of Gay and Lesbian Educators. The number in Project 21 refers to the twenty-first century, a good indication that Mr. Birle and

Robert Birle, co-founder of Project 21, with his dog Rose. Birle also helped to found BANGLE, the Bay Area Network of Gay and Lesbian Educators.

his colleagues recognize the long-term nature of their work. They're looking at the next century – but through the end of this one, they've got their hands full.

Their specific pursuits include providing testimony before state and local boards of education concerning textbook selection and curricular offerings, informing the public about educational equity issues, and furnishing schools with lesbian and gay resource material. Those resources, they believe, should be available to elementary as well as secondary school teachers, and should not only include information for sex education and family life classes, but should reach every other department too. That covers vast territory: the past and present contributions of gays and lesbians in art, language, science, and sport; discussions of the gay liberation movement; explorations of significant social and historical events.

Which is, of course, exactly the type of information many people do not want to hear.

Mr. Birle sent a year-long series of five letters to schools in Iowa, Nebraska, Kansas, Missouri, Oklahoma, and Arkansas. The response was not encouraging. One, from a Kansas City–area superintendent, was typical: "We especially do not make an effort to communicate with those special-interest groups who are neither members of our student body nor residents in our district."

That makes it plain, Mr. Birle said, that gay, lesbian, and bisexual issues will not be addressed by schools "unless we have residents, parents, students, educators, or allies who can act as contacts with their local district. Project 21, to be successful, needs to be grassroots."

Of course, getting gay people to be active at the grassroots level – especially in their own communities, where no one may know their sexual orientation – is seldom easy. Hence, the next-century focus of Project 21.

Like any such group, Mr. Birle and his cohorts have a long-term plan. Central to it is their belief that much of the battle will be won or lost around textbooks.

Both California and Texas have sweeping policies under which committees recommend or reject textbooks for the entire state. Because they are two of the most populous states in the nation, acceptance by the committees can be crucial to a textbook's success; rejection can doom it to failure. (For the 1994–95 school year, Texas considered 140 million dollars' worth of textbooks for state funding.) In these days of open meetings and sunshine laws, public input has become an accepted part of the textbook selection process – and the religious right has learned that they can strike fear in the hearts of publishers who years ago never thought twice about who was scrutinizing their pages.

To counter the cries of fundamentalists who wish to ban every mention of homosexuality (not to mention AIDS, abortion, birth control – everything short of breathing) from health education books, Project 21 stepped up to the mike.

In 1993, when the Texas Education Agency considered for adoption seven health texts for grades nine through twelve, Project 21 Austin chapter members helped ensure that the homophobes did not carry the day. Leader David E. Walker and his colleagues examined every book, debated how each depicted homosexuality, and spoke out publicly for certain texts and against others.

They found *Health America* (published by an obscure company, Little Red Hen of Pocatello, Idaho) "extremely homophobic." Two others, *Glencoe Health: A Guide to Wellness* (McGraw-Hill) and *Prentice Hall Health: Skills for Wellness* (Prentice Hall) were described as treating gay and lesbian issues "very inadequately, if at all." Mr. Walker termed *Making Life Choices: Health Skills and Concepts, Expanded Edition* (West Publishing) "by far the most comprehensive and positive of all the texts" he reviewed. However, the same book's student edition did not cover homosexuality anywhere in the main text; information was provided separately in a 48-page softbound unit, available only at the discretion of teachers and district administrators.

After months of hearings, the textbook committee rejected *Making Life Choices: Expanded Edition.* But the fifteen members also voted unanimously against the Little Red Hen book, citing extensive inaccuracies.

One accepted text, *Holt Health* (Holt, Rinehart and Winston), was recommended by Mr. Walker and his group.

Once the textbook committee made its decision, Project 21 shifted its focus to the local level, where advocates began encouraging their school districts to adopt the Holt book over others. "Books don't just appear in classrooms," Mr. Birle explained. "There's an incredible amount of behind-the-scenes work involved."

At the same time Project 21 was fighting Texas textbook battles, they turned their energies to other regions as well. Most state boards are only advisory; decisions on what's available to students are actually made at the local level. So Mr. Birle and others contacted local school boards throughout the Midwest and East Coast, slowly networking and sharing information to communicate their concerns.

While admitting that Project 21's focus on textbooks and curricula is narrow, Mr. Birle noted that the processes that affect gay and lesbian studies inclusion are quite complex. He cited one small program that kicked up a ferocious firestorm: the donation of two paperback books to forty-two Kansas City–area school districts.

Neither *Annie on My Mind* by Nancy Garden nor *All-American Boys* by Frank Mosca describe explicit acts ("The average episode of 'Beverly Hills 90210' has more references to sex," wrote newspaper columnist Jennifer Howe); both novels do, however, tell stories of teenagers as they discover and accept their homosexuality. And, because of such content, neither found its way directly onto school library bookshelves.

A few adults called school officials to express disapproval. A group of about fifteen parents, grandparents, and ministers paraded in front of the Kansas City School District office with bullhorns and signs, then set fire to a copy of *Annie* (which was included in the American Library Association's list of "Best of the Best Books for Young Adults"), noting that they had already taken their children out of public education and enrolled them in Christian schools to avoid such influences. Meanwhile, an equally small number of demonstrators gathered to counter-protest. Many districts appointed committees of parents, counselors, teachers, and administrators to review the books; most eventually decided they were indeed appropriate for teenagers.

But not all. For example, in Kansas's Shawnee Mission School District, south of Kansas City, district committee members decided to return the two books to Project 21, following two days of acrimonious public hearings. An eleven-member committee concluded that the books were "presented by a special-interest group advocating its own agenda." Interestingly, three of the five district high schools already owned copies of *Annie on My Mind,* purchased several years earlier by library staffs. The committee voted to place the two books on "restricted" status, accessible for checkout by students only with parental permission. Even that did not placate protester G. Gordon Thomas, who said, "I'd like to know whether they are going to keep a file system to say who checked out those books, and if it's going to be a matter of public record. I think it ought to be."

Mr. Birle's reaction, as reported in the *Kansas City Star,* was measured. He was particularly saddened because of the noteworthy reputation of the district, adding, "I expected better from Shawnee Mission."

But the reactions of district students were more spirited, and drew more media attention. Students at Shawnee Mission East High School protested the committee's decision by checking out hundreds of books from their school library, and gathered hundreds of petition signatures as well. The actions, said junior Erin Stephenson, were "attention-getters to show we will not tolerate censorship in our school." The mass checkouts were meant to demonstrate how few books would be left in a library if all controversial materials were removed.

Junior Travis Graf, who checked out 135 books, said students discriminated in their selections. "We looked for books that could be considered controversial by someone. We started with religion and went to war, violence, abortion..." Senior Kyra Bechtel told the *Star* that she took half the library's philosophy section "because philosophy can be influential, you know."

Assistant principal Lynn Kowalski was quoted as saying that no more than 1,000 of the 25,000 titles in the library were checked out. In fact, the total reached 2,977. Administrators attempted to stem the tide by implementing a two-book maximum by midmorning, but agreed that students could check out more with written teacher permission. "I respect their right to express themselves by removing books from our library, but it would be unfortunate if other students are denied access to books they need," said principal Marlin Stanberry.

Students and teachers worked together. Drama teacher Phil Kinen let students store books in the school's Little Theatre, while others piled them in cars and lockers. And Erin Stephenson, who started the protest, said that students would return the books when they were due. "We're going to offer to help re-sort them when they come back," he noted.

Elsewhere, reactions to the Project 21 donations took other forms. Missouri's Liberty and North Kansas City districts both accepted the award-winning *Annie* but rejected *All-American Boys* as "poorly written." The town of Olathe, Kansas, did the same thing, but then district superintendent Ron Wimmer pulled *Annie* after taxpayers and parents complained. Ironically, the book had sat on the Olathe South High School library shelf for almost ten years, though it had never been checked out. (That did not mean, one teacher noted, that no student ever read it surreptitiously.) And in another Olathe school, East High student government president Stevie Case enlisted the American Civil Liberties Union to help file a lawsuit charging censorship and seeking the return of *Annie* to the shelves. "As an informed student, I cannot stand by and allow this flagrant act of censorship to remain unchecked," Stevie said.

In Lee's Summit, Missouri, superintendent Gail Williams also refused the novels and removed the copy of *Annie* already on the shelves, saying, "We felt the book was not being used as a reference or as a resource material in any of our classes." She noted that the high school libraries had sixteen works covering gay and lesbian issues, and that a wide range of publications, including *People* magazine and *U.S. News & World Report*, offered commentary on diverse issues. A group of anti-censorship and gay rights demonstrators assembled outside the board of education building to protest *Annie*'s removal; they were denied access to a conference room to speak with board members, however, when president Bob Bruce ruled that only school district residents could address the group.

"Certainly, parents have a right to make decisions about what their children are reading," Mr. Birle said in the middle of the controversy that engulfed metropolitan Kansas City. "But by making decisions about what libraries offer, they make that decision for all parents, and for everyone's children."

In the debate that followed, Missouri senator John Russell announced he would reintroduce legislation to prohibit public schools from promoting or advocating homosexuality "as an acceptable lifestyle." (His similar bill the previous year never reached the Senate floor.) "I don't think that public or private schools should become a platform for someone's agenda even if it starts out innocent," Senator Russell said, adding that the several gay-themed elementary-level books he had read were "very subtly, in my opinion, saying, 'There is nothing different or wrong about this.'"

Steve Sheldon, political director of the Traditional Values Coalition and son of the group's leader, Rev. Louis Sheldon, weighed in from his Anaheim, California, headquarters, where officials had earlier fought similar Project 21 efforts. Mr. Sheldon argued that historical information, such as factual teachings about the persecution of gays during the

Holocaust, may be included in lessons but that, depending on how a teacher presents the material, discussions might seem to condone homosexuality as an acceptable alternative to heterosexual relationships – and that could "lead" children into "the homosexual lifestyle."

That comment, Project 21 supporters argue, shows exactly why their work is necessary: to show students – gay, lesbian, bisexual, questioning, and straight – that there is no "homosexual lifestyle," but rather that the lives led by homosexuals have enriched the world. It is precisely because they learned nothing about gay heroes or history while going through school that Mr. Birle and others in his loosely structured organization are willing to work into the next century to provide such information to new generations of youngsters.

Project 21's advocates hope to reorient the teachings of literature, history, anthropology, Greek and Roman culture, science, math, and social studies, to provide a gay and lesbian perspective that balances today's heterosexist curriculum. The group's brochure lists forty-four famous figures, ranging from Alexander the Great, Plato, and Leonardo da Vinci to Walt Whitman, Eleanor Roosevelt, and James Baldwin, and asks rhetorically whether textbooks tell that they were lesbian, bisexual, or gay.

"We want to see the contributions of gays and lesbians reflected throughout the curriculum, where it's relevant, and in an appropriate way. We are working toward the next century, toward an inclusive and fair community," Mr. Birle said.

So far this century, they've had some – though limited – success. In the 1990s, Mr. Birle's definition of wins and losses is flexible. "I sense a willingness, an openness, on educators' parts to start looking at these issues, and that's good," he said. "I'm often surprised at some of our support: the Arkansas school counselors' group, the Missouri council of social studies teachers, individual school board members.

"When I sent out letters I wasn't expecting real positive responses to our offer to present information. But I think more and more they're starting to realize that their members, be they counselors or teachers or fellow board members, need this. We're starting to get recognized; we're doing booths and actual workshops at as many conventions as possible, and more and more people are starting to ask us questions, seek us out.

"So we're working both behind the scenes, doing those sorts of things, and up-front, in your face, doing things like donating books and speaking out at public textbook meetings. They're two different types of advocacy, and both are important. We haven't won a whole lot of battles yet, but we've got so many people doing so many great things, I really feel the momentum is on our side."

And Project 21 is doing what any organization must to succeed: getting people to talk about it. "We are generating public debate and concern, and publicity of any type is great," Mr. Birle claimed. "Anytime we get discussed is a win for us. We've got right-wing radio stations discussing our focus on inclusion issues, and every time they do they cite the historical figures we name. They can't talk about us without discussing our agenda – so that's a win for us right there."

⸻

When Robert Birle and his cohorts field specific questions about curriculum – for example, how to teach about Stonewall, or who to include in gay and lesbian literature – the lesson is reinforced that this is not yet the twenty-first century. They have few curricular resources to recommend; virtually none are available. But one place they can refer interested teachers is the Project for the Study of Gay and Lesbian Issues in Schools (formerly the Gay and Lesbian High School Curriculum and Staff Development Project), an arm of the Harvard University Graduate School of Education.

The project is the brainchild of Arthur Lipkin, Ed.D. His program sounds exciting – there are plenty of educational words in the name, and it's part of Harvard to boot – but the reality is that it's an underfunded, little-known adjunct of one of the university's least endowed schools. "The ed. school is not particularly wealthy because, as one might expect, teachers are not as good contributors as doctors or lawyers," Dr. Lipkin said in his quiet, understated way. Money comes primarily through individual donors – most gay, some straight – but to its creator, the lack of funds is less important than the simple fact that it exists. He is a former high school teacher, with twenty years' experience at Cambridge Rindge and Latin School (CRLS). Yet despite being openly gay – and despite the proximity of Harvard's education school, which sits, accessible and open, just a couple of blocks from Rindge and Latin – he found virtually no gay- or lesbian-related materials to give to his high school English, social studies, and moral development students.

Mr. Lipkin – he did not yet have his doctorate – began thinking seriously about the dearth of resources in 1987, when he helped plan and run a voluntary, twelve-hour staff development workshop called "Gay and Straight at CRLS: Creating a Caring Community." That led to an all-faculty, mandatory session. But after whetting the appetite of his colleagues to introduce gay and lesbian material into their classes, he was unable to point them in any direction to find it.

A year later, engrossed in his doctoral dissertation on the workshops' impact on teachers' practices, he was once again struck by the sorry state of materials available for the growing number of educators who were inspired to bring gay and lesbian issues into their classrooms. "I found that teachers had been very affected by stories they heard from people in their own school communities – students and former students," Dr. Lipkin said. "Teachers finally understood that gay and lesbian students are all around, and that when students have questions surrounding their sexuality it's a dereliction of our duties as educators not to help. Almost everyone agreed that their awareness had been raised, but they were still ignorant of curriculum opportunities."

So was Dr. Lipkin – because there were no such curricula. He and every other reasonably competent teacher knew where to find lesson plans, videos, even unit tests on the Revolutionary War or African-American literature – but acquiring similar, appropriate material for high school students about, say, the struggle for gay rights, or James Baldwin's homosexuality, was nearly impossible.

After completing his dissertation, Dr. Lipkin served as co-chair of the fourth annual Lesbian, Bisexual and Gay Studies Conference, held at Harvard, at which over two hundred papers were presented to more than fifteen hundred registrants (primarily university scholars). When it was over he realized there was no way to transfer such wonderful scholarship to high school teachers and students. Thus the High School Curriculum and Staff Development Project was born.

He approached the education school about developing gay- and lesbian-related curricula, and earned a Harvard appointment as a research associate. His first task – after raising funds to ensure the program's existence – was to articulate his two goals. The short-term aim of the project is to write and disseminate gay and lesbian social studies, language arts, and science curricula for use in American high schools. The units, which can be integrated into existing mainstream curricula, present current and historical issues in lesbian and gay life from a multicultural perspective.

A longer-term goal is to create a center at Harvard for curriculum writing and teacher training in the area of lesbian and gay studies, for grades kindergarten through twelve. The center is planned to serve as a national focal point for anti-homophobia work in schools. Teachers and administrators would meet university scholars, create curricula for their own classrooms, and develop strategies both for challenging bigotry and for supporting gay and lesbian students. The aim, Dr. Lipkin said, is to take gay studies "out of the realm of pathology."

The rationale for the first goal is that short modules, easily incorporated into existing classes, are the most practical types of units for teachers. New courses are hard to develop and get approved; beyond that, a separate semester course in "Gay/Lesbian Studies" would most likely not attract many students (or teachers). Paradoxically, its very existence would cause other instructors to assume that all gay and lesbian subject matter was being adequately covered, leaving them little incentive to include it in their own courses. So Dr. Lipkin has prepared his own materials for teachers, including a manual to make them feel comfortable introducing the topic of homosexuality into their classroom.

The eight- to ten-day social studies unit includes primary and secondary sources, study sheets, and topics for writing and discussion. Subjects include cross-cultural representations of homosexuality, both current and historical; the importance of gay and lesbian individuals in various eras; the evolution of the modern homosexual identity; and current gay and lesbian world issues in civil rights, medicine, and politics. Called "The Stonewall Riots and the History of Gays and Lesbians in the United States," it uses the 1969 uprising as a colorful entry point, Dr. Lipkin said. "It hooks kids into asking, 'Who are these people? Where had they been? What was the big fight about?'" The unit then backtracks to explore gay history as far back as colonial times. It moves forward through the nineteenth-century development of the concept of homosexuality and the importance of World War II in the creation of homosexual communities, then continues through the twentieth-century homophile movement before concluding with the AIDS epidemic.

The literature unit includes short stories, biographies, novels, poetry, drama, films, analysis, and criticism, as well as study sheets and topics for discussion and writing. All deal with the experiences and observations of gay people, and the observations of others, from different historical periods, races, religions, cultures, and classes. "Looking at Gay and Lesbian Literature" offers study questions and guides for ten poems and short stories, by authors ranging from David Leavitt and Gloria Naylor to Henry David Thoreau and Willa Cather. A reading list of forty-eight mainstream writers such as Sherwood Anderson and Virginia Woolf, and their works that contain gay or lesbian situations and themes, is also available.

The three- to five-day science unit resulted from collaboration with a psychology and biology teacher, and can be used in either subject. "History and Nature of Homosexuality (and its 'Causes')" includes current and historic views on the biology and psychology of homosexuality, as well as the psychological roots and dimensions of homophobia. It reviews various theories of homosexuality, examines how both interest in and characterizations of homosexuality are determined by the cultural milieu, and explores causation issues in the context of the nature-nurture debate.

Those materials, as well as the teachers' manual, are now used in thirty states. Most requests come from New England, but Dr. Lipkin has shipped them as far as Alabama and Hawaii.

All three units are designed for high school students. "My background is that level," he explained. "Besides, I think there are some good materials already out there for younger kids, such as the guides for *Daddy's Roommate* and *Heather Has Two Mommies*. There are, on the other hand, no high school materials that I've seen. I thought the need was there. And I also feel it's important to reach kids when they're in high school. The struggle with coming-out issues occurs most often then – and gay-bashing is done predominantly by teenage males. High school is such a critical time."

Most units are ordered by individual teachers; some administrators ask for them on a school- or departmentwide basis. A few requests come from community youth workers. The feedback, Dr. Lipkin said, has been very positive – and he has seen some of it firsthand, in classroom observation. "Students really get engaged," he noted. "This is a subject they've been interested in anyway, even though they don't know a lot about it. So here is a chance to learn about gay history, or look at literature through a gay or lesbian lens, and do it in the context of school and the classroom."

Yet the availability of curriculum materials on gay and lesbian issues does not mean that teachers and administrators are ready to embrace them, elbowing each other out of the way in the headlong race to be first with this new stuff – nor even to want them. In fact, Dr. Lipkin said, "I think the trend is to shy away from gay and lesbian curriculum, period. We saw that in the fight over the Children of the Rainbow curriculum in New York [when a group of parents forced the school chancellor to back down from his support for teaching diversity – including the existence of gay and lesbian families – to elementary school children]. We even saw it in the Governor's Commission here in Massachusetts, to which I was an advisory board member. Two of our recommendations were dropped by the governor's office when he approved the report: one was that there be gay- and lesbian-related materials in school libraries, the other recommended incorporating gay- and lesbian-related curriculum into classrooms."

In fact, Dr. Lipkin said, "The only place that anything gay enters the curriculum today with any regularity is AIDS courses – even more so there than in the general health and sexuality curriculum. But that limits discussion of homosexuality to sexual topics, and ignores the roles of gay people in society. And offering a separate course on gay and lesbian studies is problematic as well. Fear of being labeled and stigmatized may make both gay and straight students afraid to take the course – and the homophobic students who need to be sensitized are very, very unlikely to enroll."

However, he noted, homosexual teachers themselves are as much to blame for the current sorry state of gay and lesbian curricula. "My general feeling is that gay people themselves have shied away from pushing it. The ones that are closeted aren't going to raise the issue, and the ones who are out may not want to be seen as 'pushing it.' So that's just one more reason teachers can't find a lot of materials on gay and lesbian issues for their classes."

He is aware of Project 21's attempt at the policy level to introduce gay and lesbian material into schools, and added that Kevin Jennings's recent book, *Becoming Visible,* has helped make social studies teachers more aware of these issues. He has heard too of individual teachers' efforts to develop units, such as one on the gay and lesbian experience in the Holocaust. But, he re-emphasized, "When I look around for materials, I can't find a whole lot."

A lack of suitable materials is precisely the problem Peter Wild faced a dozen years ago, when he introduced the topic of homosexuality into his sociology course at Glastonbury (Connecticut) High School. The juniors and seniors in his popular elective already spent a semester exploring the issues and problems faced by various minorities. Yet they were ignoring, in the social studies teacher's words, "the last openly discriminated-against group in American society."

Mr. Wild, who describes himself as somewhat of a liberal, noted that "de jure discrimination against blacks and every other group is over – except homosexuals." He'd already spent fifteen years at Glastonbury, an above-average, academically oriented large school filled with upper-middle-class youngsters in the suburb of the same name on the outskirts of Hartford. ("We've allegedly got 9 percent minority students, but most of them must be affluent Asians," he said wryly). Over the years, he gradually became aware that homosexuality was an issue that needed to be addressed. "There was rampant homophobia here, just as there is in any high school. I'm heterosexual; I was not coming at it as 'one of them,' trying to rally people to the cause. I just felt it was an issue we needed to talk about."

Yet when he began searching for curricular materials, Mr. Wild found himself in the wilderness. There was nothing available. So, like any resourceful teacher, he created his own. He clipped newspaper and magazine articles, and taped television shows. "I found lots of good stuff on *20/20, 60 Minutes,* and after-school specials," he said. "They cover everything from gay-bashing to what it's like to be homosexual or have homosexual parents, to different ways gays are discriminated against." He went to conferences, and built up an impressive list of contacts.

Over the past decade, "Homosexuality" evolved into a two-week unit that Mr. Wild introduces midway through his sociology course (in a typical semester he teaches two different sections, thus reaching a hundred students a year). The class explores such questions as What is a homosexual? What causes homosexuality? How are gays treated in society? What is homophobia? Where did sodomy laws come from, and why do they still exist?

But before his students grapple with those thorny issues, Mr. Wild said, they must first voice their own fears and get their own prejudices out in the open. They have to sound off, and that takes time. Once that is done – through a series of intense classroom discussions, and some written work – the students move on to examine facts, do background readings, and explore myths.

Late in the unit, Mr. Wild invites representatives from Hartford's Stonewall Speakers Association to visit. "It's very important for the class to 'confront the enemy,' so to speak," he said. "The reaction is generally, 'Wait a minute. These are people too.' The kids start seeing them not just in terms of their sexual preference, but in the entire spectrum of their lives as human beings."

Mr. Wild takes pains to present different sides of the subject. "I'm not afraid of showing pro and con," he said. "In fact, if anything I think I'm probably guilty of showing too much of the negative side of homosexuality. Sometimes I worry about my stress on negativity, and think I have to work harder to try to show that homosexuals can live happy, productive lives." He is often concerned about the students in his class, and in Glastonbury High, who are questioning their sexuality. "They're going through this hell, hearing slurs from teachers, parents, and friends. It must be brutal." That is why he appreciates the Stonewall speakers, many of whom point out how liberating coming out can be. At the same time, he realizes his goal is not to present a case for or against homosexuality; it is rather "to show and teach acceptance, tolerance, and understanding for this group of people."

Mr. Wild admitted that "when you teach a unit on homosexuality there is always a fear that people will say you're condoning it. But I don't think my portrayal is going to cause anyone to want to become a homosexual. I talk about so many negatives – maybe too much."

Yet his emphasis obviously touches students. Many who initially were very up-front about being anti-gay later confide, "Yeah, I can see another point of view," or, "Yeah, discrimination is wrong," Mr. Wild said. "When most human beings get enough information on a subject, a certain fairness creeps into their thinking. They start to say, 'Yeah, why *should* they be kept out of the military anyway?'"

Such reactions he finds immensely gratifying. "As a teacher you seldom know who you reach, or how. But I've found that, given enough time, there are attitudinal changes. I see many kids developing more tolerance and understanding. I can tell by the anecdotal evidence, the before and after surveys, and by testing, even though some kids may just spit back what they perceive as politically correct. It's nothing I can quantify, but I can sense it, hear it, feel it, and see it. I know I can't reach everyone, but I know progress does occur." However, he emphasized, "it doesn't just happen. You need a definite block of time, like the two weeks I use. The feelings are too strong to do it in just two or three days."

In the decade-plus he's been teaching his sociology unit, Mr. Wild has also noticed an increase in curricular material. However, he is not very impressed with it, so he continues to use the newspapers, periodicals, and TV shows he has amassed through the years. He has found the *New York Times* to be a good source of scientific articles, while local papers are helpful for personalizing with hometown examples such controversies as domestic partnership laws and gays in the military. "You just have to be cognizant, be aware, and keep your eyes on the *TV Guide,*" he noted. "It's a slow process. But if you use your creativity and search around, you can come up with good materials on your own."

Although more books are being published and more curricular resources are appearing, Mr. Wild attributed the dearth of good material to several factors. "Some school systems, and many teachers, are hesitant to deal with homosexuality," he said. "I've been asked, 'How do you get away with teaching it? What does your principal say?' There's a lot of apprehension about it. Fortunately, it is not an issue in this school.

"Another thing is that a lot of teachers carry a lot of baggage. They're older – like myself – and maybe homophobic. Growing up they never talked about sex at home, and of course homosexuality was always taboo. Many teachers don't want to talk about this, much less teach it. So if there's not a lot of clamor for it by teachers, there's not a lot of chance that things will be produced for them."

Mr. Wild also reserved some criticism for gays and lesbians themselves. "Frankly," he said, "I'm a little surprised the gay community hasn't done more to create teaching materials. I teach many things, and I don't know everything there is to know about this field, but I think there's been some negligence on the part of the gay community in terms of getting things out there for teachers to use. Maybe they're there and I just haven't had access to them, but if you believe as I do that the primary way to create change is through education, you have to wonder why the people who are experts on this subject haven't done more to educate others about it."

But the sociology unit is not Mr. Wild's only contribution to Glastonbury students' understanding of homosexuality. He also participates in the year-long Current Issues course, a requirement for all three hundred seniors. They pile into the auditorium at 7:45 every morning, five days a week; for forty-two minutes they hear lectures, listen to guest speakers, or stage debates on important contemporary topics.

"It's not the optimum setting," Mr. Wild admitted. "It's much more difficult to deal with a sensitive issue in a large group setting. We deal with a lot of different things, so we can devote only a week to homosexuality, and that's not as effective either." Yet the two days of talk, followed by three days of discussion, obviously strike a chord: following the debate on homosexuals in the military, more than half the students voted that gays and lesbians should be allowed to serve. "That's pretty enlightening," Mr. Wild said. "I don't think most polls would find that result."

He found something else fascinating: "In over ten years, I've never heard *any* complaints from parents or administrators. No one's ever raised an eyebrow; there hasn't been any commotion or negative feedback. I find that astounding. I think there's a fear among many teachers that this subject is too controversial but – at least in this community – there's been no negative feedback at all."

Glastonbury was a pioneer in introducing homosexuality into the curriculum; now, over a decade later, Mr. Wild sees it as a topic that's starting to creep into high schools. Yet he does not view himself as an expert. "I'm just one teacher who considered it important, and set about gathering materials," he said.

He is extremely glad that he did. "Teaching about homosexuality has been a very exciting, worthwhile, and rewarding experience," he concluded. "Anytime you can reach students – especially about a subject as important as this – well, that's the real joy of teaching."

Workshops Work

Since its founding a dozen years ago in western Massachusetts by a varied group of educators, psychologists, lawyers, and "organizational specialists" concerned about increasingly overt signs of discrimination, Equity Institute has emerged as a nationally respected nonprofit organization. Its training programs have taught nearly 100,000 corporate executives, police officials, government workers, religious figures, health care providers, board of trustee members, educators, and students better ways of working and living in a society in which their peers don't always look as if they've just strolled out of a minivan or breakfast cereal advertisement. The country is filled with men in wheelchairs, women on welfare, boys who like boys, and girls who like girls — and, the people at Equity Institute say, that's what makes this such a wonderful place.

The trick is to get everyone else to agree.

To help spread the word that differences should inspire, not frighten, the organization — now located in the San Francisco Bay Area in the small town of Emeryville — has developed programs aimed at the specific needs of clearly defined target groups. They work with police to develop interpersonal and human relations skills; they show companies and institutions ranging from Pacific Gas and Electric to the American Red Cross ways of managing diversity to produce a more harmonious, creative workplace (and prevent litigation); they even train trainers to carry the multicultural message back to entire organizations. Their Program on Jewish Awareness draws together Jews and gentiles, clergy and laity, to explore attitudes and overcome misconceptions, while their Dismantling Classism programs allow people raised in widely varying circumstances to recognize that while economic background obviously colors one's behavior and worldview, poverty need not be seen as gruesome – while wealth is not always an advantage.

Among the earliest concerns Equity Institute addressed were those surrounding homophobia; a decade later, gay and lesbian issues continue to dominate many workshops and training sessions. The topic first arose when a group of homosexual educators mentioned that their administrators ignored name-calling. From that basic beginning emerged two school-based projects, both heavily emphasizing sexual orientation; they rank today among the most popular of all the institute's offerings. (Of course, homophobia is addressed in all Equity programs, even those not specifically aimed at gay and lesbian concerns.)

One of the school programs, the Appreciating Diversity Project, helps educators, youth group leaders, and teenagers examine the root causes and damaging effects of oppression. Participants then attempt to reduce damaging behavior in their schools and communities by developing intervention and prevention techniques and strategies.

At the core of the program is *Sticks, Stones, and Stereotypes,* a video documentary and "curriculum module" designed especially for high school and first-year college classrooms. The bilingual English-Spanish 26-minute video comes with a teacher resource guide; both describe the anguish caused by name-calling and explore methods of stopping it. Personal stories are juxtaposed with true-to-life scenes. No type of prejudice is spared, said Barry Myles, associate director of training at Equity Institute, because "we believe there is no hierarchy of hatred. Hurt is hurt, and pain is pain."

However, he admitted, homophobia is one of the last bastions of hatred to remain acceptable. "It's manifested when a teacher lets an anti-gay comment go by, whereas it would not be okay in that same classroom to make a racist or sexist remark."

In the Appreciating Diversity Project, participants – and Equity Institute demands that a "diverse population" be represented – are encouraged to think about the groups into which their schools are divided, then follow those ideas through into discussions about the unintentional exclusion that occurs in classes and clubs. The desired result, Mr. Myles said, is to get people to realize that "oppression comes from systems – the way schools and societies are organized – and not from individuals themselves."

Appreciating Diversity groups often discover entrenched homophobia that few administrators, faculty members, or students even recognize: for example, a classroom project based on *The Dating Game* may send the subtle message that only heterosexuals go out together, while graduation rituals might celebrate heterosexual couples, yet exclude or frighten youngsters with same-sex feelings. "Some of what we hear when the groups report back a month after our first session is incredible," Barry noted. After meeting again groups begin setting up multicultural resource teams, and designing an action plan for the school. This may range from textbook and curriculum revisions to the institution of a "training of trainers" program.

A second Equity program is even more homosexual-themed. Project Empowerment, held six times a year at various locations around the country, brings together twenty-five to fifty lesbian, gay, and bisexual teachers, administrators, guidance counselors, and other educators for three days of examining, confronting, and overcoming fears.

"We look at how we've internalized so many messages of fear," said Barry Myles, himself a gay man and former private Christian academy teacher. "We draw analogies with other groups that have been oppressed and made fearful. We develop strategies around breaking down those fears, and spend a lot of time on ally development — how to find allies in school, and be a good ally ourselves."

Although participants typically represent a wide range of stages regarding their homosexuality, many return home from a Project Empowerment weekend ready to come out further than they have been. "The bottom line of what we do is to explore how our schools and lives might be different if we come out," Barry said. "There's not necessarily any pressure to come out during the weekend, but we do look at the entire coming-out process. For instance, school rhetoric often insists that a building is a comfortable place for everyone. We ask ourselves, Is our building really safe? If it isn't, why isn't it? Would it be more comfortable, or less, if we were more open?"

Project Empowerment leaders encourage participants to construct scenarios surrounding circumstances that might happen. They roleplay how they might react to various comments. Once issues are addressed in the safe environment of the weekend, educators feel well prepared to return to their school environment.

The retreat changes participants in many ways. "Some people go back home and come out to their principal, their colleagues, their students — everyone," Barry reported. "Some who were already somewhat out take the next step, setting up support groups for gay, lesbian, and bisexual students. Some take smaller steps, like putting up posters, assigning literature about gay and lesbian issues, ordering books or videos, or just wearing a button." Many write to thank Equity Institute for the workshop; some send scholarship money so that others can participate. (The fee, a self-assessed sliding scale of $125 to $250, includes program materials, meals, and accommodations.)

Which raises an interesting point. Though much of the institute's funds come from private sources, such as the United Way and philanthropic foundations, many donors consider Project Empowerment "high risk" or "controversial." Since its initiation in 1986, Barry said, this particular program has been the most difficult of all at Equity to get funded. "That shows about as well as anything how important it is to address issues of gays and lesbians in the schools."

Public schools are not the only ones getting the gay and lesbian message, of course; private schools are too. Nearly ten years ago the Pacific Northwest Association of Independent Schools (PNAIS) began discussing the need for diversity — the 53-year-old organization even designated a staff member to work full-time on their Project for Diversity in Education — but it took several more years before "diversity" came to include gay students.

That occurred when Kathy Sorrells, PNAIS diversity program director, started talking with the fifty-five school heads, all of whom sit on the organization's board. The feedback she heard from many was, "We don't really need to talk about this. It's not an issue." She chalked up that response to their own internalized homophobia.

Shortly thereafter, in the fall of 1993, Ms. Sorrells helped PNAIS start a support group for gay and lesbian teachers in both private and public schools. One result was that she goosed along the PNAIS heads, who agreed to discuss gay and lesbian issues at their next spring meeting. Another was getting them to debate the inclusion of sexual orientation in the organization's nondiscrimination policy. A third result was a day-long workshop in February 1994, called "Building Bridges of Respect and Support: Lesbian/Gay/Bisexual Issues in Our Schools."

That's how fifty private school teachers, guidance counselors, and interested others — some openly gay, some semi-out, some closeted, some heterosexual; more females than males; mostly white, except for three blacks and one Asian — gathered in the residential hills at the lovely Annie Wright School, overlooking the unlovely city of Tacoma, to learn, in the middle of Washington State's fevered debate on an initiative barring municipalities from passing anti-gay discrimination, all about anti-gay discrimination.

"The issues are challenging," Ms. Sorrells's greeting to the group began. "I've been challenged by them in school, and personally.

They're tough to talk about for many of us. Lots of other people *want* to be here, but for one reason or other can't be." She applauded the courage of those who did attend and expressed hope that the next gathering would be even larger.

The next speaker was PNAIS board member Fred Dust, head of the Bush School in Seattle. He noted that while the PNAIS is more broad-based than many education groups (its fifty-five members, scattered throughout seven states, include day and boarding schools, lower and upper schools, religious and nonsectarian schools), all must recognize that parents who enroll their children do so by choice. He did not mention that all also hire gay faculty and enroll gay students – whether they know it or not.

But Ms. Sorrells and Mr. Dust were mere warm-ups for the main act: Kevin Jennings of Concord Academy in Massachusetts. One of the first openly gay private school teachers in the country, he was spending the year as a Klingenstein Fellow at Columbia University, working on two books on gay and lesbian issues. He was also traveling around the country, presenting his "Homophobia 101" course to groups like the PNAIS. He began lightly: "This is my first year away from school after teaching for eight years, and I miss the petty power trips, like giving pop quizzes. So here's one."

He passed out paper – "No talking, please!" – and the presentation was under way. The first question asked, "What do you think caused your heterosexuality?" It was followed by ten more, all dealing with heterosexuality: "Is it possible heterosexuality is a phase you will grow out of?" "Why are heterosexuals so blatant, always making a spectacle of their heterosexuality by kissing in public, wearing wedding rings, etc.?" "Heterosexual marriage has total societal support, yet over half of all heterosexuals who marry this year will divorce. Why are there so few successful heterosexual relationships?" The gays in attendance immediately got the point and started laughing out loud; the straights scrunched up their faces, tapped their pencils on the table, and tried to respond.

After announcing, "Time's up!" Mr. Jennings asked for reactions from the heterosexuals. "Embarrassing ... thought-provoking ... table-turning ... challenging ... intimidating ... confrontational" were some. That launched him on a discussion of relevant terms, including "heterosexism" and "homophobia."

Mr. Jennings linked the two: "Homophobia and heterosexism both limit educational opportunities for every student in a school. They're educational issues that prevent every child from achieving his or her full potential. Whether we like or dislike gay people is irrelevant. All teachers have an obligation to serve all children in their class, whether they like them or not. The threat to kids' safety is homophobia, not homosexuality – and homophobia is just as dangerous as child abuse."

He delved deeper, into the three types of sexuality – orientation, behavior, and identity – and made the distinction between being gay (which is a behavior) and being homosexual (an orientation). "People choose to be gay," he said. "People don't choose to be homosexual."

Next he turned the question "Why are people gay?" upside down, asking, "Why do people care? It's irrelevant. You can't make someone straight, and you can't make someone gay. But you can make someone miserable."

Mr. Jennings moved on to the sources of support many youngsters enjoy – peers, teachers, family, religious institutions – and then asked participants to imagine them from a gay youth's point of view. "The profound isolation of gay and lesbian kids comes about because they have *no* traditional areas of support." This can lead to a series of problems: academic ("If you're worried about your entire life, you can't concentrate on the Constitution or the quadratic equation. Or else you do what I did – you become an overachiever, graduating magna cum laude from Harvard, and that has its own risks"); alcohol and drug abuse; inappropriate or dangerous sexual behavior; suicide. To underscore his point, he read the writings of several of his own students. Their words sent chills down many teachers' spines; several wept.

Unwilling to let his listeners off the hook, Mr. Jennings then showed an excerpt from the powerful video *Gay Youth*. The mother of a young man who killed himself by leaping off a bridge speaks of his life; interspersed are selections from his diary, in which he spirals downward from a loving, spirited son into a suicidal loner.

When the video was over, Mr. Jennings asked for comments. They came quickly. One was about religion, and Mr. Jennings attacked it like a batter knocking a fat pitch out of the park. (As well he might: the son of a fundamentalist minister, he spent his youth listening to his father preach in Southern churches – and his brother works for archconservative senator Jesse Helms.) "The radical right is destined to lose," he said, "because they oppose the fundamental American values with bigotry, hatred, and injustice. The question is, When will we win? It took hundreds of years for blacks to gain the right to be full citizens, and that battle is not yet over. Will our generation be remembered as the Germans of the 1930s, or the American college students of the 1960s? We need to recognize that the religious right comes from a place of weakness, not fear — but we have to find a way to reach them with our message."

He gave his audience hope that they could. "My mother has a sixth-grade education; she honestly thought, until she was sixteen, that Jews had horns, and she didn't speak to my brother for four years after he married an African-American woman. But she went on to found the first PFLAG chapter in North Carolina. That's education. Remember, we're educators. People can change. I think it's pretty depressing for us as educators if we think we can't effect change."

Mr. Jennings's post–lunch break message was uplifting: "One candle lights a darkened room. Each of us can be that candle." That happens, he said, as simply as putting a book with the word "gay" or "lesbian" in its title on a classroom bookshelf, or as slowly as a teacher seeking change by framing all his or her comments in terms of the school's mission statement and refusing to be dragged off that turf.

Any teacher, he noted, can serve every student. "We need gay and lesbian role models for gay and lesbian kids, and for straight kids. But we also need compassionate straight people to be role models too, because every kid must see how a good person can act. Homophobia is taught. We don't come out of the womb crying because we hate our lesbian doctor. Well, if homophobia is taught, then it can also be untaught."

Most teachers, administrators, trustees, and school heads want to be good, and want to do the right thing, Mr. Jennings concluded. "The challenge for all of us, then, is to set a climate so that people *can* act with fairness, justice, and compassion for all, all the time."

Lunch was followed by a "fishbowl" — an intense exercise in which several gay teachers sat in a circle and answered a question posed by Ms. Sorrells: "Who do you love, and how do you love them?" Participants spoke about the pleasures and pains of loving someone of the same sex — adding the ways in which students, colleagues, and supervisors reacted to, did not react to, or did not even know about — those loved ones. The speakers shared searing insights into their school experiences, and the listeners who surrounded them sat in rapt silence.

The workshop ended with a choice of four presentations. One dealt with combating homophobia and heterosexism in the curriculum; another with how teachers and parents can work together on sexual orientation issues; a third explored how an entire school can change from homophobic to supportive.

The fourth panel featured several gay and lesbian students discussing their own school experiences. One girl noted how impressed she was when, after she came out, a teacher took the time to ask questions of her because he felt he needed to know more. A boy mentioned his pleasure that most teachers now incorporate gay and lesbian information and references into many of their lectures and discussions. Another male said he got through high school because several teachers protected him. "It worked, but it didn't teach me to be self-sufficient," he said.

After the students spoke, a lesbian mother related how pleased she was that, at her six-year-old daughter's school, students sing Michael Callen's affirming ballad, "Everything Possible" ("You can be anybody that you want to be, you can love whoever you choose..."). "The kids hold hands and hug," she said. "I bawl every time I hear it."

When the panels ended, participants went home; there was no final session, no special closure. However, that did not matter, because the day had been filled with openings. The fifty women and men who left Tacoma headed back to Seattle, Oregon, or wherever filled with a sense of purpose. They knew plenty of work remains to be done at their own private schools – but they were eager to get going, and energized to involve their colleagues, trustees, parents, and heads.

Of course, not all workshops on homosexuality attract out-of-the-closet, in-your-face gays and their progressive, anti-homophobic straight friends and allies. A workshop of a different kind is run by Stan W. Ziegler, Ph.D. He is one of a very few openly gay adolescent psychologists in the country, yet the teachers who attend his sessions are usually burrowed deep in the classroom closet.

That's because Dr. Ziegler does not deal with topics like "teaching diversity" or "stopping name-calling" that any reasonably competent professional educator should be able to handle. He tackles such issues as why homosexual teachers teach ("Going back to high school for gay teachers is like returning to the scene of the crime, where so much pain and suffering occurred in their lives"), and how to react when an administrator says, "It's okay if you're out to the staff, but don't you dare tell the kids!"

Dr. Ziegler's workshops are not the easiest way to earn in-service credits.

The Long Island native has been interested in the issues and baggage surrounding homosexuality and schools ever since graduating summa cum laude from Yale University, but it was not until he nearly died from Crohn's disease in the early eighties that he decided to focus on adolescents as his lifework. Because of his own sexuality and training, he felt he could make a special contribution to teenagers. So

To help address the problems of gay teens from another angle, openly gay adolescent psychologist Dr. Stan W. Ziegler developed workshops for gay and lesbian teachers.

Dr. Ziegler, a student of both Anna Freud and Erik Erikson, co-founded the Erikson Center for Adolescent Advancement in Tarzana, California, a county residential treatment center for fifteen- to eighteen-year-old dependents of the court, and became president of the board of Gay and Lesbian Adolescent Social Services (GLASS) in Beverly Hills, where his practice is based.

His GLASS work led Dr. Ziegler to the Crossroads School and other cutting-edge private institutions. He discovered Project 10 and similar programs for gay and lesbian teenagers. The more he learned, the more interested he became; the more he worked with homosexual students, the more he realized that their issues were not completely separate from those of their teachers. Soon the idea of a workshop was born.

"There's no more important group of adults in this country for young people who are beginning to recognize that they are gay and lesbian than gay and lesbian high school teachers," he said. Those men and women can serve as vital, even life-affirming, resources – and there are plenty of them. "We know that gay people are drawn in disproportionately high numbers to the helping professions.

"Think about what it would mean if all teenagers knew several teachers in their school who were at least reasonably bright, mature, responsible authority figures who were also gay. Research shows that it's harder for people to maintain homophobic ideas when they know a Real Live Gay Person. Think about the remarkable possibility for changing the next generation's attitudes toward gay and lesbian people." Yet the vast majority of teachers are not out at their schools – and if they are, they are out only to other adults, not to students.

Dr. Ziegler has firsthand experience with that phenomenon. "I will always have some residual anger at my own high school choir director," he said, though the two have remained friends for years. "He was one of my best and favorite teachers. The madrigal group sometimes practiced in his home, and we knew he shared it with the choir director from the neighboring high school. How much he could have helped me, a young and struggling gay boy who despite being popular and president of many of the major school organizations – it's called sublimation – felt alone and very different. He might have saved me a number of difficult years if he matter-of-factly introduced his roommate as his lover or partner, or told me they were gay – or *something*." Dr. Ziegler acknowledges that this would have taken "a lot of courage" on the choir director's part in 1968 – just as it would today. Through his workshops, he is trying to do something about that.

The first day-long event, held at his home, drew a dozen participants, though twice that number had contacted him. Many were deeply closeted; a typical attitude was expressed by one woman who was appalled that Dr. Ziegler had spoken "the g-word" to her answering machine. "We looked at how you integrate yourself into your work environment," he explained. "Most gay teachers hide their personal lives at school. What does this communicate to students, both gay and nongay? Deprived of positive role models, young gays and lesbians see silence as a sign of shame. If being gay is okay, they correctly ask, then why are you hiding it? For straight students, it simply reinforces what they already know: gay people lead secret lives because they're ashamed of who they are."

Dr. Ziegler helped the teachers in his workshop understand the fear that they felt, even as adults, in a high school setting. "They realize they can be hurt – not physically, as they could have when they were teenagers themselves, but emotionally. Adults are just like kids in that when we expose ourselves, we open ourselves up to possible ridicule, embarrassment, or shame. High school kids are just as capable of being cruel today as when we were in high school. That's amazing to think about in a city like Los Angeles, but it's true."

He added, "While high school students view their teachers as smart and powerful, they don't know that inside many of their gay and lesbian teachers remains the hurt and scared teenager who doesn't want to be taunted again."

Dr. Ziegler and the participants examined the process of how they were damaged as teenagers, and their choice of teaching as a profession. "Most people don't choose teaching because they like *teaching* history or English, but because of a desire to help," he said. "That led to a discussion of how we help kids, gay kids especially, and the pros and cons of being out to them."

Other workshops followed, although Dr. Ziegler was stunned at the reaction he received after proposing his sessions to organizations he was certain would be receptive, such as the National Association of Independent Schools. "They said, 'Thanks, but no thanks,'" he reported. "I've been on all the talk shows – *Oprah, Donahue, Entertainment Tonight* – talking about these issues, and they could see by my vita that I have a reasonable amount of experience. But they just weren't interested in something like this. I'm surprised. The silence has been overwhelming."

The cast of participants changes from group to group, but one thing does not: the level of outness remains the same. As the workshops evolved, Dr. Ziegler added special exercises, such as asking everyone to bring in their own high school yearbooks. "They point to their picture, and I ask them to talk about who they were then – in the third person," he said. "It's fascinating – the most touching part of the workshop for me."

He shares his own experiences too, of course. "One day an old schoolmate tracked me down, and as we talked he said, 'You were miserable in high school?! We all wanted to be you!' But there was a lot of angst for me then, so I know what these teachers feel and why they feel it."

Participants in Dr. Ziegler's workshops also talk about how their feelings at age sixteen or eighteen relate to their emotions and perceptions now, at thirty or forty or fifty, and how that in turn fits in with their actions and feelings in the classroom. "Some people become quite emotional," he admitted. "They're spending twenty-five years in a school environment pretending to be someone they're not."

The discussion often turns to what Dr. Ziegler termed "walking the line of appropriate judgment – being helpful without getting yourself in trouble. We take more risks if we're not openly gay, but being open carries with it some risks too. When we talk about risks – real, imagined, or both – we're not necessarily trying to teach teachers to say the right words. We are trying to get someone to feel at ease to start talking in school about their private life after years of not doing so."

The session can become fairly specific. One man asked how to respond to "fag jokes" he hears in the halls; while he appeared comfortable telling students such talk was inappropriate, he was unwilling to take the next step and say, "As a gay man, I don't like to hear that."

But much of the discussion remains theoretical. Some situations are just too painful to talk about in a group.

Most workshops end with teachers exchanging addresses and phone numbers, so they can turn to each other for support and strength in the days and weeks ahead. "That's a first step, and a very important one," Dr. Ziegler noted.

The sessions attract a fifty-fifty mix of men and women, usually in their thirties and older. "I think it's easier for young gay educators today," Dr. Ziegler said. "The older ones had a harder time as teenagers, and are still finding it harder to integrate homosexuality into their lives." Though they are not yet out at school, they feel unsatisfied with the compromises they've made in life. "They're uncertain about what they're prepared to do, and they've got lots of questions – about the choices they've made, and their options of dealing with things."

The workshops fill a clear need, as evidenced by the continuing list of teachers eager to attend. Dr. Ziegler even did a large session for the United Teachers of Los Angeles. It was held during the week the Rodney King verdict was to be announced, and it was with some trepidation that the psychologist drove downtown. He found an audience of 150. "They braved all the warnings," he said. "That says a lot."

But he knows too that his sessions are just one small part of a long, agonizing process. "A lot of people who come to these things are right on the cusp, and it's taken a long time to get there," he noted. "They're ready to take whatever the next step is. They come to the workshop, they get encouraged, and then they have new courage to go forward. It takes a while.

"I wish people were doing this all over the country. I don't know if they are. There are so many teachers who could be helped by it. Gay people go into education in disproportionate numbers, and have so much to give. But ninety, ninety-five percent of us stay hidden, and that hurts everyone."

Editor's note: Dr. Stan Ziegler died in January 1995, shortly before this book went to press.

SAFE SCHOOLS

The Bay State
Leads the Way

In 1775, Massachusetts citizens stood at the vanguard of the American Revolution, battling British troops at Lexington and Concord. In 1972, the Bay State was the only state in the nation to back George McGovern over Richard Nixon in the presidential election. Now, in the 1990s, Massachusetts has become the first (and so far the only) state to ensure – legally, in writing, with four specific recommendations and a major legislative vote – the rights of lesbian and gay students to a safe, secure learning environment.

Advocates of lesbian and gay youth hope that in this instance Massachusetts is leading the country, not veering away from it.

This particular and inspiring story began in late 1989, when the state legislature passed a gay and lesbian civil rights law. The Coalition for Lesbian and Gay Civil Rights soon filed legislation to create an advisory board focusing on youth services; it died, but in early 1992, Gov. William Weld formed an innovative Commission on Gay and Lesbian Youth.

The man who had succeeded Michael Dukakis was an unlikely catalyst for such an act: born to a family that arrived from England in 1635 (Harvard's Weld Hall and numerous other area properties honor his family; a New York investment firm named for his ancestors bought out a company founded by George Bush's grandfather), Mr. Weld looks, talks, and plays squash like the patrician he is. As governor he has made deep cuts in social spending to balance the budget, befitting a man who won the 1990 election with the slogan "Tough on taxes. Tough on crime."

But beneath that WASPy, preppy exterior lurks – well, perhaps not a bleeding-heart liberal, but at least a compassionate, people-oriented person with a penchant for the underdog. He served, along with Hillary Rodham Clinton, on the staff of the House Judiciary Committee during the Watergate hearings, where he concluded that Nixon "wasn't telling the truth." He quit his number-three spot in the Justice Department in Washington after a spat with his boss, Attorney General Ed Meese. One of his favorite songs is "Lola," the Kinks' ode to cross-dressing. And his presidential aspirations are well known – though he has declared himself out of the running for the 1996 presidential race.

The Governor's Commission's twenty-seven members included the requisite human services professionals, along with three teachers, two parents of lesbian and gay children – and two high school students. Their mandate was to work to end all forms of discrimination against gay and lesbian youth, with a special eye toward preventing suicide and violence. The commission held five hearings across the state in the fall of 1992; among the ninety people who spoke publicly were many teenagers, gay and straight. Their words were covered by print, radio, and television reporters; their stories were discussed in every Massachusetts village and town.

Even today, printed in black and white as part of the official commission report, their comments evoke chills. "Throughout eighth grade, I went to bed every night praying that I would not be able to wake up in the morning, and every morning waking up and being disappointed," one eighteen-year-old said. "And so finally I decided that if I was going to die, it would have to be at my own hands."

Inspired by such testimony, the commission realized that its initial focus had to be on schools – where, according to its first report, issued in February 1993, "the prevailing unsafe climate denies equal educational opportunities to lesbian and gay youth. Virtually every youth who testified before the commission cited the need for action to change their school environment. Often the first-person experiences these youth related were horrifying – stories of violence, abuse, and harassment, from both peers and adults." Because state government has a responsibility to guarantee equal opportunity and a safe environment for all the students, the commission continued, the report homed in on creating an environment "where all students might learn, free from fear and intimidation."

"We could have focused on human service agencies, not school systems," admitted commission chair David LaFontaine, an English instructor at Massasoit Community College. "But it was obvious that schools are where gay and lesbian kids suffer the most, and where we can reach the most number of them." He made no apologies for taking a very public approach to gay youth issues. "We haven't been afraid of right-wing counterattacks, because we've been so very aboveboard talking about the need for this sort of thing."

The commission sent five major recommendations to Governor Weld, the Department of Education, and the Executive Office of Education. They asked every one of the state's three hundred high schools to establish policies protecting gay and lesbian students from harassment, violence, and discrimination; to train teachers, counselors, and school staff to respond to the needs of gay and lesbian students, including crisis intervention and suicide prevention; to establish a support group where gay and straight students can discuss important issues; to develop a library collection for students to learn more about lesbian and gay issues; and to develop curriculum that incorporates gay and lesbian themes and subject matter into all disciplines, in an age-appropriate manner.

In a historic and unanimous vote in May 1993, the Massachusetts Board of Education adopted the first four points as recommended state education policy; the fifth awaited development of discipline-specific guidelines. Approval brought no immediate practical effect – the state board can encourage, but not require, local school committees to enact policy – but its symbolic weight was enormous. Gay and lesbian youth issues had finally acquired government's imprimatur; they leaped out of the closet, into every classroom in the commonwealth.

And that was only the beginning. Unlike many official commission reports, this one did not slide into obscurity or die a quiet death. Instead, actions began speaking even louder than the report's powerful words. In July, Governor Weld stood in front of a group of educators and gay students in a Boston church to announce the first-ever state-wide effort to train teachers about lesbian and gay issues. "The concept of schools as safe havens must apply to all students, including gay and lesbian students," he said. "This is not about a different way of life; it is about life itself. We can take the first step toward ending gay youth suicide by creating an atmosphere of dignity and respect for gay youth in our schools."

Even before the governor's announcement, 110 school districts had expressed interest in the Department of Education project. Fortunately, they did not have to wait long to begin; in a launch rare for any government program, this one took off like a rocket.

One driving force behind what came to be called the Safe Schools Program for Gay and Lesbian Students, and one of the most enthusiastic bureaucrats to be found in any state department of education anywhere, is program director Jeff Perrotti. Originally hired as a consultant to work on AIDS training and education, he seized the chance to develop and nurture the $450,000 project, which is funded through the state legislature as part of its comprehensive school health curriculum. Within weeks Mr. Perrotti led a staff of twenty-five men and women (three of them full-time) whose sole mandate is to make Massachusetts schools more comfortable for gay, lesbian, bisexual, and questioning youths.

"We're framing this in the context of school safety," he explained. "It's been presented by the Department of Education as a violence prevention program, to make the school climate safer for all students. We're targeting one group that's traditionally been at risk, but also poorly addressed." The program is run by the same department unit that handles health education; the philosophy behind that, he said, is "you can't address one part of a student's life without addressing many others. Violence prevention is one part of school life, and gay and lesbian students are part of that part."

Because Bay State taxpayers cherish local control of their schools, Mr. Perrotti's group has embraced the belief that each district knows best what works for it, and what does not. "We don't have the answers for each community – just suggestions," he said. "Whatever schools want us to do, we'll do it." What districts want ranges from presentations on sexual harassment (with gay and lesbian issues simply one component), to evening community forums on gay and lesbian concerns, to in-service training, and much more.

The department's first step was to contact every high school principal, asking each to select a liaison to the Governor's Commission on Gay and Lesbian Youth, which had not disbanded following its report. Many administrators designated counselors or interested teachers; some named themselves or their vice principals. In the summer of 1993 Mr. Perrotti's group requested each liaison to develop a team of people to attend a regional workshop; ideal teams were comprised of parents, teachers, guidance counselors, administrators, and students. Nearly half of the schools that had selected liaisons formed such teams.

The regional Saturday workshops began in the fall of 1993; fifteen were scheduled for that first school year. Each brought ten or so school teams together, to introduce them to each other and the Department of

Education's resources. Mr. Perrotti termed the workshops very successful. "We had good attendance and great interaction. They came away with incredible energy and ideas." Though the focus was on high schools, several middle and elementary schools were also represented. Each team received a $100 stipend.

At the workshops, participants brainstormed about their schools. By the end of the day they had developed work plans, and received applications for grants ranging from $500 to $2,000 (the total departmental budget available was $100,000), plus technical assistance for applying. Grants could be used to develop programs or groups, such as gay-straight alliances; training materials for teachers; field trips to attend plays, gay pride marches, or similar events; film series; Outward Bound–type experiences to build group unity; speakers; conferences – "anything at all that relates to developing programs," Mr. Perrotti said. However, the department discouraged spending grants on books or curricular materials. They did not want a disaster like the New York Rainbow Curriculum battle over the inclusion of gay-themed material in elementary schools. Leaders were determined to keep the focus on violence prevention.

The department also spent its first year developing a student-based theater production that addressed gay and lesbian school safety. They made a training video for cable public-access television, planned resource manuals for students and families, organized four regional guidance counselor forums, and published a statewide directory of mental health practitioners and agencies. In the spring the department ran a large conference at which teachers, administrators, and students shared information about the use of their grants.

Though the program touched only a third of Massachusetts's high schools in its first year, many of them from suburban and rural districts (city systems were curiously slow to respond), Mr. Perrotti was not discouraged. "We're reaching out to the ones that aren't involved," he said. "We let them know what other schools are doing, and encourage them to get involved. It's an ongoing process. Our goal is to get every school to have a liaison, so they'll have access to all our resources, materials, workshops, and newsletters. The department is making it clear this is not mandatory, but we hope every school will realize it's available and important."

Mr. Perrotti, who entered his first year as director of the Safe Schools Program with high expectations, admitted that his definition of "success" was modified. "What I define as 'success' might not sound like it. But I look back on these regional workshops as wonderful things. At the end of one, a completely closeted teacher came out. She realized she could count on the support of her colleagues, after fearing it for more than twenty years. There's a direct link between how safe teachers feel, and how the students in that building feel. This woman can now serve as a positive role model, and every kid in her school can gain from that."

A similar experience occurred when he led an in-service day for 150 faculty members. "A woman stood up, came out — it was very moving — and got a standing ovation," he continued. "You can't underestimate the significance of those moments on an entire school's culture. I really feel that people meeting openly gay and lesbian people will do more than anything to change attitudes. The more we can provide an openly safe environment in our schools, the more successful we'll be. Having openly gay people at the Department of Education leading these workshops leads to people putting their toes in the water, and then going on from there."

Though his definition of success has changed, he knows from the evaluations he receives that the department's program works. "It's incredible," he enthused. "People say things like, 'This is the best use of state money I've ever experienced'; 'It's the most useful thing the Department of Education has ever done!' People are so grateful we're giving them access to open doors. It shows that policy is not just words — it's power. We see that at our level: we've got a law, we're here to help implement it, and by doing so we're doing a lot for people. All it took was support from a high level, and fortunately we got that."

And if Mr. Perrotti ever doubts the impact Massachusetts's Safe Schools Program is having, he does not have to look farther than his own desk. He has spoken nationally on his work, and requests for information and assistance pour in from across the country. "It's incredible," he said proudly. "I just got a call the other day from North Dakota."

But impressive as all that is, it's not all that Governor Weld, his commission, and the Department of Education have accomplished. Aided by hundreds of young allies — some gay, some lesbian, many straight — they have succeeded in doing the near-impossible: they moved the state legislature to pass a controversial bill.

H. 3353 is its innocuous number; "An Act to Prohibit Discrimination Against Students in Public Schools on the Basis of Sexual Orientation" is its name, and it became law on December 10, 1993, when Governor Weld affixed his signature to it four days after it passed on a voice vote, with no debate. The bill — the first of its kind in the nation

— protects lesbian and gay public school students from harassment and discrimination.

The wording of the bill was hardly momentous; it simply added sexual orientation to an existing public school anti-discrimination statute that included race, color, sex, religion, and national origin. In this case, however, words did not tell the whole story. Students did.

Angered by previous failures of similar bills, two of which were bottled up in Senate committees until they expired, students across Massachusetts engaged in what the *New York Times*'s Sara Rimer called "an extraordinary lobbying campaign." They worked for months, she said, "to affirm the rights of openly gay students to many rituals of adolescence: to form alliances and clubs, to take a date to the prom, to participate in sports." As of March 10, 1994, any gay or lesbian student in the state who suffers harassment, discrimination, or violence, or who feels unprotected by school officials, can sue his or her district for negligence. For the first time anywhere in the United States, officials will be held accountable for the learning environments in their schools. The bill does not cover private and parochial schools. However, one advocate said, "It's clearly going to set a tone and a standard for all schools in Massachusetts."

Governor Weld's chief secretary, Marty Linsky, readily acknowledged the impact of students on the bill's fate. "There were a thousand young people up here endlessly," he said. "And I think they were able to persuade members of the legislature that the problem was real and that the solution was reasonable. Their stories about their own difficulties were very compelling, very persuasive."

Among the speakers was Mark DeLellis, a seventeen-year-old senior at Belmont High School, who told legislators about the time his soccer teammates turned on him in middle school, spitting and calling him names. Andrew Lavin put himself on the line by addressing public hearings; as a result of the media attention, he became isolated and had objects thrown at him during school. Chris Hannon told of leaving high school after receiving a death threat and other harassment for revealing his homosexuality. He and several friends made the bill's passage an utmost priority: each personally called and wrote all forty senators. One indirect but ego-boosting result of their efforts was that several students received national attention. They fielded questions from reporters across the country, and appeared on television and radio stations across the land.

But effective as that was, the students' efforts involved more than public speaking. Led by Mr. LaFontaine, chair of the Governor's

Commission, 150 young lobbyists descended on the State House one October day. They divided into groups, each with a leader, and together visited the offices of every state senator.

Thirty of them met with a top aide to powerful Senate president William M. "Billy" Bulger, a conservative lawmaker from an Irish-Catholic district. His earlier opposition had scuttled the bill; at the time of the lobbying, it was stalled in the Senate Committee on Steering and Policy. After hearing the youths, Mr. Bulger helped release the bill.

Other lobbying efforts included a letter-writing campaign that elicited hundreds of pieces of mail, a candlelight vigil outside the State House, and a march down the Freedom Trail.

When the House and Senate passed the bill with an easy voice vote on December 6, the students were understandably elated. The last time one of the leaders, seventeen-year-old Brookline High School junior Sarah Lonberg-Lew, had lobbied legislators was in fourth grade. "It was to make the corn muffin the official state muffin," she said. "We baked corn muffins for them." This victory, she acknowledged, was a bit more momentous.

Governor Weld took a bit of heat for signing the bill in private, although Mr. LaFontaine noted that he had been the commission's strongest ally. "Having a Republican governor champion this issue, creating a group and funding training programs, has opened a lot of eyes. He has made this a much safer issue for both teachers and activists. And the governor forced Democrats to be much more active too, because they don't want to be perceived to be to the right of Republicans. They have to live up to their rhetoric."

Governor Weld's private signing was forgiven eleven days later when he met with student leaders and ceremonially signed several copies of the landmark legislation. Then a hundred gay, lesbian, and straight high schoolers, along with their adult supporters, gathered in the State House to celebrate the bill's passage.

Byron Rushing, the Democratic state representative who sponsored the bill in the House, told the group that they had made "an overt statement of your understanding of the respect and rights deserved by everybody. You said that because you are a human being and because you are here, you have inalienable rights that cannot be taken away by anybody. The legislature did not give you rights. You got those rights when you were born. This legislation says only that no one can take away those rights. It was your organization and your perseverance, and it was your clear, logical arguments that got this bill passed, and you should all feel great pride in your accomplishments."

But, as had been the case so often during the legislative battle, it was the students who had the last word. Mark DeLellis, the former soccer player whose teammates taunted him, said he felt new clout when dealing with his school's administration. He reported that his principal had already agreed to change the wording of Belmont High School's anti-discrimination clause. And Chris Hannon, the boy who dropped out of Boston College High after suffering extreme harassment, said, "When I first spoke, it was as a victim. But we passed the bill, and I'm not a victim anymore."

Yet developing, introducing, even passing a bill is one thing – implementing it is quite another. Citizens can petition and lobby, legislators can debate and vote, governors can sign – but ultimately it is up to the bureaucrats to put it into practice.

Making the Massachusetts legislation work is one of the challenges facing the Commonwealth of Massachusetts Department of Education – specifically, people like Jeff Perrotti. His job is to translate the act's theory into reality. Fortunately, it is a task he relishes.

"This bill is remarkable – it's a major, major thing," he began. "It gives gay and lesbian kids real protection. Schools are mandated to develop an atmosphere that prevents harassment. The effects can really be far-reaching. In the past this law has been the basis for textbook changes; it's led to reparations for people of color, changing perceptions of women's roles, different types of teacher training about discrimination and harassment. Now we're taking it one step further."

Among Jeff's biggest challenges is "letting schools know exactly what this means for them. That's a huge educational task, just letting them know that this exists. The anti-discrimination statutes have been on the books since 1971, but some schools still don't have a contact person for compliance. So we'll be doing lots of interpreting for schools, helping them revise their regulations."

Obstacles exist. One relates to the overall nature of school change, and how new programs are presented and institutionalized. "Anything that's new straddles the fine line between what's needed because it's not being done, and what's not really new or is deemed unnecessary," Mr. Perrotti explained. "If something is presented as too new, it may be seen as faddish or peripheral. But if it's presented another way, it can be diluted or simply not happen." The bureaucrats and educators assigned to the program at the Department of Education and in school district offices are keys to its success, he said, but they must have the support of insiders in each building. "If people pushing the program are seen as too 'outside,' they won't have the clout to get something going and then institutionalized," he continued. "On the other hand, if you involve too many 'tried and true' people, you run the risk that it never happens in a new and exciting way."

The challenge for Mr. Perrotti and his colleagues, then, is to bring in excited, energized people who have sensitivity to schools, which are cultures of their own filled with rigid barriers against being told what to do. That is not easy; few people feel comfortable in both the Department of Education and school worlds, he said. And both are incredible bureaucracies.

Any program's success, Mr. Perrotti noted, turns on "empowering people at the lowest level. That's where the work really goes on – but it can be incredibly frustrating. Bureaucracies are antithetical to empowering people."

However, he added one important caveat: "Students and parents have incredible power in schools. If they want something to happen, they can make it. We've come to realize how important parents are in this whole issue. Without a doubt, the most moving speakers we heard in the debate over amending the bill were the parents talking about accepting their gay and lesbian kids. PFLAG (Parents, Families and Friends of Lesbians and Gays) is often on the outskirts of the gay community, but they've been integral on this issue and to this program."

Another obstacle to the act's success is one that's seldom talked about, Mr. Perrotti said: "The internalization in our gay and lesbian community that 'we shouldn't be around kids.' This involves teachers who don't feel safe coming out, and others in our community who find it too painful or fearful to be around kids. There are a lot of internalized worries to overcome."

Yet the Department of Education director sees that as an exciting challenge, too. "To let gays know they can take care of their kids – to talk about youth suicide, and overcome the four taboos of death, suicide, youth sexuality, and homosexuality – takes a lot, but we're doing it. We're sensitizing and educating the gay and lesbian community that these are issues, that they're important issues, and that they should be talked about. And once we do it, we've found the gay community to be very, very generous with time, energy, expertise, and resources. It's an issue that involves everyone, not just kids in high school and their teachers, and the response has started to be very, very gratifying."

The amendment to the anti-discrimination bill did not take effect until March 10, 1994, ninety days after its passage. According to commission chair David LaFontaine, school administrators got the word early that the statute was on the books and ready to be enforced. "I'd bet you a million dollars, if I had it, that every principal in Massachusetts knows that this law passed, and is already rethinking the way the school deals with anti-gay violence and harassment." In that way, he said, even before the first case was litigated, "we've already won a victory."

Though he would like to think of Massachusetts as a model for the rest of the nation, Mr. LaFontaine acknowledged that his state is not a typical one. "We've had over 100,000 people in our pride marches every year," he said. "We've got a proliferation of colleges and universities, which gives us an enlightened base of citizens, and Governor Weld is an unusual figure. His unique political configuration – a socially liberal Republican governor in a Democratic state – combined with the courage of gay, lesbian, and straight kids and teachers, all came together at the right time."

However, Massachusetts is not nirvana. "I'm generally disappointed by the fact that gay and lesbian adults still do not make gay and lesbian youth a priority," he noted. "Many still seem afraid to work openly in schools for gay and lesbian youth rights, though I think that fear is misplaced. The vast majority of gay and lesbian teachers are still in the closet – even though since 1989 we've had a gay rights law on the books protecting teachers in their place of employment. The number of gay and lesbian teens coming out is really outpacing the number of adults."

Much of the teachers' fear, he claimed, is irrational. "People who had good reason to be closeted on the job fifteen or twenty years ago are now stuck in unhealthy patterns. It's not easy to re-evaluate a position taken fifteen or twenty years ago, and realize the atmosphere is more tolerant now than it was in the past. But that's just one more reason to continue working on gay and lesbian youth issues: so gay teenagers won't go into the closet, and spend years being fearful for their jobs, themselves, or their lives."

Mr. LaFontaine recognizes that his commission's work has unleashed a phenomenal reaction. "We've distributed over 10,000 copies of the report, all around the country," he said. "Several of us have spoken all over the place. I'd like to believe the work we're doing here – proving we can take a proactive stance regarding gay and lesbian school issues, and rally public support for them – is an inspiration for other states. I believe our Massachusetts model – and at the heart it means giving voice to gay and lesbian teenagers, helping them be leaders – can work all over the country. We've found that when people hear these stories, they're moved by them. They realize these students can be their own sons or daughters. Then it becomes no longer an issue of gays and lesbians pushing a particular agenda, but a simple issue of the human rights of young people."

Still, he is not ready to mark Massachusetts a success and move on. The commission's work is ongoing, he observed. "We've had impressive media visibility, but what we've done so far is just a beginning. The real work lies now in creating programs for every high school in the state. We want to translate the governor's mandate, and the huge public awareness, into school-based action.

"We know we've got years of work ahead of us," he concluded. "The liberal communities are light-years ahead of the rural and conservative ones. And we won't stop until support services are in place for every student, in every school, in Massachusetts."

The Final Chapter

This is the final chapter of *School's Out* – but it's the end in a literal sense only. The last chapter of gay and lesbian issues in America's schools has yet to be written. Still, it is far closer to completion than it was just a few short years ago.

A decade ago, who would have thought that an entire book could be written on the subject of homosexuality and education – written, in fact, using real names, real schools, and real incidents, many of them not only positive but spectacularly so? Who would have thought that in so many buildings throughout the United States, in large cities, medium-sized suburbs, and tiny towns, there would be not only openly gay teachers, administrators, coaches, and students, but also gay-straight alliances, gay-themed curricula, and gay topics discussed honestly and intelligently in workshops, classes, and the pages of school newspapers? It would have seemed like a fairy tale.

A decade ago, New York's Harvey Milk School opened its doors as the first school in the country serving the needs of gay and lesbian students. It was the object of intense media curiosity and educational scrutiny; today, its success in educating youths, building self-esteem, and saving lives is indisputable.

But much remains to be done. The Harvey Milk School has spawned only one similar school, EAGLES in Los Angeles. Teenagers and teachers alike cower in the classroom closet, afraid to come out because they fear negative repercussions, both real and perceived. The loss to other students and educators alike, in terms of wasted energy, squandered potential, and dishonest relationships, is incalculable.

Parents and boards of education still fight to keep homosexuality – debate, discussion, even its mere mention – out of schools. Nurses and librarians still fail to offer resources to timid young people with agonizing questions. And in nearly every school in America, the words "gay" and "fag" are still the ultimate put-down.

What remains to be done? Plenty.

The Students' Bill of Rights, first described by Dr. Virginia Uribe's Project 10 in Los Angeles, represents an ideal all schools should strive for. The bill states that all students have the right to:

- Attend schools free of verbal and physical harassment where education, not survival, is the priority.

- Attend schools where respect and dignity for all is a standard set by the board of education, and enforced by every principal.

- Gain access to accurate information about themselves, free of negative judgment, delivered by trained adults who not only inform but affirm them.

- See positive role models, both in person and in the curriculum.

- Be included in all support programs that exist to help teenagers deal with the difficulties of adolescence.

- Be represented by legislators who fight for their constitutional freedoms, rather than reinforce hatred and prejudice.

- Enjoy a heritage free of crippling self-hatred and unchallenged discrimination.

In addition, schools have certain obligations of which they must never lose sight. These include the obvious – protecting gay students and staff members from harassment and violence; creating a specific written policy prohibiting discrimination on the basis of sexual orientation; providing training to all administrators, educators, support staff, and students, on issues of sexual orientation and homophobia – but there are others that are less easily discerned. For example, schools should hire openly gay, lesbian, and bisexual faculty and staff, and, during the interviewing process for any new teacher, should ask about applicants' experience with, and personal attitudes toward, gay and lesbian students.

Schools should identify an advocate within the administration to address gay issues; designate (and publicize) a resource person in each school who is available to gay, lesbian, bisexual, and questioning students; and offer workshops to parents and community members on sexual orientation and homophobia. At the same time, they should reach out to gay and lesbian parents, and encourage them to share their status, stories, and concerns with school officials.

Schools should define sexual orientation harassment, and inappropriate use of language, with clear explanations of the channels for reporting such behavior, and its consequences.

They should provide hands-on support, ideally in the form of on-campus school groups. Barring that, they should provide brochures, flyers, posters, and phone numbers, for youngsters needing information about off-campus groups. Referrals can be made not only to support groups, counseling agencies, and hotlines, but also to auxiliary organizations for family members, such as Parents, Families and Friends of Lesbians and Gays (PFLAG). Counselors' and nurses' offices are excellent places to display such material.

Schools should include lesbian, gay, and bisexual concerns in all prevention programs (for example, suicide, dropout, and pregnancy). Assemblies and programs should include films, speakers, and performance groups, so students can see the diversity of the gay and lesbian community. Library and media holdings should include gay-related materials; the school newspaper and yearbook should routinely include gay-related points of view.

No one in a position of power should assume heterosexuality. In others words, boy-and-girl couples should not receive discounted tickets to the prom. Guidance counselors must be trained and encouraged to work with children of gay parents, as well as youngsters who are questioning their own sexuality. Issues of protection and respect are paramount.

Teachers bear special responsibilities. They should address harassment, jokes, graffiti, and vandalism the moment they occur, sending strong messages that derogatory behavior based on sexual orientation – real or perceived – is unfair, offensive, and harmful to everyone in a school community.

Gay, lesbian, and bisexual contributions should be introduced throughout the curriculum, and raised routinely during class – not only in history and literature, but in art, music, science, psychology, athletics, and other fields as well. Bulletin boards and other classroom materials should depict the world's diversity, including of course sexual orientation. Gay and lesbian materials should be included on all reading lists, and on possible topics for written assignments and class presentations. Teachers should also work to improve library holdings, both fiction and nonfiction.

Teachers should use openly lesbian, gay, and bisexual adults as resources for class presentations. Teachers should also educate themselves about lesbian and gay issues, especially as they relate to young people and to teachers' subject areas of expertise.

Some schools and some teachers are doing some of these things, some more successfully than others. For those doing none of them, or only a few, the list of suggestions may seem long and daunting. Obstacles block the path of every one; they range from bureaucratic disapproval to internalized homophobia. But that does not mean these are ideas that can be shunted aside or ignored; on the contrary, they are literally issues of life-and-death importance to some youngsters. They thus become topics that everyone involved in America's schools, no matter what his or her capacity or capability, is duty-bound to address. They affect not only the climate of every school in the country, but the dignity, honor, and respect of every boy and girl in each of those schools.

Ultimately, then, it is not a question of whether, why, where, or how to implement these suggestions; it is only a question of when. And the longer anyone involved in education – teacher, administrator, coach, counselor, nurse, librarian, paraprofessional, parent – waits, the greater the chance that school will be a lonely, oppressive, hurtful place for one more agonized youngster. That is a wait we simply cannot afford.

Resources

Books

Clyde, Laurel A., and Marjorie Lobban. *Out of the Closet and Into the Classroom: Homosexuality in Books for Young People*. Australia: Alia Thorpe, 1992.

Harbeck, Karen M. *Coming Out of the Classroom Closet: Gay and Lesbian Students, Teachers, and Curricula*. Binghamton, NY: Haworth Press, 1992.

Heron, Ann (ed.). *Two Teenagers in Twenty: Writings by Gay and Lesbian Youth*. Boston: Alyson Publications, 1994.

Jennings, Kevin. *Becoming Visible: A Reader in Gay and Lesbian History for High School and College Students*. Boston: Alyson Publications, 1994.

Jennings, Kevin. *One Teacher in Ten*. Boston: Alyson Publications, 1994.

Khayatt, Madiha Didi. *Lesbian Teachers: An Invisible Presence*. Albany, NY: State University of New York Press, 1992.

Mayer, Martin P. *Gay, Lesbian and Heterosexual Teachers: An Investigation of Acceptance of Self, Acceptance of Others, Affectional and Lifestyle Orientation: Their Rightful Places*. Lewiston, NY: The Edwin Mellen Press, 1993.

McConnell-Celi, Sue. *The 21st Challenge: Lesbians and Gays in Education*. Red Bank, NJ: Lavender Crystal Press, 1993.

Olson, Myrna R. *From Closet to Classroom ... A Perspective on Gay and Lesbian Individuals in U.S. Schools*. University of North Dakota Press, 1986.

Rofes, Eric E. *Socrates, Plato, and Guys Like Me: Confessions of a Gay Schoolteacher*. Boston: Alyson Publications, 1985.

Sidaway, Caroline, et al. *The Lesbian in Front of the Classroom: Writings by Lesbian Teachers.* Santa Cruz, CA: Herbooks, 1988.

Woodman, Jane (ed.). *Lesbian and Gay Lifestyles: A Guide for Counseling and Education.* Manchester, NH: Irvington Publishers, 1992.

Brochures, Handbooks, Journals, and Resource Guides

A Bibliography: Lesbian and Gay Issues in Education. The Teachers' Group of Colorado, PO Box 280346, Lakewood, CO 80228.

Affording Equal Opportunity to Gay and Lesbian Students through Teaching and Counseling. National Education Association, 1201 Sixteenth St. NW, Washington, DC 20036; (202) 822-7730.

Equity Education and Safer Schools, Colleges and Universities. Association for Supervision and Curriculum Development, PO Box 27527, Oakland, CA 94602; (510) 642-7329.

Gay, Lesbian, and Bisexual Resource/Reading Lists. Frank Colasonti, Jr., PO Box 893, Birmingham, MI 48012.

"Gay Male and Lesbian Youth Suicide." *Report of the Secretary's Task Force on Youth Suicide: Vol. 3. Prevention and Interventions in Youth Suicide.* U.S. Department of Health and Human Services, Public Health Service, Alcohol, Drug Abuse, and Mental Health Administration Publication No. (ADM) 89-1623. Superintendent of Documents, U.S. Government Printing Office, Washington, DC 20402.

"The Gay Teenager." *The High School Journal,* vol. 77, nos. 1–2. University of North Carolina Press, Box 2288, Chapel Hill, NC 27514.

Lesbian/Gay Speakers Bureau of Community United Against Violence Training Manual. Community United Against Violence, 973 Market St., Suite 500, San Francisco, CA 94103.

Making Schools Safe for Gay and Lesbian Youth: Breaking the Silence in Schools and in Families. Education Report. Governor's Commission on Gay and Lesbian Youth, State House, Room 116, Boston, MA 02133; (617) 828-3039.

Massachusetts Department of Education Safe Schools Workshop. Massachusetts Department of Education, Learning Support Services, 350 Main St., Malden, MA 02148; (617) 388-3300.

One out of Ten Students: A Resource Directory for Teachers, Guidance Counselors, Parents, and School-Based Adolescent-Care Providers. The Personal Fund, PO Box 1431, New Brunswick, NJ 08903; (908) 469-9135.

Project 10 Handbook: Addressing Lesbian and Gay Issues in Our Schools. Friends of Project 10, Inc., 7850 Melrose Ave., Los Angeles, CA 90046; (213) 651-5200.

Currriculum Materials

The Association for Supervision and Curriculum Development Program: Lesbian, Gay and Bisexual Issues in Education. PO Box 27527, Oakland, CA 94602.

Family Life Education Curriculum. Fairfax County Public Schools, Department of Instructional Services, Office of Curriculum Services, 3705 Crest Dr., Annadale, VA 22003; (703) 698-7500.

FLASH (sex education). Elizabeth Reis, Seattle-King County Department of Public Health, 110 Prefontaine Pl. South, Seattle, WA 98104.

Gay Male and Lesbian Sexuality and Issues. SIECUS, 130 W. 42nd St., Suite 2500, New York, NY 10036.

Health Lessons on Sexual Orientation and Homosexuality. Frank Colasonti, Jr., PO Box 893, Birmingham, MI 48012.

Homophobia: Discrimination Based on Sexual Orientation. GLAAD/LA, PO Box 931763, Hollywood, CA 90093.

Human Sexuality course material. c/o Barbara Blinick, Support Services for Gay and Lesbian Youth, San Francisco Unified School District, 1512 Golden Gate Ave., San Francisco, CA 94115; (415) 749-3400.

Project 21. c/o Robert Birle, 4600 N. Winchester Ave., Kansas City, MO 64117; (816) 453-1854.

Project for the Study of Gay and Lesbian Issues in Schools (formerly the Gay and Lesbian High School Curriculum and Staff Development Project). Dr. Arthur Lipkin, Harvard Graduate School of Education, 210 Longfellow Hall, Cambridge, MA 02138; (617) 491-5301.

Sexuality and the Curriculum. James T. Sears, Teachers College Press, 1234 Amsterdam Ave., New York, NY 10027.

Struggle for Equality: The Lesbian and Gay Community. PACE, 115 W. 28th St., #3-R, New York, NY 10001; (212) 643-8490.

Films, Videotapes, and Audiotapes

A Little Respect (25 minutes, color, video). Rutgers State University, Department of Health Education, University Heights, 299 University Ave., Newark, NJ 07102; (201) 648-1236.

Gay, Lesbian, and Straight Teachers Network (GLSTN; formerly the Gay and Lesbian Independent School Teachers Network) conference transcripts. Cambridge Transcriptions, 675 Massachusetts Ave., Cambridge, MA 02139; (617) 547-0200.

Gay Youth (color, video). Pam Walton, Wolfe Video, PO Box 64, New Almaden, CA 95042; (408) 268-6782.

Homosexuality: Nature Versus Nurture. (26 minutes, color, video). Films for the Humanities and Sciences, Box 2053, Princeton, NJ 08543; (800) 257-5126.

Homosexuality: What about McBride? (11 minutes, color, film and video). CRM Films, 2233 Faraday, Carlsbad, CA 92008; (800) 421-0833.

Homosexuality: What Science Understands (2 parts, video). Intelligence in Video, 123 W. 44th St., Garden Level A, New York, NY 10036.

No Rewind (video). No Excuses Productions, 3703 Rhoda Ave., Oakland, CA 94602; (510) 530-3247.

Pink Triangles: A Study of Prejudice against Lesbians and Gays (34 minutes, color, film and video). Cambridge Documentary Films, PO Box 385, Cambridge, MA 02139; (617) 354-3677.

Sexual Orientation: Reading between the Labels (29 minutes, video). NEWIST/CESA #7, 1110 IS Building, University of Wisconsin–Green Bay, Green Bay, WI 54301; (414) 465-2599.

Sticks, Stones, and Stereotypes/Palos, Piedras, y Estereotipos (20 minutes, color, video; Spanish and English). The Equity Institute, Tucker-Taft Building, 48 N. Pleasant St., Amherst, MA 01002; (413) 256-0271.

The Times of Harvey Milk. Cinecom International Films, 1250 Broadway, New York, NY 10001.

What If I'm Gay?: A Search for Understanding (29- and 47-minute versions, color, video). Coronet/MTI Film and Video, 108 Wilmot Rd., Deerfield, IL 60015; (800) 621-2131.

Who's Afraid of Project 10? (28 minutes, color, video). Project 10, Fairfax High School, 7850 Melrose Ave., Los Angeles, CA 90046; (213) 651-5200.

Resource Agencies and Organizations

American Friends Services Committee Pacific Northwest Regional Office Safe Schools Coalition. 814 N.E. 40th St., Seattle, WA 98105; (206) 632-0500.

American Library Association Gay and Lesbian Task Force. 50 E. Huron St., Chicago, IL 60611.

American School Counselor Association. 5999 Stevenson Ave., Alexandria, VA 22304; (703) 823-9800.

American School Health Association. Box 708, Kent OH 44240; (216) 678-1601.

Association for Supervision and Curriculum Development. 1250 N. Pitt St., Alexandria, VA 22314; (703) 549-9110.

Gay and Lesbian Alumni/ae Network. c/o Sue Phillips, 1507 Delmont Ln., Takoma Park, MD 20912; (301) 445-7069.

Lambda Youth Network. Box 7911, Culver City, CA 90233.

National Association of Independent Schools. Meade B. Thayer, 1620 L St. NW, Washington, DC 20036; (202) 973-9700.

Parents, Families and Friends of Lesbians and Gays (PFLAG). 1101 14th St. NW, Washington, DC 20005; (202) 638-4200.

Outreach to Rural Youth Project. PO Box 25791, Portland, OR 97225; (503) 292-3454.

Sexuality Information and Education Council of the United States (SIECUS). 130 W. 42nd St., Suite 2500, New York, NY 10036; (212) 819-9770.

Selected School Gay-Straight Alliances

Brookline High School, 115 Greenough St., Brookline, MA 02146.

Central High School, 275 N. Lexington Ave., St. Paul, MN 55104.

Deerfield Academy (Get Rid of Homophobia – GROH!), Deerfield, MA 01342.

Milton Academy (Gay and Straight People – GASP!), 170 Centre St., Milton, MA 02186.

Newton South High School, 140 Brandeis Ave., Newton, MA 02159.

Phillips Academy, Andover, MA 01810.

Staples High School, 70 North Ave., Westport, CT 06880; (203) 227-1755.

School District Programs

Harvey Milk School, 2 Astor Pl., New York, NY 10003; (212) 674-2400.

Project 10. Dr. Virginia Uribe, Fairfax High School, 7850 Melrose Ave., Los Angeles, CA 90046; (213) 651-5200.

Project 10 East. Al Ferreira, Cambridge Rindge and Latin School, 459 Broadway, Cambridge, MA 02138; (617) 349-6486.

San Francisco Unified School District. Kevin Gogin, 1512 Golden Gate Ave., San Francisco, CA 94115; (415) 749-3400.

Teacher Organizations

American Federation of Teachers Gay and Lesbian Caucus. PO Box 19856, Cincinnati, OH 19856; (513) 242-2491.

Bay Area Network of Gay and Lesbian Educators (BANGLE). Contra Costa, (510) 687-4851; East Bay, (510) 234-4627; San Francisco, (415) 648-8488; South Bay, (408) 298-1231; Sonoma, (707) 526-7931.

Connecticut Educators and Friends of Lesbians and Gays (Ed-FLAG). Jim Klopfer, 623 Springfield Rd., Somers, CT 06071.

Gay and Lesbian Educators (GALE) Network. PO Box 930, Amherst, MA 01004.

Gay, Lesbian, and Straight Teachers Network (GLSTN). PO Box 390526, Cambridge, MA 02139; (617) 536-3597.

Lesbian, Gay and Bisexual Issues in Education: A Network of the Association for Supervision and Curriculum Development. PO Box 27527, Oakland, CA 94602; (510) 642-7329.

Lesbian Teachers' Network. PO Box 301, East Lansing, MI 48826.

National Education Association Gay and Lesbian Caucus. c/o Harry Hillegas, 218 Crain Ave., Kent, OH 44240; (216) 678-4126.

National Education Association Human and Civil Rights Office. 1201 16th St. NW, Washington, DC 20036-3290; (202) 822-7700.

Pacific Northwest Association of Independent Schools. c/o Kathy Sorrells, 1906 42nd Ave. East, Seattle, WA 98112; (206) 323-6137.

Training Programs and Workshops

Warren J. Blumenfeld. 136 Hancock St., Cambridge, MA 02139; (617) 492-4639.

Campaign to End Homophobia. PO Box 819, Cambridge, MA 02139; (617) 868-8280.

Community United Against Violence. 973 Market St., Suite 500, San Francisco, CA 94103; (415) 777-5500.

DiversityWorks, Inc. 201 N. Valley Rd., Pelham, MA 01002; (413) 256-1868.

Equity Institute. 6400 Hollis St., Suite 15, Emeryville, CA 94608; (510) 658-4577.

Pat Griffin. 368 Hills South, University of Massachusetts, Amherst, MA 01003; (413) 253-7210.

Harbeck & Ferreira Consultants. 55 Glen St., Malden, MA 02148; (617) 321-3569.

kta (knox turner associates). (800) 514-2085.

Pacific Center. 2712 Telegraph Ave., Berkeley, CA 94705; (510) 841-6224.

Rheua Stakely. 10 Sumner Rd., #9, Cambridge, MA 02138; (617) 864-1098.

Staff and Curriculum Development for Anti-Homophobia Education. Dr. Arthur Lipkin, Harvard Graduate School of Education, 210 Longfellow Hall, Cambridge, MA 02138; (617) 491-5301.

Other books of interest from

ALYSON PUBLICATIONS

❑ **BECOMING VISIBLE,** edited by Kevin Jennings, $9.95. The *Lambda Book Report* states that *"Becoming Visible* is a groundbreaking text and a fascinating read. This book will challenge teens and teachers who think contemporary sex and gender roles are 'natural' and help break down the walls of isolation surrounding lesbian, gay, and bisexual youth."

❑ **CODY,** by Keith Hale, $5.95. Trottingham Taylor, "Trotsky" to his friends, is new to Little Rock. Washington Damon Cody has lived there all his life. Yet when they meet, there's a familiarity, a sense that they've known each other before. Their friendship grows and develops a rare intensity, although one is gay and the other is straight.

❑ **CRUSH,** by Jane Futcher, $5.95. Hope, joy, and pain intertwine in this wonderful teenage lesbian romance.

❑ **DEATH BY DENIAL,** edited by Gary Remafedi, $9.95. An essential book providing vital information about teenagers, sexuality, and suicide.

❑ **NOT THE ONLY ONE,** edited by Tony Grima, $7.95. These stories reflect both the joy and the fears of teenagers who are coming out.

❑ **ONE TEACHER IN TEN,** edited by Kevin Jennings, $9.95. Educators describe their efforts to be openly gay and proud.

❑ **REFLECTIONS OF A ROCK LOBSTER,** by Aaron Fricke, $5.95. A timeless and coura-geous story about growing up gay in a small New England town.

❑ **REVELATIONS,** edited by Adrien Saks and Wayne Curtis, $7.95. Twenty-two men of all ages and backgrounds tell their coming-out stories.

❑ **SOCIETY AND THE HEALTHY HOMOSEXUAL,** by George Weinberg, $7.95. The man who popularized the term *homophobia* tells gay people how to guard against its subtle influence.

❑ **TESTIMONIES,** edited by Karen Barber and Sarah Holmes, $7.95. More than twenty lesbians of varying ages and backgrounds tell their coming-out stories.

❑ **TWO TEENAGERS IN TWENTY: WRITINGS BY GAY AND LESBIAN YOUTH,** edited by Ann Heron, $9.95. "Designed to inform and support teenagers dealing on their own with minority sexual identification. The thoughtful, readable accounts focus on feelings about being homosexual, reactions of friends and families, and first encounters with other gay people." —*School Library Journal*

❑ **YOUNG, GAY, AND PROUD!** edited by Don Romesburg, $5.95. A resource book for gay and lesbian teens, rewritten for the nineties.

These books and other Alyson titles are available at your local bookstore. If you can't find a book listed above or would like more information, please call us directly at 1-800-5-ALYSON.

a